Reader's Digest

Penny Pincher's Almanac

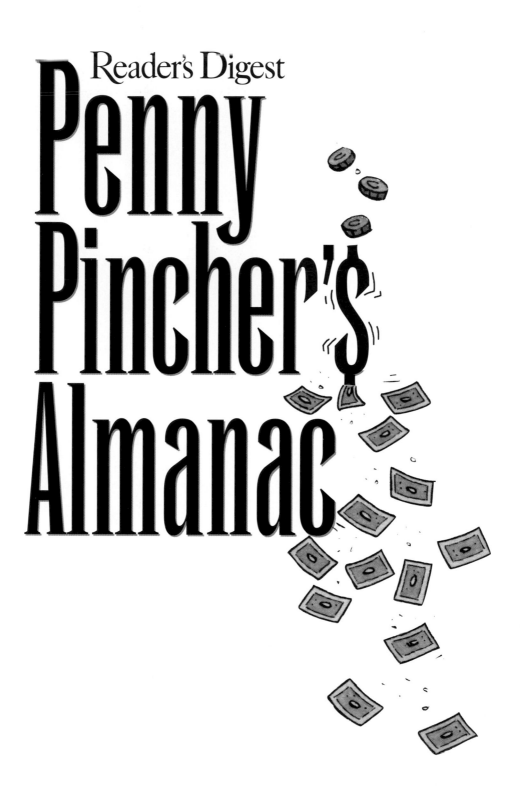

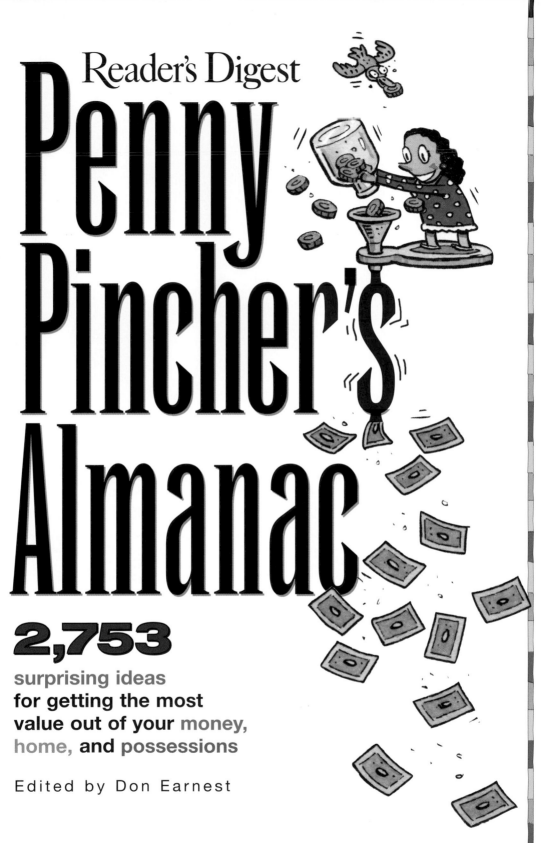

Reader's Digest

Penny Pincher's Almanac

2,753
surprising ideas
for getting the most
value out of your money,
home, and possessions

Edited by Don Earnest

Published by The Readers Digest Association, Inc.
Pleasantville, New York/Montreal

PENNY PINCHER'S ALMANAC PROJECT STAFF
Senior Editor: Don Earnest
Senior Design Director: Elizabeth Tunnicliffe
Production Technology Manager: Douglas A. Croll

CONTRIBUTORS:
Writer: Kim Elliott
Illustrator: Elwood Smith
Designer: Susan Bacchetti
Copy Editors: Susan C. Ball, Denise Willi
Indexer: Nan Badgett
Manufacturing Manager: Barbara Persan

READER'S DIGEST HOME AND HEALTH BOOKS
Editor in Chief: Neil Wertheimer
Art Director: Michele Laseau
Vice President and General Manager: Keira Krausz
Marketing Director: Dawn Nelson

THE READER'S DIGEST ASSOCIATION, INC.
Editor in Chief: Eric W. Schrier
President, North America Books and Home Entertainment: Thomas D. Gardner

Library of Congress Cataloging in Publication Data has been applied for.

ISBN 0-7621-0467-8 (hardbound)
ISBN 0-7621-0444-9 (paperback)

Address any comments about *Penny Pincher's Almanac* to:
Editor in Chief
Reader's Digest Home and Health Books
Reader's Digest Road
Pleasantville, NY 10570-7000

To order additional copies of *Penny Pincher's Almanac*, call 1-800-846-2100.

rd.com For more Reader's Digest products and information, visit our Web site.

NOTICE:
The information in this book has been carefully researched, and all efforts have been made to ensure accuracy. However, the use of this book is not a substitute for medical, legal, accounting, or other professional services. Consult a competent professional before making any major purchase, repair, investment, or health decision. Reader's Digest Association assumes no responsibility for any injuries suffered or damages or losses incurred as a result of following the information within this book. The mention of any product or Web site in this book does not imply an endorsement. All prices, store names, product names, and Web sites mentioned in this book are subject to change and are meant to be considered as general examples rather than specific recommendations.

Printed in the United States of America.
1 3 5 7 9 10 8 6 4 2 (hb)
1 3 5 7 9 10 8 6 4 2 (pb)

US4293/IC

welcome to the world of the
Penny Pincher

you'll know the real joy of penny pinching when:

- **You and your family get praised for your clothing...**
  all of which was bought at wonderfully discounted prices.

- **You eat amazing dinners for next to nothing...**
  because you use grocery-store ads to pick out your
  meats and vegetables.

- **Your car runs like a dream year in and year out...**
  because you regularly invest in smart maintenance.

- **You are fit as a fiddle and healthy as a horse...**
  yet you never go to costly health clubs or buy trendy equipment.

- **Your house is sparkling fresh and smells divine...**
  because you know the cleaning power of vinegar and baking soda.

- **Your heating bills are half those of your neighbors...**
  thanks to the caulking, weather-stripping, insulating,
  and window maintenance you've done.

- **Your weekly garbage is a fraction of your neighbors...**
  because you have embraced the power of recycling and reusing.

- **Your parties are the talk of the town...**
  not because of their extravagance but because of their
  creativity and fun.

- **Your family has exciting weekends...**
  thanks to your diligence in scoping out discount tickets
  for museums, concerts, plays, and events.

- **You drink luscious, deeply aromatic coffee...**
  but never pay exorbitant coffee house prices.

- **You do all the travel your heart desires...**
  because you've learned the tricks to find the most frugal
  flights, hotels, and meals.

- **You have lots of cash and home equity for your future...**
  thanks to smart choices to pay off your mortgage quickly.

contents

2,753

living well for
Less

The moniker penny pincher evokes a powerful image of squeezing that little copper coin until every bit of it is used up. The truth is, penny pinching is smart. The penny pincher's principles have been honed through the ages, from prehistoric hunters who used every bit of the animals they killed to environmentalists today who find clever and money-saving ways to produce almost no garbage by recycling and reusing all manner of things.

Look around. You can probably find examples everywhere of folks who have a clear understanding of their priorities, of what they want now and what they want in the future. Why pay full price when you can get the same high quality at a lower price elsewhere? Those are our words to live by, our mantra: **Penny pinchers don't live in denial; they live well for less, and have fun doing it.**

it's not just about money

Penny pinching is about more than saving money. There are many other unexpected benefits that can arise from frugality. Thriftiness has shaped us as a people and society in a number of wonderful ways. Think of the penny-pinching Pilgrims who had to make every scrap of cloth count. No one could afford to throw out a piece of fabric, no matter how small. Some inventive woman tried stitching together the scraps to make a bed covering and voila! A warm cover was made and the American art form of patchwork quilting was born in the process. Or how about the hardy pioneers, who took off across this land with nothing more than what they could carry themselves, pack on an animal, or tuck into a wagon? They used their ingenuity to survive from one season to the next, creating a legacy of independence and resourcefulness we laud today. Take the folks who lived through the Great Depression and World War II. They learned hard lessons about doing without or rationing for the future, but the same generation produced some of the greatest movies and music ever made, not to mention the WPA buildings and structures that lend their long-lasting beauty to many state and National parks today.

Each generation is faced with challenges—making the most of economic highs and digging in to weather economic lows. Penny pinchers know how to meet these challenges with humor, courage, and creativity, always keeping an eye on the long-term goal of living well.

That is the most important reason to practice the art of pinching pennies—to enable you to live the life you want. Sometimes it means creative budgeting so a parent can stay at home with small children. Sometimes that means saving small amounts throughout the year to take one stupendously big trip abroad. Sometimes it means socking away now to leave a legacy to your loved ones in the future. Whatever your personal reason for choosing to be a penny pincher, thrift as a way of life can give you the freedom to really live.

a budget is not a straitjacket

Which brings us to The Budget. There's a telling parallel between budgeting and dieting. Most diets don't work in the long run. That's because going on a diet rarely addresses why a person overeats and rarely changes their eating habits for life. So you go on a diet, lose 10 pounds, feel good, go off the diet and the 10 pounds come right back—sometimes with a few additional pounds for good measure. Or worse, while dieting, you deny yourself all treats, start feeling resentful, and go on a binge.

Saving money can backfire in the same way. If you put yourself on an extremely restrictive budget, without really assessing how you spend—what you absolutely need versus what you can live without—you will most probably wander away from your budget and be right back where you started—or worse. More troublesome still, if your budget includes no "treats" (whatever that means to you), you will probably go hog-wild one day when you simply can't take the continuous self-denial anymore.

Penny pinchers enjoy the process of spending money—wisely.

Budgeting is an art. It should take into account your current lifestyle and the life you envision for your future. It should embrace who you are and what you value. Most important, it should become such a well-ingrained part of your life, that you are hardly aware you are doing it. The art of pinching pennies is predicated on sensible, everyday living—on making prudent, healthy choices that will yield not just savings, but the financial flexibility to live in a manner that is simple, stress-free, and most important, enjoyable. Being a penny pincher doesn't mean living the life of a monk. It doesn't mean practicing constant self-denial, being a martyr, or fleeing from life's comforts and niceties. We penny pinchers truly enjoy the process of spending money—wisely. We dive into researching the best deal for car insurance. We think nothing of checking all the consumer information to buy the highest performing dishwasher for the most reasonable price. We assume everyone reads the supermarket ads each week to determine where to obtain our gourmet meal makings for the lowest possible cost. We never feel better than when someone is wowed by our "new" leather coat—

We find bargains beguiling, delight in a discount, and positively gush over a really great deal.

which we picked up at a garage sale and carefully restored with face cream. We find bargains beguiling, delight in a discount, and positively gush over a really great deal.

it's not about income

Your level of income is perhaps the least important factor in being a penny pincher. Here are three examples:

- **real-life case 1** We know a woman who was widowed when her children were 13, 11, and 7. She started teaching at a public high school and, over time, managed to buy a four-bedroom house, take all the children to museums, theater, music performances, and other cultural events. She also took each child to Europe; the youngest went three times before she turned 18! How? By recruiting and leading student groups, the woman managed to get both her and her child's trip paid so that the only money she spent was for incidentals. The woman paid off her mortgage before she retired—by paying about $25 extra each month toward her principal—and invested judiciously to ensure financial freedom during retirement. She still travels frequently (often with Elderhostel), goes to (and supports financially) the performing arts she loves, and bought her last car (a Toyota Avalon) for cash. She has also helped all three children financially over the years to achieve their own dreams. And she did it all on a school teacher's salary, a small widow's pension, and a penny pincher's creativity.

- **real-life case 2** Another family we know paid outright for their son to attend an Ivy-league medical school, leaving him free of debt at the end of his training. The father was a pediatrician so their income was decent, though not as high as many folks assumed. By scrupulous savings and an eye on the long-term, they lived fairly simply (though very comfortably) when their kids were young so they could provide this amazingly generous gift, yet still enable themselves to do the things they loved.

- **real-life case 3** In yet another family, a spouse found a way to support his wife and mother of two small children as she pursued her Ph.D. in astronomy. When her academic load increased, her husband approached his company and worked out a deal to go in very early in the morning so he could come home by 2 p.m. This freed his wife to work while he enjoyed time with his toddler and baby. They own a lovely home and travel regularly. How? Creative living through penny pinching.

learn the real value of things

Living well for less means not only knowing the price of things but also knowing the value. What's the difference? Costs fluctuate depending on all sorts of factors. Value remains a lot more constant. Buying a cheap sofa costs less money up front, but if the poor construction and inferior fabric wear badly, you'll end up spending more money to repair or replace it—bad value. A high-quality sofa that is structurally well made with sturdy fabric and that will continue to look good despite hard use may cost more at first, but the savings over time are considerable—good value. Of course, being a penny pincher also means that you found that good sofa for the absolute best price. The price was higher than the cheap sofa's, but your good-value sofa still looks great and provides comfortable seating 10 years down the line while the bad-value sofa couldn't even be donated to charity.

We cover all the major aspects of penny pinching your way to the Good Life—from caring for your body, your home and car, to travel and entertaining, with a little money management for good measure. But every penny pincher is unique—no one model will work for everyone—so as you read, assess how these ideas can be modified to fit

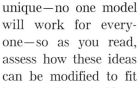

As a penny pincher, you are not fooled into believing that cost and value are the same thing.

into your lifestyle. If you can't give up Starbucks every morning, can you cut out the health-club costs and start exercising with tapes at home? Keep a pad and pen handy while you read and note aspects that resonate: driving to save gas, finding the cheapest flights, buying designer children's clothing at consignment stores, saving on prescription drugs, doing your own regular home maintenance. And always keep your eyes on the prize: You are learning to spend less on daily living to afford you the luxury to live, as you like.

Good Eats for Less

- savvy food shopping

- frugally fresh

- the penny pincher's pantry

- meal-planning for pennies

Savory tenderloin grilled to perfection . . . fresh salmon poached in a lemon-wine sauce . . . decadent chocolate mousse topped with real whipped cream . . . is this a penny pincher's menu? You betcha! As you'll discover in this chapter, cooking and eating at home is so much cheaper than eating out that you can afford to splurge a bit on getting the best ingredients and pampering your taste buds. With a few strategies, you'll be able to make your food finances go the distance. You'll learn how to use (or not use) coupons to cut costs, resist super marketing ploys to persuade you to spend too much, and score the best deals on everything from strawberries to steak, coffee to cauliflower—even soup to nuts. You'll discover that fresh food tastes better and is healthier, plus it is usually less expensive. We'll also help you go through your kitchen and set it up so you want to cook there. And we'll show you how to do the setting up the penny pincher's way: by snagging specialty items for a song, trolling garage sales to net bargains on small appliances, linens, and china, and designing your pantry so you'll be able to make mouthwatering meals economically and effortlessly.

Now, to the store!

savvy food
Shopping

BUYING GROCERIES IS A REAL TEST
OF THE PENNY PINCHER. GO ARMED WITH
SHOPPING LIST, COURTESY CARD, AND COUPONS.

Two fundamental rules should guide your food shopping. The first: Never go food shopping on an empty stomach. Hunger compels you to buy things you don't need, including high-priced "indulgence" foods. Eat a light, filling meal or snack on an apple or banana before walking into a grocery store. The second rule: Never go food shopping without a list! Learn to stick to it, and you'll save money.

strategies for supermarket savings

Never underestimate a grocery store manager's marketing savvy. No other store is organized so cunningly to get you to buy things you don't need. Only need milk? Funny how you have to walk by the fresh-baked cookies, cheese crackers, and discount videos to get it. At the register, you're surrounded by muffins, candy bars, magazines, and tabloids. So here's how to manage a supermarket frugally and happily:

have a sense of purpose Know what you are going to buy when you enter the store, and leave the store with just that. It's so obvious, yet we so often go astray.

shop the perimeter Food essentials (produce, meats, dairy, and bread) are usually on the store's perimeter. The middle aisles have the more costly prepared foods. The more you concentrate your shopping on the edges of the store, the healthier and cheaper your food-buying will be.

turn your head Eye-catching displays of cookies, chips, and convenience foods are everywhere. Ignore them. Unless they are truly staples of your home, they should be off limits.

know your aisles Every store has an aisle or two that has no temptations for you (pet food, paper goods, baby supplies, cosmetics, and so forth). Make that aisle your passageway to the departments you need at the back of the store.

study sales patterns Grocery store sales often occur in patterns. For example, we know of a grocery store that puts our favorite ice cream on a "buy one, get one free" sale one week every month. Many items regularly rotate between on sale and off. Learn the patterns, and never buy at full retail!

look up, look down, look all around Generally, the most expensive brand-name items are on shelves at eye level. Less expensive store brands are on the upper and lower shelves.

weigh it yourself Preweighed produce is convenient, but reweigh them, just in case. A 5-pound bag of carrots will end up being anywhere from 4.5 pounds to 6 pounds!

calculated savings When comparing prices, always always always compare price per pound. It's the only objective way to do it. Most stores put that number on the shelf product tags. But the tags are often missing. And always have a calculator with you. It makes comparison shopping a breeze.

twenty-four hours a day If your store is a 24-hour operation, try shopping during off hours. Just being able to take your time can help you make better choices and save money.

shopping-list tips

- Keep a stack of scratch paper in your kitchen with a pen next to it. (Make your own scratch paper by cutting or tearing used computer paper into fourths.) As soon as you use something up, deplete your stock of a pantry item, or are getting close to using up an everyday item (such as coffee or milk), add it to the list. If you shop at several stores (which you should if you are a good penny pincher), keep a list for each store.
- When you see newspaper ads with specials on foods you buy, either cut out the ad, circle the dates, and clip it to your list, or make a note directly on your list for that store noting the sale item and the sale dates.
- Organize your shopping list to the way in which the store is organized to prevent wandering (and possible impulse buying). Try to make the produce section your last stop before checking out so that your fresh fruits and vegetables won't be crushed under other food while you shop.
- Try not to visit any store more than once a week. Generally, aim for a once-a-month big shop at a price club (such as Sam's or Costco) to stock up on pantry items. You'll probably need to visit your favorite grocery store about once a week to once every two weeks for things that you buy in smaller amounts, and every two or three days for quickly used or highly perishable items, such as milk and fresh fruit and vegetables.

> **66** Will power is being able to eat just one salted peanut. **99**
>
>
> Pat Elphinstone, author

cashing in on store courtesy cards

A relative newcomer in the savvy shopper's arsenal, store courtesy cards (also dubbed club or thank-you cards), issued by a supermarket, give you additional savings on certain items. The store offers the cards in an effort to make you a regular shopper, but the savings can actually be significant, and there are no rules restricting how many stores you can have a card from. In a recent supermarket flier, we spotted Old Orchard 100% Juice, often $1.99 per can, at five for $5 using the courtesy card, and three Tombstone Pizzas (usually between $4 and $5 apiece) at three for $10 with the card! As with coupons, you will need to keep an eye on the going prices of things, but courtesy cards can help in your fight to contain food costs.

using the newspapers

Few of us have the time (or the gas) to go tooling around town checking prices from one store to the next. Many local newspapers devote a section one day a week to food, and that is also the day the grocery stores really go to town on ads or inserts. Use that day to sit down and armchair-compare prices before you go shopping.

making coupons work

Ah, the joy of the Sunday newspaper, with its enticing sheets of coupons. The dollars off! The cool stuff! The traps, the tricks, the truth: Used wisely, coupons can truly save you money on certain items, if you know how to make coupons work for you.

● Organize your coupons the way you organize your shopping list: in the same order as the store aisles. You'll find the coupons you want more quickly and will be less likely to overlook a useful coupon. As you clip them, put each coupon in a product category. Within a category, put them in expiration order, with the soonest to expire first.

● Seek out stores that regularly offer to double or triple coupons, saving you twice or three times the face value.

● If there is a special on any food on your list, be sure to check for a coupon that will give you even more savings. Combining shopping specials with coupons will reward you the most.

● Though buying the largest size of most items is usually thriftiest, you may be able to buy several smaller sizes with coupons and actually get a better price per pound.

coupon catches and hidden costs

Although coupons can indeed save you money, they can also fool you into spending money on foods you normally wouldn't buy—and doing that may actually cost you. Some money-saving maneuvers for using coupons:

● Big dollar-off coupons look good, but those coupons are generally for an already expensive item. Do the math before you grab it off the shelf.

● Think twice before switching brands. There may be a significant saving between the sale brand and your regular one, but your family may not like the product. Result? A product that sits on the shelf and wastes your money.

● Don't forget to check the cost of the store brands. Even with the price reductions offered by coupons, brand-name items may still be more expensive than store brands.

● Many foods that offer coupons are highly processed, expensive, and low in nutrients. You may pay a fancy price for foods that don't provide good nutrition.

● Sometimes a tie-in offer gives you an item free or at a bargain price if you stock up on another product at a regular price. But if the freebie isn't exactly what you want, it can take a large bite out of your week's budget, and it may never be used.

the rules of refunds

Claiming refund offers takes time and patience, but if you are buying something that you would normally buy anyway, applying for the refund puts money back in your pocket.

- As with using coupons, your best rewards come when you use your coupons in conjunction with special prices on items that also have refund offers.
- As soon as you get home, do your refunding work: Remove the part of the package designated as proof of purchase (POP). Fill out the application for the refund and mail it. Be sure to send exactly what has been specified or you'll be disqualified. The longer you wait to do this, the less likely it is that you'll actually do it and get the money back.
- Keep a log of the refunds you have requested, listing the item, the company's name and address, what was requested, and when you mailed it.

bulk bargains

- Preshredded and pregrated cheeses are usually more expensive than blocks of cheese. Buy the blocks and grate your own. Then make your own convenient packages of grated cheese in self-sealing plastic bags. Most grated hard cheese can be frozen without any problem, so grate extra and freeze it.
- Ask the deli if it has lower prices on end pieces of block cheese. If so, buy the ends, grate them, and freeze.
- Bologna, salami, and other cold cuts bought in bulk and sliced at home are less expensive than packaged meats.
- If there's a great sale on milk (and you have the freezer space), buy extra and freeze it. Whole containers will take about two days to thaw in the refrigerator.

dollarwise do-it-yourself items

- Don't buy packages of seasoned rice and noodles; they cost more and contain too much salt. Cook plain rice in low-sodium broth and add fresh or dried herbs or spices. Cook fresh noodles and toss with a little olive oil or butter and herbs. For a really quick fix, toss pasta with a little salad dressing. Or make your own seasoned rice mix to keep on hand for quick fixes.
- Buy plain cottage cheese and plain yogurt and stir in fresh or canned fruit or even a little homemade jam.
- Bags of salad are extremely popular and convenient, but they are also expensive per pound, and it is easy to prepare

RE: SOURCES

COUPONS FROM CYBERSPACE

www.nesteggz.com

www.valupage.com

You can also find coupons on the Internet, often with a novel twist. At nesteggz.com, you can save money at the register and put money into a savings account. With its "Account Credit" coupons, you only get about 10 cents off at the supermarket register, but the full value of the coupon is deposited into an online interest-bearing savings account and you can withdraw the cash value at any time. The site also offers regular "Instant Cash" coupons on all kinds of items. The valupage.com site offers register-redeemable coupons for "wish list" items. So surf for savings before you shop.

your own. Tear a head of lettuce into bite-size pieces and wash and dry the pieces in a salad spinner (a good cheap investment). Wrap the pieces in a dish towel or paper towels and store them in self-sealing plastic bags, preferably ones intended for storing greens. Consider adding sliced or diced carrots, sweet peppers, radishes, and so on. For best taste and nutritional benefit, combine several types of lettuce and add some raw spinach.

the value of price clubs

We all know those big box stores where you can buy a pack of 40 rolls of toilet paper, but do they really save you money? Yes, they do, if you use them well. You have to know the price per pound or the price per item of things you formerly bought in other stores, such as traditional supermarkets or drugstores, so you can compare costs at a price club. And you have to buy things that you use and that you have room to store. But you can net yourself a tidy savings by buying in bulk such things as meat and poultry, canned and other shelf-stable items, paper goods, toiletry items (body soap, shampoo, toothpaste, and sunscreen), juices, breakfast cereals, and coffee. You just have to be an informed consumer.

discount store savings

Another venue to consider when grocery shopping is the discount store that contains a grocery store—Wal-Mart and Kmart in particular. A recent survey by the *Arizona Daily Star*, which compared the prices of several fresh and shelf-stable products, showed that Wal-Mart had consistently lower prices on the greatest number of items, although Kmart came close. You'll have the same wide selection as in a traditional grocery store, plus the convenience of being able to purchase clothes, videos and DVDs, drugs, toiletry items, housewares, and other items these stores are known for offering at a good price.

seafood savings

Though seafood is generally considered rather expensive, the health benefits of adding fish to your diet are considerable and should be figured into your cost analysis.

● Check out local varieties. If you live on a coast, you'll have greater access to a wide variety, but even inland folks can benefit by buying locally caught fish.

● Farm-raised varieties tend to cost less. You can buy fresh catfish, salmon, and trout from farms at good prices.

● Substitute less expensive fish fillets, such as pollack, ocean perch, or whiting, in recipes calling for costlier sole.

- Frozen fish is generally cheaper than fresh fish and often tastes almost as good, especially if you're adding a sauce or will be marinating the fish prior to cooking.
- Try surimi in place of shellfish. Also labeled as sea legs, surimi is a processed product made with fish. It can be an inexpensive substitute for crab and lobster in cooked dishes such as fish cakes and pasta sauces, and because it is processed, it is also less perishable. The only drawback to surimi is that it contains ten times the salt of fresh shellfish, so don't add salt when cooking with it.
- Frozen shrimp costs half as much as fresh but tastes just as good when used in recipes where they are cooked.

buy frozen juice
Save from half to three-fourths the price of juice by purchasing frozen juice concentrates and reconstituting them. They are just as nutritious, you'll find a wide variety, and they are smaller to store, so you can buy in bulk when they're on sale. Look for those that are made from 100 percent juice and avoid juice "drinks"—they have way too much added sugar.

choice beef is cheaper
When buying beef, select choice cuts instead of prime. Prime cuts are more marbled, which makes them fattier and more expensive. To ensure flavor and tenderness in leaner (and cheaper) cuts of meat, marinate them before cooking. To really lower the fat content, trim all visible fat from meats and skin poultry before cooking.

make your own oil spray
Buy a small spray bottle and fill it with vegetable or olive oil (or one of both), and you'll be spending a lot less than if you bought the prepackaged spray cans. You will also use less oil, cut calories, and do the environment a favor!

egg economy
Always buy large eggs; they are the size most often called for in recipes and are usually a good value. The outside color of eggs doesn't affect the inside quality.

shopping bags
Save all your shopping bags: Use the larger bags for garbage can liners and the produce bags to store produce, as sandwich bags, or as handy countertop garbage bags. Or even better, make or buy cheap canvas bags; they'll last forever (practically), you can wash them when they get dirty, and they won't break on you in the middle of the parking lot!

frugally
Fresh

LET'S FACE IT: FRESH FOOD TASTES BETTER. HERE ARE SOME TIPS ON BUYING AND PREPARING ITEMS FROM ASPARAGUS TO ZUCCHINI.

Fruits and vegetables in season not only offer superior flavor, they're also better for you and they cost less. Farmers' markets, which sell locally grown produce, offer great bargains (and are fun to visit), but your grocery store can also provide penny-pinching prices on scrumptious seasonal produce. The fresh approach applies to many other foods as well, including bread and coffee. Select the freshest ingredients, store them properly to preserve their flavor, and enjoy your food a whole lot more.

admirable asparagus

Though it is rarely cheap, asparagus is delicious, nutritious, and less costly if purchased in season. (See page 27.) If you see it at a good price, buy a bunch with firm stems and heads intact. At home, place the asparagus with the ends in water (like a bouquet of flowers). Dampen a paper towel or washcloth and drape it gently over the asparagus tips. Place a piece of plastic wrap (or the bag the asparagus came in) over the towel and store in the refrigerator. The asparagus will keep for almost a week this way.

banana rama

When bananas are on sale, buy them in bulk. Look for greenish yellow, unblemished bananas; they will ripen rapidly. Contrary to popular belief, you can store fresh bananas in the refrigerator, either wrapped in newspaper or in a sealed container. Though their skins will darken more quickly, the flesh inside will be unaffected, and the cold will slow down the ripening process so the fruit will keep longer.

- Brown spots on bananas are actually a sign of ripeness, not rot. If your family objects to the spots, peel the bananas and use them in recipes.
- Once the peels turn mostly brown, mash the bananas, add a teaspoon of lemon juice per banana, and freeze the purée in an airtight container. Frozen banana purée will last six months and tastes delicious in milk shakes, cakes, and quick breads and muffins.

a hill 'o beans

Beans, dried or canned, are one of a penny pincher's best friends. A remarkably inexpensive source of protein, naturally low in fat, and containing no cholesterol, beans are easy to use in soups, stews, chili, and salads.

- If you are using dried beans, be sure to pick through them first to remove any pebbles or shriveled beans. Place the beans in a large pot and fill with cold water. Skim off anything that comes to the surface, drain in a colander, and rinse under cold running water.
- To soak or not to soak? Dried beans are usually soaked

before cooking. Place them in a large bowl or pot and cover (by about 2 inches) with cold water. The length of soaking time will vary with the type of bean.

- To help beans keep their shape, do not soak them. Instead, place them in a pot with cold water and, very slowly, bring them to a boil. Reduce the heat and simmer until the beans are tender. Then continue with the recipe.
- If you are using canned beans, be sure to rinse them well in a colander under cold running water to remove the excess salt. Then use as directed.

berry good
Don't let fresh berries get soggy! Store them in the refrigerator in the open-weave baskets from the store or in a colander, if you picked them yourself. Do not wash berries until just before you are going to eat them.

- Chill berries before washing them, because cold berries are less likely to bruise or bleed during washing than those at room temperature.
- To freeze berries, wash them and pat them dry. Lay the berries in a single layer on a baking sheet lined with a paper towel and freeze until the berries are hard (about one hour). Transfer the frozen berries to self-sealing plastic bags, label, date, and return to the freezer. Use within nine months.

best bread
Fresh bread will generally keep for five to seven days, depending on the texture; the lighter the bread, the more quickly it dries out. To keep bread and rolls fresh longer, put them in one heavy-duty or two regular plastic bags and store the bags in the freezer. Slice a whole loaf before freezing it, so that you can easily remove just the amount you need.

- If you really love the taste of fresh crusty bread—and frequently find yourself spending $3.50 or more on a loaf of fancy bread—you'll find that it pays to invest in a breadmaking machine. These appliances sell for about $100 and the cost of the ingredients for a loaf run less than $1, so, with regular use, you should recoup the cost within a year. Best of all, you get bread that's fresher and tastier than any store-bought loaf—and the house will be filled with a wonderful aroma as it bakes.

cheesy chat
- To inhibit mold growth on cheese, wrap the cheese in a paper towel that has been dampened with vinegar. Then seal it inside a plastic bag. Keep the towel moist with additional vinegar as needed.
- Cottage cheese will keep fresh longer if it's refrigerated

66 Never eat more than you can lift. 99

Miss Piggy
(as told to Henry Beard)

upside down in its original carton. And you can freeze cottage cheese, though it will break down when thawed. After thawing the cheese, just whip it until it is creamy; then use it in cooking.

citrus spectaculars

When lemons, limes, oranges, and grapefruits are at their peak, they are also least expensive. Buy in bulk, store some for eating and using in recipes, and use the rest to make a large batch of each kind of juice.

● Before juicing oranges, lemons, or limes, grate the rind and store the zest in the freezer. The next time a recipe calls for grated zest, you'll be good to go.

● After the zest is removed, submerge the fruit in hot water for 15 minutes and then roll it on a counter, pressing down as you roll; this releases the juice before squeezing.

● Pour the juice into ice cube trays and freeze it. Transfer the cubes to labeled and dated self-sealing plastic bags. Whenever citrus juice is called for, thaw one cube for each 2 tablespoons of juice you need.

● If you need only a drop or two of juice, don't squeeze the citrus—jab it with a toothpick and squeeze out the amount you need. Put the toothpick back in the hole to close it, and store the fruit in the refrigerator.

coffee talk

Save dollars a day by brewing your own gourmet coffee instead of purchasing coffee or coffee drinks at a high-priced coffee boutique.

● Invest in good quality coffee (you'll get more flavor per scoop), preferably beans. The best buy we've spotted is at Costco: They sell their store brand, Kirkland, in 2-pound bags for $8.99. The bags are marked with the Starbucks logo and say "Roasted by Starbucks." A 2.5-pound bag of Starbucks French Roast, however, sold for $15.99. Makes you wonder. Costco also had Seattle Mountain Drum-Roasted coffee beans at $7.99 for a 3-pound bag. Some so-called world market stores, such as Cost Plus or Pier One, also offer gourmet coffee beans at a reasonable price. And supermarkets are now selling their own beans in bulk for a relative bargain.

● Depending on where you live, you'll find other good buys. Latin-brand coffee, coffee imported from Mexico, and the coffee-and-chicory blend from Louisiana will all brew a cup of tasty dark-roast coffee for a lot less than you'd pay at a trendy coffee shop.

● Transfer coffee (either beans or ground) from the store bags to self-sealing plastic bags; then label, date, and store the coffee in the freezer. The less air and moisture coffee is exposed to, the longer it retains its full flavor.

- Add a pinch of salt to your ground coffee before brewing a pot to reduce bitterness and enhance flavor.
- Give your coffee that boutique touch for pennies by adding a teaspoon of ground cinnamon or a grating of orange zest to the grounds before brewing. (It smells great, too!).
- Love flavored coffees but don't want to pay $3 a cup? Cost Plus had Torani syrups on sale for $2.49 for a 6.3-ounce bottle and $4.99 for a 750 ml bottle. Available in both regular and sugar-free versions, they have vanilla, hazelnut, Irish cream, and chocolate.
- For a special coffee topping, keep a can of light whipped cream in your refrigerator. Or invest in a device to froth your own milk for a cappuccino (we found a Bodum milk frother at Bed, Bath and Beyond for $9.99!).

as corny as kansas in august

The old saying is "Corn knee-high by the 4th of July." Which is why late summer is the time to buy and eat corn. It is cheap and plentiful, and the taste is beyond compare. Corn in the husk is generally less expensive, and the husk keeps the corn fresh longer. Look for a grass-green, slightly damp husk. The silk should be light to amber brown, with no black. Feel for plump kernels through the husk rather than tear it back. Cook fresh corn as soon after purchasing it as possible for maximum flavor.

egg-axtly!

There is really nothing like the flavor of farm-fresh eggs, if you're cooking them by themselves. From-the-nest quality is a bit less crucial if you are using eggs in a recipe. Check the dates on cartons carefully. There is no nutritional difference between brown and white eggs, so buy whichever you prefer. If you are in doubt about the freshness of an egg, place it in a deep container of cold water. If it floats to the top, it's too old to use.

- Store eggs in their carton, not on the refrigerator egg shelf. This helps preserve moisture and prevents the eggs from absorbing the flavor of other foods.
- If a recipe calls for just egg whites or egg yolks, don't toss the other part of the egg down the drain. You can freeze both yolks and whites for future use.
- To freeze egg whites, use a plastic ice cube tray. Put one egg white into each cube space and freeze until hard. Pop the egg-white cubes out of the tray and store them, labeled, in a self-sealing plastic bag in the freezer.

● To freeze egg yolks, add a pinch of sugar or salt to each yolk to prevent them from coagulating. Freeze them as you do egg whites.

fresh fish on ice?
Retain the flavor of your freshly caught fish by putting it in a clean, empty milk carton. Fill the carton with fresh water and put it in the freezer. After thawing the fish for a meal, use the water to fertilize house plants.

tutti fruity
● Size matters: If you are planning to eat fruit raw, buy the smallest pieces you can find. You'll probably be able to buy more pieces of fruit per pound this way. But if you are planning to cook with the fruit, buy larger (and fewer) pieces, so you will have less fruit to wash, peel, core, pit, and chop.
● Sneaky shoppers: When a fruit is in season, check for sales on its frozen counterparts. For example, when peaches are in season, the demand for frozen peaches drops, and the market may want to sell them. Stock up and take advantage of the lower prices.

gingerroot
Many recipes call for a little fresh gingerroot, but the root loses its flavor if stored for long in the refrigerator. Instead, buy a larger piece and store in a self-sealing plastic bag in the freezer. When you need a little, take it out and grate what you need, then return the unused portion to the freezer. Another plus: Frozen gingerroot grates more easily.

herbal essence
Growing your own herbs is easy and economical. Here's how to store them for future use:
● For herbs you will use in the next few days, make a bouquet and set the stems in a cup of water. Cover the leaves loosely with a plastic bag and refrigerate. Change the water regularly, and your fresh herbs will last from a week to ten days.
● To quick-dry herbs, place them on a baking sheet and warm them in a 100° F oven until they are dry. If you have a gas oven, preheat it to 200° F, turn it off, and set the sheet of herbs inside until dry.
● Parsley, chives, and basil all freeze well. Wash the leaves and pat them dry, then finely chop and store each herb in a small labeled and dated self-sealing plastic bag.
● For other herbs, wash, dry, and chop them. Place the chopped herbs in an ice cube tray, add just enough water to cover the herbs, and put the tray in the freezer. When the cubes are frozen, store them in self-sealing bags. If you

need some oregano, for example, for spaghetti sauce, just drop a cube of the oregano into the pot.

got milk?

When you buy milk, pick a carton or jug with the latest sell date, but keep in mind that the date does not indicate when the milk will go bad, only the date by which the store has to sell it. If properly chilled, milk should last for at least a few days past the sell date.

- Use evaporated milk as a convenient substitute for fresh milk. Regular, low-fat, or skim, it has a long shelf life. To reconstitute, add an equal measure of water. Evaporated milk works well in sauces, gravies, and baked dishes. (Condensed milk is a sweetened form; use it only when specifically called for in a recipe.)
- For richer texture without extra fat, add 1 or 2 tablespoons of nonfat dry milk to skim milk, cream soups, omelets, or puddings. The powdered milk also provides extra calcium and protein.

mushroom magic

Button or white mushrooms can often be bought on sale, but the more exotic varieties tend to stay on the pricey side, so make a little go much longer this way: Mix a small amount (about 1/2 ounce) of dried specialty mushrooms with a much larger amount (about a pound) of button mushrooms. The intense flavor of the exotic dried mushrooms will saturate the mild, inexpensive button variety.

- Store mushrooms in paper bags in the main section of the refrigerator. Plastic bags and produce drawers reduce air circulation, leading to slimy, quickly spoiled mushrooms.
- Clean mushrooms with a damp towel or mushroom brush just before preparing them. Never soak mushrooms; it robs them of flavor and nutrients, such as phosphorus, magnesium, potassium, and selenium.
- Save your stems! Chop the mushroom stems and add them to stock, stuffing, or soup.

nut know-how

To keep nuts fresh longer, store them in airtight jars or cans in the refrigerator. If you will not be using them for a few months, store them in the freezer. For longer-lasting nuts, buy them in the shell. Plan to use them within a month or two, though, because they can turn rancid if stored longer.

pick a peck of peppers

Sweet peppers, with the exception of green, can often be high-priced. If you spot a good sale on yellow, orange, or red peppers, buy them and freeze the extras.

FARMERS' MARKETS

For super fresh food, go to your local farmers' market, where small farmers in the area bring their freshly harvested produce. Although a few vendors ask high prices for their boutique veggies, you can usually haggle. And if you go at the end of the day, you'll find that prices plunge—especially if it's the last day the market is open that week. At that point, the farmers want to get rid of everything.

- Peppers are among the few vegetables that require no blanching before freezing. Cut, seed, and slice or dice them, and freeze them in dated, self-sealing plastic bags.
- Don't spend money on jars of roasted peppers; do it yourself! Broil whole peppers about 4 to 6 inches from the heat, turning them often, until the skins are well charred. Remove the peppers from the broiler and transfer them to a paper bag; close the bag and let sit for about 15 minutes. The skins should be loosened by then and come off easily. Then cut, remove the seeds and membranes, and rinse. Let the roasted peppers dry completely, then cover and refrigerate them. They should keep for up to two weeks.

rootin' tootin' root veggies

When shopping for root vegetables, such as onions, potatoes, carrots, and beets, look for firm surfaces with no cracks.
- Store onions and potatoes in a totally dark, cool, dry place. Other root vegetables can be refrigerated.

sugar is sweet

Buy store brands, not national brands, unless there's a sale and the price per pound for the national brand is better.
- Don't use sugar substitutes when baking; the taste and texture will disappoint you. And don't try to use confectioners' sugar and granulated sugar interchangeably; the weight and volume are completely different.
- There is no real difference between light brown sugar and dark brown sugar, although the darker the color, the more intense the flavor. To revive caked brown sugar, sprinkle it with water and set it in a 200° F oven for 10 minutes, or microwave it for 20 seconds. If you place a slice of apple in the sugar container and close it tightly, the sugar will soften in a few days.

you say tomato

Loaded with vitamin C, tomatoes are delicious raw or cooked. Recent studies suggest that consumption of cooked tomatoes may reduce the risk of some cancers, particularly those that are more likely to plague men. Whether you grow your own or take advantage of seasonal specials and farmers' markets, tomatoes are a good buy.
- Ripen tomatoes at room temperature in a bowl with other fruit or in a closed brown paper bag. Tomatoes will not ripen in the refrigerator and actually turn pulpy and lose flavor in cold temperatures.
- At season's end, use the last of your homegrown tomatoes to make (and freeze) tomato sauce, purée, or tomato soup. You can also freeze ripe tomatoes, whole or cut up, in plastic freezer bags. After they thaw, use them for cooking.

z is for zucchini

Enjoy this vegetable with the peel on, as that's where you'll find the beta carotene and other vitamins. If you're cooking zucchini, look for firm, bright-green squashes no longer than 6 inches. But if you're planning to stuff them, then the larger the better.

- If you have a bumper crop or want to take advantage of seasonal sales, shred the zucchini and freeze in self-sealing bags. Use shredded zucchini in soups or breads.
- Fresh uncooked zucchini, sliced crosswise or cut into strips, makes a welcome addition to a crudités plate.
- Zucchini are great on the grill. Cut them into thin slices, brush the slices with some olive oil and balsamic vinegar, sprinkle with some herbs or garlic, and grill until the edges are slightly charred.
- Slice 1 pound of zucchini into long strips. Dredge the strips in flour, shaking off the excess, and dip each strip in a batter of 1/2 cup flour and 1/2 cup water or beer. Deep-fry in 3 inches of hot vegetable oil and drain on paper towels. Serve with low-fat ranch dressing for dipping, or sprinkle with balsamic vinegar before serving.

Seasonal Shopping Guide

FRUIT	PEAK SEASON	VEGETABLE	PEAK SEASON
Apples	September to March	Acorn squash	October to November
Apricots	June and July	Artichokes	March to May
Blueberries	July	Asparagus	April and May
Blackberries	June to August	Beans, snap	June to September
Cantaloupes	June to August	Beets	June to October
Cherries, sweet	June and July	Broccoli	October to April
Cranberries	September to December	Brussels sprouts	September to February
Figs	June to October	Cauliflower	October
Grapefruit	October to May	Corn	May to September
Nectarines	July and August	Eggplant	August to September
Peaches	July and August	Endive, Belgian	October to May
Pears, Anjou	October to April	Leeks	October to May
Pears, Bartlett	July to October	Okra	June to August
Plums	May to September	Peas	May to September
Raspberries	July	Peppers, green	September to October
Rhubarb	May	Summer squash	July to August
Strawberries	April to June	Sweet potatoes	September to December
Watermelon	June to August	Tomatoes	May to August

the penny pincher's
Pantry

SETTING UP YOUR KITCHEN THE RIGHT
WAY WILL SAVE YOU TIME AND MONEY.

A key element in saving money on food is a well-stocked pantry. If essential ingredients are always on hand, you're less likely to make an emergency run to a convenience store, which tends to lead to impulse buying. Another crucial factor is having a kitchen that is well organized and easy to work in so that cooking becomes a pleasure. Home-cooked meals cost a fraction of what restaurant or take-out food costs and tend to be far healthier. So creating a true penny pincher's pantry is well worth the time and effort.

out with the old!

First, go through each drawer and cupboard in the kitchen and pull out all the equipment you have. Do you really need three can openers? Keep the best for the kitchen, put the next best in a storage box for emergencies, and put the remaining opener in your garage sale pile. If you have an old or extra blender, retire it to your workshop and use it to mix paint or for other messy blending jobs. You might even want to sell it or donate it to charity.

in with the new (or nearly new)?

You can pick up small appliances at many places, and it pays to shop around. We found the Cuisinart Automatic Grind & Brew coffee maker, which freshly grinds and brews coffee using a timer, at Cooking.com and at Chef's Catalog online (**www.chefscatalog.com**) for $99.95, but Costco was offering it for only $69.99!

● Garage sales can net you fabulous finds for your kitchen and dining room. We recently picked up two brand-new, in-the-wrapper Pyrex pie plates for $3 and a beautiful set of four never-used linen place mats with matching napkins for $2! We've spotted a Crockpot slow cooker, knife sharpeners, bread makers, ice-cream makers, and all those gadgets people get for wedding gifts that often are never used, all on sale for a song at garage sales. You can also pick up china, silverware, and glassware, some of which has never been used or is gorgeous collector stuff.

● After you've assessed your kitchen, make a list of the things you'd like to have or need. Keep that list with you whenever you go out. You never know when you'll spot a sale that might have exactly what you want for much less than what it cost new.

revamping valuable space

Make your kitchen work for you. Take a long look and ask yourself how you really use the space. Where do you do most of your food preparation? Do you tend to prepare mixes for baking in one place? What about the cleaning area around the sink? As you reorganize, jot down where you put things, so you can find them easily when needed. Tape the list to the inside of a cupboard door.

- Store your dishes and glassware in a cupboard close to the sink and dishwasher.
- Designate the area closest to the stove the food prep area and keep knives, pots, and pans close at hand.
- Make the longest kitchen counter your baking area. Store your mixer, dry-measuring cups, measuring spoons, and baking pans nearby.
- Decide which small appliances you use regularly (toaster, food processor?) and keep them out on a counter, if possible, near the area of highest use.
- Store less-used appliances (ice-cream maker, slow cooker?) in a cupboard that is easy to access but out of sight. If you have cupboards with basically unusable corner areas, consider buying an inexpensive lazy Susan (or making one). Or pick up some old cookie sheets at a garage sale and use them as sliding trays for storing appliances in those back corners.
- Put useful but rarely used utensils, such as lobster crackers, holiday items, and decorative cake plates, in the most inaccessible cupboards or drawers in the kitchen. If your kitchen is orderly and easy to use, you'll be much more likely to enjoy cooking and do so on a regular basis.

66 Tell me what you eat, and I will tell you what you are. **99**

Anthemlme Brillat-Savarin, 19th-century French gastronomic chronicler

cookware 101

There are few things more frustrating than trying to cook with lousy pots and pans. But how do you invest in good cookware without going into debt? Folks who purchase the good stuff rarely part with it, so you won't often find it at garage sales or resale shops (but always check anyway, just in case). Not to worry. We found some decent prices by doing a little digging.

on the web The Chef's Catalog (**www.chefscatalog.com** or 1-800-884-2433) has long been known as a source of high-quality cooking items at decent prices. Recently, they were offering a seven-piece set of Le Creuset (enamel-coated cast iron) cookware for $229.99, down from $470. They also had a ten-piece set of Emerilware stainless steel cookware for $199.99, originally $350. Both came with free shipping (on orders of more than $99)—quite a savings when you consider how heavy cookware can be. But the real deal was in their clearance section: A commercial-quality covered saucepan in heavy-gauge anodized aluminum was just $19.99, down from $65! How's that for a bargain?

back to betty Remember Betty Crocker coupons? They're boxtop coupons—each worth a certain number of points— on Betty Crocker–brand products that you can redeem when purchasing products from the company's catalog (or now its

Good **O**ld **W**ays

Nothing beats a cast-iron cooking pan. While its enamel-coated cousins look pretty, this plain workhorse of the pioneers will last a lifetime (literally), cooks evenly, can go from campground to gourmet kitchen without a second look, and costs only a few dollars. Read and follow the care directions to the letter, and these pans will be with you for years.

Web site, too). You can still save money with them. At **www.bettycrocker.com/bettystore** we found an eight-piece set of anodized cookware for $199.95 (plus 400 points), originally priced at $399.95. In their clearance section, they had beautiful French copper cookware with stainless steel interiors. A 9.5-inch sauté pan was $119.99, originally $200, and a 2.7-quart covered saucepan was $79.99, originally $150.

web discounter Costco online (**www.costco.com**) was showing a ten-piece set with copper exteriors, aluminum centers, and stainless steel interiors by Cuisinart for $249.99. They also had a Circulon commercial cookware 12-piece set for $199.99 and a Sitram stainless steel 11-piece set for $199.99.

discount superstores Stores like Target, Kmart, Walmart, Bed, Bath and Beyond, Linens 'N Things, and Tuesday Mornings all offer cookware, often at very good prices.

department stores Don't ignore traditional outlets like Marshall Fields, Macy's, Dillards, and Bloomingdales. They all have sales and clearance shelves. Check them out. You can pick up great stuff for half price or even less!

creating counters

Few kitchens have enough counter space. Here are some quick, easy, inexpensive ways to stretch the space you have:

- For a really fast fix, pull out a drawer and place a cutting board on top; shut the drawer until the board fits snugly.
- Use baking trays with raised edges (your own or picked up at tag sales) over unused burners on your stove top.
- Find or buy an inexpensive cutting board that fits over the top of your sink. Cut a hole at one end of the board; if possible, cut the hole so that your kitchen colander can sit snugly in it. As you work, you can put prepared vegetables or fruit in the colander. When you're finished, rinse the food in the colander, remove the colander, and scrape the peelings right into the sink.
- Attach a sturdy piece of board to the back of a kitchen door, using two hinges at the bottom and a hook and eye to secure the top to the door. When you need extra counter space, unhook the board and put a chair under it for strength.

wood cutting boards are back

A few years ago, there was a huge fuss about using plastic cutting boards instead of wooden ones because you could sterilize the plastic. Turns out to be wrong. Bacteria don't incubate on wooden boards, but they grow rapidly on plastic boards at room temperature. Always wash any cutting board with soap and hot water after using it.

- To remove odors and dirt from a wooden cutting board, make a paste of baking soda and water. Rub the paste into the board, then rinse and allow the board to air dry.
- To clean a butcher's block, coat it with coarse salt and let it sit for several hours or overnight. The salt absorbs fats and oils, and when you brush off the salt, you brush off the greasy stuff, too.

the cutting edge

Good-quality knives are not only much safer to use but will save you money and time. How much does quality cost? Costco was offering a 12-piece set in a block by J. A. Henckels (high quality) for $168.99. Sound pricey? A seven-piece  Henckels set at Target was going for $149.99 and an 8-piece set of Wusthof (top quality) was selling for $299.99 on the Chef's Catalog website (**www.chefscatalog.com**), and that was the discount price!

- You actually need only four knives: a small paring knife, a larger chef's knife, a curved-edge cleaver, and a serrated bread knife. Buy the best quality you can afford (and use them for 25 years or more). Cheap tip: Check in Chinese shops for a time-saving curved-edge vegetable cleaver, usually priced around $25.
- Sharpen your good knives after each use. Run the blade along a butcher's steel for ten or so strokes. Your knives will stay sharper much longer. A whetstone or electric sharpener can also be used to keep knives sharp.
- Store knives in a wooden block or on a magnetic strip with the tips pointing up. Use a wooden cutting board, because hard plastic and stone tend to dull knife blades.

slow and steady slow cookers (aka the Crockpot)

There's an appliance most likely hiding in the back of your kitchen closet that can save you a ton of money: the slow cooker. This old standby has come back into popular use—and if you don't have one, you can probably pick one up at a garage sale for a few dollars. The slow cooker is a valuable cooking tool for the working family. You can set up a pot roast in the morning and have it ready to eat by the time you get home. Most models have a timer, so you can set the cooking time even if you're not home. Because they use less energy than an oven, you save there, too. Spaghetti sauce, chili, boeuf bourguignonne, chicken cacciatore, Irish stew, pea soup, clam chowder, and beef or pork pot roast are only a few of the dishes that cook to perfection in a slow cooker. It does wonders with cheap, tough cuts of meat, making it a money-saving appliance in the first degree.

penny-pinching potholders

Don't throw out that old mattress pad! You can turn it into fabulous potholders. Here's how:

- To make a square potholder, cut an 8- x 15-inch rectangle from the fabric. Ideally, one of the long sides should be a selvage or other finished edge. Fold the rectangle in half, right sides together. Stitch along the two unfinished edges. Turn the pocket right side out. Fold a 4-inch-long piece grosgrain ribbon in half to make a loop, and pin the ribbon ends between the open pocket edges at one corner. Topstitch the open pocket edge closed, catching in the free ribbon ends in the stitching.
- To make a mitt holder, cut two 8- x 15-inch rectangles. Stitch the rectangles together, right sides facing out. Then repeat the above directions, but do not topstitch the open edge of the pocket closed. Instead, stitch the ribbon ends to one corner of the open edge for a hanger. (If the open edge is not a selvage or finished edge, make a small rolled hem and stitch it in place.)

do-it-yourself kitchen tools

- Make a sturdy funnel by cutting a clean plastic 1/2- or 1-gallon jug (milk, orange juice, or the like) in half with a sharp, heavy knife or kitchen shears. Use the half containing the spout for your funnel. (Use the bottom half as a saucer for a potted plant, to start seeds in, to store cleaning products under the sink, as a portable dog water dish, or for just about anything else.)
  - If you need a temporary funnel for dry ingredients, clip one corner of a small paper bag. For cool liquids, cut off the corner of a heavy plastic bag.
- Don't spend money on a cake-decorating bag. Spoon icing into a self-sealing plastic bag and seal it. Squeeze all the icing to one corner and cut a small opening in the corner. Practice your design on the side of the icing bowl or another test surface before working on the cake.
- The same technique can be used for making melted chocolate designs. A big plus is that you can melt the chocolate right in the bag (immersed in a bowl of hot water), making cleanup a breeze.
- Old herb and spice bottles with shaker tops are invaluable. Wash them well and let them dry thoroughly. Then fill them with flour, cornmeal, cinnamon sugar, confectioners' sugar, cocoa powder, or anything else you might need for sprinkling on baked goods or coating surfaces where dough will be rolled out.
- Don't have a flour sifter? You don't actually need one: Sift flour through a kitchen sieve.

the amazing self-sealing plastic bag

These bags are a tremendously useful item that you can use again and again, for all sorts of storage solutions. Buy them in bulk at a price club, which lowers the cost per unit. Then wash and reuse them until they are worn out. They can last for months at a time this way, and they take up much less space than hard plastic containers. Be sure to press all the air out before sealing them.

● Make your own prepackaged mixes. (See pages 46–49.)
● Freeze fresh fruit or vegetables in season. (See page 27.)
● Buy big packages of chicken and meat and break them down into serving-size portions. Label and date the bags.
● Store your flour or other dried goods in bags, if bugs are getting into them.
● Make big recipes of stews, soups, chili, and such and freeze family-size portions in bags.
● Don't buy moist towelettes to take on picnics or other outings. Dampen a washcloth and squeeze a little antibacterial soap on it. Place the washcloth in a self-sealing bag, and it's ready to clean when you are.

hand blender

Most kitchen gadgets are just a waste of money and precious kitchen storage space. But one real time-saver is the hand-held blender. You can use it to puree foods—from spaghetti sauce to baby food—right in the pot. (Of course, you have to let the food cool a bit first.) You can also use the blender to make instant milkshakes and smoothies right in the glass.

the right baking pans

If you bake, getting the right baking pans can make a huge difference in the results you get. What you want are heavy duty, shiny metal pans. They won't warp like lighter weight pans. And they'll produce cookies, cakes, pastries, and breads that are golden in color. With dark-colored pans, which absorb heat, you are more like to get burnt or dry results. Also look for pans that have a nonstick finish.

viva la vinegar

Store vinegars according to type: Keep plain vinegar in the cupboard; its acidity gives it an almost indefinite shelf life. Refrigerate flavored vinegar to help retain its taste longer.

honey: don't toss it out

If that jar of honey has crusted over (called sugaring), place the open jar in boiling water until the original texture is restored. You can also liquefy honey in a microwave.

NEED TO CHECK YOUR OVEN TEMPERATURE?

Here's how to check the temperature of your oven if you don't have a thermometer: Turn on your oven, set it to 350° F, and let it warm up. Then put a tablespoon flour on a baking sheet in the oven. After five minutes, the color of the flour will tell you the approximate temperature:

● Tan indicates 250° to 325° F.
● Golden means 325° to 400° F.
● Dark brown is 400° to 450° F
● Almost black is 450° to 525° F.

Make sure you have a good selection of shelf-stable foods as well as essentials for your refrigerator. Keeping a well-stocked pantry saves you time and money. If you have food items on hand, bought at the best price, you won't have to run out to an expensive convenience store to pick something up at the last minute. Not all of your pantry items need to be bought. Many of the items listed below can be homemade, such as applesauce, bread crumbs, canned fruits, and peanut butter, if you have the time and the desire. And, obviously, this list is just a place to start; what you and your family eat will determine what you need to keep on hand. If you do run out of an ingredient now and then, you'll find some helpful charts on the following pages listing substitutions and food equivalents.

the well-stocked pantry

● in your cupboards

Applesauce

Baking powder

Baking soda

Bouillon cubes: chicken, beef, and vegetable

Bread crumbs

Cake mixes

Chocolate, unsweetened

Chocolate chips, semisweet

Cocoa powder

Cornmeal

Cornstarch

Corn syrup

Dried fruits: raisins, currants, and prunes

Fish, canned: tuna, salmon, clams, and oysters

Flavorings: vanilla, almond, etc.

Flour, all-purpose (cake, whole-wheat, or other flours are determined by the cook's needs)

Fruits, canned: peaches, pears, pineapple, mixed

Gelatin, flavored and unflavored

Honey

Jams, jellies, and preserves

Maple syrup

Mayonnaise

Meats and poultry, canned: chicken, corned beef

Milk: canned evaporated and condensed

Milk, nonfat dry

Molasses

Mustard, prepared

Oatmeal

Oils: olive, canola, or other vegetable (peanut oil if you do a lot of deep frying)

Pasta: thin noodles (spaghetti, vermicelli, angel hair), egg noodles, other dried pasta as used

Peanut butter

Pickles, dill and sweet

Pickle relish

Rice

Salt, table (kosher or sea salt as used)

Seeds: celery, poppy, sesame

Soups, canned and dried

Soy sauce

Spices: allspice, cardamom, cayenne pepper (ground hot red), chili powder, cinnamon (ground and stick), cloves (ground and

whole), coriander, cumin, curry
powder, ground ginger, mace,
mustard, nutmeg, paprika, peppercorns, turmeric

Sugar, granulated white, brown,
and confectioners'

Tomatoes, canned: diced, sauce,
paste, whole

Vegetables, canned: corn, artichoke hearts

Vegetable shortening

Vinegar: white, cider, balsamic, red
wine, and white wine

Worcestershire sauce

● in your refrigerator

Butter, salted and unsalted

Cheese: Parmesan, cheddar, mozzarella

Eggs, large

Margarine

Milk: 1 percent or skim, unless you
have babies or toddlers who
need the higher fat content

Yogurt: plain

herb and spice substitutions

If you happen to be out of the herb or spice that a recipe calls for, don't despair. Another one that you already have on hand will work just as well and taste as good, too.

HERB OR SPICE	SUBSTITUTE
Allspice	Cinnamon, plus a dash of cloves
Aniseed	Fennel seed
Basil	Oregano
Caraway seed	Aniseed
Chives	Scallion tops
Cinnamon	Nutmeg
Cloves	Allspice
Cumin	Chili powder
Dillweed	Fennel tops
Ginger	Cardamon
Mace	Allspice
Parsley	Tarragon
Thyme	Rosemary

emergency substitutions

INGREDIENT	AMOUNT	USE INSTEAD
Baking powder	1 tsp.	1/4 tsp. baking soda plus 1/2 tsp. cream of tartar
Broth, chicken or beef	1 cup	1 bouillon cube or envelope instant broth dissolved in 1 cup boiling water
Buttermilk	1 cup	1 cup plain yogurt
Flour, cake	1 cup	1 cup sifted all-purpose flour less 2 tbsp.
Flour, self-rising	1 cup	1 cup all-purpose flour plus 1-1/2 tsps. baking powder plus 1/8 tsp. salt
Chocolate, unsweetened	1 square (1 oz.)	3 tbsp. cocoa powder plus 1 tbsp. butter
Chiles, canned		Roasted green pepper plus dash hot pepper sauce
Chili sauce	1/4 cup	1/4 cup ketchup plus 1 tsps. chili powder or hot sauce
Cornstarch	1 tbsp.	2 tbsp. all-purpose flour
Corn syrup, light *(not for baking)*	1 cup	1-1/4 cups granulated sugar plus 1/3 cup water
Cracker crumbs, fine	3/4 cup	1 cup fine dry bread crumbs

emergency substitutions *(continued)*

INGREDIENT	AMOUNT	USE INSTEAD
Cream, heavy *(not for whipping)*	1 cup	3/4 cup milk plus 1/3 cup melted butter
Cream, light	1 cup	3/4 cup milk plus 1/4 cup melted butter
Cream, sour	1 cup	7/8 cup plain yogurt or buttermilk plus 3 tbsp. melted butter
Garlic	1 clove	1-1/8 tsp. garlic powder
Half-and-half	1 cup	7/8 cup milk plus 1-1/2 tbsp. melted butter
Herb, minced fresh	1 tbsp.	1 tsp. dried herb
Honey	1 cup	1-1/4 cup granulated sugar plus 1/4 cup water
Ketchup or chili sauce	1/2 cup	1/2 cup tomato sauce plus 2 tbsp. sugar, 1 tbsp. vinegar, and 1/3 tsp. ground cloves
Lemon juice	1 tsp.	1/2 tsp. vinegar
Milk, whole	1 cup	1/2 cup evaporated milk plus 1/2 cup water; or 1 cup water plus 1/3 cup instant nonfat powdered milk and 2 tsp. melted butter
Mustard, prepared	1 tbsp.	1 tsp. dried mustard
Onion	1 small	1 tbsp. instant minced onion
Pork, ground	1/2 lb.	1/2 lb. mild sausage
Pumpkin puree, canned	15 oz.	2 cups pureed cooked fresh pumpkin or winter squash
Sugar, brown	1 cup	1 cup granulated sugar plus 2 tablespoons molasses
Sugar, confectioners'	1 cup	2 cups granulated sugar ground to powder in food processor
Tomatoes, crushed	2 cups	1-3/4 cups tomato puree
Red pepper sauce	4 drops	1/8 tsp. cayenne pepper
Tomato paste	1 tbsp.	1 tbsp. ketchup
Vinegar	1 tsp.	2 tsp. lemon juice
Wine or sherry	Any	Vermouth, apple cider, white grape juice, or broth

food equivalent and yields

FOOD	AMOUNT	YIELDS
Almonds, shelled	1 lb.	3-1/2 cups
Apples	1 lb.	3 cups pared, sliced
Apricots, dried	1 lb.	2-3/4 cups
Bananas	1 lb.	3 to 4 medium bananas
Beans, canned	15-1/2oz.	2 cups drained
Beans, green (fresh)	1 lb.	3 cups uncooked or 2-1/2 cups cooked
Beans, dried	1 lb.	2 cups uncooked or 6 cups cooked
Berries	1 quart	3-1/2 cups

food equivalents and yields *(continued)*

FOOD	AMOUNT	YIELDS
Bread crumbs, fresh	1 bread slice	1/2 cup
Broccoli	1 lb.	2 cups cooked
Butter	1/4 lb.	8 tbsp. or 1/2 cup, melted
Cabbage	1 lb.	4 cups shredded
Carrots	1 lb.	2-1/2 cups diced
Cheese, blue	4 oz.	1 cup crumbled
Cheese, hard	1/4 lb.	1 cup shredded
Cheese, cottage	1/2 lb.	1 cup
Cheese, Parmesan	4 oz.	1-1/4 cups grated
Chicken, broiler or fryer	3-1/2 lb.	2 cups cooked, diced meat
Chocolate	1 oz.	4 tbsp. grated
Coffee, brewed	1 lb.	45 (6 oz.) cups
Coffee, instant	2 oz.	25 (6 oz.) cups
Corn	2 ears, shucked	1 cup kernels
Crackers, graham	16	1-1/4 cups crumbs
Egg whites, large	8	About 1 cup
Flour, all-purpose	1 lb.	4 cups sifted
Flour, whole-wheat,	1lb.	3-1/2 cups
Graham cracker crumbs	15 crackers	1 cup
Lemon	1 medium	2 to 3 tbsp. juice; 2 tsp. grated rind
Milk, instant *(nonfat dry)*	1 lb.	4 quarts
Mushrooms, fresh	1/2 lb.	1 cup sliced, cooked
Oatmeal	1 cup	2-1/4 cups cooked
Onion	1 medium	1/2 cup chopped
Orange	1 medium	6 to 8 tbsp. juice; 2 to 3 tbsp. grated zest
Pasta, uncooked	8 ounces	4 cups cooked
Peach or pear	1/4 lb.	1/2 cup sliced
Peas, dried	1 lb.	2-1/4 cups uncooked or 5 cups cooked
Pecans, in shell	1 lb.	2-1/4 cups chopped nutmeats
Pepper, bell	1 large	1 cup diced
Potatoes, 3 medium	1 lb.	2-1/4 cups cooked or 1-3/4 cups mashed
Prunes, dried	1 lb.	2-1/2 cups or 4 cups cooked
Raisins	1 lb.	2-3/4 cups
Rice	1/2 lb.	1 cup dried or 3 cups cooked
Spaghetti noodles	1 lb.	6 to 8 cups cooked
Spinach	1 lb.	1-1/2 cups cooked
Sugar, brown	1 lb.	2-1/4 cups firmly packed
Sugar, confectioners'	1 lb.	3-1/2 cups
Sugar, granulated	1 lb.	2 cups
Tea	1 lb.	125 cups, brewed

meal-planning for
Pennies

WITH A LITTLE PLANNING, HOME-COOKED
MEALS CAN BE NOT ONLY CHEAP BUT
DELIGHTFUL AND NUTRITIOUS AS WELL.

**"What's for dinner
tonight?"
This question drives
many working parents
or spouses right to
a restaurant or take-
out place, and the
monetary (not to
mention calorie) costs
can be considerable
over time. Eating at
home is cheaper
and healthier by far.
And with a little
thinking ahead,
home cooking
can be fun, creative,
and yummy, too.
But whether meals
are homemade or
not, try to eat them
together as a family.**

make a list

To make cooking at home—not to mention the shopping—easier, try to pencil in a week's worth of meals at a time. Don't feel you're locked into a particular meal, but use the list as a way to take the hassle out of coming up with a new meal every night. If you don't want to decide on an entire meal, pencil in the main course; then you can play around with the side dishes.

a family affair

Turn menu planning into a family project. Ask various members to list their favorite dishes, and then compile menus using those dishes. Make everyone agree ahead of time to eat the planned dishes without complaint. If Tuesday night's fare isn't to your daughter's taste, she'll at least know that she'll get her favorite dish on Wednesday. Once you've planned the meals, assign tasks to each person in the family. This relieves the main cook of some of the burden of meal preparation, teaches kids about cooking, makes the waste of food less likely, and makes the meal run more smoothly. Even small children can set the table.

variety is the spice of life

- Don't fall into the rut of cooking the same things over and over. Share recipes with friends and family, keep your eye out for new ideas in magazines, thumb through cookbooks while you watch TV at night. Some supermarkets even provide recipes in their meat, produce, and other food departments. You'll enjoy cooking more and your family will enjoy home-cooked meals more if there's a little variety now and again.
- Change the meal pattern: Instead of including a meat or poultry, a vegetable, a grain, and so forth in every meal, serve a hearty stew, a satisfying soup, a creative casserole, a shepherd's pie, or a main-dish salad.
- Surprise your family with breakfast for dinner. Egg dishes, pancakes, waffles, even hot cereals can provide a much-needed break from the ordinary. These dishes are also fast and easy to prepare, which gives the cook a break, too.

do it your way

As you use a recipe over time, you'll develop your own way of doing things, you'll make alterations that work better for you and your family, or you'll figure out recipe shortcuts. Write all these things on the recipe card or in the margin of the recipe book itself. If you trust it to your memory, you'll end up forgetting or remembering too late.

winning food combinations

If you put together a menu that works particularly well, write it on a recipe card, including the sources of all the dishes included. Then when you have an event coming up, you'll have an instant place to find a winning menu.

stale bread redux

Buying day-old bread can be a big saving (up to 50 percent off the price of fresh). And sometimes bread we already have gets stale before we can use it. So try one of these creative uses for bread that's no longer fresh:

- Revive stale bread and rolls by spraying them lightly with water, putting them in a paper bag or aluminum foil, and warming them in a 375° F oven for about five minutes for rolls, 10 to 15 minutes for bread.
- Stale bread makes divine French toast. Soak slices in a mixture of eggs and milk (add a dash of nutmeg for verve) and toast on a griddle or in a large nonstick frying pan. Serve with maple syrup, preserves, fruit yogurt, or, for dessert, with frozen yogurt or ice cream.
- Turn slices into croutons: Cut the bread into cubes and sauté them lightly in olive oil or safflower oil. Store in an airtight container for about ten days, or freeze.
- Make your own bread crumbs: Dry bread slices in an oven at 300° F for about ten minutes. Break the bread into the bowl of a food processor or blender and whirl until the crumbs are the size desired. Store in self-sealing bags in a cupboard for about two weeks, or freeze for longer storage.

simple spreads

Take a tip from upscale restaurants and serve one of these elegant (and surprisingly low-cost) spreads with crusty bread for an appetizer:

- Wrap whole, unpeeled heads of garlic in aluminum foil and roast them in a 400° F oven for one hour. Cool slightly, then cut across the top (not the stem end). Arrange the garlic heads on a serving tray with sliced bread. Squeeze a clove or two on a slice and spread out the creamy pulp.
- Serve small bowls of extra virgin olive oil with bread. Dip the bread in the oil. It tastes out of this world and is a lot healthier than fat-laden butter.

> **❝Ask your child what he wants for dinner only if he's buying.❞**

Fran Lebowitz, humorist

presto pizza

One of the most versatile of foods, pizza can be made from just about anything. It is easy to make (one of the more forgiving of doughs), and you probably have the basic ingredients on hand. Use your imagination to create culinary sensations of your own.

● For really easy dough, use your bread maker. Just pour in the ingredients, and in about 90 minutes, you'll have fresh dough ready to go.

● If you are in a hurry and can't make your own dough, ready-made pizza dough is available in most supermarkets. Or use prepared bread dough; day-old French, Italian or sourdough bread; English muffins; pita bread; or even tortillas, for south-of-the-border style pizza.

● If you don't have pizza sauce and don't have time to make it, stir oregano, basil, powdered garlic, a pinch of sugar, and a half-pinch of salt into tomato paste. The intense tomato flavor stands up to any topping.

chicken, chicken

When it comes to meat, chicken is the penny pincher's first choice. Not only is it cheaper than other meats, but if you are careful to skim off the excess fat and to avoid frying, it's also a lot healthier.

whole chicken Often on sale for as little as 49 cents a pound, whole chicken is about the best deal of any entree food in the universe. With a little practice and a strong knife or a good pair of poultry shears, you can cut one into pieces in about a minute, saving about $1 a pound in the process.

cut parts If you insist on buying chicken parts, avoid wings. They have become so fashionable that they are no longer the incredible deal that they use to be. Thighs and drumsticks generally deliver the best value.

chicken breasts If you want to splurge, keep an eye out for boneless chicken breasts on sale. Periodically, you'll find them in family size packages for as little as $1.99 a pound. Take any that you don't cook right away, wrap them individually in aluminum foil, and freeze them for later use.

chicken soup Two dollars worth of bony chicken parts—backs and necks typically sell for 49 cents a pound—are all you need to make a huge pot of wonderful chicken broth that can be frozen for three or four family soups (see recipe, page 104). It runs a quarter the cost of canned broth and is even more cost effective when compared to canned soups. And it tastes a lot better.

fast, delicious spaghetti sauce

Fancy brands of spaghetti sauce go for up to $4 a jar. And it's just too easy to use them when you need to put together a pasta dinner in 15 minutes. But in the same amount of time, you can create your own frugal homemade version of those costly sauces for about one-fourth the cost. Just take a can of crushed tomatoes, mix in some herbs (such as basil, oregano, and bay leaf), add a couple of splashes of olive oil and vinegar, and simmer for a few minutes. That's it! Experiment. There's no hard and fast recipe to follow. And you'll be surprised at how good it tastes.

baked potato base

A simple potato, baked in the oven or in a microwave, can form a terrific (and cheap) base for lunch or dinner, depending on what you put on top:

- Chopped broccoli and Cheddar cheese
- Leftover chili, chopped onions, and a dollop of sour cream or plain yogurt
- Salsa, canned corn, chopped olives, and a splash of hot sauce
- Leftover cooked ground meat, a little tomato sauce, and Parmesan cheese
- Cooked chopped spinach and a little feta cheese

OTHER DELICIOUS BAKED VEGGIES

Potatoes—and winter squash—may be the most popular vegetables to bake, but they are by no means the only ones fit for the oven. The vegetables below are all delicious when baked.

Asparagus: Arrange trimmed, peeled or unpeeled asparagus in a shallow baking dish, drizzle with melted butter or olive oil, and shake pan to coat each spear. Bake, uncovered, 10 to 12 minutes at 425° F until lightly brown.

Beets: Arrange scrubbed, unpeeled, small whole beets in a shallow baking dish, add 1 tablespoon vegetable oil, and turn beets in oil to coat. Bake, uncovered, 40 minutes at 375° F, turning occasionally. Raise heat to 425° F and bake for another 15 to 20 minutes until tender.

Carrots: Turn whole or chunked peeled or unpeeled medium-size carrots in 1 tablespoon oil or melted butter in a shallow baking dish. Bake, uncovered, 30 minutes at 375 °F, turning occasionally. Raise heat to 425° F and bake 20 minutes more until tender.

Onions: Peel sliverskin onions, turn in oil in a shallow baking dish, and bake, uncovered, 30 to 35 minutes at 350° F until tender and brown. **Note**: Large onions can be peeled, halved, and placed cut side up in a baking dish. Brush with oil and bake, uncovered, 1 to 1-1/2 hours at 350° F until soft and brown.

Parsnips: Turn whole or chunked peeled medium-size parsnips on oil or melted butter in a shallow baking pan and bake as directed for carrots (see above).

Summer squash (pattypan, yellow, zucchini): Scrub, cut yellow squash and zucchini in 1- to 2-inch chunks, pattypan in wedges, and bake, uncovered, 45 minutes at 450° F until fork-tender and nicely browned.

Turnips: Peel and quarter medium-size white turnips, then bake as directed for carrots (see above).

boutique water at bargain prices

Instead of buying expensive flavored waters, make your own. Add a splash of lemon, lime, grapefruit, or cranberry juice to plain seltzer water or club soda. These homemade beverages are tastier and easier on your pocketbook.

gourmet grinds for penny pinchers

As mentioned earlier, making your own gourmet coffee is a whole lot cheaper than frequenting one of those boutiques that gouge you for $3 a cup. And a thermal mug will let you tote your superb java anywhere.

- For years, most Americans used a percolator, which boiled water and forced it up through a basket full of ground coffee. Then the trendy crowd started using cone-shaped filters with a Melitta or Chemex glass pot, slowing pouring boiling water over the grinds so that the coffee trickled through to the base like sand in an hourglass. Automatic drip makers were next in line, doing the same thing with less effort. Now there's a tremendous variation in pots and methods, including French press, automatic espresso/cappuccino, grind and brew, and more. Each has it proponents and each can produce a good cup of coffee.

- Use 2 tablespoons of ground coffee for each 3/4 to 1 cup of water. (We like to add one for the pot, too.) You can always tone down coffee that tastes too strong but can't do anything with weak watery coffee except throw it out.

- If your water is highly chlorinated or tastes off, use filtered water, either store bought or home purified. Don't use distilled water; there needs to be some minerals in the water to bring out the flavor in the coffee.

- For real espresso, you need a pump-operated machine—a home version of the machines used in espresso bars. You can get one starting at around $100, but a good one runs closer to $300. An alternative is to get a steam-operated espresso machine, which cost anywhere from $50 to $90 or so. Unless you are a real coffee connoisseur (read snob), who drinks espresso several times a day, you are not really going to notice enough of a difference or get enough use out of the machine to warrant the extra cost. With the right coffee and grind, a steam machine can produce a very good cup of espresso.

- Even better for a serious penny pincher, that little stove-top aluminum or stainless steel pot with a cinched waist simply can't be beat for taste or price. Known as a moka, it is found in virtually every Italian home. We found one at Bed, Bath and Beyond for $12.99 (the best price we saw after checking four other stores). It comes with instructions and, when the right coffee is used (try

Medaglia D'Oro Caffé Espresso in the red, white, and green can if you don't want to grind your own gourmet beans), we challenge anyone to make a better cup of espresso at home with a fancy machine.

wine with dinner

Wine is a civilized drink with dinner, and it doesn't have to cost a fortune. In fact, more expensive is not always better when it comes to wine. Check out a book on wine at the library and learn a few basics, then shop around until you find a good supplier, whether in your local supermarket, price club (they usually have an excellent selection), or wineshop. Learn what should cost more, get to know certain reliable vineyards, read about cutting-edge countries and what they are producing (often good wine values for your money), and then drink what you enjoy and don't worry about rules. And don't overlook jug wines and even boxed wines; they are often great bargains, especially when you are having a crowd over.

● Invest in a wine saver, a gadget that forces the air out of an opened bottle of wine and then reseals it. Resealed bottles can last up to a week in the refrigerator.

● If your leftover wine has gone off slightly, use it in sauces, marinades, or salad dressings in place of vinegar.

brew your own brew

There has been an explosion in the world of beer making, and now the word microbrew is on just about everyone's lips (if you like beer, that is). The only problem is that those boutique beers can cost a pretty penny. If you really enjoy the rich flavor of microbrewed beers, you may want to consider brewing as a hobby. Look in your Yellow Pages under Beer Brewing and find a good supplier. Suppliers will have equipment, books, and even kits for brewing specialty beers. And they usually love to talk about brewing, so you can learn quite a bit from them. The initial outlay for equipment will vary, depending on how fancy you want to go (it's not necessary to go high end) and how much equipment you already have that you can adapt, but the eventual savings in premium beer will more than pay for the start-up costs. And it's fun, too.

reinvent the leftover!

● Leftover steak? Slice thin and serve on greens with horseradish dressing for a spicy salad. Or serve in warm pita bread with sliced onions and cucumber sauce.

● Seasoned ground meat? Make a savory omelet with a little Cheddar and Monterey Jack cheese. Or spread some refried beans over a large tortilla, sprinkle with some of

BUTTERMILK PINCH HITTER

If you need buttermilk for a recipe but don't have it on hand or don't want to buy more than you need for a single recipe, make your own substitute. Put 1 tablespoon of lemon juice or vinegar into a measuring cup and pour in 1 cup of milk. Let the mixture set for about five minutes. It will become sour milk, which you can use to replace buttermilk in your recipe.

the ground beef, add a little cheese, and microwave for about one minute. Top with salsa and sour cream or plain yogurt and fold both sides in to make a burrito.

● Leftover chicken? Dice it and whip up a stir-fry. Or shred the chicken and fill a taco bowl with lettuce, tomatoes, chopped olives, a little Cheddar cheese, and the chicken. Top with salsa and a bit of sour cream for added zing.

● Leftover fish steaks? Serve over salad greens with a vinaigrette or ranch dressing. Or toss with cooked pasta, steamed veggies, and a little cream sauce.

● Chop or grind leftover meat, chicken, fish, or vegetables; season the mixture; then pack it into sweet peppers, large mushroom caps, or giant pasta shells. Bake with a sauce for added flavor and moisture.

● Leftover white rice? Sauté it in a little vegetable oil until it is hot and golden. Stir in some chopped green onion and, if you have it, chopped ham or chicken or cooked shrimp until everything is well mixed. Make a hollow in the center of the pan, break two to three eggs in the hollow, and scramble them. Add some cooked peas and a little soy sauce and toss to mix everything together. Voilà! Homemade fried rice!

superchef to the rescue

A penny pincher wouldn't dream of throwing away food; however, we all have the occasional kitchen emergency. Check these quick cooking-disaster saves.

slow burn

● Get the food to a fresh pot as fast as you can. Fill your sink halfway with cold water and set the new pot in the water to stop the cooking. This will also erase any burned flavor.

● If a dish develops a burned taste, try laying a damp dish towel over the pot for a few minutes. If the food is a bit drier, rice or couscous for example, a slice or two of fresh white bread may do the trick.

sticky stuff

● If your hot rice or pasta is sticking in the colander after draining, run hot tap water over it until it loosens.

● If your breakfast or dinner is stuck on the bottom of a frying pan, fill a large, shallow pan with cold water and set the frying pan in the water. Using a flexible spatula, try to gently pry up the food.

boil, boil, and trouble

● If you see a potential boilover in time, take the pot off the stove and quickly stir the liquid to cool it down a bit.

● To prevent a boilover before you start cooking, lightly coat the rim of the pot or pan with a little oil or grease.

salt overboard
- Rinse boiled vegetables with fresh hot water.
- Add a sliced raw potato to soups and sauces; it'll absorb some of the salt. Be sure to discard the potato before serving your soup.
- Add a pinch or two of brown sugar to salty stews; the sugar will cut the saltiness without adding sweetness.

fat attack
- Refrigerate the dish until the fat solidifies, and then just skim off or spoon out the fat.
- Place a paper towel or lettuce leaf on top of a liquid isurface (soup, stew, or chili); either will attract the heavier fat components, making them easier to remove.

sweet endings

These taste tempters are fast and easy to prepare and low in cost. You can keep most of the ingredients on hand.
- Chop and mix together two or more fresh fruits. Sprinkle with a little fruit juice (orange juice is lovely) or a couple of tablespoon of orange or almond liqueur.
- Save the liquids from canned fruit. Heat the liquid with a little cornstarch to thicken it, and pour it as a sauce over fresh fruit, cake, pudding, or ice cream.
- Faux sorbet: Pour your favorite canned fruit, preferably packed in heavy syrup, into a plastic container and place the container in the freezer. When the fruit and syrup have frozen, and just before dessert time, empty the fruit-syrup mixture into a food processor or blender and whirl for a few seconds. For an elegant touch, add 2 tablespoons of rum or a liqueur just before whirling. Spoon your homemade sorbet into glass dishes (or wineglasses) to serve.
- Tolerant trifle: If a cake breaks apart when you're removing it from the pan, improvise! Place the pieces in a large glass bowl and add layers of fruit (fresh or thawed frozen), chopped nuts, and whipped cream or vanilla pudding.
- Slice fresh strawberries, bananas, and kiwi into individual serving bowls. Drizzle a tablespoon or so of chocolate sauce over the fruit and serve.

Although convenient, paper napkins are wasteful and cost you in the long run. Take a tip from our forebears and switch to cloth napkins. Make your own from cotton remnants: Cut a 12-inch square and machine- or handstitch a small rolled hem. Or check for cloth napkins at clearance or white sales. For a family of four, plan on a set of 12 napkins per week. Just toss dirty napkins in the laundry. Cloth dish towels also last longer, look nicer, and make good monetary sense.

make your own mixes

Ready-made mixes are a godsend to busy cooks. They are convenient, you can keep them on hand for use as needed, they can shorten your time in the kitchen, and so on. But they tend to be expensive and contain more salt than anyone needs. The solution? Make your own mixes and keep them in self-sealing plastic bags, bottles, or jars (depending on the mix), labeled for use.

savory meat mix

- 2 tablespoons olive oil
- 2 medium onions, peeled and chopped
- 2 cloves garlic, peeled and finely chopped
- 1 stalk celery, chopped
- 2 carrots, chopped
- 2-1/2 pounds lean ground beef, chicken, or turkey
- 2 teaspoons dried basil, crumbled
- 1 teaspoon dried oregano, crumbled
- 1 teaspoon salt
- 1/2 teaspoon black pepper
- large pinch sugar
- 1 tablespoon Worcestershire sauce
- 1 (14-1/2 ounce) can diced tomatoes in sauce

① Heat the oil in a large, deep skillet over moderate heat.

② Add the onions, garlic, celery, and carrots to the skillet and sauté for ten minutes, stirring occasionally. Crumble the meat or poultry into the skillet, breaking it up with a large spoon; cook, stirring occasionally, until the meat is no longer pink. Add the basil, oregano, salt, pepper, sugar, Worcestershire sauce, and the tomatoes with their sauce; stir until well mixed. Reduce the heat, cover the skillet, and simmer for 20 to 25 minutes.

③ Remove the skillet from the heat and let cool completely. Spoon off any visible fat and then divide the mixture among three to four (1-pint) self-sealing freezer bags. Squeeze all the air out of the bags, label, date, and freeze.

Will keep for three months stored in the freezer. MAKES 3-1/2 TO 4 PINTS.

skillet supper italiano

- 1 package (10 ounces) frozen Italian-style vegetables
- 1 pint savory meat mix, thawed
- 2 cups cooked ziti, penne, fusilli, or wagon-wheel pasta
- 1 can (8 ounces) tomato sauce
- 1 cup (8 ounces) part-skim ricotta cheese
- 1/4 cup Parmesan cheese

① In a skillet, cook the mixed vegetables according to the package directions.

② Stir in the savory meat mix, cooked pasta, and tomato sauce. Cover and cook over moderate heat for about ten minutes, stirring occasionally. Add a little water if necessary to prevent sticking.

③ Stir in the ricotta cheese until well mixed. Sprinkle the Parmesan cheese over the top; do not stir. Cover the skillet and cook just until the mixture is heated through, about ten minutes. Serve from the skillet. MAKES 4 TO 6 SERVINGS.

chili con carne

- 1 pint savory meat mix, thawed
- 1 tablespoon chili powder
- 1 teaspoon cumin
- 1/2 teaspoon cayenne pepper
- 2 cans (15-1/2 ounces each) red kidney beans, drained and rinsed
- shredded Cheddar cheese (optional)

Combine the meat mix, chili powder, cumin, cayenne pepper, and kidney beans in a medium saucepan. Cover and cook over moderate heat for about ten minutes. If you wish, serve over cooked rice or with tortilla chips, and sprinkle each serving with a little Cheddar cheese. MAKES 6 SERVINGS.

make your own mixes

speedy pizza

- 1 pint savory meat mix, thawed
- 6 sourdough English muffins, split
- 1 cup grated mozzarella cheese
- 3 teaspoons dried oregano, crumbled
- 1-1/2 teaspoons dried basil, crumbled
- hot pepper flakes (optional)
- thinly sliced olives, onions, green or red peppers, mushrooms, and thin slices of pepperoni (optional)

(1) In a small saucepan, simmer the savory meat mix for about five minutes or until heated through.

(2) Meanwhile, toast the sourdough muffin halves, then arrange them in a single layer on a cookie sheet. Spoon some of the meat mix over each muffin half. Sprinkle with some of the cheese, oregano, basil, and hot pepper flakes if desired. If you wish, top with sliced vegetables or pepperoni or a combination.

(3) Broil the pizzas for three to five minutes or until the cheese is lightly browned and bubbly. MAKES 12 INDIVIDUAL PIZZAS.

basic biscuit mix

- 6 cups all-purpose flour (or 3 cups all-purpose and 3 cups whole-wheat flour)
- 3-1/2 tablespoons baking powder
- 1 cup nonfat powdered milk
- 1 tablespoon salt
- 1 cup solid vegetable shortening

In a large bowl, combine the flour, baking powder, powdered milk, and salt; mix well. With a pastry blender, cut in the shortening until the biscuit mix resembles coarse meal. Put in a self-sealing plastic bag, label, and date.

Will keep six weeks at room temperature. MAKES ABOUT 8 CUPS OF MIX.

homestyle biscuits

- 2 cups basic biscuit mix
- 1/2 cup skim or 1 percent milk

(1) Preheat the oven to 450° F. In a medium-size bowl, stir the biscuit mix and milk with a fork until just blended.

(2) On a lightly floured surface, gently knead the dough ten times. Roll the dough out to a 1/2-inch thickness and cut out 2-1/2-inch rounds. Place the rounds on an ungreased baking sheet.

(3) Bake for 10 to 12 minutes or until golden brown. Serve hot. MAKES ABOUT 10 BISCUITS.

variation Add 1/2 cup shredded Cheddar cheese or 1/2 cup grated Parmesan cheese.

waffles

- 2 large eggs, separated
- 1-3/4 cups basic biscuit mix
- 1 cup skim or 1 percent milk
- 3 tablespoons butter or margarine, melted
- 1 teaspoon vanilla (optional)

(1) Preheat a waffle iron. In a large mixing bowl, lightly beat the egg yolks. Add the biscuit mix, milk, melted butter or margarine, and vanilla (if desired); stir until just moistened. In a medium-size bowl, beat the egg whites with an electric mixer until stiff peaks form. Gently fold the egg whites into the batter until no white streaks remain.

(2) Cook according to the waffle iron manufacturer's directions. MAKES ABOUT FIVE 8- X 4-INCH WAFFLES.

pancakes

- 2 cups biscuit mix
- 2 large eggs, lightly beaten
- 1 cup skim or 1 percent milk

(1) Combine biscuit mix with eggs, milk, and vanilla (if desired) and stir until the ingredients are barely blended; do not overmix (or the batter will be lumpy).

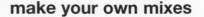

make your own mixes

② Spray a griddle or large flat skillet with nonstick cooking spray. Over moderate heat, bring the griddle to hot but make sure it is not smoking. Spoon the batter onto the griddle using about 1/4 cup per pancake and cook until bubbles form across the top, for about two minutes. Flip the pancakes and cook for two minutes more. Serve immediately. MAKES ABOUT 10 TO 12 PANCAKES.

variation If desired, stir 1/2 cup blueberries, sliced strawberries, sliced bananas, or mini chocolate chips into the batter.

best brownie mix
- 2 cups white sugar
- 1-1/2 cups brown sugar
- 2-1/2 cups all-purpose flour
- 1-1/2 cups unsweetened cocoa powder
- 2 teaspoons baking powder
- 1-1/2 teaspoons salt
- 2 cups solid butter-flavored vegetable shortening

In a large bowl, mix together the white and brown sugars, flour, cocoa powder, baking powder, and salt. With a pastry blender or two knives, cut in the shortening until the brownie mix resembles coarse meal, working in batches if necessary.

Will keep for six weeks, refrigerated, in a self-sealing plastic bag or tightly sealed container.

best brownies
- 3 cups brownie mix
- 2 large eggs
- 2 teaspoons vanilla
- 1/2 cup coarsely chopped pecans or walnuts
- 1/2 cup semisweet chocolate chips or peanut butter chips

① Preheat the oven to 350° F. Combine all the ingredients in a medium-size bowl and stir until just blended, about 40 strokes. Pour the mixture into a greased 8-inch-square baking pan and smooth the surface of the mix.

② Bake for 30 minutes or until a knife inserted in the center comes out clean.

③ Place the pan upright on a wire rack and let the brownies cool to room temperature. Cut into squares and serve. MAKES 16 BROWNIES.

cornbread mix
- 3 cups sifted all-purpose flour
- 3 cups yellow cornmeal
- 1-1/2 cups instant nonfat dry milk
- 3 tablespoons white or brown sugar (optional)
- 3-1/2 tablespoons baking powder
- 2-1/2 teaspoons salt
- 3/4 cup solid vegetable shortening

Combine the dry ingredients and mix well. Using a pastry blender or two knives, cut in the shortening until the mixture resembles coarse crumbs.

Will keep six weeks, refrigerated, in self-sealing bags or airtight containers. MAKES ABOUT 8 CUPS.

classic cornbread
- 2-1/2 cups cornbread mix
- 3 eggs, lightly beaten
- 1 cup water

① Preheat the oven to 425° F. Combine all the ingredients in a large mixing bowl and stir until just mixed. Pour into a greased 8-inch-square baking pan.

② Bake about 17 minutes or until a knife inserted in the center comes out clean. Cut into squares and serve hot with butter. To store, cover the pan tightly with aluminum foil.

Will keep three days refrigerated; two months in the freezer.

variation Stir in a 4-ounce can of jalapeño or mild green peppers, drained and chopped.

make your own mixes

seasoned coating mix

- 2 cups sifted all-purpose flour
- 1 tablespoon paprika
- 2 teaspoons dried marjoram, crumbled
- 2 teaspoons dried thyme, crumbled
- 2 teaspoons onion powder
- 2 teaspoons garlic powder
- 1 teaspoon dried rosemary, crumbed
- 1/2 teaspoon salt
- 1/4 teaspoon black pepper

Combine all the ingredients in a self sealing plastic bag. Seal the bag and shake it to combine all the ingredients.

Will keep six months in a cool, dark place. MAKES ENOUGH TO COAT 20 PORK CHOPS OR FOUR CHICKENS.

variation for fish To 2 cups of flour, add 2 tablespoons dried tarragon, 1 tablespoon dried dill weed, 2 teaspoons dried parsley flakes (all herbs crumbled), 1 teaspoon onion powder, 1 teaspoon garlic powder, 1/2 teaspoon salt, and 1/4 teaspoon white pepper. MAKES ENOUGH TO COAT 30 FISH FILLETS OR FISH STEAKS.

seasoned baked chicken

Low in fat, easy to make, and very tasty.

- 2 tablespoons vegetable oil
- 1 broiling or frying chicken (about 3 pounds), cut into eight pieces
- 1/2 cup seasoned coating mix

① Preheat the oven to 425° F. Coat a large, shallow baking pan with nonstick cooking spray.

② Brush the vegetable oil over the chicken pieces. Pour the seasoned coating into a large self-sealing plastic bag. Add two chicken pieces to the bag, seal it, and shake until both pieces are evenly coated. Remove the chicken pieces from the bag and arrange them in a single layer on the prepared pan. Repeat until all the chicken pieces are coated.

③ Place the chicken in the oven and immediately reduce the heat to 350° F. Bake, uncovered, for about one hour, or until the chicken is no longer pink near the bone; darker meat may need five to ten minutes more. MAKES 4 SERVINGS.

seasoned baked pork chops

The double-duty coating adds sensational flavor and keeps the chops moist. For thicker chops, add five to ten minutes.

- 4 (1-inch thick) pork chops, trimmed
- 6 tablespoons seasoned coating mix

① Preheat the oven to 425° F. Coat a large, shallow baking pan with nonstick cooking spray.

② Lightly dampen each pork chop with water, shaking off the excess. Pour the seasoned coating into a large self-sealing plastic bag. Add one pork chop to the bag, seal it, and shake until the chop is evenly coated. Remove the pork chop from the bag and arrange on the prepared pan. Repeat until pork chops are coated.

③ Bake the pork chops in the preheated oven, uncovered, 15 to 20 minutes or until the chops are no longer pink on the inside. MAKES 4 SERVINGS.

seasoned baked fish

- 2 tablespoons vegetable oil
- 2 pounds fish fillets (or steaks)
- 6 tablespoons seasoned coating mix, variation for fish

① Preheat oven to 375° F. Coat a shallow baking pan with nonstick cooking spray.

② Lightly brush some vegetable oil over each fish fillet, coating each side. Spread the coating in a shallow dish. One at a time, dredge each fillet until it is well coated on each side, shaking off any excess. Arrange the fillets on the prepared pan.

③ Bake uncovered, 10 to 20 minutes (depending on the fillet's thickness) or until it flakes easily. MAKES 4 SERVINGS.

Beauty on a Budget

- dressing for less
- chic looks for little investment
- cosmetic caper...

Appearances can be deceiving. That elegant woman in the red wool suit with the creamy silk blouse, snazzy shoes and matching purse, peaches-and-cream complexion, and just the right makeup might have spent thousands of dollars to achieve this perfect look . . . or did she? Surprise! The suit was actually picked up at a steep discount during a pre-inventory sale at a high-end department store. The blouse was a thrift store coup (never worn with the tags still attached). The shoes and purse found at the fifteenth outlet store she rummaged through. The complexion was achieved literally with peaches and cream. And the make-up was purchased at her local drugstore for a fraction of the cost of department store counterparts. Not that you'll ever know this. What that woman has accomplished is a high-end appearance at bargain-basement prices—and it's strictly her happy little secret that the money she saved is racking up interest in a money-market account. This is the real goal of penny pinchers: to enjoy looking like a million bucks when you only spent $49.95!

What are you waiting for!

dressing for
Less

WHEN IT COMES TO CLOTHING,
YOUR SHOPPING MANTRA SHOULD
BE "FRUGAL AND FABULOUS."

**A chic wardrobe doesn't have to cost a fortune. In fact, retail markup is ridiculous—often as much as 200 percent. And that's not necessarily for the highest quality merchandise!
We all want to dress well, but do we have to pay through the nose to look good? Nope. We just need to adopt the penny pincher's shopping strategy: Buy quality, not quantity; buy off-season or on sale; and take care of the clothes you have so that they'll last.**

before you buy:
planning a fabulously frugal wardrobe

To plan your new wardrobe, start with your current clothing. Take all the clothes you own out of your closet and drawers and make three piles:

PILE 1 is for the ragbag. These clothes are irreparably damaged or stained. (Remove and save the buttons before tossing them.)

PILE 2 includes clothes that are hopelessly outdated without being retro, clothes that no longer fit, and clothes you haven't worn in the past year. Sell these items at a garage sale or give them to charity.

PILE 3 gets the keepers—pieces you still wear that look and feel good on you and are in good condition. Now you're ready to figure out what you need to buy to complete a wonderful working wardrobe.

fashion plus musts

For a dynamic working wardrobe, you'll need a well-made blazer or two, two skirts, and two pairs of slacks. The skirts and slacks should not all be the same color, but they should all go well with the jacket. Solid colors will be more versatile and date less quickly than patterns or plaids will, but you don't have to think only in dark solid colors. Look for fabrics you can wear year-round, such as lightweight wool, challis, sturdy cotton, linen, and silk, and buy the highest quality basic pieces that you can. By investing in well-made basics, you'll actually save money, because the clothes will last longer and look better even after numerous cleanings. Always check the label on a new garment for the care required to avoid spending more on dry cleaning than you have to. It's well worth the money to dry-clean a suit, but do you really want to pay to clean shirts and blouses, too?

the rule of three

When you're considering a clothing purchase, be sure each piece passes the rule of three: Can you think of 3 things to wear it with, 3 places to wear it to, and 3 ways to accessorize it?

For example, you spy a poppy-red, washable silk blouse on sale. You can wear it with your linen suit and a scarf for the office, with a paisley challis skirt and your antique gold earring and necklace set for dinner out, and with black wool slacks and a brocade vest for high casual entertaining (three outfits, three places, three accessories). If you can't quickly come up with three pairings, places, and presentations, forget it! It's just not worth the cost.

time to shop: stores galore

Clothing stores are much more varied than they once were. At both high-end department stores (such as Nordstrom and Saks Fifth Avenue) and discount stores (such as Kohl's and T. J. Maxx), you can find bargains and less-than-bargains— it's your job to be a savvy shopper.

high end These stores (Nordstrom, Saks, Barneys, and the like) cater to the well-to-do and carry designer labels with correspondingly high prices. Does that mean a penny pincher should never shop at them? No! Even the priciest department stores have sales, including clearance sales, where you can pick up extremely well-made clothing at reduced prices. Now, these prices won't be cheap, but if you're looking for a Donna Karan dress or a Calvin Klein suit, you can find it at a high-end department store sale for a fraction of the original price. Cost is relative.

mid-range These department stores (Macy's, Dillard's, and the like) also have designer sections, but they carry a large inventory of mass-market designer labels, such as DKNY (Donna Karan), Chaps (Ralph Lauren), and Lizwear (Liz Claiborne). These stores sometimes have fabulous sales. (At Macy's post-Christmas sale, we picked up an $80 cocktail dress for $19.99!) You just need to know the sales calendar. (See page 54.)

discount clothing chains These stores (T.J. Maxx, Kohl's, Daffy's, and the like) carry a hodgepodge of clothing, including designer fashion, all at significant discounts. For example, T.J. Maxx sells brand names at 20 percent to 60 percent off retail. On their Web site recently, Kohl's was selling Gloria Vanderbilt stretch capris for $21.99, discounted from about $36. And Daffy's was advertising men's Italian sports shirts for $26.99 to $29.99, discounted from about $98 to $118. So the savings can be terrific. Check the items carefully, though, because they can be manhandled as folks tear through them looking for the best bargains.

specialty stores In these stores (Gap, Banana Republic, Abercrombie & Fitch, and the like), the retail prices, like those in high- and mid-range department stores, are often fairly steep, but their clearance racks can yield fantastic finds and are well worth a visit.

"Fashions fade; style is eternal."

Yves Saint Laurent

JANUARY

Holiday clothing; winter coats; cashmere and other wool sweaters; gloves, hats, and scarves; costume jewelry; lingerie; purses; shoes

FEBRUARY

Valentine's Day and Presidents' Day specials; men's apparel; fine jewelry; winter boots

MARCH

Winter clothing; boys' and girls' shoes; infants' clothing

APRIL

Spring dresses and raincoats; hosiery; lingerie; women's shoes

MAY

Mother's Day and Memorial Day specials; cosmetics and beauty products; handbags; housecoats; jewelry; shoes; sportswear

outstanding outlets

Are factory outlet stores and malls really full of great bargains? Sometimes. Are they worth the trip? That depends—on how close they are, on what you're shopping for, and on how astute you are about prices. You can find some outstanding bargains at outlets (up to 75 percent off the retail price), but a designer or upscale item is still going to cost you, even if it's deeply discounted. At an L.L. Bean outlet, for instance, we found that the clothes weren't much of a bargain (half off, but still $60 for a casual dress), but Teva sandals (normally $40 to $80) were priced at $29.99. That's still not cheap, but it's not bad for a high-end product. Most people don't shop at outlets regularly (unless they live close to one). More often, shoppers visit outlets while on vacation or during a big shopping season (back-to-school, December holidays). Unfortunately, what you find will be the luck of the draw, but for a major shopping trip, try the following:

- Do your homework before you go: Know the general prices of the merchandise you're shopping for (wool coats, dress slacks, silk blouses).
- Look for outlet malls that are anchored by a few well-known names (Gap, Burlington Coat Factory, Saks) and that have at least three stores you're interested in.
- Get there early and walk the stores to get an overview of what they carry and the prices, making notes to yourself so you won't forget to go back later.
- Examine the merchandise carefully. Some big-name companies produce special lines just for their outlets, and the quality isn't always as high as their retail counterparts.
- Unless you're shopping for kids, leave children at home. Outlets require concentration.
- Wear comfortable shoes and bring snacks and water. You'll last longer and won't have to stop to eat.

how super are superstores?

Stores such as Target, Kmart, and Wal-Mart can be super sources of inexpensive clothing, but you have to know how to use them. Although these stores sell mostly casual clothing, they are also good places to pick up trendy gear at a minimal cost. Both Target and Kmart have their own house brands (Cherokee, Route 66), which tend to cost less than national name brands and are quite well made. All three chains have contracts with celebrity designers (such as Kathy Ireland, Jaclyn Smith, Mossimo), allowing them to offer more trendy looks at lower prices. Always make a point of checking the clearance racks (usually toward the back of the department) at the end of a season. The managers really like to move merchandise, so you can pick up stuff for 75 percent off or more (say, a $16 sweater for $4.99).

price clubs

These big box stores may surprise you. Price clubs offer a variety of clothing, including major clothing lines, often at fantastic bargains. On a recent expedition to Costco, we spotted women's Speedo swimsuits for $21, crinkle-cloth dresses for $15, and designer shorts for $12. SAM's Club offered Polo jeans for men at $24.99 and their store brand, Members Mark, men's jeans for $11.98. The only drawbacks to clothes shopping at price clubs are that you can't count on seeing the same merchandise from one visit to the next, there often aren't any dressing rooms, and the stock tends to be strictly seasonal. But keep your eyes open when you visit. You may snag a really good deal on well-made merchandise.

thrift stores

We're not just talking your mother's thrift store here. Although your local Salvation Army or Goodwill shop can still delight or disappoint, there are a few new wrinkles.

consignment stores These are popping up all over (especially for children's clothing), and you can score excellent deals at them. You can find them in the Yellow Pages under Consignment Shops—often with cute names like Once Again or Second Time Around. Although they sell mostly used clothing, their standards are pretty high. The clothing must be in good condition for sale. At a consignment store, you can sell, buy, or trade gently used, good-looking clothes. Buffalo Exchange, a consignment chain thriving in the Southwest and West, hires "trendspotters" to ensure the fashion aspects of the inventory. You'll find a lot of vintage 1960s, '70s, and '80s clothing at consignment stores, but you'll also discover traditional looks and even some new clothing.

thrift stores These range from Goodwill warehouses to opera society stores, and the merchandise can be just as varied. In high-end thrift stores, located in upscale neighborhoods or run to benefit a charity or cultural institution (such as an opera company) that attracts a fairly well-to-do clientele, you may find Armani, Valentino, or other designer clothing—some of it barely worn. The downside is that you will pay more for the clothes; the upside is that what you pay will still be a fraction of the full price. You also have the other end of the thrift-shop spectrum—stores that offer well-worn, uninspiring collections of rags.

That's both the challenge and the fun of thrift-store shopping. You have to go in with low expectations, be open to possibilities, and be willing to go home with nothing. Whatever your past opinion of such stores has been, it does make good financial sense to check out better thrift stores and consignment shops in your area. See what you can find, you'll probably be pleasantly surprised.

JUNE

Father's Day specials and men's clothing; bathing suits; boys' clothing, lingerie and sleepwear; hosiery; women's shoes

JULY

July Fourth specials; bathing suits; children's clothing; handbags; lingerie and sleepwear; men's shirts and shoes; sportswear; summer wear

AUGUST

Back-to-school specials; summer clothing; men's coats; women's coats; cosmetics

SEPTEMBER

Labor Day specials; fall clothing

OCTOBER

Columbus Day specials; fall and winter clothing; lingerie and hosiery; women's coats

NOVEMBER

Election Day and Veterans Day specials; Thanksgiving specials; boys' suits and coats; lingerie; men's suits and coats; shoes; winter clothing

DECEMBER

Holiday specials; children's clothing; coats; hats; men's furnishings; cruise wear; shoes (The Christmas-to-New Year week is a great but crowded sales time.)

coupons for clothes?

Now here's some good news: Coupons are not just for food.

- ◉ Check major department store ads in your newspaper. They often have coupons for 10 to 20 percent off in certain departments. Combine that with a sale, and you can snap up some dazzling duds at truly bargain-basement prices.
- ◉ Outlet malls also frequently offer books of coupons (sometimes for a small fee) for their stores.
- ◉ If you have a store credit card, check the inserts with your bill each month. You may find a coupon tucked in there to lure you back to the store. And department stores sometimes have special sales offering an extra 10 to 20 percent off for using their card.
- ◉ Support your favorite nonprofit organization by investing in one of those community discount-coupon books. You won't just find dollars off on restaurants; you'll also find some terrific savings at clothing stores.

getting discounts on discounted items

Some tips to save you even more at the checkout counter:

button-off bargains If you find a garment you really like and a button or two is missing, you may be able to buy the piece at a discount, especially if it is an end-of-season item. A good discount can more than pay for new buttons. If you already have a set in your button box, so much the better. (You do have a hoard of buttons, right?)

highly irregular Items marked as irregular may not be perfect in size or color, but they are usually free of substantial damage and are often a real deal. Those marked as seconds or thirds should be examined with a fine-tooth comb, however, as they may have serious flaws. You may still decide to buy such items; just look carefully first to see whether you can live with, cover, or repair the flaws.

women unite: raid the men's room!

It's grossly unfair that, by and large, men's clothing is less expensive (and often of better quality) than women's. When shopping, especially during sales, be sure to go through the men's and boys' sections to see what you can make work for you. Try an oversized men's polo shirt with your capri pants or a men's crewneck sweater with khakis.

working clothes

Many department stores, mid-price to low-end, and super-stores carry heavy-duty men's work clothes, usually aimed at those who wear khaki pants as part of a uniform. These pants are made to last and are a fraction of the price of name-brand khakis. If you want a pair of nice casual pants that will be with you for years, this is a good option. Wear them with a nice shirt, and who'll know the difference?

life extenders for new clothes

Check all the stitching before wearing a new piece of clothing. If you see any loose thread ends, fasten or trim them or pull them to the wrong side of the garment and secure them.

- Reinforce stitching on patch pockets by sewing a tiny triangle at each top corner of the pocket.
- Use iron-on patches on the inside of the knees of pants, especially jeans. You can use this trick on shirt or jacket elbows that will get a lot of rough wear, too. Hidden iron-on patches are particularly useful for kids' clothing.
- Use cotton underarm shields to protect your favorite dresses from perspiration stains. Either tack the shields on or sew on snaps to secure them.
- Check the stitching on all fasteners—buttons, hooks and eyes, snaps—and resew them securely if any are loose. Machine-stitch around the edges of Velcro pieces to keep them from pulling away from the fabric.
- Let your clothes air out or dry before you put them away. Don't wear the same items day after day; allow at least 24 hours for moisture to evaporate.
- Use a cotton ball soaked in witch hazel to wipe away body oils around your neck and wrists before getting dressed to avoid staining collars and cuffs.

the right coat

Coats can end up costing you big bucks unless you're a smart shopper. When you shop for a coat, keep in mind that this item will get a lot of wear and tear, so pick a coat that is well made. Try these coat-buying tips:

- Buy at the end of the season. Department stores often have great sales on high-quality coats that they want to get rid of before the new season starts. Depending on where you live, January and February are often the best months.
- Make your coat do double duty. Instead of buying a wool coat for warmth and a raincoat for wet weather, buy a raincoat with a zip-out lining. It will see you through all but the worst cold weather (when you can wear a sweater underneath). In fact, any waterproof shell with a warm, removable lining can easily get you from fall through spring. At the Burlington Coat Factory site (**www.bcfdirect.com**), we found a Bill Blass microfiber rain jacket with removable lining for $79.99, originally priced at $175!
- Check out thrift stores. They sometimes have great coats, especially if you like a funky, retro look.
- Visit your local Army-Navy store for a good bargain in a warm, well-made pea jacket for other casual wear.

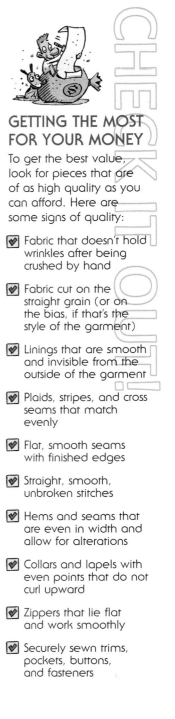

GETTING THE MOST FOR YOUR MONEY

To get the best value, look for pieces that are of as high quality as you can afford. Here are some signs of quality:

- ✔ Fabric that doesn't hold wrinkles after being crushed by hand
- ✔ Fabric cut on the straight grain (or on the bias, if that's the style of the garment)
- ✔ Linings that are smooth and invisible from the outside of the garment
- ✔ Plaids, stripes, and cross seams that match evenly
- ✔ Flat, smooth seams with finished edges
- ✔ Straight, smooth, unbroken stitches
- ✔ Hems and seams that are even in width and allow for alterations
- ✔ Collars and lapels with even points that do not curl upward
- ✔ Zippers that lie flat and work smoothly
- ✔ Securely sewn trims, pockets, buttons, and fasteners

SENIOR STEALS

MALL ON THE NET
www.wiredseniors.com/mall

Surfing the Web recently, we found this terrific site for seniors. It hooks you up with the Seniors Discount Mall. They have listings for dozens of things, from antiques and collectibles and apparel to health and beauty, sports and travel — all offering special discounts for seniors. One of the apparel sites is Silvert's, a company that sells attractive clothing that is easy to put on and take off using Velcro closures and with discreet openings in the back. They specialize in clothing for people with arthritis, but also offer comfortable outfits for the wheelchair-bound, and people with other physical disabilities.

bathing beauty

A good quality swimsuit can be a good investment. Cheap bathing suits usually don't last very long, but if you don't swim often or plan to wear a suit only a few times, quality may not matter that much to you. Here are some buying tips:

- Look for end- or beginning-of-season sales (typically May through August).
- Check out price clubs at the beginning of the summer season and superstores during holiday sales.
- If you find a suit you love at a bargain price, buy two. You'll double your savings and won't have to shop again soon.
- Take care of your suit. Rinse it in cold water after each use to remove salt or chlorine and hand-wash or machine-wash it on the gentle cycle. Do not twist or wring it out.

silk savoir faire

Although luxurious, silk is actually quite durable. (Hot-air balloons used to be made of silk.) Silk keeps you cool in summer, because it's breathable and light, and keeps you warm in the winter, especially if it's layered with other clothing. If you treat silk right, it will last and stay beautiful longer.

- Hang silk clothing on plastic or padded hangers. Wooden hangers can snag silk, and thin metal hangers frequently leave small creases or imprints in silk garments.
- Treat new stains on silk by dampening a clean washcloth with club soda and sandwiching the stained silk between two layers of the washcloth. This will lessen staining, but wash or dry-clean the garment as soon as possible.

making leather last

A brand-new leather coat is a hefty investment, which is why dedicated penny pinchers often buy used ones at thrift or consignment stores or garage sales and clean them up. But a new leather coat will usually last for years (especially if you stick to a classic style) and can truly keep the wind out (which is why bikers wear them). Besides, for many people they are the ultimate in cool. So if you make the investment, protect it!

- Waterproofing your leather garment can protect it from minor staining. The products sold for waterproofing leather work fine on shoes and boots, but for soft leathers, you might be better off using a temporary fluorocarbon spray such as 3M Scotchguard every few weeks.
- Cold cream is as good for leather as it is for your face, tending to make it cleaner and softer. Rub it in with your fingers and wipe off excess with a cloth or paper towel.
- Removing stains from leather is tricky, so it's best to leave them to an expert.
- If you want to darken leather, use a cloth dipped in ammonia. Apply as evenly as possible to avoid streaks.

new clothes from old

If you have some old favorites stashed in your closet or drawers that are no longer in style or are worn out in places but not all over, try overhauling them in one of these ways:

- Transform a too-tight pullover sweater into a classy cardigan. Measure the exact center of the front, mark it, and machine-stitch down each side of the centerline. Cut from top to bottom between the lines of stitching. Finish the edges with ribbon or decorative sewing tape.

- If the sleeves of a sweater are stretched out of shape or are too short, use the above stitch-and-cut idea around each armhole to turn the sweater into a sweater-vest! Then use the cut-off sweater sleeves to make leg warmers for kids!

- If you've been a bridesmaid more times than you care to think about and have a slew of essentially unusable dresses clogging the back of your closet, look closely at each: Can it be made into a cocktail dress by taking up the hem and removing some decoration? Or might removing the sleeves or altering the neckline do the trick? A trip to the notions area of a fabric store can often provide just the right touch.

- How about that outdated dress in a great fabric? Cut the top from the bottom and, with a little stitching here and there, you can have a great blouse or a great skirt.

- Denim, wool, or corduroy dresses can be transformed into jazzy jumpers. Cut away the collar or reshape the neckline into a V or a scoop. Be sure to cut the armholes slightly larger to accommodate a blouse underneath. Cut facings from the sleeve fabric or face the new neck and armholes with bias binding.

- Turn a full slip that just doesn't work anymore into a half-slip: Cut off the bodice, stitch a casing at the top, and insert elastic. If the top is in decent shape, hem the bottom of it to make a new camisole.

GOOD OLD WAYS

If you have a worn-out garment that you can't even donate to charity because of wear or stains, snip off the buttons before you cut the fabric into rags for cleaning or making rag rugs. Keep the buttons in a self-sealing plastic bag in your sewing box, and you'll always have replacements for lost buttons when you need them.

101 uses for men's t-shirts (OK . . . we exaggerate)

sweet dreams Men's large or extra-large T-shirts are ideal for sleepwear, which should be light, comfortable, and non-binding—and they cost a lot less than women's sleep shirts.

cover-ups Colorful all-cotton men's T-shirts, size large or extra-large, make terrific cover-ups for the beach or pool or just for hanging out in your backyard.

tunic topper Wear a man's large or extra-large T-shirt over slim-fitting jeans or capri pants.

minidress A man's extra-large tee can become a cute minidress with a belt, matching tights, and a jacket.

not-your-donna-reed apron A man's T-shirt makes an excellent apron for cooking or crafting. A roomy T-shirt covers your whole upper body and is easy to move around in.

the james dean look Buy a snug-fitting men's white T-shirt and wear it with boot-cut blue jeans.

boys allowed If you're petite, don't ignore the boys department (boys are just little men, you know) for all kinds of neat shirts and sweaters as well as tees.

stalking perfect stockings

It may sound crazy, but your panty hose will last longer if you freeze them when they're brand new. After wetting them thoroughly and wringing out excess water, put the panty hose in a plastic bag and store them in the freezer. When you need stockings, thaw them out and let them dry.

- Panty hose resist runs much better and go on more easily if you starch them very lightly first.
- To stop a run in a stocking, rub the run with wet soap, spray it with hair spray, or dab on clear nail polish. When a pair of panty hose finally does give up the ghost, try some of the recycling tips on the facing page.

- When you see a really good sale on microfiber tights, buy, buy, buy! They last much longer than panty hose, keep your legs warmer in winter, are easier to clean, and are almost always in style. You can find tights made from other fabrics that are less expensive than microfiber tights, but the cheaper tights tend to lose their shape rather quickly, and no one wants to wear baggy tights.

if the shoe fits . . .

Don't buy shoes strictly by size. Walk around in them for several minutes before making a final decision. A size 7 shoe, for example, can vary in size, depending on the style and manufacturer, or your feet can swell up to a half size larger if you've been walking a lot. If you're shopping for shoes that you'll be wearing regularly to work or for sports, buy the best-quality shoes you can afford. They will last longer and look better longer, if you take care of them.

- Coat good shoes with a stain-repellent product or even plain shoe polish to protect them.
- Don't wear the same shoes every day. Wear them one day and let them air the next.
- If the heels are starting to wear down, take the shoes to a repair shop—and consider putting protectors on the heels.
- Don't spend a bundle on shoes or sandals that you will be wearing without stockings or socks. Your sweat will wear the shoes out faster. And summer styles tend to change rapidly. So save on summer footwear and get a really great pair of leather boots for the fall and winter.
- Avoid wearing your good shoes on the streets. Keep your nice shoes at the office and wear a pair of inexpensive

sports shoes to and from work or when you're going outside on an errand. Your shoes will thank you and so will your feet, ankles, and legs, not to mention your back!

○ New shoes can be slippery. To avoid slippage, lightly sand the soles or apply nonslip bathtub appliqués, strips of adhesive tape, or bicycle tube repair patches to the soles.

dyeing to be worn

Use fabric dyes to renew jeans, jackets, slacks, dresses, and just about anything else. If you find a somewhat faded denim jacket or jeans at a thrift store or garage sale, use dye to give them a new look and a new lease on life.

twice as nice

If the collar of a shirt is starting to fray, don't get rid of the garment. Carefully remove the collar at the seam where it is joined to the shirt, turn the collar over, and reattach it with the unworn side showing. Or sew the seam closed and leave the shirt collarless. If the cuffs are fraying, cover them with bias or satin binding (depending on the style of the shirt). If you use a contrasting color for the binding, also bind the edges of the collar, and it'll look like a completely different shirt.

sanding sweaters

Don't spend your money on those little shavers for sweaters. Instead, gently rub medium-grade sandpaper across the sweater's surface to remove the pills. Clean the sandpaper so that you can use it over and over again.

old reliable denim

Turn that pair of old jeans into a skirt. Cut the jeans to the desired skirt length, leaving an inch for hemming. Then remove the inseam stitching. For a straight skirt, just sew those edges together and hem the bottom. To add flair, cut triangular pieces from the leg material you cut off and sew the triangles into the openings formed by the inseam edges.

○ Keep jean hems from unraveling by attaching a wide strip of iron-on mending material inside the bottom hem.

○ Gussy up a plain denim jacket with decorative stitching, buttons, braid, or any other trim your imagination dictates.

○ Give your old straight-leg jeans a new flare or bell-bottom effect. Working from the bottom up of each outside leg seam, remove 6 to 12 inches of the stitching. Cut two triangular pieces of material from old jeans or contrasting fabric to add the amount of flare you want to each leg. Stitch the triangles to the edges of the outside seams.

○ Add eye-catching stripes of colored rickrack, embroidered braid, or metallic ribbon to the bottom of your jean legs. Use several stripes of varying trims for extra pizzazz.

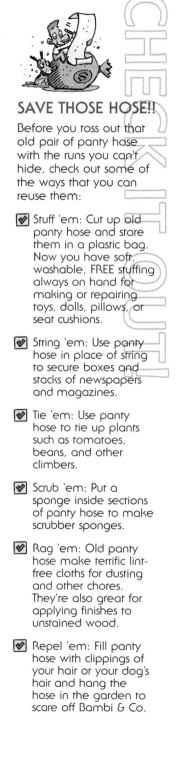

SAVE THOSE HOSE!!

Before you toss out that old pair of panty hose with the runs you can't hide, check out some of the ways that you can reuse them:

☑ Stuff 'em: Cut up old panty hose and store them in a plastic bag. Now you have soft, washable, FREE stuffing always on hand for making or repairing toys, dolls, pillows, or seat cushions.

☑ String 'em: Use panty hose in place of string to secure boxes and stacks of newspapers and magazines.

☑ Tie 'em: Use panty hose to tie up plants such as tomatoes, beans, and other climbers.

☑ Scrub 'em: Put a sponge inside sections of panty hose to make scrubber sponges.

☑ Rag 'em: Old panty hose make terrific lint-free cloths for dusting and other chores. They're also great for applying finishes to unstained wood.

☑ Repel 'em: Fill panty hose with clippings of your hair or your dog's hair and hang the hose in the garden to scare off Bambi & Co.

make your own shoe-cessories

Don't buy shoe trees for your boots—make 'em. Tie two or three paper-towel cylinders together or use large soft-drink bottles or rolled-up newspapers to preserve their shape.

- If you find your feet are often cold, make shoe liners from pieces of sturdy quilted fabric (old mattress pads are ideal), felt, or scraps of thin carpeting. First, make a pattern by tracing your feet on paper. Then cut out the liners and slip them into your shoes or boots.
- To spruce up plain pumps, attach a clip earring to each shoe. Put a dab of florist's clay under each clip to keep it from falling off or marring the shoe.

shoe shine

- To remove salt stains from winter boots, wipe them with a solution of 1 cup water and 1 tablespoon white vinegar.
- Cover ugly scuff marks with a matching color of acrylic paint, indelible felt marker, or crayon. Typewriter correction fluid makes a great cover-up for scuff marks on white shoes; try a bit of India ink on black shoes.
- Remove light scuff marks with an art-gum eraser. To remove tar and grease stains from white shoes, try a little nail-polish remover.
- To speed-clean patent leather, rub a little petroleum jelly over the shoes and buff. Or try a spritz of glass cleaner.
- Don't throw out hardened shoe polish. Put the metal container in a bowl of hot water until the polish is soft again.
- If you need a quick shine, rub hand lotion or cream over your leather shoes and buff with a tissue.

smooth suede shoes

- Perk up the nap on suede shoes by rubbing a dry sponge or a stiff upholstery brush over them after each wearing. To get rid of stubborn scuff marks on suede, gently rub with very fine sandpaper. (An emery board works great.)
- Steam-clean suede shoes by holding them over a pan of boiling water. Once the steam has raised the nap of the shoes, stroke the suede with a soft brush in one direction only. Let the shoes dry completely before wearing them.

on canvas

- Extend the life of canvas shoes by spraying a fabric protector or starch over them before wearing.
- Clean canvas sneakers quickly with a spray-on carpet cleaner. Scrub with a toothbrush, let dry, and then brush with a dry brush.
- Help your canvas tennis shoes keep their shape longer: After washing and drying them, stuff the shoes with paper towels, cover them with liquid starch, and let them dry.

purse perfection

Purses, like shoes, can be a major investment. Again, before you buy, consider how you will use the purse, the season in which you'll use it, and the wear and tear it will face. Also consider what you will put in it; do you need a pocket for a cell phone, for example?

- For your everyday purse, which gets the most use, invest in a high-quality leather purse in a neutral color. (Black is always good, as is cream.) Check out holiday sales at department stores, factory outlets, price clubs, and shoe stores. A high-quality purse in good condition is hard to find at a thrift store, but it is not impossible.
- Microfiber purses can take a lot of abuse and maintain their good looks.
- Save on summer bags. They usually don't last more than one season, so buy straw or canvas bags on sale and wear them till they fall apart. (Superstores sometimes offer good variety and great sales on casual purses.)
- Evening bags that are real gems can often be found at thrift stores and garage sales. Search carefully, especially through boxes of evening bags. Clutch purses from the 1940s, '50s, and '60s can be picked up for a pittance and can add swank to an outfit.
- If you have a special occasion and can't find the right purse, pick up a cloth purse in the right color and decorate it yourself with trims from a fabric or craft store.

pamper your purses

If you've spent serious money on a high-quality leather purse, it will last a long time, if you take care of it.

- When you're storing the bag, gently stuff it with tissue paper or newspaper to maintain its shape. Then place it in an old flannel or cotton pillowcase to protect the exterior.
- Clean and condition your leather purses by wiping them with a damp cloth and mild soap, or apply a colorless leather conditioner with a dry cloth.
- Keep the metal trim on your bag from tarnishing by coating it with clear nail polish.
- Bring the shine back to a patent-leather purse by spraying it with a little glass cleaner and gently drying and buffing it with cotton cloths or paper towels.
- Replace a broken purse strap with a heavy chain necklace or belt.

chic looks for little
Investment!

TO BE A DAZZLING DRESSER,
YOU HAVE TO SEE THE
POSSIBILITIES IN A VARIETY OF ACCESSORIES.

The little black dress is a fashion staple because it is so versatile. Go formal by adding an heirloom necklace, be exotic with a shawl, jazz it up with an eye-catching belt, or acquire elegance with a hat. Only you need know that the necklace is a garage-sale find, the shawl started as a remnant, the belt is Granddad's tie, or the hat is an end-of-season steal trimmed with ribbons and roses. It's not what you have but what you do with it that counts.

hats off

Try a few simple tricks to keeping nice hats looking like new (or to perk up second-hand steals):

- Brush interior leather hatbands with a little melted paraffin to prevent oil and dirt from accumulating.
- Brush and sponge a straw hat regularly. If it's especially dirty, run a hand vacuum over it.
- Add sheen to a dull straw hat by applying a light coating of glycerin or hair spray.
- After laundering a beret, slip it over a dinner plate to dry. Just be sure you use a plate that's the same size as the hat!
- Keep a felt hat looking fresh by using a soft brush on it after each wearing. Store the hat in a plastic bag.
- If you're caught in the rain with your best felt hat, blot the raindrops with a tissue. Then rub a wad of tissue paper over the rain spots using a smooth, circular motion. A coffee can works great as a hat stand while your hat dries.
- Revive a tired felt hat by holding it over steaming water for a second or two and then brushing with the nap.

hat tricks

You can make an old hat look like new or give an old favorite a new personality with a few simple trims. Craft or fabric stores carry a wide selection of materials you can use as hat trims, including raffia, ribbons, braid, tassels, fake flowers and greenery, buttons, and beads. Such stores often have excellent sales. Ask to have your name put on their mailing list to receive advance notice of special sales.

- Long scarves are an excellent quick-change adornment.
- Twist or braid raffia to use as a hatband. Tie the band in place and trim the ends.
- Real or fake flowers can be tucked into hatbands or stitched on in clusters or singly.
- A broad ribbon or a strip of decorative trim can add interest to a hat.
- Men's silk ties (male relatives' discards or thrift-shop finds) can be wrapped around the crown of felt hats.
- Upholstery trims or tassels, used judiciously, can add real drama to a winter hat.

be sure to wear some flowers in your hair

Fresh flowers are among the simplest—and, if you have a garden, cheapest—ways of adding glamour and elegance to an evening ensemble. You can wear flowers in your hair, on your clothing, attached to a ribbon tied around your wrist, or pinned to a hat.

- ⦿ A white gardenia pinned next to a chignon not only looks lovely but also adds a wonderful fragrance.
- ⦿ Roses, either single large blossoms or sprigs of tiny tea roses, are always in fashion.
- ⦿ Daisies last for hours and create a summery look.
- ⦿ A nosegay of chrysanthemums in rusts, browns, and yellows will signal the advent of autumn.
- ⦿ Variegated ivy, either tucked behind a flower or on its own, can be a real eye-catcher.
- ⦿ Be daring: Fresh sprigs of herbs, such as thyme, rosemary, purple sage, bay leaves, and lavender, are quite ornamental.
- ⦿ For a Christmastime adornment, use sprigs of holly, preferably with berries. Just be careful not to prick yourself.

fits like a glove

When trying on a new gloves, clench your fist to see how comfortable the glove feels. Make sure the glove opening falls right at your wrist and palm joint and that the seams are well sewn.

- ⦿ To keep gloves looking as good as new, always pull them back into shape right after removing them.
- ⦿ Remove stains on leather gloves by rubbing them with an art-gum eraser or white cornmeal.
- ⦿ If you get an oily stain on leather gloves, dust them with cornstarch and leave it on overnight. In the morning, brush off the residue.

belt up

- ⦿ Fix a belt that is too small by adding another hole. With a pen, make a dot where you want the hole. Lay the belt on a piece of scrap wood. Place the point of an awl, ice pick, or large nail on the dot and tap it vigorously a few times with a hammer to pierce the leather.
- ⦿ As with metal purse trimming, keep metal belt buckles bright with a coat of clear nail polish. The polish also helps prevent scratches.

the look of lace

If you need a dressy blouse and all you have is plain cotton, add lace to the cuffs and collar edges. Or add a lace collar to a plain dress for instant elegance. In the notions and bridal sections of fabric stores, you'll find a variety of laces, including traditional, cotton crochet, eyelet, and even Battenburg-style lace, giving you plenty of options for lots of looks.

> ❝Nothing makes a woman more beautiful than the belief that she is beautiful.❞

Sophia Loren

special scarf effects

Scarves and shawls are a simple, quick way to add color and flair. They can also provide just the right finishing touch to a simple outfit. But they can be pricey when bought at department stores. Keep a lookout for bargains at garage sales and flea markets. Search the remnant bins at fabric stores for beautiful pieces of silk, rayon, challis, gauze, lace, or any other fabric that hangs well. Take the pieces home, cut them to size, hem them, and voila! Gorgeous designer scarves at penny-pincher prices.

○ Wear a large silk or lace scarf as a shawl over a cocktail dress for an elegant evening look.

○ Tie a brightly colored oblong scarf around the band of a straw hat, letting the ends hang down your back, for that country-fair charm.

○ Brighten up a solid-color T-shirt dress by tying a scarf around your waist or a shawl around your hips.

○ To dress up a plain winter coat, drape a scarf or shawl around the shoulders and partially under the lapel.

○ Do you have an heirloom lace tablecloth you never use? Fold it in half and use it as a shawl.

○ Twist together or braid two to three oblong scarves in contrasting colors to use as a belt.

○ Wrap a large (45- to 54-inch-square) scarf around your body under your arms, at your waist, or low on your hips to form a sarong. Pull the fabric taut and knot the top ends where you want the opening to fall.

button, button

You can use interesting buttons in an endless variety of ways. Be on the lookout for them at garage sales and flea markets, and don't pass up big bags o' buttons at fabric stores.

○ Sew buttons around the band of an old denim or plain fabric hat. Buttons are a particularly useful decoration for a kid's hat, making it instantly identifiable without putting the child's name in it.

○ Trim a plain vest or jacket with a set of buttons along the bottom edge or the lapel. Group buttons of the same color but different styles for added interest.

○ Transform a plain blouse, dress, or jumper by changing the buttons from drab to dazzling. You'll get a custom look for very little cost.

○ Make buttons stay on longer by dabbing a bit of clear nail polish over the threads to strengthen their hold.

○ Instead of sewing on buttons with thread, use dental floss; it's stronger and keeps the buttons in place much longer.

new looks from old

Try the following to give old jewelry a rebirth or to create new pieces out of found objects:

○ Hang a baby's ring on a chain for an instant heirloom necklace.

○ Drill holes though coins collected on a special vacation and string them on a bracelet or necklace chain. Or use an inexpensive craft-store kit to create unique earrings.

○ Collect subway tokens from foreign travels and hot-glue them to a pin backing.

○ Use a single stud-type pierced earring as a lapel pin.

○ Stitch single earrings to hatbands for eye-catching decorations.

pinups

If you own or find a brooch with the pin on the back broken, don't toss it:

○ Stitch it to a hatband.

○ Put it on a chain to make a necklace.

○ Sew it to a jacket (but remember to clip it off when cleaning the jacket).

○ Repair the brooch yourself by using hot-glue or super-strength glue to attach it to a new pin backing.

beaded beauties

Beading is a simple craft, and the variety and modest price of beads make beading a skill worth learning. Look for beads at craft or fabric stores or specialty bead stores. You can find bags of beads and bead kits on the markdown aisle. When you see a good price, stock up and keep them on hand for a variety of projects.

○ Sew or glue beads to formed or stretchy fabric headbands.

○ Sew tiny pearl-like beads along a blouse or jacket edge.

○ Buy an inexpensive black or white cloth clutch purse and cover it with matching beads for an instant antique.

○ Dig out that old felt beret from your closet and create a pattern of contrasting beads all over the top and edges.

jewels from nature

Many items found on a walk through the woods or on the beach can be fashioned into unique jewelry. Small pine cones (shellacked or sprayed with metallic paint), beautiful pebbles, shells, tiny starfish or sand dollars, eye-catching small pieces of wood, nuts, and the like can be hot-glued to pin backings (available at craft stores). Or drill small holes in unusual pieces of wood and string them from leather thongs. The possibilities are limited only by your imagination, and you'll not only have a lovely and unique piece of jewelry but will be wearing a beautiful memory, too.

QUICK FIXES FOR JEWELRY

● To repair chips on gold- or silver-plated jewelry, use a fine-pointed paintbrush and a can of gold or silver spray paint. Spray a small puddle of paint on a piece of cardboard, dip in the brush, and touch up your jewelry.

● To unknot a chain, lay your necklace on a piece of wax paper. Put a drop or two of baby oil or salad oil directly on the knot. Use a pair of needles to gently untangle the knot. Then blot the oil with tissues.

● If the post on a pierced earring has broken off, use a nail file to smooth off any residual glue on the earring back; then apply super-strength glue, and mount a new post.

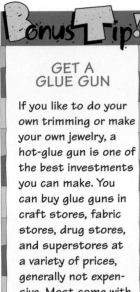
string of beads

Go one step further with beads and make your own necklaces. If you're using thread or string, dab clear nail polish on one end and let it dry before starting to string beads.

- To keep the whole strand from coming apart if the string breaks, tie knots between the beads.
- Out of string? Use waxed dental floss, nylon fishing line, or yarn coated with beeswax.

some classy combinations:

- Thread wooden beads on a leather thong.
- Alternate long silver beads with small, round dark blue or turquoise beads.
- String beads in different shades of the same color for a subtle effect.

how green was my neck?

Costume jewelry opens up vistas for accessorizing, but unfortunately a number of folks are sensitive to some of the metals used and end up with bizarre green spots on ears, wrists, and necks. The solution: clear nail polish. First, clean the jewelry thoroughly (see facing page) and let it dry completely. Then apply a coat of clear nail polish to the part of the jewelry that touches your skin.

she sells seashells

Lots of us have collections of seashells, and we know they are beautiful. What we don't see is how useful these lovelies from the sea can be.

- To whiten shells, bleach them overnight in a 50–50 mixture of chlorine bleach and water. For hard-to-whiten shells, increase the proportion of bleach. To let shells bleach naturally, set them out in the sun.
- Create charming buttons by carefully drilling holes in small shells. Then stitch or tie the buttons to sweaters, vests, dresses, or jackets.
- Embellish hair décor by hot-gluing shells to rigid headbands, barrettes, or combs. Before gluing, roughen the surface of the piece with an emery board.
- Make a unique necklace or pair of earrings. Carefully drill a small hole in one edge or at the top of small shells and string or thread them on dangle earring bases. For a very dramatic seashell necklace, suspend one large shell from a black satin cord.
- Hot-glue a selection of smaller shells to a pin backing.

keeping your ice in trays

Use plastic ice cube trays to organize your earrings and rings. The trays don't cost must to start with, but if you keep and eye out, you'll find them at garage sales for pennies.

treasure troves of ties

Ties can be used for many kinds of projects. You can even remove their stitching, spread them open, and use the fabric for quilting projects or to make clothing. And the truly terrific thing is that you can buy ties for a song at garage sales, thrift stores, and flea markets. Sometimes department stores and discount stores offer good sales on new ties. And don't forget to raid the closets of all your male relatives (especially the older ones). You never know what you'll find!

men's department: tie-ins

Men don't get to do much in the way of accessorizing, but they often have a whole collection of ties right under their noses that could be used to good effect. Just by changing a tie, you can change an outfit from fairly casual to fairly formal. You might start collecting (or giving as presents) special ties for special occasions or to highlight a profession, hobby, or sport. Ties for holidays can be fun, too.

- If a silk tie has lost its oomph, use a little steam heat. Hang the tie in a steamy bathroom or wrap a damp cloth over the soleplate of an iron and pass the steaming iron lightly over the tie.
- If you get a water spot on a silk tie, let the spot dry, then rub the spotted area vigorously with a hidden part of the tie. More often than not, the spot will disappear.

TWINKLE, TWINKLE, LITTLE JEWEL!

Jewelry is simple to clean and restore to its former beauty. Here's how:

- **Amber:** Put 2 drops linseed oil on a cotton ball and rub; wipe off residue.
- **Amethyst, aquamarine, emerald, garnet, jade, sapphire, ruby, topaz, tourmaline:** Immerse in 1/2 cup warm water with 1 tablespoon ammonia; scrub.
- **Costume jewelry:** Sprinkle a layer of baking powder; brush off. Shine pewter with silver polish. For brass, copper, chrome, or steel, use brass cleaner.
- **Diamond:** Soak in 1 cup hot water with 1/4 cup ammonia and 1 tablespoon detergent for 20 minutes; scrub with a toothbrush. Rinse, dip in rubbing alcohol, and air-dry.
- **Gold:** Soak in 1 cup warm water with 1/2 cup ammonia for 10 to 15 minutes. Then gently scrub with soft toothbrush and rinse. Air-dry.
- **Ivory:** Rub with denatured alcohol.
- **Lapis lazuli, malachite:** Use detergent in cool water and soft toothbrush.
- **Pearl:** Soak in mild soap and water solution. Rinse and buff with a flannel cloth. Do not soak a string of pearls; clean each individually with a soapy cloth.
- **Silver:** Wash in a mild detergent; then use silver polish.
- **Turquoise:** Shine with a chamois; then polish with a dry toothbrush.

cosmetic Caper...

WHAT YOU REALLY NEED
VS. ALL YOU REALLY DON'T

Do I need it? Is pricier better? Which do I need? These questions have plagued womankind for, well, a long, long time. The bad news is that, given our society, you will probably be buying at least some cosmetics. The good news is that you can put together an excellent cosmetic kit for very little, especially for skin care products.

Rx: H_2O

One of the best things you can do for your skin—and for your overall health—is also one of the cheapest and easiest things to do: Drink water. Not juice, not soft drinks, not coffee, not sports drinks. Good old plain water. At least six 8-ounce glasses a day. Eight glasses would be better. To make it easy on yourself, buy a sports bottle that holds 24 ounces, fill it with water, and drink it down three times a day.

a clean face on the cheap

You don't need to buy special cleansers to achieve healthy, clean skin. A mild, unscented soap with a neutral pH (such as Dove or Basis) is the best bet for every member of the family. And you can use it on your face as well as your body, saving you money on extra products. If you want to exfoliate, simply rub soap over a washcloth, then gently rub the soapy cloth over your skin.

go for yogurt

If you want to treat yourself to a special facial cleanser, boil 1/3 cup of water and pour it over 1 teaspoon of either chamomile tea (for dry or normal skin) or peppermint tea (for oily skin). Let the mixture steep until it is completely cool; then strain it and discard the solids. In a small bowl, beat together 5 tablespoons of plain yogurt with the tea mixture until they are well mixed. For dry to normal skin, stir in 1 teaspoon of wheat-germ oil or sesame oil; for oily skin, stir in 1 teaspoon of lemon juice. Pour the mixture into a sterilized jar with a tight-fitting lid. The mixture will keep in the refrigerator for up to five days. Always shake before using.

do-it-yourself cleansing cloths

A hot item in drug stores and beauty shops is prepackaged cleansing cloths for your face. You pull out one of these little guys, get it wet, wash your face, then toss it. Now we can see immediately that this is a waste of resources and money (these cloths are not cheap), but the convenience factor woos us against our better judgment. What to do? Make your own. For "at home" wipes, cut up those old, very soft but stained

T-shirts into 4-inch squares. Keep them in an old, clean butter tub near your bathroom sink and use them with your pH-balanced soap. You won't find a cloth that is gentler on the face. If you make or purchase a net washing bag, you can toss the used cloths in there and then just throw the bag in with your regular washing.

○ For cleaning cloths on the go (when traveling), purchase cotton gauze pads in bulk. When you want to wash your face, wet a pad, rub it over a bar of pH-balanced soap, apply to your face, rinse, then toss the pad.

○ If you want a bit more exfoliation, sprinkle a little cornmeal on your dampened cloth and wash as usual; the cornmeal will provide just the right amount of friction without being too harsh on your delicate facial skin.

skin to beat the band
Save money on moisturizers: Baby oil or plain mineral oil can be just as effective as expensive cosmetics in softening your skin or removing makeup. For daytime use, sunscreen with a sun protection factor (SPF) of at least 15 can do double duty as your moisturizer and your skin protector.

peaches-and-cream complexion
Did you know you can use peaches and cream to help you get a peaches-and-cream complexion? Blend one ripe peach with enough heavy cream to make a soft, creamy mixture. Massaged into the skin once a day, this stimulating, rich moisturizer can help you achieve a real peaches-and-cream complexion. Store it in the refrigerator.

fun in the sun
About 80 percent of all wrinkles are due to the sun's ultraviolet rays. A tan is actually sun-damaged skin, and the rays also play a role in skin cancer. Do your face and body a favor by getting into the daily sunscreen habit.

○ Look for sunscreen with an SPF of at least 15 that filters out both ultraviolet A (UVA) and ultraviolet B (UVB) rays. A store's private-label brands are usually less expensive than name brands (unless you find a really good coupon) and are just as effective. Buy the biggest bottles you can find; you'll save more per ounce.

○ When you go out in the sun, wear a wide-brimmed hat— a classic look that protects your face, too.

○ If you can, avoid spending time outdoors between 10 a.m. and 3 p.m., when the sun's rays are at their harshest.

○ Much of the sun damage to skin occurs during childhood. A bad burn when you were five could turn into skin cancer when you're 40. So be sure to get your kids to start the sun-safety habit early.

> 66 I'm tired of all this nonsense about beauty being only skin deep. That's deep enough. What do you want—an adorable pancreas? 99

Jean Kerr

making up is hard to do

You don't have to spend a small fortune on makeup. The brands sold in drug stores or discount stores will give you ample variety to choose from as to skin type and personal preference and will be much cheaper than similar products sold at a department store cosmetics counter. Clip coupons for brands you really like (October and May are good beauty coupon months) and watch for newspaper ads about sales.

must haves:
- Foundation: to even out the complexion and cover flaws
- Blush:to give a healthy glow
- Mascara: to enhance the eyes
- Lipstick: to enhance the lips

nice to haves:
- Eyeliner pencil
- Eye shadow
- Face powder
- Lip liner
- Concealer for under-eye circles or blemishes

Makeup is perishable, especially eye makeup. Bacteria from your eyes can be introduced to the product and vice versa. Replace your shadows and pencils every six months; your mascara, every three months.

double duty does it

Makeup can really add up, so look for products that do two things to get double your money's worth. For example, buy a foundation or moisturizer with sunblock, a combination foundation-and-powder compact, an eyeliner pencil that can also tend to your eyebrows, or an extra-moisturizing lipstick or lip liner for color and comfort.

toned up

A toner tightens the pores temporarily. You don't actually need a toner for good skin care, but many people like the feeling of cool, tight skin after they use a toner. Instead of shelling out for commercial products, keep a bottle of witch hazel in the refrigerator and get the same fresh feeling for a whole lot less. If you want to pamper yourself a bit (and who doesn't?), try this herbal milk toner:

- Bring 2/3 cup of milk to a boil and pour it over an herbal teabag in a cup or bowl. Cover the cup and let the mixture steep while it cools. If you have dry to normal skin, use whole or 2-percent milk and chamomile tea; if you have oily skin, use 1-percent or skim milk and peppermint tea. When the mixture is completely cooled, strain it through a piece of cheesecloth or unbleached muslin. Pour the mixture into a sterilized jar or bottle with a tight-fitting lid. The toner will keep in the refrigerator for up to five days. To use: After cleaning your face, soak a cotton ball in the toner and wipe it over your skin.

acne

Though instinct might tell you otherwise, acne-prone skin needs to be treated extremely gently. If you are using a harsh exfoliation method or are rubbing too hard and long with a washcloth when you clean your face, you will actually increase oil production and eruptions, so easy does it. Follow these acne-treatment tips:

○ Avoid the sun. Although exposure to sun seems to clear up acne, the results are temporary. A week or two later, the oil-producing sebaceous glands go into high gear, often increasing breakouts.

○ A paste of baking soda and water applied at bedtime will help dry up and draw out pimples overnight.

frugal facials

Although a wonderful way to make your skin feel renewed and revitalized, a professional facial can set you back quite a bit. The good news: Homemade facials are every bit as good, and you probably have the ingredients on hand.

○ Start by filling a bowl with hot water. Drape a towel over your head and keep your face directly over the steam for about 10 minutes.

○ Next, gently blot your wet face. If you wish, apply a mask (see Make Your Own Masks, below) and let dry. Wash off the mask with cool water.

○ Soak a cotton ball or soft cloth in witch hazel and gently rub over your face.

○ Finish by moisturizing.

make your own masks

○ To help relieve inflammation and irritated facial skin, apply a compress of cool skim milk for 10 minutes, rinse it off with cool water, and then apply a thin coating of face cream.

○ For a deep-cleansing mask, stroke milk of magnesia on your face with cotton balls, avoiding the eye area. Leave the mask on for 10 minutes. Then gently remove with a warm washcloth and apply a moisturizer.

○ For dry skin, combine 1 egg yolk with 1 teaspoon of honey and 2 tablespoons of plain yogurt. Apply to clean skin with cotton balls, being careful to avoid the eye area. After 15 minutes, rinse thoroughly with cool water.

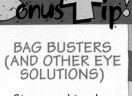

BAG BUSTERS (AND OTHER EYE SOLUTIONS)

• Store used tea bags in a self-sealing bag in the refrigerator to use on mornings when your eyes are puffy. Place a damp tea bag on each eye for about 10 minutes.

• Cut two slices of raw potato. Lie down and put a slice over each eye. Rest for 15 minutes, then wash away any filmy residue. For red, swollen eyes, substitute cucumber for the potato slices.

• Soak a clean cloth in weak chamomile tea. Then hold the compress over your eyes for 10 to 15 minutes to soothe itchy eyes.

○ For oily skin, make a paste of honey, oatmeal, and lemon juice (use about 2 tablespoons of each). Apply the paste to your face and leave on for 10 minutes. Rinse with warm water. If you're out of oatmeal but have a box of Cheerios or a generic version of it on hand, just grind up a small amount of the cereal and substitute it for the oatmeal in this mask.

○ For normal skin, make a paste of 1/3 cup of finely ground almonds and enough witch hazel to moisten. Apply to face, being careful to avoid the eye area. Leave on for 15 minutes. Then wipe off the mask with tissues and rinse your face with warm water.

ban rays

The sun is also hard on your eyes (some doctors say ultraviolet rays can encourage the formation of cataracts), so sunglasses are a year-round necessity. Luckily, expensive is not better. You can pick up classy shades in a variety of styles for $10 or less at drug stores, discount stores, and outlets. Just be sure to look for a sticker that specifies that the glasses give 100 percent UV blockage for the best protection.

the eyes have it

○ Before putting on eye shadow, apply a light coating of cream foundation makeup over the area, blending with your little finger. Be careful not to get the foundation in your eye. Then brush on your eye shadow. The powdery shadow will bind to the foundation and stay in place a lot longer than if you apply it directly to the skin.

○ Tame unwieldy eyebrows by using a dab of petroleum jelly on a clean, soft-bristled toothbrush. Gently brush your eyebrow hairs up and out.

lasting lipstick

○ Your lipstick will last much longer if you use the following method of application: Pat face powder over your lips, apply the lipstick, blot and powder again, then apply a final layer of lipstick.

○ To repair a broken lipstick, use a lighter or long fireplace match to slightly melt the bottom of the broken piece and the top of the remaining lipstick. Press the melted pieces together gently and seal the edges with a clean match or a toothpick. Place the lipstick in the refrigerator until it is completely cool.

GOOD OLD WAYS

Take a tip or two from days gone by making your own hair rollers:

• Cut narrow strips of cotton cloth and knot each strip in the middle. Roll a section of your damp hair around the knot and use the loose ends of the cloth to tie the curl in place, or secure it with a bobby pin.

• For a permed look, bend pipe cleaners into U shapes. Section your damp hair into thin strands. With the bend in a pipe cleaner toward the top of your head, weave a strand of hair around the pipe cleaner, going in and out and around both sides of the pipe cleaner. Then twist the pipe-cleaner ends together to secure it.

• For larger curls, cut a paper-towel roll into four sections. Roll damp hair around each section and pin in place.

a cut above

The key to good-looking hair is almost always a good hair-cut. Sometimes it pays to spend a little more at a salon for a professional style. (Skip the blow-dry.) But a fancy (expensive!) salon is not the answer. That $60-a-cut stylist could give you just as bad a cut as a $12-a-cut stylist. If you see someone with hair like yours (thick and curly, fine and straight, flyaway, and so forth) whose style you like, make a point of asking her where she got her hair cut; the answer may surprise you.

- If you live in a city with a professional training salon for hair stylists, check their prices and hours. These are not schools for novices; they are places where professional stylists go to learn a new or specific technique. If you have the time to seek out such places, you can often get an excellent cut for a small fee.
- To lengthen intervals between haircuts, trim your own bangs (if you have them). Spray your hair with water and use a comb to bring down a fine layer of fringe. Holding your comb just above the length you want and trim off the excess hair. Keep bringing down layers, using a comb and fingers, trimming each layer as you go.

shampoo stretch

Commercial shampoos are highly concentrated and much stronger than you really need, especially if you wash your hair every day. Try diluting shampoo by about half with water. Your hair will get just as clean, and you'll save money, too.

highlights for hair

dark hair Simmer 1 teaspoon of allspice, 1 teaspoon of crushed cinnamon, and 1/2 teaspoon of ground cloves in 1 cup of water. Strain the mixture, discarding the solids, and let it cool. Pour the mixture over freshly shampooed hair. Then rinse well.

red hair Brew a cup of regular orange pekoe tea, or dilute some strained beet juice. Pour the cooled liquid through your freshly shampooed hair, wait five minutes, and then rinse well.

brunettes or redheads Pour cooled black coffee over your freshly shampooed hair and then rinse well.

blondes Combine 1 cup of chamomile flowers with 2 cups of boiling water; simmer for 30 minutes. (Do not bring to a full boil.) Remove the pan from the heat and let the mixture cool for about two hours. Strain the mixture, discarding the solids. Pour the liquid through your hair several times, catching the excess in a bowl. The lightening effect will be increased if you dry your hair in full sunlight and use the rinse regularly.

TEN TRICKS FOR AN OLD TOOTHBRUSH

Never throw out a toothbrush! It still has many uses. (Run it through the dishwasher to clean and sterilize it if needed.) Here are a few ideas:

1. Use to clean jewelry, with or without a cleaner.
2. Use to clean small appliances, such as hair dryers, food processors, and juicers.
3. Use as a mustache or beard brush.
4. Use as an eyebrow brush.
5. Use as a cleaning brush for shoes.
6. Use as a cleaning brush for carpet spots.
7. Use to scrub grout between tiles.
8. Use as an infant's hairbrush.
9. Use as a nailbrush.
10. Dip in kerosene and use for cleaning oily gunk from motors.

dandruff destroyers
- Shake 1 tablespoon of table salt into dry hair. Massage gently into your hair before shampooing. Don't use this treatment if you have any cuts or abrasions on your scalp!
- Yogurt is reported to help even difficult cases of dandruff. Work a liberal quantity of plain yogurt into your scalp and hair and let it set for an hour. Shampoo as usual.

kitchen hair care

cornstarch For a fast, dry way to clean your hair, just sprinkle some cornstarch over it, especially along the part. Leave the cornstarch in your hair for about five minutes. Then brush it out.

vinegar To add shine to dark hair, stir 1 tablespoon of vinegar into 1 cup of water. Pour the mixture over your hair and then rinse well with plain water.

lemon juice To lighten and brighten blond hair, combine the juice of 1 lemon with 1 cup of water. After shampooing, work the lemon mixture into your hair and then rinse it out well with plain water.

mayonnaise For an old-fashioned conditioner that leaves hair smooth and shiny, coat your hair with mayonnaise, pin it up, and wrap it in plastic wrap or use a shower cap or plastic bag. Leave the mayonnaise on your hair for 30 minutes; then shampoo as usual.

olive-oil combo Combine 3/4 cup of olive oil, 1/2 cup of honey, and the juice of 1 lemon. Rinse your hair with water and towel it dry. Work a small amount of the conditioner into your hair (store the remainder in the refrigerator), comb to distribute evenly, and cover your head with a plastic bag, plastic wrap, or shower cap. Leave on for 1/2 hour. Then shampoo and rinse with water.

hair spray away

To get rid of a buildup of hair spray in your hair, work 1 tablespoon of baking soda into your lathered hair when shampooing. Rinse thoroughly.

pool rules for hair
- Before swimming in a chlorinated pool, wet your hair thoroughly and work some conditioner through it. The water saturates the hair shafts, making them less likely to absorb the chemicals, and the conditioner protects the exterior of the shafts.
- Always rinse your hair completely after getting out of the pool—not just at the end of the day, but every time you get out of the pool.
- If your hair starts looking like you're from the Emerald City (green, that is), mix the juice of a lemon in a pint of

water. Pour the mixture over your hair and rinse. Or try rinsing with club soda, tomato juice, or several aspirin dissolved in warm water.

happy hair dryer

Keep your hair dryer working better and longer with regular maintenance. First, unplug the dryer. Then use an old toothbrush to remove dust, lint, and hair from the air-intake filter at the back of the dryer. This helps prolong the motor's life.

glad hands

The key to keeping hands soft and young-looking is moisturizing and protecting them regularly. Creams are more effective than lotions, because lotions contain a high amount of water and preservatives; creams do not. Instead of spending money on several different products, find a thick sunscreen cream (SPF 15 or more) and use that as your daily hand moisturizer. This is a good idea for a body moisturizer, too, especially if you live in a sunny climate. Sun damages the skin more than anything else does.

○ For an inexpensive fix when you won't be going outdoors, slather petroleum jelly, baby or olive oil, or vegetable shortening on your hands. Do this before bedtime and wear cotton gloves while you sleep for a real hand saver.

○ A cost-effective moisturizer is the beauty secret of farmers and fishermen—and cows! Bag Balm is a highly concentrated ointment used to soothe and soften cow udders. Though you can find it in feed-and-seed stores, its growing popularity has moved it into many drug stores, too.

happy feet

Soften your feet by soaking them for 20 minutes in a bowl of hot water mixed with a cup of warm olive oil and the juice of a lemon. Then dry your feet and rub petroleum jelly all over them. To keep the moisture in, put on a pair of thin cotton socks.

○ If your toes, nails, or the skin on your feet are discolored, rub the discolored areas with half a lemon. For extra bleaching and softening, cup the lemon on your heels for 15 minutes. Be sure to moisturize afterward.

bathing beauty

For the perfect bath, be sure the water is neither too hot nor too cold. If you want to add oil to your bathwater, do so after you've soaked for five to 10 minutes. The presoak period allows your skin's pores to open and absorb the water. Then, when you add the oil, it will coat your skin, creating a barrier to hold in the moisture.

○ To soothe dry skin, add a few tablespoons of olive or vegetable oil to your bathwater instead of expensive purchased bath oils.

○ Add a cup of lemon juice to your bathwater to give it a clean, fresh scent and to tone and tighten your skin.

○ For a winter warmup, add a couple of tablespoons of ground ginger to your bathwater. The ginger will intensify your feeling of warmth.

○ Relieve dry, itchy skin by adding 1 cup of salt to your bathwater and letting it dissolve completely before bathing. If you want added luxury, use sea salt instead.

○ If you're lucky enough to grow your own roses, toss some fresh rose petals into your bathwater. The oils from the fragrant petals will leave your skin feeling velvety smooth.

OIL ESSENTIALS

Throughout this book you will see formulas or recipes calling for essential oils. These highly concentrated oils are obtained by distilling leaves or flowers. They are volatile and flammable and evaporate at low temperatures. Essential oils are potentially toxic if inhaled or used incorrectly. Most of them must be diluted in a fixed oil (fatty, nonvolatile oil) before they are applied to the skin. Lavender and tea-tree oils are exceptions but should be used sparingly. You can find essential oils at health food stores and often at craft stores, since they are used in making perfumes and scented bath products. They come in very small bottles, and the cost may give you pause. (They are not cheap!) However, in any given recipe, you use only a drop or two of essential oil, and the products you can make with essential oils can compensate for the investment.

scents for cents

Make your own cologne or perfume, and you'll smell sweet at a fraction of the cost of purchased scents.

classic cologne Pour 1 cup of rubbing alcohol into a jar that has a tight-fitting lid. Add 1/2 cup of dried lavender flowers and 1 tablespoon of olive oil. Cover and let the mixture sit for two days, shaking occasionally. Strain the liquid into a bottle, discarding the solids, and add 1 cup of distilled water and 3 drops bergamot essential oil (see Bonus Tip box, left). Cap tightly and shake to mix.

lemon-fresh splash Combine 1/2 cup of rubbing alcohol with 3 teaspoons of lemon extract and the juice of 1 lime in a bottle that has a tight-fitting lid. Cover and shake well. Store in the refrigerator. Makes 5 ounces.

spicy scent Combine 1/2 cup of rubbing alcohol with 1/4 cup of whole cloves in a small jar with a tight-fitting lid; add 1 teaspoon of orrisroot (available at health food stores). Cover and shake well. Let the mixture stand for two days, shaking occasionally. Strain the liquid into a spray bottle, discarding the solids. To use, dab on behind your ears or on your wrists or spray lightly over your skin. Store out of the reach of small children.

odor eaters

Instead of using pricey deodorants, try one of these homemade solutions to unwanted body odors. But remember none of these controls perspiration.

- Pat a little baking soda on freshly washed and dried skin under your arms. The moisture still on your skin will help the soda stick. If the soda isn't soft enough, mix it with a little cornstarch.
- Pat a mixture of equal parts of white vinegar and water under your arms. Or just pat cider vinegar, either diluted or full strength, under your arms and let dry.
- Mash a dark-green leaf of romaine lettuce to extract a drop of chlorophyll. Spread it under your arms and let it dry.
- Combine a few drops of lavender essential oil (see Bonus Tip box, facing page) with a teaspoon of water and apply the mixture lightly to freshly washed skin.

powder power

Cornstarch makes a good substitute for talcum powder, and it's safe if you happen to breathe a bit in. Rice powder is also wonderful, especially for use on the face.

sharp shaving

Using a sharp blade to shave is just the beginning. The following can help you make the most of your shaving time.
- Ouch! If you nick yourself while shaving, wet a tea bag with cold water and press it on the cut.
- Apply sunscreen instead of aftershave to smooth your skin and shield it from the harmful rays of the sun.

after your shave

This mixture soothes shaved skin and smells just wonderful:
- Combine 2 cups of rubbing alcohol, 1 tablespoon of glycerin (available at health food stores and some drug stores), 1 tablespoon dried lavender, 1 teaspoon dried rosemary, and 1 teaspoon ground cloves in a jar with a tight-fitting lid. Put the jar in the refrigerator and let the mixture steep for three to four days, shaking the jar occasionally. Strain the mixture into a second jar or bottle with a tight-fitting lid and discard the solids. The aftershave will keep in the refrigerator for up to two months.

Frugal Health and Fitness

- home remedies from a to z

- diet right: low-cost strategies for good health

- exercise economics

Reality check! Seeking out the best clothes, whipping up dazzling accessories, and making your own luxurious cosmetics is a waste of money if you don't take care of your health first. Your health is the best investment of all—and you can safeguard it more economically than you might imagine. Instead of running off to the doctor (big bucks) or the drugstore (smaller but still significant bucks) every time you feel an ache or pain, open your kitchen cupboard. Chances are, relief will be staring you in the face. Mustard alone can help relieve arthritic joints, pamper achy feet, and soothe a sore throat! Instead of joining a pricey gym teeming with pretty people and even prettier equipment, put those dollars in your vacation account and try some of our body- and budget-friendly workouts. Just think. Once that vacation account is healthier, you'll be able to take the leaner, stronger, healthier you on that tropical vacation you've been dreaming about!

Getting healthy is not a matter of money.

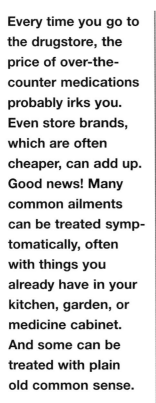

homemade remedies
from A to Z

DON'T WASTE MONEY AT THE DRUGSTORE FOR EVERY LITTLE ACHE AND PAIN. RELIEF IS AT HAND, OFTEN IN YOUR KITCHEN PANTRY.

Every time you go to the drugstore, the price of over-the-counter medications probably irks you. Even store brands, which are often cheaper, can add up. Good news! Many common ailments can be treated symptomatically, often with things you already have in your kitchen, garden, or medicine cabinet. And some can be treated with plain old common sense.

allergies

The best way to cut down on airborne allergies is to keep the air in your home as clean as possible. Before investing in expensive machines, try the plant approach: philodendrons, ferns, and dracaenas filter many allergens from the air naturally. For maximum benefit, have one plant for every 100 square feet of space.

arthritis

If you suffer from the daily pain of arthritis, here are a few tricks you can try:

- If your knees are swollen and painful, fill four small, self-sealing bags with ice. Hold or secure one bag over and one bag under each knee and keep it there for 15 to 20 minutes. Repeat several times a day until the swelling goes down and the pain is relieved.
- Try rubbing a little plain mustard over the afflicted joints as a pennywise alternative to costlier creams.
- Wear stretch gloves at night to reduce morning arthritic pain, stiffness, and joint swelling in your hands.
- If your arthritis causes you to have difficulty holding a pen, push the pen through a small rubber ball. Or wrap masking tape around and around the pen until it's large enough for you to hold.
- Exercise may be your most important weapon against the effects of arthritis. Physical activity strengthens the muscles and prevents the joints from stiffening further. Ask your doctor about an exercise program specifically designed for your needs, or see page 108 for great low-impact, low-cost workouts.

colds and flu

The common cold and influenza (the flu) are both viral diseases, and you cannot take something to cure them once you have them. What you can do is treat the symptoms.

cold symptoms Fatigue, a scratchy or sore throat, hoarseness, coughing, sneezing, a runny or stuffy nose, watering eyes, and a headache. Colds do not usually cause a fever over 100° F. Cold symptoms usually last from five to seven days.

flu symptoms Initially similar to those of a cold, but symptoms can become more severe, causing fever in adults and even higher fever in children. Flu often causes muscle and joint pain, weakness, and loss of appetite. Flu symptoms may disappear in a few days to one or two weeks, but full recovery can take from two to three weeks.

medical prevention People in high-risk groups—such as those older than 50 years old, adults and children who suffer from chronic illnesses such as diabetes or asthma, and people with weakened immune systems—should get flu shots every year between October and mid-November. People in high-risk fields, such as teaching or health care, should also consider getting flu shots. Flu vaccination will usually protect a person from the most common flu strains expected in a particular year.

what you can do

- Go to bed! Don't go to school or work, because you will likely prolong your illness and will spread the virus.
- Drink plenty of fluids, especially liquids that don't contain caffeine. Water is the best choice, but juice, low-sodium broth, or sports drinks are good, too. One 8-ounce glass per hour will help flush your body tissues and keep you well hydrated so that your body can fight the virus. (To encourage a child to keep hydrated, freeze different kinds of fruit juices on wooden sticks to create homemade Popsicles.)
- Wash your hands often with warm soapy water, whether you are the patient or the caregiver. Be sure to wash all glasses and utensils in hot, soapy water and either boil the family toothbrushes to sterilize them or use this opportunity to replace toothbrushes.

66 *So many people spend their health gaining wealth, and then have to spend their wealth to regain their health.* **99**

A. J. Reb Materi, author

constipation

If you're eating enough high-fiber foods, constipation shouldn't be a frequent problem. Whole-grain breads, bran cereals, fresh or dried fruit (especially apples), and leafy vegetables are all good choices. If you suffer from chronic constipation, see your doctor. For the occasional bout, include more high-fiber foods in your diet and avoid "binders," such as rice, bananas, and yogurt, for a few days. Also remember to drink water, which keeps the digestive system lubricated. Don't spend your money on laxatives and enemas—they sometimes tend to make the problem worse. If you find you do need a laxative, here are two natural, cheap remedies:

homemade laxative Combine 2 cups tomato or vegetable juice, 1 cup sauerkraut juice, and 1/2 cup carrot juice. Drink 1 cup of the mixture at a time. Store the rest in the fridge.

fruit and fiber Soak about five prunes in orange juice or water overnight. Eat the prunes and drink the soaking liquid before you eat breakfast.

corns and calluses

Soften corns and calluses by soaking your feet in 2 gallons of warm water with 1 tablespoon of Epsom salts for 15 minutes. Then use a pumice stone to rub off the top layers of dead skin. Apply moisturizing lotion (or petroleum jelly) to the feet while still damp. Then put on thin cotton socks.

congestion

● Make your own saline nose drops to fight nasal congestion: Mix 1/4 teaspoon table salt in 1 cup water. With a dropper, place two or three drops in each nostril 1/2 hour before meals and at bedtime.

● Use a humidifier: Purchase an inexpensive model and follow the manufacturer's instructions for use and cleaning. Or place pans of water around your house, especially on radiators if you have them.

coughs

Few things are more exhausting than a hacking cough. Try a homemade cough syrup or cough drop to relieve this annoying problem.

cough syrup Combine 3 tablespoons lemon juice and 1 cup honey; slowly stir in 1/4 cup warm water. Take 1 or 2 tablespoons once every three hours to relieve coughing. Store in the refrigerator.

caution Never give honey to a child under the age of one; to be safe, wait until the child is at least two years old.

cough drops In a medium-size saucepan, boil 1 quart washed and chopped horehound leaves and stems (available at health food stores) in 2 cups water for 30 minutes. Strain the mixture and discard the solids. Stir in 3 cups sugar. Place a candy thermometer in the mixture and boil to the hard crack stage (300° to 310° F). Stir in 1/4 cup (1/2 stick) butter and remove the pan from the heat. Pour the mixture into a greased shallow pan and let it cool completely. When cool, break into pieces. Wrap each piece in waxed paper, twisting the paper ends, and store in a tightly covered jar.

dazzling dentures

If you wear dentures, don't waste your hard-earned money on fancy cleaners. Combine 1 tablespoon of household bleach and 1 teaspoon of water softener in 1 cup of water. Place removable full dentures (those with no metal parts) in the solution and soak for 1/2 hour. Remove the dentures and

Are you suffering from chest congestion resulting from a cold? Make an old-fashioned mustard plaster for relief: Sift together 1 tablespoon of dry mustard and 1/4 cup of flour. Slowly stir in just enough lukewarm water to form a paste. Spread the plaster on a piece of cotton cloth big enough to cover the chest area. Cover with another piece of cloth. Then place the mustard plaster on dry skin covering the chest. Check frequently and, when the skin begins to turn red (in about 10 to 20 minutes), remove the plaster. Do not use the plaster for more than 30 minutes at a time. Rub petroleum jelly over the reddened skin to hold in the heat. Use the plaster twice a day until the congestion clears up.

NOTE: Do not to use the plaster on the eyes, face, or open skin and make sure that the person isn't allergic to mustard. Do not use on young children.

brush and rinse them thoroughly with plain water. Store your dentures in plain water when you're not wearing them.

- To get rid of calcium deposits on dentures, soak them overnight in 1/2 cup of white vinegar ever two weeks. Then brush and rinse thoroughly.

ear problems

- For temporary relief of an earache, hold a hot compress against your ear. Leave it in place until the compress has cooled. Repeat as often as needed.
- Remove earwax safely and gently by flushing with a 50-50 mixture of hydrogen peroxide and warm water. Lie on your side and use a dropper to fill your ear with the solution, then turn your head, holding a towel at the ready, and let the ear drain. Repeat twice a day until the wax softens and washes out.
- If an insect becomes trapped in your ear canal, try to float it out with water. If this doesn't do the trick, try rinsing your ears with drops of vegetable or mineral oil to kill the bug. Then have a doctor remove it from your ear.

feet that ache

Add 3 tablespoons of plain mustard to a pan of warm water and stir until the mustard is completely dissolved. Soak your feet in the warm mustard-water mix for at least 15 minutes, or until the water has completely cooled.

halitosis

Chronic bad breath may indicate a more serious disorder, but for everyday problems try one of the following:

chew herbs Chewing fresh parsley or fresh mint leaves helps freshen breath.

mouthwash Bring 2 cups water to boil in a small saucepan. Remove from the heat. Add 3 teaspoons fresh or dried parsley, 2 teaspoons whole cloves, 2 teaspoons ground cinnamon, and 2 teaspoons peppermint extract. Let the mixture steep for about an hour. Strain the mixture into a jar or bottle with a tightly fitting lid; discard the solids. Will keep for two weeks in the refrigerator.

hangovers

Naturally, it's better never to have one of these, but . . . . Here are some tried-and-true preventive measures and remedies.

- Drink water! Many hangover symptoms are actually caused by dehydration. A glass of water between each alcoholic drink will help slow down and dilute your overall alcohol consumption and prevent dehydration. And don't forget to drink one last glass of water just before bedtime.

- When finished drinking, take two ibuprofen tablets with a big glass of water. This may help stave off a headache. **caution** Never take acetaminophen when drinking alcohol; it can cause liver damage.
- Get some fresh air. Twenty minutes of walking outdoors and breathing deeply can do wonders. Though it may be the last thing you want to do when hung over, a little aerobic exercise (carefully done) can provide relief.
- Pump a little caffeine—it constricts the arteries dilated by alcohol and may relieve your headache.
- A vitamin C supplement or a couple of spoonfuls of honey may help your body eliminate the alcohol more quickly.

headaches

Try easing a tension headache with a gentle facial or neck massage or by applying a heating pad or hot compresses to the forehead and the base of the skull.

heartburn

- Tight garments and belts increase pressure on the abdomen. Don't wear them or loosen them after meals.
- Avoid lying down right after a meal. It can take several hours for the stomach to empty its contents into the intestine. Once that happens, regurgitation—and heartburn—are less likely. Don't eat near bedtime for the same reason. If you must lie down, try to lie on your left side. In this position the esophagus is above the stomach, so that gravity helps keep the stomach acids down. (Lying in this position is helpful during pregnancy as well.)
- Try not to consume effervescent substances, such as soda water, which cause belching. Belching allows acid from the stomach to flow back into the esophagus.

- Avoid bending over soon after meals; bending can cause the stomach contents to back up into the esophagus.
- Obesity increases pressure on the abdomen. Losing weight may help heartburn.
- At the first sign of gastric distress, eat a banana! Bananas contain natural antacids, which can provide fast relief for people with sensitive stomachs who suffer from heartburn pain.

heat rash

Heat rash, or prickly heat, occurs when pores become blocked and perspiration can't be released. Young children are prone to it, but adults can be affected too. To ease itching, steep 3 rounded teaspoons (1/2 ounce) fresh thyme leaves or 1 rounded teaspoon dried thyme leaves in 1/2 cup boiling water for five to ten minutes. Strain through a fine sieve and discard solids. Pour into bathwater and soak yourself.

heat relief

As you can probably guess, the best way to stave off heat exhaustion is to stay out of the sun and drink plenty of water whether you feel thirsty or not!

- If your home doesn't have air-conditioning or an evaporative cooler, head to cool public places during the hottest part of the day: libraries, malls, museums, or even a well-chilled supermarket.
- A tepid shower or bath can help lower your body temperature, but don't take a cold bath or shower, because that will signal your body to warm itself up.
- Small, light, cool meals are a better choice than hearty ones, and avoid junk food.

hiccups

- A spoonful of sugar will make the hiccups go away. Just quickly swallow 1 teaspoon of granulated white sugar for fast relief.
- A teaspoonful of bartender's bitters, followed by the juice of a fresh lemon wedge, can get rid of hiccups.
- Drink ten sips of water, swallowing after each. Don't take a breath until after the tenth sip.
- Hold your breath for as long as you comfortably can, then exhale very slowly. Repeat this exercise several times.

hives

Take an antihistamine and then rub the affected area with an ice cube or take a cool bath. Apply calamine lotion, witch hazel, or zinc oxide to relieve itchiness as well.

insect bites

prevention Try to avoid going outside early in the morning and one to two hours after sunset, the times when insects are most active. If you do go out, try the following:

- Wear clothing that is light in color, such as pale green, tan, khaki, or white.
- Wear long sleeves, long pants, socks, and shoes when outdoors during prime insect time.
- Rub baby oil or imitation vanilla extract on your skin as a nontoxic way of repelling mosquitoes and other biting insects.
- Look for oil of pennyroyal, eucalyptus, and citronella at a health food store; they are all natural mosquito repellents. Mix about 10 drops of oil with an ounce of olive oil, sunflower oil, baby oil, or almond oil and spread the mixture on exposed skin.
- Mosquito repellent: Combine 3 cups rubbing alcohol, 1-1/2 cups red cedarwood shavings (available in pet stores), and 1/2 cup eucalyptus leaves in a large jar or

PENNY-PINCHING COLD PACKS

Cold packs are handy to have around, but you needn't spend money on them. A self-sealing bag with a few ice cubes will do the trick. And if the injury is in a spot that's difficult to wrap, use a small bag of frozen peas instead. (Peas or a combination of carrots and peas works well because the small frozen vegetables are easy to maneuver.)

bowl. Cover and let stand for five days. Strain the mixture and discard the solids. Apply the mixture to the skin as needed. Store in a tightly sealed jar. Makes two cups.

● Be careful of the normal products you use on your skin. Suntan lotions, perfumes, and colognes, as well as scented soaps, lotions, shampoos, deodorants, shaving lotions, and hair sprays, may actually attract mosquitoes.

once bitten . . .

● If you get bitten by an insect, first wash the affected area with soap and cold water. Then use cold compresses and elevation to ease the swelling.

● Make a paste of 1/4 tablespoon meat tenderizer and 1 to 2 teaspoons water. Rub the paste over the stung area as soon as possible. Repeat in an hour if it still stings. Meat tenderizer contains papain, an enzyme from the papaya fruit that breaks down insect venom.

● For a quick fix, dab a little ammonia or vinegar on the bite.

caution Allergic reactions to bites and stings can be severe. If you or a family member has a serious allergy, have your physician prescribe an insect-bite kit and carry it with you at all times. If you don't know whether you are allergic (and remember that you can develop allergies later in life), call 911 if you develop hives, shortness of breath, or any other potentially life-threatening symptoms.

menopause

Vitamin E to the rescue! Some doctors recommend 200 to 400 mg of vitamin E a day to reduce night sweats and hot flashes. Check with your doctor because vitamin E can intensify the effect of blood thinners, such as Coumadin and aspirin. Take a vitamin E supplement or eat foods that are high in vitamin E. Some E-rich foods include sunflower oil, safflower oil, wheat germ, mayonnaise, whole-grain cereals, nuts (especially hazelnuts), seeds, egg yolks, and some leafy green vegetables.

● Dress in layers that you can take off or put on as needed to reduce the discomfort of hot flashes. Keep your home cool, especially your bedroom. Keep consumption of caffeine, alcohol, and spicy foods to a minimum.

motion sickness

Instead of buying costly motion sickness drugs, which can have side effects such as drowsiness, dry mouth, or blurry vision, try chewing candied ginger.

nausea

stress-induced Soak in a warm bath. If desired, put four to eight drops of lavender essential oil or sandalwood scent into your bathwater.

queasy stomach Sip peppermint tea or eat peppermint candy after you comsume a large meal. Menthol in the mint can help soothe a sensitive stomach.

pregnancy-related Try eating several small meals during the day, rather than three big ones. Avoid heavy or greasy foods. Before going to bed, have something starchy, such as rice pudding or soda crackers.

flu-related Ginger ale or other clear sodas may help, and they'll act to replenish the fluids that your body has lost. Avoid caffeinated sodas; caffeine functions as a diuretic and further dehydrates your body.

after nausea subsides Stick to bland, fat-free foods until you feel better. Good choices include dry toast, bananas, applesauce, rice, clear soups, and soda crackers. Drink lots of water and fruit juices. (Be wary of citrus juices, because they contain a considerable amount of acid and may cause indigestion in an already sensitive stomach.)

nosebleeds

Nosebleeds are often the result of dry, cracked nasal membranes, so keep the air in your house humidified, especially at night. During dry times of the year, when you plan to be outdoors, dab a little petroleum jelly in your nostrils. To stop a nosebleed:

- Sit in a chair and lean forward slightly. Gently pinch the nostrils together and hold them in this position for five minutes. Check to see whether the bleeding has stopped; if it has not, repeat the gentle pressure until it does stop.
- Once the bleeding has stopped, don't blow your nose for several hours, try not to lean over or lift anything heavy, and don't exert yourself any more than is absolutely necessary.
- If the bleeding is particularly heavy or pressure is not working quickly enough, apply a cold pack (see page 88) to the nose and cheeks. Or hold a little crushed ice in a washcloth directly on the upper lip under the nose until the bleeding stops.

osteoporosis

This "brittle bone" disease has no cure, so your best defense is a strong offense. The sooner in life that you begin to address the possibility, the longer you can stave off the disease. There appears to be a genetic link, and certain people seem more prone to it, so if the condition is in your family history or if you feel yourself to be at risk, ask your doctor about a bone-density test. This painless X-ray procedure can tell you if you have the disease or if you are at risk for it.

- Get enough calcium from food and supplements.
- Get enough vitamin D in your diet. It allows the body to absorb calcium and stimulates the growth of bone cells.

ER USES FOR EVERYDAY ITEMS

Do you know how many things you already have on hand that can be used in an emergency?

- ☑ Cloth or disposable diapers: Use as compresses to control bleeding, bandages for large cuts, or padding for splints.

- ☑ Sanitary napkins: Use as compresses, bandages, or padding.

- ☑ Linens: Tear into strips for bandages or slings.

- ☑ Diaper pins or large safety pins: Use to secure bandages.

- ☑ Blankets: Tuck around accident victim to keep warm; prevent shock.

- ☑ Magazines and newspapers: Roll up and use as splints.

- ☑ Umbrellas: Another good choice for splints.

- ☑ Table leaves or doors: Use as stretchers. But not if you suspect head, neck, or back injuries!

- ☑ Electric fans: Use to cool heatstroke victims.

- ☑ Large handkerchiefs or scarves: Use for bandages or slings.

- ☑ Tap water: For flushing eyes, irrigating wounds or burns, washing cuts, and rehydrating someone who is dehydrated.

- ☑ Wrapping and duct tape: Use to secure bandages and apply pressure to wounds.

- Participate in weight-bearing exercises, such as brisk walking, jogging, tennis, and weight lifting, to build dense bone tissue before menopause and to delay bone loss afterward. See pages 108–115 for some great exercise ideas.
- For an inexpensive supplement that does double duty, chew some sodium-free antacid pills, which consist mainly of calcium carbonate. These are just as effective—and less expensive—than traditional calcium supplements.

pill-taking

If a pill sticks in your throat, chew a bite of a banana thoroughly, then swallow it. The banana should dislodge the pill.

poison oak or ivy

"Leaves of three, let them be." Recite this simple rhyme every time you go into the woods. It's also an easy way to teach children how to recognize poison ivy. But if you have a close encounter with poison ivy or poison oak, try this:
- Soak the affected area in a mixture of 1 quart warm water and a cup of uncooked oatmeal. Pat dry and apply calamine lotion to the area.

premenstrual syndrome (pms)

Be assured, this is not in your head. Many women suffer from varying degrees of PMS, ranging from mildly annoying to completely debilitating. Here are tips to help with mild symptoms. If you find yourself unable to function at certain times of the month, see a gynecologist immediately and bring a detailed list of what happens to you and when.
- Two weeks before your period, cut down on (or cut out) caffeine and alcohol and try to limit your intake of sugar, salt, and fat. These foods can promote water retention, mood swings, and other unpleasant symptoms of PMS.
- Eat at least every three hours. Fruits, vegetables, complex carbohydrates, and low-fat dairy are good choices.
- Evening primrose oil, sold in health food stores, is thought by many to relieve breast soreness and other PMS symptoms. To try it, take the herb three days before you expect symptoms to start and continue until your period begins. The usual dosage is 1,000 mg twice a day.
- Exercise regularly, even if you don't feel like it! Aerobic exercise releases endorphins into the bloodstream. These proteins can help relieve pain and lift your mood. Exercise can also help relax your body.
- Generic ibuprofen can relieve menstrual cramping because it targets those specific pain receptors and also works as an anti-inflammatory. Aspirin can also relieve inflammation. Acetaminophen is not an anti-inflammatory, so it is less likely to help.

sleep

Although getting enough sleep is one of the most important things you can do for your health, it can be elusive for many people. How much you need depends on your age and genetic predisposition, but aiming for eight hours is still a good general rule. (Children need more, so consult with your pedi atrician to determine a child's sleep schedule.) The following tips may help you get to sleep, and they don't cost a thing!

- Set and maintain a sleep routine: Go to bed and wake up at about the same time every day. Staying up later and sleeping later on weekends disrupts your sleep rhythm.
- Exercise aerobically four to six hours before you go to bed. If you exercise right before bedtime, you'll be too stimulated to sleep. Swimming is a great, relaxing choice.
- Stop any intake of caffeine six hours before bedtime. Caffeine takes that long for the body to process. Nicotine is also a stimulant and should be avoided.
- A drink of alcohol can make you feel relaxed and sleepy initially, but a few hours later the sugar kicks in and can wake you up or make you sleep restlessly. Try to stop intake of alcohol about four hours before bedtime.
- Wind down before going to bed by reading or watching television. Sit in a comfortable chair or couch and wear comfortable clothing.
- Take a warm bath to further relax your body.
- Too much sleep can be as disturbing to your body's rhythms as too little sleep. Short naps during the day are better than trying to sleep longer at night.
- Use your bedroom only for relaxing activities; don't do work there. Your body reacts to very subtle cues, and if your bedroom is a calm, quiet place used for relaxing, your body will react appropriately.
- If exterior noise is a problem, use good earplugs. White noise, such as running a fan or something similar, works well, creating a consistent background sound that blocks out unwanted noise.

snoring

- Sleep on your side. Most people who snore sleep on their backs. Tuck pillows in strategic places to keep you on your side. Or sew a pocket into the back of a T-shirt and put a tennis ball in it. When you roll onto your back, the discomfort will force you to turn back to your side.
- Check your weight. Being overweight is a major factor contributing to snoring. Even losing 5 or 10 pounds can dramatically reduce snoring frequency and intensity.
- Use a cool-mist humidifier in your bedroom at night to keep your nasal passages from drying out.

● Avoid drinking alcohol and smoking before bed. Alcohol relaxes the muscles of the throat, and smoking promotes nasal congestion, both of which can cause snoring.

sore throat

Here are three gargles to can help:
● Dissolve a teaspoon of table salt in a cup of warm water.
● Add 3 tablespoons of cider vinegar, 2 drops of hot red pepper sauce, and a pinch of salt to 1 cup warm water.
● Combine 2 tablespoons of plain mustard, 1 to 2 tablespoons of lemon juice, 1 tablespoon of salt, 1 tablespoon of honey, and 1-1/2 cups of boiling water; stir until well mixed. Cover and let the mixture cool for 15 minutes.

splinters

● If you can see the splinter but it is too deeply embedded to pull out with tweezers, try soaking the affected area in warm water for 10 to 15 minutes. As the wood swells, it may push the splinter out far enough for you to grab it.
● Coat the splinter with white, nontoxic glue. After the glue has dried, peel it off slowly. The splinter may pull out with the dried glue.
● If the splinter is small and there is no sign of infection, leave it alone. Most small splinters will break down or come out on their own over time.

sports injuries

A simple formula to keep in mind for sports injuries is **RICE**. This stands for **R**est, **I**ce, **C**ompression, and **E**levation, and it is remarkably effective.

rest Stop whatever it was you were doing immediately. When you injure a muscle, it needs time to heal or you will keep reinjuring it—leading to costly doctor visits. A minor injury usually needs to heal only a day or two before you can resume gentle exercising. More severe injuries need longer and it is crucial not to resume exercising until you are fully healed. If you are taking ibuprofen or another pain reliever, don't let that mask the fact that your injury has not yet healed. You could do yourself permanent, expensive damage.

ice Ice reduces pain and swelling, helps stop bleeding, and encourages the body to begin the healing process. For comfort, wrap your ice pack in a towel or old T-shirt.

compression Use a stretch (Ace) bandage to wrap the injured area just tightly enough to support it, without cutting off circulation. This will also help reduce pain.

elevation If you've injured a limb, raise it above the level of the heart, if at all possible, or at least above hip level. Elevation helps to limit swelling and keeps you from accidentally moving the injured part.

The final part of the equation is **patience**. Our bodies are remarkable in their ability to heal but we need to give them time to do this. Once your immediate pain has gone, begin using the injured area very gently and slowly, building back up to your previous level of activity.

sunburn

The best choice is to avoid sunburns altogether. Slather on sunscreen every day and reapply it as needed. Stay out of the sun from 10 a.m. to 3 p.m. if at all possible. Sunburn in childhood can lead to skin cancer in later life, so start a sun protection program while you or your children are young and stick with it throughout life.

● Soothe sunburns by putting ice wrapped in a towel on the burned area several times a day. The ice will reduce swelling and ease the burning sensation.
● Liquid from a leaf of aloe vera can both soothe burns and speed the healing process. The plants are very easy to grow, so you can supply your own.
● Combine 4 tea bags (cheap black tea), 2 cups fresh mint leaves (or 1 cup dried mint), and 4 cups water in a saucepan. Bring the mixture to a boil; reduce the heat and simmer for five minutes. Remove the pan from the heat and let the mixture steep for 15 minutes. Strain the mixture into a jar and discard the solids. To use: Dab the mixture on sunburned areas with cotton balls or a washcloth.

toothache

If you have persistent tooth or gum pain, see a dentist to fix the problem. Here are some strategies for quick relief:

● Soak a sterile cotton ball or piece of cotton gauze with oil of cloves (available at drug stores and health food stores), or make a paste of finely ground cloves and water. Pack the cotton or paste in the aching tooth's cavity or place it over the sore area. Cloves will naturally numb the area, but you may also feel a stinging in your lips and tongue.
● If your tooth has just started to ache, try drinking a hot liquid. For an ongoing ache, try sucking on an ice cube.
● Mix a teaspoon of salt in warm water and gargle once an hour, swishing the solution over the aching area.
● Try a form of acupressure: Massage the web of skin between your thumb and index finger with an ice cube. Rubbing that part of the right hand will affect the right side of your mouth; the left hand, the left side.
● If a filling has fallen out, make a temporary replacement by combining eugenol and powdered zinc oxide (both available at most drug stores) into a stiff paste. Pack the paste into the cavity, then bite down hard to further force it in and shape it. Then get to a dentist as soon as possible.

GIVE YOURSELF A HAND

There is one simple thing you can do that will greatly reduce your risk of getting sick, and it is cheap, cheap, cheap: Wash your hands. Several times a day, wash your hands with soap and water and avoid touching your eyes, nose, and mouth. Whenever you come home from shopping or work or school, the first thing you should do is head for the bathroom or kitchen sink and wash your hands. If you touch money, wash your hands. (Money is notorious for spreading germs.) Wash your hands even if you don't think they are dirty. You would be surprised (and probably totally disgusted) by what you can't see with the naked eye.

diet right:
low–cost strategies for
Good Health

A HEALTHFUL DIET CAN BE
MOUTH WATERING, SOUL SATISFYING,
AND CHEAP AS WELL.

The word diet conjures up visions of minuscule portions of rabbit food. But that's not a good diet. If you can't see yourself eating certain foods for life, you won't. The terrific news for penny pinchers is that a diet beneficial to your health and well-being can also be helpful to your pocketbook. It's a win-win situation. The best way to cut health care costs is to prevent health problems in the first place. And a balanced diet is a lot less expensive than doctor visits, hospital stays, or rehabilitative care.

rule 1 fresh is best

Learn this rule. Love it. Live it. The farther you get from fresh, the less nutritional value a food has and the worse it tastes so it is a waste of money! If you buy fruits and vegetables in season, both for variety and cost, you'll save even more.

rule 2 water, water everywhere

Provided you don't spend a fortune on designer brands of bottled water, water is one of the best, and cheapest, things you can consume. Drinking six to eight 8-ounce glasses of water a day helps keep your skin soft, fight off diseases, and maintain your digestive system. Water is good for your body in many other ways, too.

rule 3 pyramid power

Learn the Food Guide Pyramid (see box, facing page) from the United States Department of Agriculture (USDA). Think of it as an easy way to balance your diet. And guess what? No food is forbidden! If you eat enough from each food group, you'll cover all your nutritional and taste needs. Where does the penny-pinching come in? Easy! The pyramid emphasizes grains, fruits, and veggies. If you really make an effort to eat all of those that you need, you'll find yourself eating considerably less fat and protein, which (especially with meats and cheeses) tend to be pricier.

combinations for success

The pyramid can also help you see ways to combine servings. For instance, you can combine oat cereal with a sliced banana and skim or low-fat milk, giving you one serving each from the grain, fruit, and dairy groups. Just be sure to eat a variety of foods; if you limit your range too much, you'll end up feeling deprived. Find a balance you can follow for life.

how green was my salad?

If you want to get the most nutrition for your money, remember this easy color key: The darker the green, the more nutrient-rich the vegetable. Romaine lettuce, for example, has six times more vitamin C and five times more beta carotene (which the body can convert into vitamin A) than iceberg lettuce has. Deep-colored greens, such as spinach, watercress, chicory, and arugula, pack even more nutrients. If your family just loves iceberg lettuce (which does contain decent amounts of folate, a water-soluble B vitamin), try mixing it with a darker-leaf lettuce, like romaine. That will give it added nutritional punch.

dressing light

- Substitute low-fat or nonfat yogurt or sour cream for up to half of the mayonnaise in any creamy salad dressing. This is a particularly healthy, tasty, and cost-effective combination for coleslaw, potato salad, and egg salad.
- Combine puréed tomatoes with low-fat or nonfat yogurt to make a tangy, tempting healthful salad dressing for pennies. Whisk in a little canola oil to bind the dressing.
- Flavored oils and vinegars can add dash to a dressing, while lowering the fat and calories. How? You use less, and they're easy and economical to make. (See page 100.) A nut oil imparts an earthy essence to a dressing, while a fruit vinegar adds zing!
- Juice it up! Try using orange, lemon, or lime juice, apple or pear cider, or leftover wine instead of vinegar in your salad dressing. An added boon: Using a citrus juice dressing on spinach salad allows your body to absorb more of the iron in the spinach.

❝The only way to keep your health is to eat what you don't want, drink what you don't like and do what you'd druther not.❞

Mark Twain

CLIMBING THE PYRAMID

Following the USDA's Food Guide Pyramid is an easy way not only to balance your diet but also to save money. Here is a summary of the recommendations, starting at the base of the pyramid.

- **The base:** breads, cereals, rice, and pasta (food from grains)—5 to 11 servings per day (1 serving equals a slice of bread, 1 ounce of cereal, or 1/2 cup of cooked rice or pasta).
- **Second level:** vegetables and fruit—3 to 5 servings of vegetables per day (1 serving equals 1 cup leafy greens or 1/2 cup cooked veggies) and 2 to 4 servings of fruit or fruit juice.
- **Third level:** proteins and dairy—2 to 3 servings of protein (meat, poultry, fish, eggs, dried beans and peas, nuts) per day and 2 to 3 servings of dairy products (milk, cheese, or yogurt). One serving equals 3 to 4 ounces of either protein or dairy.
- **Tip-top:** fats, sugar, salt, and alcohol—although you need a certain amount of fat for good health, no more than 30 percent of your daily calorie count should come from fat, preferably unsaturated or monounsaturated. Sugar and alcohol are nonnutritive, or "empty," calories, so enjoy them in small portions. Limit salt when you're cooking, since most foods already contain sodium—more than enough for a normal diet.

- Cheap trick: Mix up your salad dressing in a nearly empty mayonnaise or mustard jar. You will make use of all the jar's contents and create a tasty dressing, too.

brighter is better value

The same color-to-value rule applies when buying other vegetables, as well as fruits. Look for bright colors for the best nutritional merit for your money. Vitamin C and beta carotene are found in orange cantaloupes, carrots, sweet potatoes, and oranges. Or think green and go for broccoli, brussels sprouts, kale, and spinach.

vegetable verities

- Start steaming now! When you boil vegetables, you lose many nutrients—and boiling takes longer. Steaming is faster and preserves the color, flavor, and nutrients better. If you do boil veggies, save the cooking water so that you can use it later when making soup, gravy, or sauce. Then you'll still get the benefit of the nutrients.
  - Sneak veggies into other dishes: Grated carrots and zucchini can be added to tomato sauces, meatloaf, and muffins. Sneak corn and chopped broccoli into chili and stews.
- Don't toss the tough stems of broccoli, asparagus, cauliflower, mushrooms, and other vegetables. Instead, steam them until they are soft, then purée them to use in soups or sauces

use less, save more

Whenever a recipe calls for oil, try cutting the amount by one-third to one-half. For example, when a recipe for hummus calls for 1/2 to 1 cup of olive oil, start with 1/4 cup and add only enough to achieve the texture and taste you like. If the recipe needs to be smoothed or thinned further, try adding a little broth, plain yogurt, or lemon juice, depending on the type of recipe. The only exception to this approach is in baking, where the exact amount of butter, margarine, or shortening is essential to the final product. Otherwise, the amount of fat you cook with is a matter of taste, not generally a requirement.

hidden helper

For a richer texture without extra fat, add 1 or 2 tablespoons of nonfat powdered milk to skim milk, cream soups, omelets, or puddings. The powdered milk also provides extra calcium and protein, and it costs less than using cream. Of course, your store's house brand of nonfat powdered milk is just a good as the national brands.

S-O-S (save on salt)

- Want to de-salt canned vegetables and beans? Drain off the liquid and rinse the food under cold water. More than a third of the salt will be washed away.
- Fool yourself (and your family, too) into using less salt at the table. Cut a small piece of tape and place it over the top of your salt shaker, leaving only two or three holes open. You probably won't even notice the difference, but every grain saved helps you.
- Don't immediately add salt to recipes even if they call for it. Instead, add the herbs and spices, cook, and then taste. Not seasoned enough? Add a bit more of the herbs and spices. You may find that this tastes so good, you won't want to add the salt at all. Garlic and onion are particularly potent flavor boosters (and good for you to boot). A notable exception to this is baked goods; always use the amount of salt listed in baking recipes because it's essential to the chemical process.

vitamin thrift

Some folks swear by vitamins. They seem to think that downing vitamins ensures that they're eating a healthful diet. But they can cost you a fortune. Vitamin pills are fine as supplements, but don't squander your money or your health on a storeful. To lower your outlay on vitamins, look for big bottles at price clubs or other discount stores, or check the prices of store brands, which tend to cost less per pill. You can also find some good deals on the Web (check under discount vitamins), but you'll have to pay shipping costs, so do the math before you buy. Just keep in mind that a vitamin is not a substitute for a balanced diet and that vitamin pills are not miracle cures for anything, despite the hype.

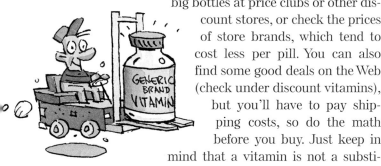

sensible stock options

It is a real waste of money to throw out the water that you've cooked vegetables, chicken, meat, or shellfish in. Strain these precious liquids and freeze them in ice-cube trays. After the liquid freezes, pop the cubes out of the trays and store them in well-marked, self-sealing plastic bags in your freezer. They will be instantly available for producing soups and stews that are incredibly rich and much more nutritious. Or try cooking rice or pasta in the broth to add both flavor and nutrition. You can also use this ice-cube trick with home-made chicken stock (see recipe on page 105).

SUPERSAVER SNACKS

The great news is that nutritious nibbles are often cheap, too. So the next time you or your family has a nosh attack, try one of these taste tempters:

- ☑ Go for the bagel! Thick, chewy, full of flavor but surprisingly low in calories with almost no fat, bagels are a better choice than muffins or croissants.

- ☑ Fancy a fig bar? Or a graham cracker? Both are low in fat and calories, and fig bars contain fiber-rich fruit. Store brands are often half the price of name brands!

- ☑ Baked is better. If you simply must have chips, look for a store brand that is baked, not fried. An ounce of baked potato chips has only 1.5 grams of fat, versus 10 grams in its fried cousin. And baked chips taste just as good.

- ☑ Skimp on salt. Choose low-salt pretzels, rice cakes, and unbuttered popcorn, which are all low fat, too.

- ☑ Crispy crudités. Keep raw baby vegetables (such as carrots) or sliced regular-sized vegetables handy in the refrigerator at all times. Add some dried onion and dill to yogurt for a low-cal, low-cost dip.

skim off the cream

When a soup recipe calls for cream, a cheaper and more healthful alternative is to add puréed vegetables. Save leftover cooked vegetables and whirl them in a blender or food processor, then stir into your soup. If you must have that creamy taste, substitute 2-percent milk or some nonfat yogurt for cream.

double the pleasure, double the savings

When you're cooking soup, stew, or chili, make a double batch. When it has cooked, put the pot in the refrigerator for an hour or so, until the fat congeals on the surface. Skim off the fat and discard it. Then pour half the mixture into a large container with a lid and store it in the refrigerator or freezer for use later as a quick, nutritious, low-cost dinner.

"eat your soup—it's good for you!"

What Grandma said then is just as true now. This one-pot wonder is delicious, economical, and diet-friendly. Start with a homemade stock. (See page 105.) Add a protein-rich component, such as beans, meat, or poultry (using small amounts of cheaper cuts of meat or poultry). Throw in whatever vegetables you have on hand, and a grain such as rice, barley, or pasta. Ta da! You have a mouth-watering, money-saving main dish!

mock mayonnaise

This palate pleaser has no cholesterol, only 18 calories per tablespoon, and costs less than purchased imitation mayonnaise. For added flavor, stir in a tablespoon of ketchup or hot red pepper sauce.

- 2 cups cold water
- 2 tablespoons cornstarch
- 1/4 cup olive oil
- 1/4 cup white vinegar
- 1/4 cup plain low-fat yogurt
- 2 teaspoons prepared yellow mustard
- 1 teaspoon prepared horseradish

(1) In a small saucepan, whisk together the water and cornstarch. Cook over moderate heat, stirring constantly, until the mixture comes to a boil. Boil for one or two minutes or until the mixture is clear. Transfer the mixture to a bowl.

(2) Whisk in the remaining ingredients in the order listed. Will keep for two weeks, tightly covered, in the refrigerator. MAKES ABOUT 2 CUPS.

mock whipped cream

Much lower in saturated fat than whipped heavy cream, this elegant mimic is cost-effective. You can keep the ingredients on hand indefinitely, unlike its dairy relative.

- 1 (5-ounce) can evaporated skim milk
- 2 tablespoons cold water
- 1 teaspoon unflavored gelatin
- 2 tablespoons sugar
- 3 tablespoons corn oil or safflower oil

(1) Pour the evaporated milk into an empty ice cube tray or a pan and place it in the freezer. When crystals form around the edges (in about 20 minutes), the milk is cold enough to whip.

(2) Meanwhile, combine the cold water and the gelatin in a small ovenproof dish without stirring. Heat about 1 inch of water in a small saucepan; remove the pan from the heat. Set the dish with the gelatin mixture in the pan and let stand until the gelatin dissolves, about five minutes. Remove dish from the pan of water, stir the gelatin solution, and let it cool.

(3) In a medium-size bowl, beat the iced milk until stiff peaks form. One at a time, gradually beat in the sugar, the oil, and the gelatin mixture. Continue beating until the mixture forms stiff peaks again. Cover the bowl and set it in the freezer for ten minutes; then transfer the bowl to the refrigerator. The mixture will become stiff. Before serving, stir to soften it. Will keep three days, covered, in the refrigerator. MAKES 4 SERVINGS

mock sour cream

This impressive impersonator contains no saturated fat and has just 11 calories per tablespoon. Try it as a luscious topping for fruit, soups, and vegetables, but don't try to use it in cooking.

- 1 cup milk
- 4 teaspoons powdered buttermilk
- 1/2 teaspoon unflavored gelatin
- 1/2 cup plain low-fat yogurt

(1) Combine the milk and buttermilk powder in a medium-size saucepan. Sprinkle the gelatin on top and let stand until gelatin softens, about five minutes.

(2) Cook over low heat, uncovered, stirring occasionally, until the gelatin dissolves. Remove the pan from the heat and whisk in the yogurt.

(3) Transfer the mixture to a medium-size bowl, cover, and refrigerate for one hour or until the mixture has thickened. Will keep for five days, tightly covered, in the refrigerator. MAKES 1-1/2 CUPS

flavored oil

Oil infused with the taste of a specific herb or spice can add a wallop of flavor, so that you can use less oil. This homemade version costs considerably less than anything you can find in a store. Make only small quantities at a time, since these delicate oils are perishable.

● Several sprigs of herbs or spices of choice (Herbs with little moisture content, such as rosemary, thyme, summer savory, coriander seeds, or whole chilies are good choices.)

● olive oil (enough to fill a bottle of your choice)

① Lightly bruise the herbs, spices, or chilies by gently pressing down on them with a rolling pin, just enough to release the flavor.

② In a small saucepan, warm the olive oil over low heat. Add the herbs or other flavoring and remove the pan from the heat. Let stand for about 15 minutes.

③ Carefully transfer the herbs or spices from the saucepan to a sterilized bottle and then pour the oil over them.

④ Seal the bottle and store in the refrigerator for at least two days to let the flavoring infuse the oil.

⑤ Strain the oil into a second sterilized bottle and discard the solids. Add a fresh sprig of the herb for decoration.

Will keep for up to one month in the refrigerator.

herb or spice vinegar

Also a real flavor powerhouse (and not cheap to buy), vinegar can be infused with herbs or spices. Be creative with the following flavorings!

● Fresh herbs, such as rosemary, tarragon, thyme, celery seed, and winter or summer savory, or spices, such as whole cloves or allspice, mace, gingerroot, or a combination of several spices (about 1 cup per 1-1/2 gallons of vinegar)

● A good quality cider or white wine vinegar (enough to fill any bottle of your choice)

① Lightly crush the herbs and pack them into a hot, sterilized bottle. Or pour the spices into the bottle.

② In a small saucepan, bring the vinegar to a boil. Pour the hot vinegar over the herbs or spices in the bottle.

③ Seal the bottle and let it sit for two weeks. (Spiced vinegar may need three weeks.)

④ Strain the vinegar into a second sterilized bottle and discard the solids. Add a fresh sprig of the same herb for decoration, if desired.

Will keep for up to a year in a cool, dark place. Refrigerate after opening.

good combinations

● White wine vinegar with hot chilies, lemon slices and fennel, orange zest and white peppercorns, or nasturtium flowers and a few nasturtium leaves

● Red wine vinegar with fresh sage leaves or shallots and green peppercorns

● Cider vinegar with mashed blackberries

penny-pinching, frugally fit, fantastic recipes

berry vinegar
For an elegant addition to a fruit salad, use berries that are in season to make this flavorful vinegar.
- 2 quarts of fresh berries, such as raspberries, blueberries, blackberries, or strawberries
- 1/2 cup sugar
- 1 tablespoon vanilla, almond, orange, or mint extract
- 1 quart cider or white wine vinegar

① Set the berries in a noncorrosive bowl. Sprinkle on the sugar and flavoring and toss to coat the berries completely.

② Pour the vinegar over the berries. Cover the bowl and let stand at a cool room temperature for 24 to 48 hours.

③ Strain the mixture through cheesecloth or a kitchen sieve into a large measuring cup; discard the solids.

④ Pour the vinegar into a sterilized bottle.

Will keep in the refrigerator for six months.

low-fat salad dressings
Here are some low- fat combinations you can use to dress up your salads. You'll find that these salad dressings are kind both to your heart and to your pocketbook.

dill dressing
Combine:
- 5 tablespoons plain nonfat yogurt
- 2 tablespoons chopped fresh dill, or 2 teaspoons dried dill
- 1 tablespoon white wine vinegar
- 1 small sweet onion, finely chopped
- salt and black pepper
- 1 teaspoon coarse-grained mustard

thousand island dressing
To the dill dressing, add:
- 2 tablespoons chopped green olives
- 2 tablespoons diced green pepper
- 1 tablespoon chopped scallion
- 1 tablespoon chopped parsley
- 2 teaspoons tomato pureé
- white of 1 hard-cooked egg, diced

low-fat vinaigrette
Whisk together:
- 1/4 cup vinegar or lemon juice
- 1/4 cup water
- 2 tablespoons olive oil
- 1 teaspoon sugar
- salt and pepper

yogurt dressing
Blend or whisk together:
- 3 tablespoons plain nonfat yogurt
- 2 tablespoons chopped parsley
- 1 tablespoon olive oil
- 2 teaspoons Dijon mustard
- 1 teaspoon lime juice

soy dressing
Combine:
- 1/4 cup reduced-sodium soy sauce
- 1/4 cup chopped fresh cilantro or parsley
- 2 tablespoons olive oil
- 1 teaspoon honey
- 2 cloves garlic, crushed

lemon and basil dressing
Combine:
- 2 tablespoons lemon juice
- 2 tablespoons olive oil
- 16 fresh basil leaves, torn into pieces
- 1 garlic clove, finely chopped.

citris vinaigrette
Whisk together:
- 4 tablespoons orange juice
- 2 teaspoons lime juice
- 4 teaspoons sunflower oil
- 1 tablspoons snipped fresh chives
- salt and pepper to taste

sensational salt substitute

This tasty trickster adds flavor without adding sodium. Use it in your shaker in place of regular table salt. Sour salt, powdered orange peel, and powdered lemon peel can be found in the spice section at most supermarkets.

- 1/2 teaspoons cream of tartar
- 1 tablespoon each garlic powder, powdered orange peel, arrowroot, and sugar
- 2 tablespoons each black pepper, celery seed, and onion powder
- 1-1/2 teaspoons sour salt (powdered citric acid)
- 1 teaspoon each white pepper, dill weed, and dried thyme, crumbled
- 1/2 teaspoon plus a pinch powdered lemon peel
- 1/2 teaspoon cayenne pepper

Combine all the ingredients in a small electric spice grinder, coffee grinder, or blender. Grind for 10 seconds or until the mixture is fine. With a funnel, pour some of the salt substitute into a shaker-top container. Store the remainder in a container with a tight fitting lid, and store it in a cool, dark, dry place. MAKES 1 CUP.

sensational spice mix

To wake up your taste buds without adding sodium, sprinkle this mix over chicken parts or fish before baking, grilling, or sautéing, or add to fresh or stale bread crumbs to make a spicy coating for pork or beef.

- 1/4 cup paprika
- 4 tablespoons dried oregano
- 4 teaspoons chili powder
- 2 teaspoons garlic powder
- 2 teaspoons black pepper
- 1 teaspoon cayenne pepper
- 1 teaspoon dry mustard

Combine all the ingredients in a shaker-top container with a tight-fitting lid. Shake until the spices are well mixed. Store the mix in a cool, dark, dry place. MAKES ABOUT 3/4 CUP.

herb dressing mix

Make your own dressing mix that is bursting with fresh taste and contains none of the preservatives of store brands.

- 1/2 cup parsley flakes
- 1/4 cup each dried oregano, basil, and marjoram, crushed
- 1/4 cup sugar
- 2 tablespoons fennel seed, crushed
- 2 tablespoons dry mustard
- 1 tablespoon black pepper

Combine all the ingredients in a quart-size jar with a tight-fitting lid. Cover the jar and shake thoroughly until well blended.

Will keep 6 weeks in a cool, dark, dry place. MAKES 2 CUPS.

to make herb dressing

Combine 2 tablespoons of the Herb Dressing Mix with 1-1/2 cups of warm water, 2 tablespoons olive oil, 5 tablespoons white or tarragon vinegar, and 2 cloves garlic, crushed, in a small bowl. Whisk the ingredients together and let the dressing sit at room temperature for 30 minutes before using. Whisk again, then pour the desired amount of dressing over a salad.

Will keep 1 week tightly covered and refrigerated. MAKES 2 CUPS.

low-sodium mustard

Enjoy the full flavor of this delicious condiment without the high cost or high-salt content of purchased brands.

- 1/2 cup mustard seed
- 1/3 cup dry white wine
- 1/2 cup white vinegar
- 1/2 cup water

 frugal health and fitness

- 2 tablespoons honey
- 1/4 teaspoon ground allspice
- 1/8 teaspoon each ground cinnamon and ginger

(1) Combine the mustard seed, white wine, and white vinegar in a medium-size bowl and let stand for 3 hours at room temperature. Transfer the mixture to a food processor or blender, and add the water, honey, allspice, cinnamon, and ginger. Process until fairly smooth.

(2) Transfer the mixture to the top of a double boiler. Bring water to simmering and cook, stirring occasionally, until thickened, for 10 to 12 minutes. Pour the mustard into a sterilized jar with a tight-fitting lid, and let cool to room temperature. When the mustard is cool, cover tightly and store in the refrigerator.

Will keep for 1 year in the refrigerator. MAKES 2 CUPS

cent-sible sauces

Start with this basic sauce mix and make a low-fat, easy-to-use classic white sauce. Then try any of the variations that follow for a tantalizingly thrifty taste. Make the sauces fresh as needed.

basic sauce mix:

- 1 cup all-purpose flour
- 1 cup instant nonfat dry milk
- 1-1/2 teaspoons salt

Combine all the ingredients in a jar, cover, and store at room temperature. MAKES 2 CUPS OF DRY MIX OR ENOUGH FOR 8 CUPS OF PREPARED SAUCE.

white sauce: Place 1/4 cup of the basic sauce mix in a medium-size saucepan and gradually whisk in 1 cup of nonfat or low-fat milk. Set the pan over moderate heat and cook, stirring constantly, for about two minutes or until the mixture thickens. Reduce the heat to low and simmer, stir-ring constantly, for two minutes more. MAKES 1 CUP.

curry sauce Add 1 teaspoon of curry powder to the basic sauce mix and pre-pare as for white sauce. Serve with roast chicken, poached fish fillets, or eggs.

mushroom sauce Sauté 1 cup of chopped mushrooms in 1 tablespoon of margarine or butter. Prepare the white sauce. At the end of the cooking time, stir in the mushroom mixture. Serve with chicken or vegetables.

mustard sauce Prepare white sauce, stirring in 2 tablespoons low-sodium mus-tard (see recipe, facing page) along with the milk. Serve with pork chops or ham.

paprika sauce Add 1 or more table-spoons of paprika to the basic sauce mix and prepare as for white sauce. Serve with veal or chicken.

parsley sauce Prepare as for the white sauce, adding 2 tablespoons of minced parsley after adding the milk. Serve with fish fillets or vegetables.

apple butter

An irresistible alternative to sugary jams, jellies, fatty butter, margarine, or peanut butter, this apple butter is packed with vitamins and spiced to perfection. Take advantage of pick-your-own apple or-chards, if possible; otherwise, stock up on seasonal specials.

- 4 pounds assorted apples (Cortland, McIntosh, Northern Spy), quartered (Do not core or peel the apples; the pectin adds body to the butter.)
- 2 cups apple cider
- 1 vanilla bean, split
- 2 cinnamon sticks
- 4 whole cloves

(1) Place the apples in a large dutch oven or stockpot. Cover and cook over low heat about 50 minutes or until the apples are

soft; if the mixture begins to show signs of burning, add a few tablespoons of water.

(2) Force the apples through a food mill or sieve into a large saucepan; discard the solids. Add the cider, vanilla bean, cinnamon sticks, and cloves. Cook the mixture, uncovered, stirring frequently, over low heat about one hour and 15 minutes or until very thick.

(3) Let the mixture cool slightly, then remove the vanilla bean, cinnamon, and cloves. While it's still warm, transfer the apple butter to hot, sterilized 1/2-pint jars with tight-fitting lids.

Will keep one month tightly covered in the refrigerator. MAKES 2-1/2 CUPS.

penny-pinching peanut butter

This make-your-own peanut butter is pure, delicious, and a lot less expensive than the purchased variety.

- 2 cups shelled, salted dry-roasted peanuts
- 1 tablespoon plus 1 teaspoon vegetable oil

for creamy peanut butter: Process the peanuts with the oil in a food processor or blender until creamy, working in batches if necessary. Stop the machine occasionally and scrape down the sides.

for chunky peanut butter: Coarsely chop about 1/3 cup of the peanuts in a blender or food processor and set aside. Process remaining peanuts and oil until creamy and then stir in the chopped peanuts.

Will keep for one month tightly covered in the refrigerator. MAKES 1 CUP.

de-light-ful dip

A terrific use for mock mayonnaise, this dip can be served with raw veggies, such as carrots, celery, cucumber, zucchini, broccoli florets, or red, green, orange, and yellow sweet peppers.

- 1 cup mock mayonnaise (see p.99)
- 1/4 teaspoon sesame oil
- 1 teaspoon soy sauce
- 1 clove garlic, minced

Combine all the ingredients in a small bowl and stir until well mixed. Transfer the dip to a serving dish.

salsa cruda

This salsa is a terrific, tasty, no-fat wonder. If you want a hotter salsa, use the jalapeño peppers; if you want a mildly spicy salsa, use the green chilies. Serve the salsa with baked tortilla chips, or use it to top fish fillets, pork chops, grilled boneless chicken breasts, eggs, or anything else you please.

- 1 pound fresh tomatoes, chopped, or 1-1/2 cups canned diced tomatoes
- 2 tablespoons fresh cilantro, coarsely chopped
- 1 tablespoon red onion, finely chopped
- 1 clove garlic, finely chopped
- 1 to 2 fresh jalapeño peppers, seeded and finely chopped, or 1 small can chopped green chilies
- 1 tablespoon lime juice

Combine all the ingredients in a small bowl and toss to mix gently. Let the salsa sit at room temperature for about one hour so the flavors will blend.

MAKES ABOUT 1-1/2 CUPS.

gourmet popcorn

Here's a thoroughly satisfying snack that's high in flavor and low in calories.

- 8 cups plain popcorn (air-popped for lowest calorie count, or use the lowest fat and calorie microwave popcorn available)

southwest popcorn: Lightly spray the popcorn with canola oil. Sprinkle with 1/8 cup dried tomato bits and 2 teaspoons chili powder. Toss to mix thoroughly.

passage-to-india popcorn Lightly spray popcorn with canola oil. Sprinkle with 1/2 cup golden raisins and 2 teaspoons curry powder. Toss to mix thoroughly.

popcorn italiano Lightly spray the popcorn with olive oil. Sprinkle with 1/2 cup of Parmesan cheese, 1 teaspoon dried oregano, and 1/2 teaspoon dried basil. Toss immediately until well blended.

homemade chicken stock

Thrifty cooks have made their own stock for generations. It tastes better, is generally higher in nutrients and lower in fat and salt than purchased brands, and is a great way to use up chicken bones and aging vegetables. Best of all, it follows the penny pincher's motto: Why buy it when you can make it yourself?

Whenever you are cooking chicken, save the backs, necks, gizzards, and bones in a self-sealing bag in the freezer. When you have enough, make stock.

1 Brown the chicken parts and bones in a large dutch oven or stockpot over moderate heat. Browning imparts a richer flavor and color.

2 Add chopped aromatic vegetables, such as onion, garlic, celery, and carrots, and your favorite herbs. Do not add salt.

3 Add enough cold water to cover the mixture by 1 inch and lower the heat. Simmer for 1-1/2 to 2 hours, adding water as needed to keep the bones covered.

4 Strain the broth into a large pot or bowl and discard the solids. Set the container in the refrigerator for a few hours. When the fat has congealed on the surface of the stock, skim off the fat and discard it. Freeze the homemade stock in ice-cube trays, muffin tins, or plastic containers in specific amounts (1/2 cup,

1 cup). When a recipe calls for stock or broth, simply add the amount you need — no need to defrost before using.

brown beef stock

For this basic brown stock, use cheap beef bones, such as marrow and shinbones or knucklebones. If necessary, ask the butcher to break the bones into pieces small enough to fit in your stockpot.

- 4 lbs. meaty beef bones
- 2 onions, thickly sliced
- 2 carrots, thickly sliced
- 2 stalks celery with leaves, sliced
- 6 sprigs fresh parsley
- 2 small bay leaves
- 2 sprigs fresh thyme or 1/2 teaspoon dried thyme
- 10 black peppercorns
- 1 tablespoon salt, optional

1 Preheat the oven to 400° F. Place the bones, onions, and carrots in a roasting pan and roast until the bones turn a rich brown, 30 to 45 minutes.

2 Transfer the mixture to a large stockpot and add the remaining ingredients and 5 quarts of cold water, or enough to cover the bones.

3 Add a little water to the roasting pan and stir to scrape up the browned particles. Add this liquid to the stockpot.

4 Bring slowly to a boil, skimming the surface with a slotted spoon to remove any scum. Reduce the heat, partly cover, and simmer gently for 3 to 4 hours.

4 Strain the broth through a fine sieve lined with cheesecloth into a large pot or bowl and discard the solids. Set the container in the refrigerator for a few hours. When the fat has congealed on the surface of the stock, skim off the fat and discard it. Transfer to small containers and refrigerate or freeze. MAKES 3 QUARTS

penny-pinching, frugally fit, fantastic recipes

lentil soup with root veggies

Lentils and other dried beans are a good source of low-fat protein and are especially healthful with prepared with other vegetables. Instead of adding salt at the table, serve the soup Mediterranean style—with a squeeze of lemon juice.

- 2 cups brown lentils, rinsed
- 1 tablespoon olive oil
- 1 large onion, diced
- 2 stalks celery, diced
- 2 cloves garlic, finely chopped
- 8 ounces turnip or parsnip, diced
- 2 quarts brown or chicken stock
- 1 tablespoon tomato paste
- 1/4 teaspoon dried thyme
- 1 bay leaf
- 1/8 teaspoon each salt and pepper

(1) In a 4-quart saucepan, heat the olive oil and saute the onion, celery, and garlic until soft and golden, about six minutes.

(2) Add the turnips and carrots, and 1/4 cup stock. Simmer until slightly soft.

(3) Add the lentils, tomato paste, thyme, remaining stock, and bay leaf and stir. Bring to a boil and simmer, partially covered, until lentils and vegetables are tender, about 50 minutes. Season with salt and pepper. Discard bay leaf.

MAKES 9 CUPS.

gazpacho

Serve this cool soup with cornbread, French or Italian bread, or baked tortilla chips for a tangy summer supper.

- 1 clove garlic
- 1 medium red or yellow onion
- 1 (14-ounce) can low-fat, low-sodium beef broth or consommé
- 3 tablespoons olive oil
- 2 tablespoon balsamic vinegar
- 1/4 teaspoon cayenne pepper
- 5 large fresh tomatoes, peeled, quartered, and seeded

- 4 to 5 sprigs fresh cilantro or parsley
- salt and black pepper, to taste
- low-fat sour cream or plain yogurt, for garnish (optional)

(1) Combine the garlic, onion, and broth in the bowl of a food processor or electric blender; whirl until liquefied.

(2) Add the olive oil, vinegar, cayenne, tomatoes, and cilantro to the broth mixture. Whirl until the mixture is puréed. Stir in salt and pepper to taste.

(3) Chill the soup before serving; if desired, top with a dollop of low-fat sour cream or plain yogurt.

MAKES 4 TO 6 SERVINGS.

chickpea and red pepper salad

A high-protein, low-fat meal in one dish. Serve with warmed pita bread, if you like.

- 2 cups chickpeas, cooked or canned (drained)
- 1/4 cup chopped parsley
- 1/4 cup diced, drained, and rinsed canned roasted sweet red peppers
- 2 medium-size stalks celery, diced
- 1/2 cup diced red onion
- 1 cup diced, seeded plum tomatoes
- 1 clove garlic, minced
- 3 tablespoons lemon juice
- 2 tablespoons olive oil
- 1/4 teaspoon black pepper
- salt, to taste
- mixed lettuce

Combine all the ingredients, except lettuce, in a large bowl and toss to mix well. Spread the lettuce over a serving platter or large, shallow bowl and mound the chickpea salad on top.

grilled asian shrimp

Imbue succulent shrimp with the flavors of the Orient for a mouthwatering main dish. To cut costs, use frozen shrimp. Serve over fluffy rice.

- 1 pound jumbo shrimp, peeled and deveined
- 1/4 cup lemon juice
- 1/2 teaspoon salt
- 2 tablespoons dark sesame oil
- 1 large minced clove garlic
- 1 tablespoon soy sauce

(1) Place the shrimp in a large, self-sealing bag with the lemon juice, salt, sesame oil, garlic, and soy sauce. Seal the bag and shake to mix. Let the shrimp marinate for one hour.

(2) Meanwhile, prepare the grill. Grill the shrimp over moderately hot coals 3-1/2 minutes per side or until cooked through. Or preheat a broiler and broil the shrimp, 4 inches from the heat, for four to five minutes. MAKES 4 SERVINGS.

fettuccine alfredo light

All the luscious flavor of the old favorite but lower in fat and calories.

- 2 tablespoons butter or margarine
- 1/3 cup minced shallots
- 1 tablespoon cornstarch
- 1 cup 1- or 2-percent milk
- 1 cup evaporated skim milk
- 1/2 teaspoon salt
- pinch ground nutmeg
- 3/4 cup grated Parmesan cheese
- 1/4 teaspoon black pepper
- 1 pound fettuccine, cooked and drained

(1) In a medium-size saucepan over moderate heat, melt the butter or margarine. Add the shallots and sauté until they are soft, about three to four minutes. Stir the cornstarch into the shallot mixture until it is well blended.

(2) Stir in milk, evaporated milk, salt, and nutmeg, and bring to a boil over high heat, stirring constantly. Reduce the heat to moderately low and simmer, uncovered, until the sauce thickens, for four to five minutes.

Stir in the Parmesan cheese and pepper.

(3) Transfer the fettuccine to a heated serving bowl. Pour the alfredo sauce over the pasta and toss to mix well.
MAKES 4 SERVINGS.

super soda pop

A natural carbonated beverage filled with vitamins and free of refined sugar—a healthy substitute for regular soda pop.

- 1/4 cup frozen orange, grape, or apple juice concentrate
- 3/4 cup club soda
- ice cubes

Pour the frozen juice concentrate into a 12-ounce glass. Add a few tablespoons of club soda and stir until the concentrate is dissolved. Fill the glass with ice cubes, add the remaining club soda, and mix well. Serve immediately. MAKES 1 SERVING.

coffee orange granita

Here is an elegant dessert that you can make ahead. And since it has no fat, you can enjoy it free of guilt.

- 1-1/2 cups water
- 2 tablespoons instant espresso powder
- 2 tablespoons orange juice

(1) Combine the water and espresso powder in a medium-size saucepan. Bring the mixture to a boil over high heat. Remove the pan from the heat and let cool until just warm.

(2) Stir the orange juice into the coffee mixture until well blended.

(3) Pour the coffee mixture into an 8 x 8-inch square pan. Place the pan in the freezer. When the mixture begins to form ice crystals, stir with a fork. Repeat two or three times during the process.

To serve, scrape across the surface of the granita with a spoon so that the frozen mixture comes up in thin shavings.
MAKES 4 SERVINGS.

exercise Economics

TO KEEP DOCTOR'S BILLS AT BAY,
FIND AN EXERCISE YOU LIKE AND CAN STICK WITH.

We all know them—folks who spend a chunk of cash to join a health club and slowly stop using it but keep on paying membership fees. Or folks who buy the exercise equipment du jour (rowing machines, eliptical trainers), use it for a few months, and then turn it into an impromptu drying rack. Here's a penny-pinching news flash: You don't need to spend a lot of money to get fit. The impor-tant thing is to find some kind of exercise that you like to do and then do it regularly.

exercise exchange

If you love working out at a gym—using the equipment or the pool—and enjoy the opportunity it gives you to meet people—but are alarmed by the cost (even the YMCAs and YWCAs are getting pricier these days), think about a work exchange. Can you teach an aerobics dance class? A stretch-ing for seniors group? Beginning swimming for tadpoles? People who work at these places, even part time, get a significant discount on membership or can use the facilities free of charge! And if you expand your horizons to the parks and recreation departments of most cities, the classes you could teach are practically limitless (art, crafts, languages, mechanics, and so forth). Check it out!

walk the walk

If an exercise exchange doesn't appeal to you, there's great news, penny pinchers! One of the best aerobic exercises is free and easy to do at any age: walking. Although higher-impact aerobics may burn more calories per hour, such exercises are often harder on the joints. Lots of people quit because of injuries incurred while running or doing step aer-obics. Walking, on the other hand, can help keep you fit painlessly, if you follow some tips:

- Start at an easy pace and set goals that are specific and attainable. For example, start with a 15- to 20-minute walk three days a week. Then add five minutes to your walk every week and eventually add another day. Or try a hill slowly, then increase your pace.
- Motivate yourself with an incentive. Plan walk dates with a good friend and catch up on each other's news while you get fit. Or listen to exciting books on tape while you walk so that you look forward to the next chapter. (The library is a fabulous free resource for books on tape.)

ride a bike

Riding a bicycle is great for your body and great for the envi-ronment. It saves you money on gasoline and wear and tear on your car. If you don't own a bike, investing in one will be money well spent—and there are some bargains out there!

- Call your local police department information number and ask when confiscated bikes are auctioned off. This can be an outstanding way to pick up a pretty good or excellent bicycle for very little money. If the bike is a bit on the battered side, just pick up a can of bright spray paint for metal and make it look like new.

caution Always wear a helmet when riding a bicycle, regardless of your age or experience.

put the i in isometrics

This type of exercise requires no cash at all! Isometric exercises are those in which opposing muscles are contracted in such a way that there is little shortening but a great increase in tone of the muscle fibers involved, such as when you press your hands together for a few seconds and then relax them. You can do simple isometric workouts just about anywhere—during a train ride, at the office, in front of the TV. Ask your librarian to help you find some good books with isometric exercises to get you started.

caution Avoid isometric exercises if you have hypertension, heart disease, or other medical problems.

down by the river, down by the sea . . .

As many girls and boys can attest, jumping rope is not only hard work, it is fun. With its rhythmic motion, it is an ideal exercise, easily building leg and arm muscles and functioning as a terrific aerobic workout. (Ten minutes of jumping can equal 30 minutes of jogging.) All you need is a rope and good athletic shoes (see page 112), both of which are highly portable for workouts when you're traveling, too.

- Make your own jump rope. Start with about 10 feet of clothesline: Measure by stepping on the middle of the rope; the ends should come to about the middle of your chest. Tie a knot at each end of the rope, then wrap plastic electrical tape around 4 to 5 inches of the rope in front of each knot.

run for your life!

Running is a fantastic aerobic exercise—if you don't have joint or back problems. You'll need to invest in good running shoes (see page 112), but that should be the only major cash investment. You can run at home or on vacation, alone or with a partner. The roads and sidewalks are free.

in the swim

OK, this one does require a pool and a swimsuit. But it's worth mentioning because swimming is such great exercise! It gives you a cardiovascular workout, uses almost all the major muscle groups, and places virtually no strain on your

> 66 Your body is the baggage you must carry through life. The more excess baggage, the shorter the trip. 99

Arnold H. Glasow, author

joints and ligaments. People often start in childhood and keep swimming their entire lives! It's especially great when you're pregnant or recovering from an injury.

pools for the parsimonious Check with the parks and recreation department in your area. These community-run pools usually offer classes and free-swim times, and are usually cheap. Another source can be YMCAs and YWCAs, or similar clubs, though they may require memberships, which can end up costing more than you want to pay regularly.

saving on suits If you swim a lot, you'll want to get a good suit. Badly made suits tend to fall apart—which is not only inconvenient and potentially embarrassing, but can also get be expensive, because you have to keep replacing them. See page 58 in Dressing for Less for some ideas on suiting up in an economical fashion.

firming your figure with housework

Doing housework is hard work! Try any of the following and you'll build muscles while you make your home beautiful:

- Do your warm-up by washing dishes, dusting, or scrubbing the bathroom.
- Get some excellent aerobic exercise by vacuuming, sweeping, mopping, or polishing. Blast some tunes to keep you going (for 20 to 30 minutes optimally).
- For limber muscles, bend and stretch to pick up clothing, newspapers, and other stuff strewn on the floor. Stand with your feet apart, arms at your sides, and bend slowly from the waist until you can touch the floor; slightly bend your knees if you feel strain in your back. Count to 10, pick up the object (nothing heavy), and slowly stand, uncurling one vertebra at a time.
- Plié to pick up heavy items. Stand with your feet shoulder-width apart, feet turned out slightly. Keeping your back straight, weight over your knees, slowly lower your body until you can pick up the item. Using your thigh muscles, slowly rise back to a standing position.
  - Stretch for the top shelf. Stand with your feet should-width apart, dusting cloth in one hand. Slowly go up on half-point, wipe the shelf, then slowly lower yourself. Repeat ten times.

exercise a-go-go

Put a little exercise in your daily routine and you'll get fit faster—and probably stick to the exercise longer. The following require no equipment or special venue:

- Whenever possible, walk, jog, or bike to work. If you take the bus or train, get off about a mile from work and walk the rest of the way. If you drive, check out parking garages

about a mile from work and walk from there. The garages farther from your office may be cheaper, too!

- Park in the outfield. Instead of parking as close to a store, school, or stadium as possible, park farther out and walk to your destination.
- Bag lifting can be a good muscle builder. Remember to lift from your thighs, not from your lower back.
- Mall walking continues to grow in popularity. If you live in a climate with icy winters or really hot summers, walking up and down a mile-long mall (buying nothing, of course) can help you get fit in a comfortable atmosphere. And you can comparison shop while you walk.

get some phone action
With the widespread popularity of cordless phones and cell phones, you can now combine time on the phone with exercise:

- Put on some wrist or ankle weights and lift away while chatting.
- Use that cellular phone right: Talk the talk while you walk the walk!

reach for the sky: stretching for life
This series of stretches is designed to strengthen your back. The whole sequence takes about 20 minutes and requires only a chair and a pillow.

warm up Walk or jump rope for 10 minutes (or more).

chair stretch Sit upright in a sturdy, straight-backed chair. Slowly bend forward toward the floor, headfirst, until you begin to feel a slight pull in your back. Hold the stretch for 10 seconds. Repeat five times.

shoulder squeeze Sit upright in the chair. Look straight ahead and pull your shoulder blades backward. Hold for 5 seconds, then relax. Repeat five times.

knee-to-shoulder stretch Lie on the floor with both knees bent and your feet flat on the floor. Slowly pull one knee to your chest, hold it for 10 seconds, and then release. Repeat the exercise five times with each leg.

cat stretch On your hands and knees, lower your back toward the floor (swayback), lift your head toward the ceiling for greater stretch, and hold for several seconds. Slowly, in a single motion, make an arch with your back, bringing your chin to your chest, and hold again. Repeat five times.

the hydrant On your hands and knees, pull one knee to your chest. In a sweeping motion, push that leg back so that your thigh is parallel to the floor and the sole of your foot is toward the ceiling. Return the knee to the chest. Repeat five times for each leg.

half curl Lie on your back on the floor with a pillow supporting your head and upper back. Keeping your knees bent,

TOP TEN MONEY-SAVING MOTIVATIONS TO EXERCISE

1. It improves your self-image—saves on cosmetics!
2. It helps fight depression—saves on therapists!
3. It's a great way to meet new people—saves on personal ads!
4. It increases your energy—saves on coffee!
5. It helps stabilize (and maybe reduce) weight—saves on diet clubs or foods!
6. It helps keep your love life perky—saves on Viagra!
7. It helps you sleep better—saves on sleeping pills!
8. It reduces your risk of having a heart attack or stroke—saves on health care costs!
9. It improves your body's ability to fight infections—saves on antibiotics!
10. It can improve your chances for a long, healthy life—saves on nursing homes!

feet flat on the floor, and arms out in front of you, reach for your knees until your shoulders lift off the pillow. (For a harder exercise, cross your arms over your chest while you lift your shoulders.) Repeat five times.

the twist Sit on the floor, legs extending straight in front of you and your back straight. Bend your left leg and cross it over your right leg. Bring your right arm across your left thigh and grab your left hand. Use both arms to twist your upper body away from your right leg until you feel a stretch. Hold for 10 seconds, release, and repeat using your other leg.

couch potato crunches

Try these simple exercises while you watch TV:

- Work off tension while watching the evening news with isometric exercises. (See page 109.)
- Jog or walk in place while catching up on your favorite sitcom (30 minutes).
- There are usually four commercial breaks during an hourlong show. For each break, do one set of each: crunches, squats, push-ups, and leg lifts.

the economics of equipment

If you absolutely have to have equipment to work out with, don't buy new and don't buy on impulse. Check and see whether you can rent a piece of equipment for a month before deciding to buy, because you need to know you will use it before spending the money. Then scour the ads, go to garage sales (often a gold mine for practically new sports stuff), and bargain, bargain, bargain. In a local shopping paper, we spotted a triple-action bike for $20, a CardioGlide machine for $60, a Life Fitness treadmill for $250, and a health-club quality StairMaster, originally bought at $3,200, for $700. The last two items may still sound expensive (and they are), but those represent considerable savings over brand-new machines.

if the shoe fits . . .

The most important piece of exercise equipment that you can invest in is a good pair of athletic shoes. Notice that we don't say expensive athletic shoes. Anyone who pays $70 or more on shoes to exercise in probably shouldn't be reading this book. The more high-impact the exercise (running, tennis, and the like), the more you'll need to pay for shoes. But you should be able to pick up a decent pair of athletic sneakers for under $40. If you check the ads in the newspaper, comparison shop, and see what's available at outlet stores and discount stores, you should be able to whittle the price down to about $20 or even less.

sweat clothes?

Why would anyone pay $80 for a set of clothes to sweat in? People do, but penny pinchers are not among them. We're talking about clothes to get really hot, dirty, and sweaty in. Stick to cheap cotton (or cotton blends) for T-shirts, shorts, tank tops, and sports bras. Most discount stores now offer women's sets of bras and bike shorts for $7. Look for clearance sales to lower prices even further. And don't forget to check out the men's and boys' departments to pick up higher quality merchandise at a penny pincher's price, especially for sweatpants and sweatshirts.

dance fever

If you hate to do what is commonly called exercise but love to dance, you're in luck! Dancing can be one of the best aerobic exercises possible, but you have to get your heart rate up and keep it up for at least 20 minutes—so save the slow dancing for another time. Besides the so-called serious dance workouts, ballet and jazz, you can also keep fit with swing dancing, Latin dancing, line dancing, square dancing, ballroom dancing, just about any type of folk dancing, and even dancing to good old rock 'n' roll. Check your local paper, especially the entertainment section or the community calendar, for dance events or clubs. Lots of recreation centers sponsor all kinds of dances, some on a regular basis. Some require a partner, but many will try to pair up singles if possible. And if you like the kind of dancing you can do alone, just put on some music and get grooving—and keep moving!

do-it-yourself equipment

Don't spend money on things you can easily make yourself.
hand weights Use 1-pound cans of soup or vegetables or fill clean 1-liter soda pop bottles with water or sand.
ankle weights Fill an old athletic sock (no holes) with dry sand, raw rice, dried lentils or beans, or clean cat litter. Keep weighing the sock as you fill it until it reaches 2 to 3 pounds. Tie or sew the ends closed, leaving room in the toe and the top of the cuff. Either use the empty ends to tie the weights to your ankles or sew pieces of Velcro to each end to use as fasteners. (If you want to be sure the filling won't leak out, fill a plastic bag first, then put the bag in the sock.)
mats A folded beach towel or old blanket will do just fine for most exercise purposes. If you need something that is more solid or provides more cushion, pin together two old towels and stitch together two long sides and one short side of the towels. Slip a piece of foam (from a fabric store) into the pocket formed. If you

HIGH QUALITY/LOWER PRICES
www.newbalancecloseouts.com

Looking for high-quality athletic shoes or apparel at a reasonable price? This Web site offers high-end exercise gear by New Balance at up to 70 percent off. The selection is good and the savings is significant. We found men's Elite Windproof Running Tights for $45, down from $79.99 (a $34.99 savings), men's and women's running shoes for $59.99, down from $84.99 (a $25 savings), and men's Dunham hiking boots, originally $104.99, on sale for $69.99 (a $35 savings). On one visit, the site was offering an off-season 20 percent discount off the lowest price—excellent bargains.

wish, sew Velcro to close the open side. Then you can take out the foam and wash your mat cover whenever you want.

get a grip Here's a tried-and-true trick: Squeeze an old tennis ball in your hand to strengthen your grip.

working out with tapes

If you really enjoy a "class" for exercise, one way to skip the cost of a gym is to use exercise tapes. You can find tapes showcasing Tae Bo, yoga, step aerobics, dance aerobics, weight training, tai chi, stretching, and just about any other type of indoor exercise you can imagine. However, not all tapes are equal in terms of the quality of exercise or instruction, so it's a good idea to preview them before making the investment. Your local library may have a pretty decent selection of exercise tapes available—and you can check them out for free. Video rental stores also usually have a section just for exercise tapes. Check for days when they charge less (a two-for-one Tuesday, for example), and try that new tape to see if you (a) really like it and (b) are motivated to use it regularly.

the office athlete

Don't waste all that time that you're stuck at work. You can incorporate nearly all the following workouts into most schedules and offices:

- While sitting on a sturdy chair, lean slightly forward, grip the sides of your chair, and alternately raise your left and right knees to your chest.
  - While sitting with your back straight, put your foot through the handle of your purse or briefcase. (Shorten the strap if it's an over-the-shoulder length.) Slowly lift your leg until it is horizontal (the full leg parallel to the floor). Slowly lower the foot but do not touch the ground. Repeat ten times, then switch and work the other leg.
  - Take the stairs! Cut out your elevator use and you'll never need a StairMaster machine!
- Take a walk at lunchtime. Look at a map and figure out a walk that equals 1 mile. Then walk that route every day before eating. Increase the distance as your stamina and speed increase.

mix it up!

This section has emphasized types of exercise that don't require much if any monetary investment. For the best over-all fitness level, you should try to aim for 20 to 30 minutes of some kind of exercise each day. But you don't have to do the same thing each day—in fact, it's actually better for your body (and your mind) to mix it up. The fancy name for this is cross training. You should make some form of aerobic exercise the foundation of your routine (dance, walking, running, swimming, biking) and add some weight-resistance work on top of that. But don't forget that walking the dog, gardening, housecleaning, and a lot of other everyday activities, can be counted in your goal of 20 to 30 minutes a day. And if you vary what you do from day to day, you'll be less likely to become bored and more likely to work all the muscle groups, leading to better fitness overall.

AEROBIC REPORT CARD

Aerobic exercise is basically sustained movement of the large muscle groups that works the heart, circulatory system, and lungs. To keep your heart in tiptop condition, you need to do some form of aerobic exercise regularly. This helps lower your blood pressure and reduce your risk of coronary disease. It also releases endorphins—which make you feel great! The chart below grades each exercise based on its aerobic benefit. The higher the grade, the better it is for your heart and body.

Exercise	Benefit Level	Calories per hour
Aerobic dancing	A	360–480
Bicycling (12 mph)	A	410–600
Golf (walking with clubs)	C	300–360
Jogging (5 mph)	A	600–700
Jumping rope	A	800
Skiing, cross-country	A	700–1,200
Skiing, downhill	C to B	500–600
Swimming (crawl)	A	275–750
Tennis (singles)	B	400–480
Walking	B to A	300–480

FOR WOMEN OVER 40

www.aswechange.com
or 1-800-203-5585

As We Change was started by three businesswomen, aged 40-plus to 50-plus, who felt there was a dearth of information and products for their age group. Their site and catalog is devoted to women's needs related to health, beauty, exercise, and more, and it features a wide variety of products, including nutritional supplements, natural hormone replacement, exercise equipment, active wear, and lingerie. In the sale section, we spotted some good bargains: Two-to-one calcium-magnesium supplements, originally $15, on sale for $9; a front-closure "arthritis" bra, originally priced at $34, reduced to $22; and Dr. Schwab's Anti-Ozone Mask, originally $24, only $9!

Home Sweet Home

When you invite someone into your home, whether you live in a studio apartment or a 2,500-foot four-bedroom home, you reveal a lot about yourself. The vibrant warmth and sense of comfort your guest experiences may not be put into so many words, but it is certainly felt. Will they notice that your sense of style comes from the bold paint you sponged on your dining room wall? Will they know the glowing wood floors were refinished by you? That the comfy, well-built, sofa is a garage-sale find? Every choice you make for your home—the energy-efficient dishwasher, the refurbished Morris chair, the bathroom wallpaper that hides structural irregularities, the vinegar and baking soda you use to clean just about everything—-contributes to the beauty and comfort in your life. They also have a significant effect on your budget—and not just at the time of purchase. Buying the right piece for your lifestyle and environment, and then caring for it meticulously can mean the difference between costly repairs or untimely replacement and long-lasting, beautiful life.

Well worth a little TLC, no?

cleaning
House

ALTHOUGH FEW PEOPLE ENJOY
CLEANING, WE ALL NEED TO DO IT,
ESPECIALLY THOSE OF US WHO ARE PENNY PINCHERS.

Cleaning things on a regular basis makes them last longer and work better. If you get on a cleaning schedule, you'll find you build momentum so that you clean more efficiently and thus save time.
If you make some of your own cleaning supplies, you will not only save a bundle but will also help the environment and create a home that's more healthful for yourself and your family.

keep dirt out!

The easiest way to cut down on cleaning time and costs is to prevent dirt from entering your house the first place. Place an all-weather, heavy-duty mat just outside every exterior door and put a thinner mat or throw rug just inside every exterior door. The larger the inside mats are, the cleaner the floors will stay. Even if your home is carpeted wall-to-wall, small throw rugs or mats will keep dirt from being tracked in and wearing down the carpet fibers.

vacuum-cleaner savings

Investing in a good quality vacuum cleaner can save you hours of cleaning time and add years to your furnishings by keeping them clean. You'll find good prices at some department stores, discount stores, and appliance stores. Watch for sales, coupons or specials, and buy the best vacuum you can. It will save you money in the long run.

Here are some tips to get the most from your vacuum cleaner:

- Look for a lightweight model that you can move around easily. Also look for a long cord and easy-to-use controls, accessories, and bag-changing procedures.
- Empty or change the bag frequently! Even a half-full bag saps up to 40 percent of a vacuum's suction power.
- Reuse vacuum bags! Durable bags can be reused three or four times. Just clip off the top, empty out the dirt, fold the top edge over once, and staple it closed.
- Save wear and tear on your vacuum cleaner by picking up hard objects, such as coins, beads, rocks, and paper clips, by hand before you vacuum an area.
- Lint, hair, and thread that collect on bristles can interfere with the cleaning action of the brushes. Use the vacuum's hose to remove lint and hair. Clip threads off or unravel them after unplugging.
- Attach a 30-foot extension cord to your vacuum to eliminate unplugging and plugging the vacuum as you clean.
- Use the brush attachment on your vacuum to gently clean lampshades, baseboards, woodwork, and heating vent covers. Cleaning these will cut down on dust in the air.
- Vacuum upholstered furniture and throw pillows once a

week. The fabric will look new far longer, and you will never have to sweat to get rid of ground-in dirt.

caring for carpets and rugs

If you take care of a good carpet or rug, it will reward you with years of service.

- Turn area rugs periodically so that they wear evenly.
- Brush carpet edges and seams with a liquid resin (available at fabric and craft stores) to lock the yarns in place.
- Sew bias binding tape around the edge of a braided rug to protect the edge from wearing out.
- Remove the indentations in carpets caused by furniture by steaming them with an iron. Let the steam penetrate to dampen the fibers; then fluff them with your fingers.
- At least twice a year, vacuum the padding and floor beneath an area rug. Be sure to clean wall-to-wall surfaces frequently, as you can't vacuum carpet padding.
- Deep-clean your carpets twice a year, at the end of winter and summer. Hire a professional service or rent a carpet shampooer from your supermarket. If you have your carpets professionally cleaned, ask whether they will give you a discount if you move the furniture before they come. Some companies will discount up to 20 percent, because not having to deal with furniture will save them time and allow them to fit more jobs into that day.

66A place for everything and everything in its place.**99**

Isabella Beeton,
The Book of Household
Management

carpet spills and stains

- Attack carpet stains as soon as possible. Use clean towels to soak up most of the spill. Then pour club soda over the stain and let it sit for a few minutes. Finally, blot the spot with a clean sponge. Repeat until the spot is gone.
- If a spill discolors your carpet, try a 50-50 solution of white vinegar and warm water. Dab the spot with a clean white towel and then blot it with a second clean white towel. Repeat until the spot is gone. Cover the area with a third clean white towel and let it dry completely.
- If chewing gum gets stuck on your carpet, rub an ice cube over it first until the gum hardens. Then use a blunt knife or spatula to scrape off the gum.

wall cleaning

If your walls look a bit grimy and dull, don't rush out to buy cans of fresh paint. Washing your walls costs only a fraction of the expense of painting them, and it can leave your walls looking bright and new. Use a clean sponge mop with a self-squeezing mechanism. Fill two buckets: one with cleaning solution and one with clean water. Clean a small section of the wall at a time, beginning at the bottom; if you begin at the top, the solution may drip down and permanently stain the paint below. Dry the clean sections with a cotton towel before moving on to the next area.

wood paneling

Here's how to clean unwaxed varnished or shellacked wood paneling: Combine 1/2 cup turpentine, 3/4 cup boiled linseed oil, and 1 tablespoon white vinegar. Rub the mixture over the paneling, let the mixture sit for 15 minutes, and rub with a clean cloth until the paneling is clean and polished.

window-washing wisdom

Wash windows on a cloudy, dry day; windows washed in direct sunlight tend to streak, because the cleaning solution dries before you get a chance to wipe it off.

- Before washing windows, use the brush attachment with your vacuum cleaner to clean any dust, soot, cobwebs, or dead insects from the window frames and sills.
- Wash using the crosshatch pattern: Wipe the outside of each pane vertically and the inside horizontally (or vice versa). This method makes it easy for you to tell which side any streaks are on.
- Wash like the pros with clear water, changing it as soon as it becomes dirty. If windows are particularly dirty, add 2 to 3 tablespoons of white vinegar to 1 gallon of water.
- Rubbing alcohol makes an excellent (and cost-effective) window cleaner. Rubbing alcohol removes grease, evaporates quickly, does not freeze, and leaves no residue.

washable wallpaper

Most wall coverings can be simply vacuumed, except for delicate silk coverings, which require professional cleaning. If vacuuming doesn't get your wallpaper clean, here are some other wallpaper-cleaning tricks to try:

- To clean nonwashable wallpaper, rub it gently with an art gum eraser, a dough-type wallpaper cleaner (available from paint and hardware stores), or try using crustless slices of fresh bread.
- Beat a mixture of 1/4 cup liquid dishwashing detergent and 1 cup warm water to form stiff foam. Scoop up the dry foam and apply with a cloth or sponge to soiled, nonwashable wallpaper. Gently wipe off the foam with a clean cotton cloth.
- Clean a grease spot on wallpaper by blotting it with a clean paper towel. Hold a fresh paper towel over the spot and press with a warm (not hot) iron. Change the paper towel as it becomes greasy.

get the dirt out of the screens

Dirty window screens block out sunlight and make spots on windows when it rains. Regular maintenance should include vacuuming or brushing screens while they are in place. About once or twice a year, wash them.

● To wash a screen, lay it flat on a smooth, cloth-covered surface, such as an old sheet on a picnic table. Scrub the screen gently with a brush dipped in soapy water and rinse with a hose. Let air-dry.

lamps: dust your lightbulbs!

Dust or wipe a lamp base with a damp cloth and clean any metal parts with the appropriate polish. Never submerge the lamp base in water, because it can damage the wiring. Also dust your lightbulbs with a dry cloth. Does that sound finicky? A dust-free bulb shines up to 50 percent brighter than a dirty one, so you save money and use less energy.

water-ring cures

A water ring on wood furniture can be devastating, especially if it is a good piece.

● Rub the ring with a rag dipped in denatured alcohol or turpentine. If this doesn't work, then use a soft cloth to rub lightly with a toothpaste (not a gel) that contains a gentle abrasive.

● If toothpaste doesn't work, sprinkle salt on the ring and rub it with a rag dipped first in lemon oil, then vinegar.

● If you have a new water stain on a wood table or counter, try rubbing it gently with a mixture of equal parts mayonnaise and fine fireplace ashes.

● Once the ring has been removed, polish the entire piece of furniture thoroughly.

candle wax conundrum

Candle wax drippings on dining tables are common, and some just seem to come off more easily than others. If you get a stubborn patch, try warming it with a hair dryer to soften the wax; then sponge it away with vinegar diluted with water. Rinse with clear water and dry well. Remember: Never scrape wax off with a knife! You'll only end up scratching the finish on the surface of the table. To get wax off a candlestick, try putting it in the freezer for a couple of hours. When you take it out, the frozen wax will come right off.

sofa shaver saver

Shaving cream can remove dirt and fresh stains from upholstery and rugs! Just spread it over the area to be cleaned, brush it lightly, and rinse off with warm water. If you're concerned about a delicate fabric, test an inconspicuous area.

TEN USES FOR BAKING SODA

1. Carpet sweetener: Sprinkle baking soda over entire carpet, wait an hour, then vacuum.

2. Drain cleaner: Pour 1/2 cup baking soda and 3/4 cup white vinegar in drain. After it stops bubbling, flush with very hot tap water.

3. Spill soaker: Pour baking soda over spill. Let it absorb, then vacuum.

4. Fire extinguisher: Keep a box of baking soda next to your stovetop to quash grease fires.

5. Silver polisher: Dip half a raw potato in baking soda and rub. Wipe with a damp cloth, then a dry one.

6. Silverfish slayer: Sprinkle a 50-50 solution of baking soda and sugar near baseboards.

7. Safe scourer: Scrub kitchen or bath fixtures with a thick baking soda–water paste.

8. Stain buster: Pour baking soda and warm water into coffee and tea pots to remove stains.

9. Odor eater: Use a baking soda–water solution to deodorize a diaper pail and kitty litter box.

10. Oven cleaner: Spread thick baking soda–water paste over baked-on grease; let sit overnight. Then scrub with a plastic scrubber and rinse.

soot and cinders!

Although it may seem like a chunk of money going up the chimney, if you use your fireplace at all, have it cleaned professionally once a year. A licensed sweep (look in your Yellow Pages) can remove the buildup of flammable creosote, which is the cause of most chimney fires. To save money, join with your neighbors to negotiate a lower group rate.

● Line the floor of your clean fireplace with a piece of heavy-duty aluminum foil before building a fire. After the fire is out, simply fold the foil over the mess and throw it out. (Or better still, use the ashes in your garden and recycle the aluminum.)

● Search antique or junk stores for a cast-iron fireback. When set against the back wall of your fireplace, this will both protect the brick and reflect heat into the room.

● Clean soot and smoke from fireplace bricks with a 50-50 solution of bleach and water. Spray the solution onto the bricks, scrub the bricks with a soft brush, and then rinse thoroughly with water. Wear vinyl gloves and be careful not to get the mixture in your eyes.

sparkling sinks

Abrasive cleansers can scratch porcelain and stainless steel sinks. Instead, try one of these easy cleaning ideas:

● Soak paper towels with bleach and spread them over the bottom of a porcelain sink. Let the towels sit for about 30 minutes; then remove them, and rinse the sink thoroughly with cold tap water.

● Wash stainless steel sinks with hot water and dishwashing soap, then wipe them dry. For a dingy sink, use a paste of baking soda to clean and polish the sink to a soft shine.

● If your stainless steel sink has become scratched or slightly pitted, rub it gently with a very fine grade of steel wool and then buff it to a sheen with a clean cloth.

clean counters

The countertops are probably the most visible part of your kitchen. Giving them a little attention every day will almost eliminate the need for a major cleaning job, except to get behind countertop appliances.

● Every evening after dinner, wipe down your counters with hot, soapy water to discourage bacteria. Rinse thoroughly and wipe dry.

● For stains such as mustard, tea, or fruit juice, rub a laminated plastic countertop with a damp cloth and baking soda. If the stain persists, wipe it with a cloth moistened with a little chlorine bleach.

● Erase those little purple marks from price stamps by wiping with a little rubbing alcohol.

stinky sponges

Kitchen sponges sometimes develop a nasty odor that just permeates the kitchen. Before tossing out that stinky sponge, pop it into a mesh laundry bag and run it through your laundry with a load of white towels. (Use bleach.) Put the washed sponge in the sun to dry. (The sun kills certain bacteria.) Don't run sponges through the dryer, and never put them in a microwave, because sponges are flammable.

taking care of your range

Don't wait to care for your range until it is coated with grime.

- Wipe off cooking spills and grease spatters while the range top is still warm using warm, sudsy water and a cloth or sponge; clean the sponge frequently while you work.
- Wipe off the top of the hood—a real grease collector—whenever you wipe off the range top.
- Unless you have a continuous-cleaning oven, wipe out the oven with a soapy sponge after each use to prevent grease buildup; otherwise, the grease will burn and harden each time you use the oven.
- Place oven racks on an old bath towel in the bathtub and soak them in a solution of ammonia and hot water. Then scrub to clean them.
- Before using your oven's self-cleaning function, wipe off the frame and the part of the door liner that's outside the oven seal. These areas aren't reached during automatic cleaning, but they do get enough heat to bake on soil, making it harder to remove later.
- To clean under an electric range with a bottom drawer, remove the drawer so that it will be easier to get at the floor. For a gas range with a broiler below the oven, remove the broiler drawer.

THE STAR FOR ENERGY SAVING

www.energystar.gov

The Energy Star, backed by the U.S. Environmental Protection Agency, is one of the most helpful appliance-shopping tools to come along in quite a while. Each appliance is tagged with a yellow energy rating card that tells you the estimated cost of running the appliance and whether it is in the high- or low-use category. The Energy Star is awarded to appliances that meet certain energy- or water-use standards. It makes sense to buy the most efficient appliance model possible. To read more about the program (and to find stores in your area that carry Energy Star products), check out this Web site.

APPLIANCE SHOPPING STRATEGY

When shopping for a large appliance, check all the consumer information you can access online or at a library. Look for efficiency ratings and repair records in particular. As with many products, if you opt for the high end, you'll likely pay for features you don't really need. Make a list of what you really want (delay timer on a dishwasher, icemaker, double ovens). Then look only at models that meet your requirements.

- Don't be afraid to haggle. Most of us just assume that "the price is the price." Not so. Salespeople have more leeway to negotiate than you might think. Be pleasant but know your stuff before you start talking price.

- Buying appliances is one area where a "new credit card discount" can really be worthwhile. Most stores now offer 10 percent off a purchase when you apply for a new card that day. If you're buying a $700 refrigerator, that's $70 off! Just make sure that when the new card comes through you think twice before you use it. Store credit cards frequently charge high interest rates.

- Just say no to extended warranties. They cost more than they're worth.

defrosting

If you own a refrigerator-freezer that is not frost-free, be sure to defrost it as soon as the frost is about 1/4 inch thick; the thicker the layer of frost, the harder the unit has to work and the less efficient it will be. Letting too much frost build up also makes it more difficult to defrost.

● Turn off the unit, move everything out, and place pots of hot water in the freezer to speed the process. Never use metal utensils to try and "hurry" the ice out—you could cause serious (and costly) damage to the freezer. If you must scrape, use a dull plastic scraper and never scrape against metal parts.

● To further speed up the defrosting process, set your hair dryer on hot and blow away the ice.

● When all the frost is gone, wipe out the freezer unit with soapy water and dry with clean cloths. Before turning it on again, dip a cloth in glycerin and wipe the freezer coils with it. This will help you remove the frost more easily the next time you defrost.

● Stuck ice cube tray? Apply a dishtowel soaked in hot water to the tray's edges for a few seconds.

● Frost in your frost-free? Check the defrost timer behind the grille. With the refrigerator running, use a screwdriver to turn the slotted knob slowly clockwise until you hear a click and the refrigerator goes off. Wait 5 minutes for defrost water to appear in the drain pan. If the frost doesn't melt or if the problem recurs, call for service.

cheap cleaning rags

Do not buy cloths for cleaning, ever! The best cleaning rags are made from old cloth diapers, T-shirts, and linen or terrycloth dish towels. Although it is tempting to grab paper towels for cleaning, it's an expensive habit; save paper towels for microwaving and some other uses suggested later in this section.

● To get into those hard-to-reach corners, slip an old sock over one end of a yardstick or broom handle and secure it with a rubber band.

quick cure for dingy dishwasher: Kool Aid

It is so discouraging to open your perfectly good dishwasher and be greeted by a stained, dingy interior. Don't snatch up one of those pricey cleaners—try a little Kool Aid! Yes, I know, sounds nuts, right? But just put one or two little packets of unsweetened, citrus-flavored Kool Aid in the soap dispenser and run your empty dishwasher through a normal cycle. The process will leave the interior sparkling. And at a cost of only about 10 cents a packet, this is a true penny pincher's miracle worker.

large-appliance bucks

Your kitchen is home to more large (and expensive) appliances than any other room in your house: refrigerator, range/oven, and dishwasher. And that's not even counting things like microwaves! If you are redoing your kitchen or starting from scratch, it might cost less to buy all your large appliances at the same time. A multiple sale can sometimes give you negotiating power. You can find decent prices and selections at several sources:

department stores These stores often sell large appliances. Sears, in particular, is known for its excellent sales and wide selection—and its Kenmore brand is generally highly rated. J.C. Penney also sells appliances and has some worthwhile sales. Department store clearance outlets sell floor models, scratched or dented pieces, and last year's inventory. The prices are often terrific, especially if you are flexible about the bells and whistles.

price clubs There is less selection, but price for quality is usually competitive.

appliance stores To get your business, you may find that these smaller local stores are willing to negotiate.

electronics superstores These chains sometimes offer good selection, reasonable prices, and good sales.

home improvement centers These warehouse stores (Home Depot, Lowe's) usually have a smaller selection but are worth checking out.

daily shine for your bath

To cut down on weekly big cleanings, take about four minutes a day to keep your bathroom sparkling.

● Store cleaning cloths and a spray bottle full of cleaning solution (vinegar and water work great and cost nothing) in the bathroom. (If you have small children, store the solution in a secure cupboard.)

● Once a day, wipe down all the surfaces with the cleaning solution. Start from the top (the mirror) and work down to the bottom (the floor), paying attention to the sink, tub, and toilet on the way.

● Use a cloth moistened with vinegar to rub away water spots and soap scum from chrome faucet handles and drains. Dry and polish with a soft cloth.

shining showers

When glass shower doors turn filmy, wipe them down with a soft cloth saturated with distilled white vinegar or a water softener solution. Shine with a dry cloth.

● The best time to clean a shower or bathtub is right after you've used it, when the steam has loosened the dirt. Just wipe off the damp surfaces with a clean cloth.

- Clean grungy grout with full-strength vinegar instead of with budget-busting bathroom cleaners.
- Wipe soap spots or film from tile with a solution of 1 part vinegar to 4 parts water. Rinse and dry with a soft cloth.
- Clean stained tub or sink surfaces with a paste made of equal parts cream of tartar and hydrogen peroxide. Spread the paste over the stain and scrub lightly with a brush. Let the paste dry and then wipe or rinse it off.

tile cleaning tricks

- Wipe off soapy film on ceramic tile walls or floors with a solution of 1 part vinegar to 4 parts water. Rinse thoroughly with clean water. Buff tiles to prevent streaking.
- For stained or mildewed grouting, apply a bleach solution (3/4 cup liquid chlorine bleach to 1 gallon water) with a cloth, sponge, or old toothbrush. Make sure to wear rubber gloves and rinse thoroughly.

clean shower curtains

Remove mildew from a plastic shower curtain by machine-washing it with regular laundry detergent. Add one or two towels to the washing load to act as buffers. Hang the curtain on its own rod to dry. If the curtain is stiff and unmanageable when you take it out of the washer, pop it (and the towels) into the dryer for a few minutes to soften, remove it promptly, and hang it while it is still warm.

tidy bowls

Those fancy in-tank cleaners cost an arm and a leg. Yet they don't clean a bowl that is already soiled, and although they may slow down the accumulation of residue, they don't stop it. In other words, they don't really clean your toilet. So save your money and clean the old-fashioned way: Sprinkle the interior of the bowl with household cleanser and use a toilet brush to scrub around the inner rim and the bowl.

- For stubborn stains, use cleanser with bleach or add bleach to the bowl, let it soak for an hour, wipe gently with a brush, and then flush it all away.
- Flush a cup of baking soda down the toilet every week or so to help prevent the buildup of bacteria in the tank as well as to guard against clogging or backing up in the tank and drain field.

fresh air ideas

- Make your own air freshener: Mix 8 ounces of water with 10 or more drops of an essential oil—rosemary, eucalyptus, pine, lavender, or any of the citrus fruit oils—in a spray bottle. Add more drops of essential oil if you want a stronger scent. Essential oils are available at health food stores. They kill airborne bacteria and evaporate cleanly, leaving no sticky residue.

- Keep your closets smelling fresh and sweet by hanging pomanders in them. Insert whole cloves into an unpeeled orange, lemon, lime, or apple, covering most of the surface of the fruit with the cloves. To make it easier to insert the cloves, first make holes through the peel using a nail or pick. Tie a pretty ribbon around the finished pomander and hang it wherever you need it.

- Musty closet? Fill an old pan (from a store-bought pie or left over from a microwave meal) or an old margarine tub with charcoal briquettes, and place it in the closet. The charcoal will absorb moisture and odors. Replace the briquettes once a month (save the old briquettes for barbecuing).

- When you do your vacuuming, squeeze a few drops of lemon juice into the dust bag of your vacuum cleaner before you start it up. You'll find that your whole house will smell better.

- Buy bags of cedar shavings at discount pet supply stores. Stitch together small bags of cheesecloth or muslin, and tuck the bags in your linen closet and dresser drawers or hang them from your clothes closet rods.

- If you grow your own lavender (an easy-to-grow and drought-tolerant plant), snip off the heads of the stalks and let them dry. Then make your own sachets using muslin, cheesecloth, or pretty scraps of any other fabric you have on hand.

GOOD OLD WAYS

NATURAL HOUSEHOLD AIDS

INSTEAD OF	USE
Ant killer	vinegar and water
Drain cleaner	boiling water, once a week
Furniture polish	3 parts olive oil and 1 part water
Aphid spray	pureed garlic, red pepper, liquid soap, and water
Black spot killer	baking soda, liquid soap, and warm water
Houseplant fertilizer	weak, tepid tea solution, weekly
Houseplant pest spray	mild soap-and-water solution, weekly
Mothballs	cedar chips
Oven cleaner	vinegar and baking soda
Brush cleaner	liquid detergent suds (for latex paint)
Paint softener	white vinegar and water
Roach repellent	bay leaves

the simplest air freshener of all?

Just cut a lemon or orange in half, set one half on a saucer and place wherever the air needs a bit of brightening (or odors need to be absorbed).

laundry for
Less

COST-CONSCIOUS WASH DAYS
SAVE ON ENERGY AND CLOTHING.

For most of us, doing laundry is a fact of life. But investing in the right washer and dryer can save you money for years, or cost you money, if you buy the wrong model. Even if you live in an apartment and have no choice of washer or dryer, using the right techniques will not only save you money but will also make doing laundry a more satisfying experience: Your clothes will be cleaner, stains will come out, and your clothes will last longer.

washers and dryers—cost and effect

Like most major appliances, a washing machine and a dryer are a big investment, and an important one (to which anyone who has had to lug laundry to a Laundromat can attest). The two major points to consider are cost and effect.

COST Setting your sights either too upscale or too cheap will land you with an appliance that is either much fancier than you need or one that doesn't work efficiently and thus costs dearly to use or repair.

EFFECT To determine the effect you need, make a list of the features most important for your family and the key climate factors in the area you live in. If you live in the arid Southwest, for example, a low-water-use washer makes good sense. You'll be able to air-dry your laundry much of the year, so a fancy dryer is not as important. If you live in the generally damper Midwest, efficient water use is not quite as urgent, but an efficient dryer can be a time and money saver.

look for the energy star

The Energy Star program (see Resources box, page 123) is particularly helpful when shopping for washers and dryers, since both water and energy efficiency are included in the ratings. Energy-efficient washers come in both front- and top-loading models. Front-loaders tumble laundry instead of agitating it, which uses less water and is easier on your clothes. Some top-loader designs now use high-pressure sprays to soak and rinse clothing instead of filling the tub with water each cycle. A typical household does about 400 loads of laundry a year, using about 40 gallons of water per load. The new, efficient washing machine models use only 18 to 25 gallons per load—a substantial savings. In addition, the efficient models generally use 35 to 50 percent less energy! So though they will probably cost a good bit more initially, an energy-efficient washer and dryer could put money back in your pocket within a few years.

Much depends on how expensive power and water are in your area. If they are cheap, an efficient model's lower operating cost isn't likely to make up the purchase-price difference over a washer's typical 10-to-15-year life span.

shopping for washers and dryers

When it actually comes to buying washers and dryers, it's no different than buying kitchen appliances. (See page 123.) Before your start, gather all the information that you can about the various models with the features that you want. It pays to shop around, check ads, and wait for sales. Department stores and their clearance outlets, appliance stores, price clubs, electronic superstores, and home centers can offer great bargains if you strike at the right time. Be ready to haggle. And remember to skip the extended warranty.

keep your washer on an even keel

Use a carpenter's level to ensure that your washer and dryer are not installed off level, either front to back or side to side. If either machine is even slightly tilted, it can cause extra vibration and noise. Use a wrench to adjust the feet until your washer and dryer are in a perfectly level position.

save while washing

Set some clothes-washing ground rules for yourself, and you'll save water, electricity, and money over the years.
● Run only full loads. Running small loads wastes electricity and water. If necessary, toss in tablecloths, dishtowels, or seldom-washed items to fill up the load.
● Use cold-water rinses, because cold water uses less energy. Though laundry detergents clean your clothes better in warm water (at least 65° F), the rinses can always be cold. If you want to wash in cold water, liquid detergent may be your best bet, because it dissolves more quickly.
● Check with your energy and water utilities to find out whether they offer lower rates early in the morning or late at night, whether weekday rates are less than on weekends, and whether they have any tips on lowering your operating costs. Each region of the country is different with respect to energy and water resources, so it pays to find out how best to use the resources in your area.

don't overdo the detergent

If you find a lot of lint on your laundry, it's a sign that you are using too much detergent. Though it is tempting to add extra detergent when you have really dirty clothes, it actually doesn't clean any better. And excess detergent may not be fully washed away in the rinse cycle, so it can leave a film on fabrics that attracts dirt and causes garments to look dingy.

washer tricks

● Reduce the lint that can stick to dark-colored garments in the dryer by adding 1 cup of white distilled vinegar to each load of laundry during the final rinse.

66 Again last night I dreamed the dream called laundry. 99

James Ingram Merrill, poet

- If you experience an "attack of the suds" (foaming over), just sprinkle salt on the foam to help settle it down.
- Prevent mineral buildup in your washing machine by filling the tank with water and adding 1 cup of white vinegar. Run the mixture through a complete wash cycle.

Take a tip from our foremothers and put up a clothesline. The environment will thank you for it, your clothes will thank you for it, and your utility bill will thank you for years! Sunshine actually kills certain odor-causing bacteria so that your clothes will smell fabulous naturally. No more spending money on laundry products that claim to give clothes an "air-dried freshness." Another plus: Line-drying is easier on fabrics. In fact, most shrinkage occurs in the dryer, and fibers are worn down in the dryer. So line-drying will make your clothes last longer and look better, too. Sounds like a win-win situation to us.

dryer dilemmas
If your dryer suddenly won't run, don't immediately call the repair service. First, be sure the door is completely closed. Second, check that the dryer is plugged in. **NO KIDDING!** The vibration from the dryer can eventually work a plug out, so it behooves you to take a look. Third, check the circuit breaker or fuse to make sure it hasn't tripped or blown. On a gas dryer, check that the pilot light is on. If all of the above failed, then it's time to call the repair service.

double-duty dryers
You can purchase a special accessory that allows you to vent moisture from the dryer indoors instead of outdoors during the winter when the air inside your house dries out from heat. A single dryer load can add more than a gallon of water to the air inside the house. Beats running a humidifier.

dry-clean in the dryer
A new weapon in the fight to keep clothes clean at less cost is the dryer dry-cleaner bag. Do they work? Yes! Follow the directions carefully, and you will be quite pleased by how great your clothes look—and the money you've saved.

makeshift drying rack
Don't throw out that old, torn umbrella. Remove the fabric, turn it upside down, and hang it from your shower curtain rod for an instant drying rack for hand washables.

shake 'em up!
Need to remove some soil from small items, such as underwear, before washing? Presoak them for up to an hour in cool, soapy water, then place the garments in a large jar with some suds, secure the lid, and shake. Rinse thoroughly.

blankie in the wash
When you purchase a new blanket, check the washing label carefully. Many newer blankets (or even comforters) are machine washable—even those made of wool. Follow the washing instructions on the label to the letter.

curtain bodybuilder
To give stiffness to limp curtains, add 2 tablespoons of powdered milk to the rinse water the next time you wash them.

The added body provided by the milk will also help the curtains resist dust and dirt, keeping them clean longer.

freshen up spreads and curtains

To quickly freshen bedspreads or curtains between expensive seasonal dry cleanings, place them in the dryer with a sheet of fabric softener. (Store brands are cheapest.) Tumble on the air-only setting for approximately 20 minutes. This trick also works well with pillows that are starting to smell a bit musty.

● To fluff a down comforter, add three or four clean tennis balls to the dryer when tumbling it. The balls will help redistribute the feathers. Spin it on the air-only setting for 15 to 20 minutes.

spots on the run

When you're traveling and need to quickly treat a greasy or oily spot on a favorite garment, try rubbing the spot with a clear gel or liquid shampoo that doesn't contain oxides.

double-duty soap

Read the label on the soap you use for dishwashing by hand. Generally, it can also be used to wash your delicate garments. If the soap is formulated to be easy on your hands, it is gentle enough for even your fine hand washables.

musty odor buster

Get rid of unpleasant, musty odors in hand washables by presoaking them in a mixture of 4 tablespoons baking soda and 1 quart water. Let the clothes soak for about one hour before washing as usual.

HOMEMADE LAUNDRY AIDS

Brightener: Add lemon juice to the wash water.

Whitener: Soak yellowed linens in sour milk and then launder as usual.

Booster: Soak your whites in a mixture of 1 cup vinegar and 1 gallon warm water before washing to get rid of detergent residue and make the whites whiter.

Scrubber: Make a paste of vinegar and baking soda and rub it into stains before washing. Thoroughly soak perspiration stains with vinegar before laundering.

TEN TERRIFIC STAIN FIGHTERS

1. Alcohol (rubbing or denatured): Helps fight grass or dye stains.

2. Ammonia: For almost any stain, combine 1 teaspoon in 1/2 cup water. NEVER use with chlorine bleach; this causes a deadly gas!

3. Chlorine bleach: Follow label directions. Not for items that call for non-chlorine bleach. NEVER mix with ammonia!

4. White vinegar: Safe for all fibers, but may affect some colors. Use 1 part to 3 parts water on food stains; saturate perspiration stains.

5. All-fabric (oxygen) bleach: Mild and safe on most fabrics; good for wine stains.

6. Petroleum jelly: Use to soften hardened paint, rubber cement, or tar before washing.

7. Club soda: Great for rinsing out stains on clothing, upholstery, rugs, and linens.

8. Nonacetone nail polish remover (banana oil): Removes glue or lacquer from clothing.

9. Enzyme detergent: The enzymes help remove stubborn stains. Not for mohair, wool, or silk.

10. Hydrogen peroxide (3%): Use straight on wool or silk; mix with ammonia for a bleach. Great for bloodstains.

decorating on a
Dime

WITH DECORATING, AS WITH CLOTHING,
IT'S NOT SO MUCH WHAT YOU HAVE
AS WHAT YOU DO WITH IT.

Whether you're starting from scratch or redoing a room, begin with an honest appraisal of the area, its strong points (light, high ceilings) and its weaknesses (awkward door placement, no closets). Browse through decorating or architecture magazines and clip photos of looks you like. Just remember: That $8,000 chair in the picture isn't necessary to create the ambiance you want. You just need imagination, a flair for style, and the patience to wait for the right piece at the right price.

use your imagination

The biggest secret of a fabulous decorator is imagination— the ability to see the possibilities in almost anything. The key certainly isn't spending the most money. And you'll be surprised at what you can do yourself at no cost at all.

assess potential Look at objects to see what they could become: An old milk can could be transformed into a lamp, the base for a small table, an umbrella stand, or a planter. Be creative as you see each object's potential.

express yourself Do you love music? Look for old sheet music with great covers whenever you're at an antique or junk store, garage sale or thrift store, or at a going-out-of-business sale at a music store. Hang the music on the wall above your piano, framed or unframed. Do you sew? Keep an eye open for antique (or just old) sewing equipment and display it on the walls and shelves of your sewing room.

not just for floors Small decorative rugs, either antiques or reproductions, can add color and life to a cold or boring wall. And they help muffle sound.

or beds Quilts or beautiful afghans can be hung on a dowel on a wall or draped over the back of a chair or sofa to add color and warmth—and be handy for snuggling under.

keep a sense of scale

If you have really big rooms, don't use Lilliputian furniture. Conversely, if you have small rooms, don't furnish them with gargantuan pieces or too many pieces. Look carefully at each room and decide the scale; then select pieces that match the scale of that particular space.

furniture: less is more

Don't worry if you don't have loads of furniture. In decorating, less is often more anyway. If you're using vibrant color on the walls and have an attractive rug picking up some of that color, you'll need only a few pieces of simple furniture, enlivened with a throw or some pillows, for a charming room. Bulky furniture can become obstacles for traffic flow through a room, it can create a cluttered feeling really fast, and it can detract from your one or two really good pieces.

make the most of color

Neutral walls have gone the way of the dodo. Color is in and is gloriously vibrant. Let your walls make as much of a statement as your furnishings (for a fraction of the price).

● To create a sense of flow from room to room, select a dominant color for your main room, then pick up different shades of the same color and use them in subtle ways throughout the house.

● It's no great surprise that desert colors—oranges, reds, browns, and yellows—are often used in decorating in the Southwest or that deep greens, earthy browns, and dark reds show up in mountain homes. Those are predominant colors in nature in those regions. The dominant natural colors of any part of the country can be used to subtly tie the interior of one's home to the world outside.

the effect of color on space

You can fool the eye with the way you use paint, making a room appear either larger or smaller just by the choice of color. Cool colors and lighter tints tend to make walls look farther apart; rich, dark colors bring walls dramatically closer, creating an intimate look even in a large room.

color moods

Different colors tend to elicit different emotions, although the relationships can vary from culture to culture. By and large:
cool colors Shades of blue, green, purple, and similar cool colors tend to have a calming influence—excellent for bedrooms if you want to create a soothing haven.
warm colors Shades of red, orange, and yellow tend to have a strong, dramatic, inviting effect—a look you might want for a living or dining room.
light, bright colors Lighter shades of yellow and the spectrum of whites can be cheerful and sunny—great in a kitchen or family room.

papering your walls

Although paint is the easiest way to add color to your walls, wallcoverings have come back into their own. Wallcoverings are easier to hang than ever before and come in a wide variety of styles. If you have walls that are in less than perfect condition, a wallcovering can disguise the flaws without the expense of replastering.

frugally fabulous floors

Don't make any decisions about new flooring until you've carefully considered whether you can revitalize the old flooring. Wood floors may need only a new coat of wax. Or you can rent a sander to redo seriously scuffed wood.

❝Blue color is everlastingly appointed by the Deity to be a source of delight.**❞**

John Ruskin, essayist and critic

- Consider the wear and tear on a surface before you decide what to do with it. Wood floors enhance living rooms and more formal areas; rooms with heavier traffic, such as kitchens, bathrooms, and family rooms, need something that's tougher and won't require as much maintenance.
- If your wood floors are so badly worn that sanding, staining, or bleaching can't revive them, try rescuing them with paint, which can cover a multitude of sins, pits, and blemishes and can really brighten a room, to boot! Although the range of colors is small, deck paint is ideal for hard-use areas because it's durable and washable.
- Add tremendous character to a stained floor by stenciling a border around the edges of the room. Flowers and vines, small checkerboard patterns, Greek key patterns, or geometric designs are eye-catching choices.
- Another idea: Paint a "rug" on a section of flooring.

give an old floor a new look

If you have a clean, flat, structurally sound floor that needs some sort of covering, consider sheet vinyl. It is resilient, water resistant, easy to clean, and relatively inexpensive. Moreover, it comes in many patterns and colors, in 6- and 12-foot widths. You won't even need an adhesive; simply move the furniture, unroll the vinyl, and trim it to fit.

forest-friendly floors

Do you love the look of hardwood floors but abhor deforestation? Try bamboo! Bamboo floors are increasing in popularity for good reasons: They are as hard as maple, take stain beautifully, and are an environmentally friendly alternative to endangered woods. One bamboo plant cut to the ground can regenerate itself to a height suitable for floor-grade wood every four years (as opposed to the decades it takes a tree to grow into a usable size). Brands include Bamtex by Mintec (**www.bamtex.com**), Sun Brand by Bamboo Flooring International (**www.bamboo-flooring.com**), and many others. The cost is similar to putting in a hardwood floor because once bamboo is in, you don't have to sand or seal it as you do other woods.

picture-perfect floors

Another increasingly popular flooring that is far less costly than hardwood is laminate. The surface of laminate flooring can be made to look like anything, from hardwood to tile to marble. Basically, a print of the desired surface look is laminated onto a fiberboard core backing. Laminate is easy to install (no adhesive is used; the flooring "floats," or lies unattached, on the subfloor), is extremely easy to care for, and is quite durable.

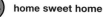

carpet costs

With carpeting, you generally get what you pay for. It pays to buy high quality because a good-quality carpet will last much longer and look much better after years of use than poor-quality carpeting will. It is also sound sense to purchase the right padding and have professionals install both. Because your floors really set the tone for your decor, carpeting is an area in which long-term savings should outweigh up-front costs. With carpet warehouses, home centers, and even department stores competing for your business, you should still be able to purchase high-quality carpeting for a reasonable price.

wonderful windows

Good news for the penny pincher: The best-decorated window is usually the least-decorated window! After all, the main function of a window is to let in light and air, so the less fussy the treatment, the better.

- If you're lucky enough to have a great view, use the window treatment to frame it, not hide it. A simple drape on either side of the window can function when you need privacy but won't detract from the view.

kitchen face-lifts for less

You may want a new kitchen, but do you really need new appliances or a new floor plan? If not, a kitchen face-lift might save you hundreds of dollars.

- Cabinet refacing: Even if you have this done professionally, you will pay much less than it would cost to have new cabinets installed. You can save even more, by doing the refacing yourself. This usually involves gluing new veneer over the old finish on all the vertical surfaces. You can get the veneer and instructions at home centers. You can also get new cabinet doors and drawer fronts to replace your old ones, refinishing the cabinet frame before installing the new doors and drawer fronts.

- If you don't want to go through the effort of a full refacing, take off all the cabinet doors and drawers and paint yourself a brand-new look. You can match the doors and the frames or, if you want some drama, paint them different colors. Paint the frames white and the doors and drawer fronts bright red, then look for a vintage '50s dinette set with a red tabletop and red-cushioned chairs. Or stencil a design of herbs on the doors and drawer fronts and paint the framework a pale green.

- Don't forget hardware! Knobs, handles, and drawer pulls come in an infinite variety these days; there's something for everyone's taste. If you've saved big money redoing your own cabinets, you can splurge a bit on hardware.

ARTISTIC GROUPINGS

Don't feel you have to have a matching set of chairs. Look for chairs you like at thrift stores or garage sales, preferably all wood unless you're going for a funky fifties dinette look. In fact, a disparate group of wooden chairs can make for a much more interesting dining set. If you want to tie them together somehow, paint or stain them the same color. Or make seat pads of the same fabric.

● Putting in your own tile backsplash can really change the look of the room. Like hardware, the variety of tiles available is staggering. You can go French country blue, Spanish-style bright, Southwestern saltillo, floral, or just about any other route you can think of.

● If you have a window that lets oodles of light into your kitchen, remove all curtains or coverings and install glass shelves to make a window herb garden. You'll always have fresh seasonings for your cooking as well as a gorgeous window, especially if you use interesting containers.

mirror tricks

Mirrors, mirrors everywhere are a tremendous help in decorating for dimes. You can use them framed or unframed, as tiles, or as pieces of furniture.

● Add height to a small, low-ceilinged room (such as a powder room) by covering the ceiling with inexpensive, easy-to-install mirror tiles. Use the recommended adhesive.

● Place a large framed mirror in a small entryway to reflect light, increase the sense of space, and allow you to give yourself the once-over before going out.

● Do you have a darkish room with only one window? Set a mirror on the wall opposite the window to give the illusion of another window and to increase the light.

● A series of small framed mirrors in varied shapes can be arranged down a darkish hallway or on the wall next to a staircase to catch light and add a bit of sparkle.

● For a recessed window, line the sides of the window recess with mirror tiles to reflect more light into the room.

● Look for attractive antique frames at flea markets, garage sales, and thrift stores. You may have to look beyond the so-called art in the frame. When you find a winner, remove the art and replace it with a mirror. Hang it above a dresser, a mantelpiece, or a powder room sink.

an indoor eden

Few things add more beauty to a room than plants. Put them in eye-catching pots to double your visual pleasure. Select plants that are right for the light available in the area where you want to display them. Some easy growers that don't require a lot of extra care include:

boston fern (*Nephrolepis exaltata* 'bostoniensis') This parlor plant with arching fronds flourishes in a north light.

cast-iron plant (*Aspidistra elatior*) This low-care evergreen has broad, shiny leaves and prefers porous, enriched soil.

ficus or weeping fig (*Ficus benjamina*) This popular shiny-leafed evergreen can thrive for years, then suddenly die.

grape ivy (*Cissus rhombifolia*) Gorgeous dark foliage with bronze underleaf tints, this plant thrives on moderate sun.

jade plant (*Crassula argentea*) This excellent house plant has a thick trunk, fleshy leaves, and tiny pink flowers.
philodendron (*Philodendron oxycardium*) With heart-shaped leaves, this trainable vine can take a lot of neglect.
spider plant (*Chlorophytum comosum*) This evergreen has soft, curving leaves and little miniature plants on long stems that can be cut off and potted. Grow in a well-lit window.
wandering jew (*Tradescantia;* several varieties) This fast-growing, long-trailing plant is great for window boxes.

learn to do it yourself

A great way to save money on creating a designer look is to learn to do many of the installations yourself. There are any number of books you can borrow or buy to learn techniques, but sometimes a class can make what you want to do really clear. Check with your local home center; home centers often offer regular classes (free or for the cost of materials) in laying tile, planning a xeriscape garden (xeriscaping refers to landscaping methods that reduce water requirements), painting techniques, and more. The parks and recreation departments of many cities also offer low-cost classes in slip-covering furniture, the art of Feng Shui, raising herbs, and more. You can even check with a university nearby to see what kind of extension classes it offers.

TRUNK TRICKS

A trunk—old or new, footlocker style or hope chest—can be one of the most versatile things around your house. New footlocker trunks can be had year-round at discount stores, but often go on sale during back-to-school months as parents ready their college-bound kids for dorm life. You can pick these trunks up for around $20 or less. But if you hunt through the attics and basements of older relatives and friends, you might find some wonderful old steamer trunks or wooden chests that can add charm to any room and provide terrific storage space.

- Set a trunk just inside your back or front door as a convenient place to sit and remove muddy shoes (and store out-of-season shoes, boots and sandals).
- Put a trunk at the foot of a bed to store extra blankets, comforters, pillows, or even sheets for that bed.
- For a handy patio coffee table, use a weather-resistant or weatherproof trunk to store pool toys, towels, extra seat cushions, games, picnic linens, table ware, bird food, or just about anything else you'd rather have outdoors.
- A good-looking wooden trunk makes a beautiful and useful coffee table or end table and adds storage space to your living room.
- Old-fashioned steamer trunks—the kind with drawers and space to hang clothes—make eye-catching armoires for a guest room or a little girl's room.
- Keep an old footlocker next to your fireplace to store firewood.
- A trunk or footlocker is a natural for a child's toy box, but be sure it has a brace or device to keep it from slamming on little fingers.

frugal furniture
Facts

An antique oak hutch, a grand piano, a rich cherry wood dining table, an elegant brass bed—think of how your eyes are drawn to such star pieces when you enter a room. Now add a cozy farmhouse table, an inviting armchair, a handy nightstand for your books, and a whatnot to display your Hummels, and you have your supporting players. With furniture, as with appliances, you should buy the best you can. You'll enjoy your handsome, good-quality furniture for years to come.

buying new furniture

department stores and furniture stores Both of these stores have a wide selection of furniture, from low-end pieces made with particleboard and veneer to high-end solid wood pieces. Both venues are worth checking out, especially when they are advertising sales.

price clubs These outlets usually have some furniture year-round, though the selection tends to reflect seasonal needs. The quality is generally high and the prices are often excellent: for instance, an oak double bookcase (48 inches wide by 84 inches high) for $199.99. You can find an even wider selection on their Web sites. On the Costco Web site, we spotted a mission-style Morris chair in solid oak with black Italian leather seat cushions and matching ottoman for $549.99, plus $121 for shipping!

discount superstores You won't find fine furniture at these stores, but they do offer a variety of everyday furnishings that make excellent fillers or supporting pieces. Dining-room chairs, computer desks, stools, side tables, and so on can be had for very reasonable prices.

consignment store bargains

Selling both new furniture (sometimes floor models) and used, consignments stores can yield some excellent buys. A recent ad offered a used carved teak rolltop desk for $698 that would sell for $1,600 new! Or a new Bassett solid maple china hutch/buffet for $348, marked down from $700. Consignment stores are well worth investigating.

thrift store bonanzas

Furniture is a category in which thrift stores shine. We know a couple who purchased a complete bedroom set—full bed with headboard and footboard, two nightstands, a dresser with mirror, and a bureau, in beautifully finished solid cherry—for less than $500! As you canvas thrift stores, you'll find that some stores carry more furniture than others and that some seem to acquire better pieces. If you are looking for a specific piece or style, tell the salespeople what you want; they may be willing to call you if it comes in.

great garage sale finds

Scouring garage (tag or yard) sales can also pay off handsomely. Look for ads or signs indicating that the sale will include furniture and go as early as possible. Make sure to check out garage sales in more affluent neighborhoods. Though you may pay a tad more, you also may find higher quality furniture. Tables, dining chairs, consoles, sofas, and end tables are among the pieces often sold at garage sales.

flea market facts

Although flea markets are a wonderful source of furniture, old and new, you have to work them like an expert to get the best merchandise at the best price.

go early Take your cue from crafty antiques hunters and arrive as the vendors are setting up their booths.

shun costly repairs Worn wicker may be selling for a song, but wicker costs an arm and a leg to reweave, so it's best to pass it by. Mildewed upholstery is almost impossible to freshen, so just leave it alone.

chat up the vendors Vendors are often collectors and tend to know who is selling what. They also frequently own shops or have some pieces at home that they might be willing to bring the next weekend.

comparison shop A number of the vendors may have similar pieces. Check each piece carefully and bargain. Vendors will often come down 10 percent if you ask.

stay late Vendors don't want to have to repack wares, so they may be willing to lower their prices significantly toward the end of the day to make a sale. You can often score some excellent bargains this way.

> **❝I had three chairs in my house: one for solitude, two for friendship, three for society.❞**

Henry David Thoreau

auction patter

Like flea markets, auctions—if you know how to work them—can yield marvels.

arrive early Look over pieces that you're interested in during the presale period. Ask the attendant or auctioneer what the piece is likely to bring—that will usually give you a good estimate of the item's true worth.

avoid bidding wars Decide in advance what your top bid for an item will be and stick to that price. Otherwise, you may go home with a really overpriced piece.

stay late Some of the best bargains can be snagged after most of the bidders have gone home.

other auction options

● Moving and storage auctions often provide fabulous deals on furniture. Movers periodically auction off unclaimed goods out of their warehouses. Check newspaper classified ads or contact local movers for dates.

- Business bankruptcies can yield bargains. For example, when a restaurant closes, it may auction off additional items, such as a car or a computer. Most bidders will be there for the tables, chairs, kitchen appliances, and supplies, so you may get the other stuff for pennies.

antique advice

If you decide to invest in an antique, make sure that you know what you are paying for. Consult collectors' guidebooks listing the prices of similar items sold at auction within the last year. (Most public libraries have such books.) Also check prices at other antique stores. If the item is very costly, consult an appraiser.

- If the piece has had alterations or repairs, you can often get the dealer to reduce the price. Check for such clues as legs made of a different wood, new screws, or machine-cut braces. Then bargain.

faux antiques

If you love the look of antiques but tremble at the price tags, buy a new or relatively new piece at a garage sale or thrift store and distress it yourself. The goal is not a perfect finish—quite the opposite! You're trying to create the illusion of use over the years, not a pristine patina.

- Create a random pattern of dents on wooden furniture by banging the surfaces using a piece of wood studded with nails, a ring of keys, a chain, stones, or other blunt or jagged objects. Sand away any splinters or rough spots.

MAKE YOUR OWN MILK PAINT

A staple of the 19th century, milk paint produces a soft, flat finish that can add a patina of age even to new furniture. Lime, whiting (finely powdered calcium carbonate), and paint pigment are sold at paint stores and some home centers; litmus paper can be found at pharmacies. Make milk paint for immediate use. If you must store it for a day or two, refrigerate it. If you need to strip off milk paint, use household ammonia. On most furniture, put a coat of shellac on top to increase the milk paint's longevity.

3 tablespoons white vinegar	4 cups milk
1 ounce slaked lime	2 to 2-1/2 lbs. dried pigment
litmus paper	whiting as desired

1. Combine the vinegar and milk in an old pan and heat gently until the mixture curdles. Stir in the lime until well mixed.

2. Test the mixture with litmus paper: If the paper turns red, it is too acid—add more lime; if it turns dark blue, it is too alkaline—add more sour milk. Keep testing until the pH is balanced.

3. Stir in the whiting until you reach a paint-like consistency. Then slowly sprinkle in the pigment, stirring constantly, until the color is as desired. MAKES 1 QUART.

- Smooth sharp edges with sandpaper. Make sure all the corners and edges are slightly rounded so that the furniture gives the appearance of years of loving use.
- Be colorful! For authenticity, select colors that were commonly used in a particular historical period or architectural style. Experiment on pieces of scrap wood until you've pinpointed the color that you like the best.
- Use old-fashioned paints for an old-fashioned finish. Milk paint, used for centuries, has made a huge comeback in furniture and decorating styles. Made of milk protein, pigments, and lime, milk paint is sold in home centers, paint stores, and some hardware stores. For a more authentic look and a lot less money, make your own (see box, facing page) and paint an unfinished piece in a classic style.

refinished to perfection

Another way to gussy up a piece of used furniture is to refinish it. If you haven't done much refinishing, practice on an inconspicuous part of the piece. Your technique will improve as you work, so save the most visible parts until last.

- Take apart a big piece of furniture before refinishing it. This will make working on any section a lot easier, and you're more likely to get the results you want.
- Take off the hardware and, for easier reassembling when you're finished, mark each handle, hinge, caster, and screw with tape and a pencil, noting its original position. Keep all the hardware in a labeled self-sealing bag so that you don't misplace anything.
- To check whether a liquid refinisher will work on your piece of furniture, soak a cotton ball in nail polish remover and press it against the surface. If the ball sticks, refinisher will do the job; if the ball doesn't stick, you will need to strip the piece with paint remover.
- Unlike paint remover, refinishing liquids (sold in home centers, hardware stores, and paint stores) just remove the top layers of old finishes, so you don't have to scrape or sand as much. You can't use refinishers on all finishes, however, so check the label carefully.
- Before you start applying stain, test the stain you want to use on a section that won't be seen, such as the bottoms of chair seats and the undersides of tabletops.

sofa, so good

Buy the highest quality sofa you can afford; it will last much, much longer than a cheaply made sofa and will look good far longer. The best-made sofas have a hardwood frame, joints secured with dowels or screws, and fitted blocks at the inside corners for added strength. Spring coils, eight to twelve per seat, offer greater comfort than horizontal steel springs.

- Take the fabric protection option. These guards are applied at the factory and come with a warranty. Do-it-yourself store-bought aerosols don't bond as well. Later, when water stops beading on the fabric, it's best to have new fabric guard professionally applied.
- If possible, get extra fabric when you buy an upholstered sofa or have an older sofa reupholstered. If you need to recover a cushion later, you will have a perfect match.
- Be sure to vacuum your sofa once a week and flip the cushions at the same time.
- If your sofa is starting to feel a bit softer than you like, buy a 1/2 inch-thick piece of plywood to fit under the cushions. Your old sofa will feel like new. You can also do this with armchairs that have started to sag.

bewitching beds

Although solid bedsteads are quite attractive, they can also be a significant investment, especially if you want real wood. To create the appearance of a headboard, try one of these fool-the-eye ideas for a less-expensive option:

- Hang a new or heirloom quilt at the head of your bed. Use an inexpensive wooden dowel and add decorative finials for extra interest.
- An unusual Oriental or Native American rug can be hung at the head of a bed to eye-catching effect.

look aloft

One option to consider for furnishing a child's room or a guest room/office is a loft-style bed. To accommodate a loft, the ceiling should be at least 12 feet high. This height allows for a minimum of 6-1/2 feet of standing room below the loft and 4-1/2 feet above (enough to sit up in a bed or sit in a chair at a desk), plus 1 foot for the platform of the loft.

- The loft options are pretty amazing: You can have a single or double bed above, and under it an office setup, book-cases, bureau drawers, even a little fort for children. The prices of lofts vary considerably, so check around. Price clubs offer lofts occasionally; check their Web sites for options year-round. Unfinished-furniture stores can offer real wood at a decent price, and you can stain or paint the pieces to match your decor.
- You can also construct a loft yourself pretty easily, especially if you have some woodworking skills and the right tools. Plans are available in furniture-making books (check the library), or you may be able to download instructions off the Web.

- Be sure to take into account the ventilation needs of someone sleeping near a ceiling. The loft area will be warmer in the winter (heat rises), but also warmer in the summer. If the room doesn't have air conditioning, remember that fans can make a big difference in airflow.

mattress matters

Few things affect a good night's sleep more than a mattress, so buying a well-made mattress can be a real investment in good health. Once you've found and purchased a good-quality mattress, take care of it, and it will last much longer, protecting you and your investment.

- Count the number of coils. Full-size mattresses should have at least 300 coils inside; queen-size, at least 375; king-size, a minimum of 450 coils. In choosing between two mattresses that have the same coil count, check the thickness of the steel of the coils. The lower the number, the thicker the wire and the longer the mattress will keep its support firm.
- Turn your mattress frequently to maintain even support. Switch the mattress end to end as well as turning it over. Some manufacturers recommend turning every two weeks for the first three months, then turning every two months for the life of the mattress. To keep track, put a bit of masking tape with the date last changed somewhere on the mattress.
- If you have an older good-quality mattress that has become a bit softer than you like, don't rush out to a store, unless it's a lumber store! A sheet of plywood, 1/2- to 3/4-inch thick, can be slipped between the mattress and the box spring to make a fine bed support. You'll get extra years from your mattress at a fraction of the cost of a new one.

wonderful wicker

You can find wicker furniture at garage or yard sales and thrift stores for a song. As long as the weaving is sturdy, don't pass a piece by because it is saggy or a bit scuffed. It is easy to bring wicker back to radiant life. And don't just look for wicker patio furniture. You can also find headboards, side tables, dining tables and chairs (perfect for a breakfast nook), bookcases, towers (for storing towels in the bathroom), love seats, rocking chairs, and so on.

- To tighten a saggy wicker chair seat, turn the piece upside down. Using a damp sponge, wet the underside of the seat (except for the chair's rim). Let the chair dry for 24 hours or overnight; the cane probably will have shrunk back into shape.
- Give a new look (and longer life) to wicker with latex

APPRAISE YOUR APPRAISER

....

www.appraisers.org or 800-272-8258

....

Whether you are in the market for an antique or you have been going through Great Aunt Sally's attic and aren't sure what you've found, you need to know you can trust your appraiser. Check with the American Society of Appraisers to find a licensed, reputable appraiser in your area who specializes in the field that you need. This organization maintains a directory of members, all certified specialists, who must meet high standards to join the society. Still, it pays to call any reference numbers and check on an appraiser's past work.

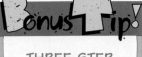

paint. Be daring with your color selection: Match the decor of a particular room, go primary for fun, use forest green for a woodsy effect, or chill out with classic white.

- Create an antique look by using a deep-color latex paint and diluting it. Use a ratio of 1 part water to 2 parts paint. Apply the paint solution with a brush and, before it has dried completely, wipe the raised surfaces with a cloth to remove some of the paint.

- If you want to change the look of wicker fast, spray-paint it with latex-based paint. Set the piece in a large cardboard box with one side cut off. Work in a well-ventilated space, preferably outdoors, on a dry, calm day.

bookcase bonuses

Unless you have to fit an exact space, it's usually easier to buy bookcases than to build them. Try unfinished furniture stores, used office furniture outlets, and thrift shops for solid cases that only need a quick coat or two of paint. If you do need a custom fit, building a bookcase is one of the easiest types of furniture projects to do, even for those with minimal carpentry skills. If building isn't for you, an unfinished furniture store will often custom-craft bookcases for a bit more than their normal price for ready-made pieces.

- If you have a bunch of mismatched old bookcases acquired during various prior lifetimes, you can often pull them together into one harmonious whole by grouping them and then painting all of them the same color—usually white or the color of your walls.

- Whether you are buying bookcases or building them, make sure the shelves are at least 8 inches deep and 9 inches high to accommodate books of average or small size, such as standard novels and paperbacks. This also is a good size for videotapes and DVDs. For larger books, such as art and reference books, the shelves should be 12 inches deep with 13 inches of clearance. The small plastic storage units that hold CDs also fit nicely on this size.

- Transform a plain wall with ordinary windows into an attractive architectural feature by constructing bookshelves above, below, and on either side of the windows. Fill some of the shelves with books, but leave space to display cherished objects or collections.

- Block out noise in apartments and townhouses. If you share one or more walls with neighbors, install floor-to-ceiling bookshelves along the walls separating the apartments to help muffle noise. You'll find that books are great sound absorbers.

- Make mini-libraries in unexpected places—on a wide landing, under a staircase, above a doorway, or in the corner of a room, and build a custom-shaped bookcase.

Try to match the books to the space. For example, take the door off an upper kitchen cabinet and turn it into shelves for your cookbooks.

fabric matters

When you're choosing an upholstered piece, such as a sofa or armchair, it's important to examine the quality of the fabric. A piece may look great, but you want it it to wear well, too.

cotton Quite versatile, strong, and comfortable. If untreated, it's less stain resistant than some synthetic fibers.

wool Very strong, long-lasting, naturally water-resistant, and generally soft to the touch; some people are sensitive to wool.

linen High-end and pricey, linen is strong and durable, and keeps its crisp look.

silk Also high-end; extremely strong, resilient, and luxurious.

rayon Comfortable, smooth, and soft synthetic fiber, but tends to wrinkle when used alone. Best in a blended fabric.

nylon Strong, long-lasting, resistant to rot, mildew, and abrasions; it doesn't absorb liquids well.

acrylic Manufactured fabric that offers many qualities of wool, it's fade-resistant but tends to pill.

olefin Manufactured fiber that resists soil and abrasions, it is often used in blends.

polyester The new generations of polyester are still extremely strong and resilient, but don't have as many drawbacks (comfort, for example) as their predecessors. Great in blends.

purchasing options

Obviously, the best way to buy a piece of new furniture is to go into the store and pay cash. But there are times in our lives when we need something to sit (or sleep) on and we simply don't have the whole price in our pocket. What to do?

- Don't fall into the "rent-to-own" trap. Like leasing a car, the agreements are often fuzzy and you could end up paying almost twice what the piece is worth.

- Furniture stores are some of the only stores left that offer lay away plans. This is where you put down honest money, then pay over time until you own the piece. Then the piece is yours to take. This means paying for something you don't get to use, but there is no interest charged as there would be if you bought on credit—a great piece should be worth waiting for, right?

- If you have to wait for delivery, don't lend the store your money. Put down as small a deposit as you can, then save for the next six to eight weeks so that when the piece is ready for delivery, you can pay the rest without strain.

Penny-Smart Parenting

○ bargain-basement babies

○ lower cost kids

○ free-time fun

CHAPTER  5

So . . . you're at the park and you spot this family: man, woman, infant, toddler, and young child (about six). They look like an ad in a fashion magazine with the infant in a bouncy seat wearing a bright Gymboree outfit, the toddler sporting a Baby Gap jean jacket, and the child in OshKosh from head to toe. You are ready to scoff at the waste of money—don't. The infant's outfit was bought at an end-of-season sale for 75 percent off and the bouncy seat was a garage sale bargain; the toddler's jacket was picked up at a consignment store for $10 (less than half the original cost); and the child's duds were an outlet mall score. Plus, the family is enjoying a home-packed meal using an old bedspread as a picnic blanket, and they are playing with a red rubber ball, not the latest computer game. It might also surprise you to know that the baby sleeps in an old drawer converted to a bassinet, the toddler stores all her toys in big plastic baskets bought at a dollar sale, and the child happily helps to plan meals that he just loves. Sound impossible? It's easy to do when you know how.

Raise your kids to be penny pinchers.

bargain-basement
Babies

ONE OF THE MOST LIFE-CHANGING
EVENTS YOU CAN EXPERIENCE
CAN ALSO BE ONE OF THE MOST COSTLY.

Don't fall prey to the notion that an infant needs a lot of baby stuff to be happy. The fact of the matter is that infants, bless their little hearts, need remarkably few things, many of which you can make yourself, buy economically, or fashion out of items conveniently on hand. So close your eyes to the hype and embrace the less-is-more route through babyhood.

baby super-duper stores

The enormous stores that cater to babies and toddlers with row upon row of cribs, changing tables, strollers, and so on are unquestionably convenient, since you can pick up anything under the sun for your baby. But are they cheaper than baby departments at traditional stores? As usual, that depends. In a comparison of Babies"R"Us, Target, Sears, and Burlington Coat Factory, we found a decent range of cribs, changing tables, strollers, playards (playpens), bassinets, car seats, diaper disposal systems, and clothing at very similar prices for comparable items. Basically, you should make a list of **"must haves"** and then check the stores near your home to determine which ones have the best prices that day on the items you need.

price clubs for babies

If you're shopping for baby furniture, strollers, car seats, and so on, price clubs may have one or two models to choose from, but such stores don't stock the same baby items consistently. That being said, on a recent visit to Costco, we saw a Cosco Alpha Omega convertible car seat (for children weighing 5 to 80 pounds) for $99.99—a price competitive with that at discount superstores. Costco was selling a 128-count pack of Huggies disposable diapers for $29.99, while Target was advertising jumbo packs (30 to 42 per pack) for $10.88. Clearly, on that day, Costco was offering a lower price per unit. You can also find fairly high-quality baby clothing at good prices in price clubs.

resale heaven

A popular penny-pinching destination that makes loads of sense is the children's resale shop. These stores, which have sprung up all across the country, buy used clothing, furniture, and other baby items and then resell them. Clothing for infants and toddlers tends to be worn for a very short time, so you can pick up like-new clothes at these stores—even high-end clothes from Baby Gap and Gymboree—for a few dollars. Though the furniture and toys selection is not as wide, you can still find great stuff for pennies.

garage sale chic

The one clothing area in which garage (or tag) sales can be fabulous is baby stuff. Babies outgrow clothes so fast, their clothes tend to stay in better shape than those for older children. Be sure to go through boxes of baby stuff; they can be treasure troves of barely used, high-quality items. You can also pick up infant swings, chairs, bedding, mobiles, and just about anything else your baby needs at garage sales.

go to the back of the store

Specialty children's stores, such as Gymboree and Baby Gap, have darling, well-made baby clothes but at budget-breaking prices. Don't despair. Specialty stores also have sensational sales, particularly at the end of a season, when they're trying to clear out stock. Walk on by the new stock and head to the back racks, where the clearance items hang. You can pick up things for 50 percent to 75 percent off. If you make a point of shopping for your child a year in advance, you may pick up some fabulous pieces at penny-pinching prices.

zero need for 0–3 months

Although those itsy-bitsy onesies are too cute, avoid buying many newborn clothes. Instead, go for the 3–6 month sizes for newborns; they grow amazingly fast. Then keep a size ahead for older babies. Most 6-month-old babies wear clothes size 9–12 months, 1-year-olds wear size 2, and so on.

baby shoe scam

Babies don't need shoes, so the only reason they're sold is because adults think they look cute. In fact, most pediatricians recommend going barefoot as much as possible well into early childhood to allow a baby's feet to develop. When toddlers do need shoes, choose soft, flexible ones with soles that won't slip but will move with the child. And buy cheap, because children go through shoes like water through a sieve.

diapers: cloth vs. disposable

Ah, the endless debate pitting the environment against convenience. So how do you decide which is more economical for your family? Do the math.

cloth diapers These last forever (practically), first as diapers and later as the best cleaning cloths you'll ever find. Though the initial investment is higher for cloth diapers, plastic pants, and pins, than for a big package of disposables, it's a one-shot expense. A set of cloth diapers will keep a baby supplied from birth through potty training, depending on how you fold them, and will produce no landfill waste. On the other hand, there's a utility cost: You must use water to

>
>
> **66** A child, like your stomach, doesn't need all you can afford to give it. **99**
>
> Frank A. Clark, author

wash them and electricity or gas to dry them. If you live in an area where water is plentiful for washing and sunshine for drying, cloth diapers make more sense, both economically and environmentally.

disposable diapers These diapers are not reusable, but they offer great convenience and are more absorbent than cloth, so you don't have to change them as often (good for you, but not so good for the baby). Moreover, the cost of disposables has come down over the years, and you can buy them in bulk for a good price at discount stores or price clubs. Disposable diapers don't use water resources, but they do produce waste (unless you want to spend more and buy biodegradable disposables). If you live in an area where water is at a premium and you can't count on drying clothes outside, disposable diapers may be a more economical and environmentally sound choice.

prudent diaper pails

If you decide to go with cloth diapers, you will need a diaper pail. Any large bucket with a tight-fitting lid will do, but be sure little fingers can't open the pail. (Even a few inches of water in any pail or tub poses a drowning hazard to children.) Buy or make a mesh bag with a drawstring opening that fits the diaper pail. Fill the pail about two-thirds full with water and add a cup of white vinegar. The vinegar, which kills bacteria, will keep the pail from smelling and will also help whiten your diapers when you wash them. When the diapers reach the top of the water line, just pull the mesh bag out and dump it (and the diapers) into your washing machine.

wipe out extra costs

You do not need to buy wipes for your baby. You can make them yourself instead:

● Buy a bundle of discount washcloths at a price club or discount store (or buy a few at a time when you see them at garage sales and thrift stores). Keep them in the bathroom near your baby's changing area. When it's time to change the baby, dampen a washcloth in the sink (if the baby has a really dirty diaper, dampen one washcloth and rub a little soap over it, then dampen a second to rinse) and use that to clean the baby's bottom. Toss the dirty washcloths in your diaper pail to wash with the diapers.

INTRODUCING YOUR BABY

Don't spend money on those fancy commercial birth announcements. A little creativity on your part will mean much more to those who receive these homemade cards:

● Get a copy of the hand and foot impressions made after birth and photocopy them on the front of plain white cards. Inside the cards, write the baby's name, date of birth, vital statistics, and whatever else you want to share.

● Cut triangles from pale pink or pale blue paper. Fold each triangle as you would a diaper. On the inside write the pertinent birth information. Secure each triangle with a diaper pin and mail in envelopes that are one size larger than the folded triangles.

● Take a picture of your baby at the hospital or on the first day home. Glue the photo to the top of a white piece of paper and write your baby's information underneath. Then take the sheet to a copy center and get color copies made.

- To make your own disposable wipes, cut a roll of paper towels in half crosswise. Put a half roll in a plastic container with a tight lid. Combine 1-1/2 cups of water with 1 tablespoon of liquid baby bath soap. Pour the mixture over the towels to saturate them and cover the container. When you need a wipe, tear off a sheet from the roll.

discount diaper bags

Here are some cheap ways to to carry all that baby gear:

pack it in, pack it out Buy a sturdy backpack—a student version at a discount store is fairly inexpensive—and use that to tote your baby's things around.

get vested Check out Army-Navy stores or thrift stores for those multipocketed vests popular with photographers and fishermen. Put those pockets to good use and free your arms for more important things, such as carrying the baby!

canvas your friends A popular giveaway item at many conventions is a sturdy canvas bag with a logo (free advertising) printed on the side. If no one in your family has access to one, ask around among your friends. Someone is sure to have an extra bag that can be turned into a diaper bag with ease.

carry on Rummage through thrift stores or garage sales for old carry-on luggage. Such bags usually have lots of compartments and are comfortable to tote around.

creative cradles

When babies are tiny, you don't have to spend money on fancy bassinets:

- Line a large wicker basket with a folded baby quilt to make a nest for your baby.
- An old dresser drawer makes a secure bassinet.
- A Moses basket (available at some import stores and on several Web sites) is a wicker basket with a handle on each side. It's made to carry a small, sleeping baby and can easily be carried from room to room with you.

beddy-buys

Buying a crib can be a big investment, but it doesn't have to break the bank.

- A used crib can be a great bargain—just check out the classifieds. But don't buy one unless it meets all current standards for crib safety (see Getting a Good Crib, page 153).
- Check out sales at baby superstores, discount superstores, and even department stores. Ask about floor models, because they tend to be discounted.
- Though they sound good on paper, transitional cribs that turn into toddler beds are more expensive than a regular crib, and their usefulness is debatable.

● Toddler beds are not necessary. Once your child can climb out of a crib (or starts trying), switch him or her to a regular bed. If you are uncomfortable with the height of a regular bed, buy an inexpensive side rail or put the mattress on the floor until the child is older.

BYOB (build your own bibs)

Purchased bibs are an unnecessary expense when you can make them or improvise:

● Stitch two ties—cut from grosgrain ribbon, seam binding, or twill tape—to a short end of a dish towel or hand towel to make an easy-to-wash bib.

● Cut an old T-shirt up the back and hem the cut edges. Add a Velcro or snap closure at the hemmed ends of the neck band to make a bib that amply covers your baby's clothes.

changing tables for change

You don't need to buy a special changing table for your baby. They are convenient, but you can easily adapt a sturdy dresser to meet your needs. Look for a dresser that comes up to your waist. (Higher or lower will strain your back.) Buy or make a pad to lay the baby on and keep everything you need for changing diapers in the top drawers. You must never leave a baby unsupervised on a changing table. If you don't have a dresser that will work, old dressers can easily be found at garage sales or thrift stores, and they are easy to paint to match your baby's room.

pads for pennies

You can make your own changing pad for very little: Pin together two bath-size towels and trim them to fit the top of your dresser or table. Stitch together the two long sides and one short side of the towels to form a pocket. Buy a piece of inexpensive foam (available at fabric stores) to fit into the pocket. Now you have a changing pad you can wash as needed; for convenience, make two or three pads, so you always have a clean cover on hand.

● Another easy cover for a changing pad is made of old pillowcases—either those you have on hand or picked up at garage sales or thrift stores or at a discount store.

storage savings

It's a good idea to keep things organized in your changing area. Empty margarine tubs make fantastic storage containers. They're just the right size for diaper pins, cornstarch (for powder, with a powder puff tucked on top), homemade ointments, damp washcloths, and just about anything else you want to keep handy but covered.

shake it

It's nice to have powder to shake quickly over your baby's bottom after cleaning. Fill old spice bottles (with shaker tops) with cornstarch or homemade baby powder (see Bonus Tip box, right), and you'll always have a sprinkle on hand.

budget blankets

A child can become mighty attached to a "blankie," which can lead to scenes of tragedy when the blanket falls apart from all that love. A trip to your local fabric store can provide a solution to the cost of a good blanket and the tears when it disintegrates. Polar fleece fabric is soft and fluffy, can be thrown into the washing machine innumerable times, and is practically indestructible. And if you buy remnant pieces in late winter or early spring, you can get a square yard for $3 to $5 (or less)! Another plus: The edges don't ravel. You can add satin binding around the edges or make a simple rolled hem, and you have a blanket that will last! If you're really smart, you'll buy 2 yards and make two identical blankets so that when one is being washed, your baby will have the spare.

frugal flannel

Every parent can use a supply of soft flannel blankets for the baby, but you don't have to buy them at a store. If you have old flannel sheets, cut them into pieces approximately 36 inches square and make simple rolled hems around the edges. If you don't have flannel sheets, look for them at garage sales, thrift stores, or end-of-winter sales or white sales.

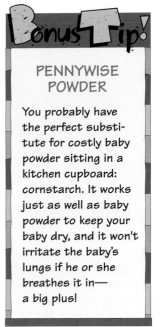

PENNYWISE POWDER

You probably have the perfect substitute for costly baby powder sitting in a kitchen cupboard: cornstarch. It works just as well as baby powder to keep your baby dry, and it won't irritate the baby's lungs if he or she breathes it in— a big plus!

GETTING A GOOD CRIB

Here is a list of musts to check out before you purchase or use a crib:

- The crib has not been recalled by the U.S. Consumer Product Safety Commission (www.cpsc.gov/kids/kidsafety)
- The slats are no more than 2-3/8 inches (60 mm) apart.
- Slats are not missing, loose, cracked, or splintered.
- The crib has no sharp or jagged edges.
- The mattress fits tightly into the crib: No more than two fingers fit between the edge of the mattress and the crib side.
- The mattress support is securely attached to the crib headboard and footboard.
- The screws/bolts holding the crib parts together are tight and none are missing.
- The corner posts are 1/16 inch (1-1/2 mm) high or less.
- The crib has no cutouts in the headboard or footboard.
- The drop-side latches are too difficult to be released by a young child.
- The mattress is covered with a well-fitting crib sheet. Never use adult sheets.
- Never put pillows, comforters, stuffed animals, or other soft items in the crib.
- Always remember: Never lay an infant on his or her tummy to sleep.

bathing babies

You don't need to buy a special baby bathtub. Those are more for the comfort of Mom and Dad than for the baby. For years babies were bathed in the sink, and that still works pretty well. Line the sink (preferably a large kitchen sink) with an old towel to prevent slipping.

● Pull on a pair of cheap white cotton gloves before bathing your baby. The gloves will give you a slip-proof grip on your little one.

papering with memories

Save the paper from your baby-shower gifts to use to line the drawers of your baby's dresser. You'll save on liner paper and relive precious memories each time you open a drawer.

extending the juice

Although most babies love juice, they don't require it full strength. So, don't waste your money on "baby" juices. Buy plain juice concentrates (the least expensive, but be sure they are marked 100 percent juice with no added sugar) and reconstitute as per the package directions. When you are filling a bottle or sipping cup, fill the container about one-third to half full, then top it off with plain water. Your juice will last longer, and your baby will consume less fruit sugar, which can contribute to early tooth decay.

frugal baby food

Once your baby is given the go-ahead to start solid food, don't spend your money on those cute little jars of baby food. It is easy, healthier, and much cheaper to make your own baby food. Using a food mill, food processor, or blender, simply purée cooked carrots or peas or canned fruit in water (not syrup). As the child grows older, just purée whatever you are having for dinner.

● To make it easier on yourself, search garage sales or thrift stores for an electric coffee grinder. Take it home and wash it well with hot, soapy water. Then use that to grind up your own baby food. The cup is a terrific size for babies.

● If you want more convenience, pick up some small plastic cups that have tight-fitting lids at garage sales or thrift stores. Then make large batches of food for your baby and store the leftovers in the cups, ready to use in a moment.

baby-sitting co-ops

If you have a group of friends with children, try setting up a baby-sitting co-op to save money and your sanity. Draw up a schedule of times that each set of parents can sit. Each time

AU NATURAL

The fewer chemicals a baby's skin comes in contact with, the better. At your local health food store or natural grocery (and even at some discount superstores or chain drugstores), you can find baby care products that are made with natural ingredients, as opposed to strong chemicals. You can also find loads of books with instructions for making your own baby care items. But a general rule is the gentler, the better.

parents baby-sit for the co-op, they earn points. Then when they want to go out, they use points to have another set of parents watch their children. To begin with, someone will need to coordinate the group and keep tabs on the points (to make sure no one is shirking the baby-sitting part). Once the co-op is running smoothly, you can expand it to include other parental needs, such as chauffeuring and toy swapping.

the economics of ear infections

Ear infection is common in childhood and, until relatively recently, prescribing antibiotics was the norm. However, many infections are caused by viruses, not bacteria. Viruses cannot be treated with antibiotics. Unfortunately, parents do not like to have a fussy, clearly uncomfortable child at home, and they hate to leave a doctor's office without some kind of a remedy. Doctors, tired of being berated by parents to "do something," sometimes bend under pressure. Consequently, antibiotics are sometimes prescribed and taken unnecessarily. This situation has contributed to antibiotic resistance, which is a very dangerous problem because the number of resistant strains of microbes is growing faster than new antibiotics are being developed.

what to do? As a parent, be informed and ask questions. If your pediatrician prescribes an antibiotic, ask whether the infection is clearly bacterial. If your child suffers from recurrent infections, ask about alternative treatments. And never press your doctor to give you an antibiotic when he or she clearly doesn't think that is the way to go. If necessary, seek a second opinion.

baby teeth bargains

For a long time it was thought that the health of baby teeth didn't matter; only healthy permanent teeth mattered. **WRONG!** Putting a baby to bed with a bottle of milk or formula or, even worse, juice can lead to tooth decay in infants! That practice can affect the way the child learns to eat or can lead to later dental problems. If a baby must have a bottle while in bed, give him or her water.

● Gently clean your baby's gums and early teeth with a damp washcloth. As your child grows, buy a soft-bristled toothbrush and child-safe toothpaste and teach your youngster how to use the brush properly.

● At about age 3, your child can start flossing and brushing alone. (You may have to help for a while.)

● Start taking your child to a dentist at about age 2. Look for someone with a family practice or see a pediatric dentist so that the experience is pleasant. The habits you instill in your tiny children will, hopefully, stay with them for the rest of their lives.

ONLINE CHILD HEALTH INFORMATION

www.whyimmunize.org
The Arizona Partnership
for Immunization

www.kidshealth.org
The Nemours Foundation

www.fda.gov
The U.S. Food and Drug Administration

www.vaccinesafety.edu
Johns Hopkins University Institute for
Vaccine Safety

There are many terrific Web sites dealing with children's health. As always when you surf the Net, be careful of who set up the site, because there is a ton of misinformation out there. The sites above are some good ones to start with. In addition, many children's hospitals and medical schools have Web sites with special sections for parents and children.

lower cost
Kids

CAN YOU RAISE CHILDREN IN THIS DAY
AND AGE WITHOUT GOING BROKE?

**Of course you can!
You can even save for
their higher education
and have some family
fun without blowing
your budget. You just
have to learn for
yourself (and teach
your children) what
is really necessary
and what can easily
be improvised or
done without. You'll
have to fight Madison
Avenue, but it's
well worth the effort,
in terms of money
management rewards
and the sense of
achievement in
teaching your
children good values.**

meal planning with kids

Planning meals is a great way to teach children how to put together a balanced diet. If your child loves spaghetti, show how pasta is a grain, tomato sauce counts as a vegetable (and fruit), Parmesan cheese on top gives you a little dairy, and protein is provided by a meatball or two. Toss the pasta with a little olive oil, and you have a meal that includes all the food groups! (See the food pyramid, page 95.) Involving your children in meal planning also increases the stake they have in cooking, may make them more open to trying new foods, and takes the burden off the primary cook to come up with menu after menu. The economical benefit: Children are more likely to eat food they've helped choose or prepare.

junk the juice boxes

Juice boxes may be handy, but they are high in cost per unit, and they create a lot of waste. Instead, pick up a reusable plastic bottle (sports bottles work well) and fill that with the juice of choice (made from frozen concentrate and cut with water to reduce costs even further). For a treat, once in a while use half juice and half seltzer or sparkling water.

buy in bulk; dole out in dribs 'n' drabs

Food producers love to offer small sizes of a product to entice parents (and children) with portions that are "just right." Don't be fooled by cute packaging. You're paying for it big time. Instead, buy the largest size container of raisins, crackers, cookies, and so on, and transfer them to small plastic containers or bags that can be washed and used again.

food size matters

Small children like small food, but prepackaged bite-size foods cost more. Luckily, you can feed your children portions that match their size and still hold down food costs: Blocks of cheese are less expensive than slices per unit, but your children will enjoy it more if you cut the cheese into sticks or cubes. Baby carrots, bought in big bags for economy, are friendlier than big carrots. For no-cost fun, cut kids' sandwich bread with cookie cutters.

brown-bagging it

Get back in the habit of making lunches for children to take to school: It's cheaper, and you'll have better control of what your children are eating. Be sensitive to what is cool to carry lunch in (lunch boxes or brown bags), but don't let that dictate your youngsters' diet. Start tucking a cloth napkin (a bandana makes a fun one) in and remind your children to bring back any reusable packaging. You'll create less waste and won't be spending your money on disposable objects, which is money down the drain. As your children grow older, you can turn over the job of making lunch to them (with a little supervision, of course).

a different diet

As children grow into teens, they begin exploring who they want to be, which can be very trying for their parents. This may manifest itself through diet: Your children may announce that they want to become vegetarians or that they don't want to eat certain foods, and so on. First, make it clear that you are not a short-order cook who makes different dishes for each family member and that your family does not waste food. Then ask if they want to start helping to plan and prepare meals to accommodate their new diet. Encourage them to research food so that they know what they need nutritionally and how to get it. If you don't automatically say no, you may be surprised at what a learning experience diet planning can be for the whole family.

66A baby is an inestimable blessing and bother.**99**

Mark Twain

kids' clothing

Buying clothing for children is not very different from buying clothing for yourself, with one notable exception: Kids go through a lot of clothes quickly. They grow at an astonishing rate (you can never predict when a growth spurt will occur), and they play hard, which can be hard on clothes. You really don't want to spend a lot of money on any one piece of apparel, because chances are you won't get good value for the investment. For children's clothing, here are some smart shopping destinations:

department stores As with adult clothing, you can often find excellent buys in children's wear during sales and on the clearance racks at both high-end and mid-range department stores. But you'll frequently pay more at these stores than at cheaper alternatives, despite a sale.

discount department stores Ross, Marshall's, T.J. Maxx, and other discount stores can offer fabulous prices on name-brand clothing for the younger set. As is always true with discount stores, you won't know for sure what they have until you get there. To get the best selections, ask the store manager to tell you what days shipments arrive.

specialty stores As with baby clothes, stores such as Gap Kids and Gymboree have well-made clothes for older children that are truly adorable, but they're equally budget boggling. Luckily, these stores have some excellent sales. Always give the clearance racks a quick once-over: You never know when you may find a steal!

outlet malls You can do some serious shopping during back-to-school or holiday sales events, but make sure you know the cost of basic kids clothing before you go, or you might not get the most from an outlet.

discount superstores Wal-Mart, Kmart, Target, and other discount superstores can really save you money, especially if you look for sales and check all the clearance racks on a regular basis. T-shirts, jeans, leggings, sweatshirts or sweaters, dresses, shorts and skirts, pants, and underwear are all available in styles that children like, that wear reasonably well, and that are budget-friendly.

secondhand when you can

Resale, consignment, and thrift stores, so fabulous for babies' and toddlers' clothing, lose a bit of their usefulness when children outgrow those sizes, because older children tend to wear out their clothes before the togs can make it to a resale store. However, a few exceptions to this rule make a trip to your favorite secondhand store well worth your while:

● Kids' coats and jackets—these are usually pretty well made, so they last a bit longer.

● Seasonal specialty clothing—ski pants and snowsuits are often outgrown in one season of wear, so they are more likely to be resold.

● Dressy dresses and jackets—these are worn so seldom, they generally still look good enough for resale once they're outgrown.

● Teens sometimes find bygone styles are retro and hip. Encourage your teen's penchant for fashions of the past; they're cheaper than buying new name-brand clothes.

hand-me-downs

If you have siblings or cousins (or really good friends who substitute for brothers and sisters), make sure they all know how much you love hand-me-downs for your kids. If your sister's family is a few years older than yours, she can pack away anything useful and pass it on to you when your kids are ready (or even before). If a friend is relocating from St. Paul to San Antonio, her kids may want to get rid of their winter wear before the move. And sometimes your little girl grows out of an adorable dress after having worn it only once or twice. Pass it on to your niece or your best friend's daughter. It's a great way to save money and share memories, too.

saving for something special

Preteens and teenagers face unprecedented pressure to wear what everyone is wearing, which can lead to wildly inappropriate or outrageously expensive clothing. Don't wait until your children become teens to explain the facts of clothes life to them. Start them young in understanding that just because a friend has something doesn't mean that they have to have it too. And encourage them at an early age to save up for those special things that they really want. If your son, for example, absolutely must have a certain pair of expensive soccer shoes, help him set aside a portion of his allowance each week until he has saved enough so that can buy the shoes himself. This will drive home the value of money, the benefit of saving, and the appreciation of buying something for which one has to work and wait.

extending elements

Sometimes kids seem to just grow straight up, not out. So their pants or skirts or dresses still fit in the waist and hips but are too short. Letting out the hem is sometimes a solution but doesn't always work and is impossible with jeans. Luckily, at least for girls, something old can be new again:

for pants Buy some trim, braid, or ribbon at a fabric store and sew several strips of different material along the hem of the pants to extend them.

for skirts or dresses Consider buying lace or other trim and adding it to the bottom hem. If you sew, you might buy a remnant of fabric that matches or contrasts with the dress fabric and stitch a bottom tier to the hem.

short-sleeved

Kids' arms also grow at an alarming rate, leaving their cuffs too short while the body of a shirt, sweatshirt, or sweater still fits well. Transform the piece into a short-sleeved variation of the original (or in the case of a sweater, turn it into a sweater vest).

shoes for fast-growing feet

There is something positively uncanny in the way children's feet grow—often much faster than the rest of their bodies. So spending lots of money on shoes for kids is usually foolish. The most important factor is room to grow, so as soon as your child complains of lack of toe room (or you notice that your youngster is walking on the sides of his or her feet or doesn't want to wear a particular pair of shoes), buy new shoes. But never spend a lot.

discount superstores Stores such as Kmart or Wal-Mart often have a decent selection of inexpensive children's shoes.

AT RISK

www.nfpa.org/riskwatch.com

As a parent (or grandparent), your biggest concern is the safety of your children. And though we all try hard to anticipate and prevent injuries, it is hard to foresee some of the things that can hurt children. The National Fire Protection Association Web site, offers an injury prevention program focused on children ages 14 and younger. The program provides safety information about cars, burns, poisons, water recreation, bikes, choking, and more. Though the program is designed for use in schools, parents and other caregivers, as well as kids, can use the information. This Web site is well worth a visit.

discount department stores Stores such as Marshall's often offer upscale footwear for low prices, though the selection will not be consistent.

discount shoe stores Payless, ShoeSource, Famous Footwear and similar discount chain shoe stores offer a good selection at good prices, especially if you shop during their 2-for-1 or buy-2-get-1-free sales.

price clubs These stores usually don't carry much in children's shoes, but it's worth checking them out, especially during back-to-school season.

creating separate private spaces

If you have two children or teens sharing a room, you probably face demands for more privacy than your house can accommodate. Here are some low-cost suggestions for creating the illusion of separate spaces:

- An inexpensive freestanding bookcase, ranging from waist height to ceiling height, can be placed between the two beds. Or look for open metal bookcases (available at office liquidation stores), and bolt one side to the wall to prevent tip-overs. Then the kids can have a bit more privacy and a great place to store their stuff.
  - Use folding screens: Make simple frames from one-by-threes and join them with hinges (or you can use light interior doors). Cover them with fabric or wallpaper, or turn them into freestanding bulletin boards. Let each child decorate his or her side of the screen.
  - Take a tip from the old movie *It Happened One Night* and hang either a clothesline or a curtain rod between the beds and make a curtain (old sheets are excellent for this) to fall between the beds.
- If the kids are a bit older, go back to the '60s and hang a curtain of beads between the beds.

double-duty beds

When it's time to buy a big bed for your child, consider a captain's bed, which consists of a mattress set on a frame that has drawers under the bed. If space is limited or you have children sharing a room, this is a real space saver, providing storage and a sleep space in one piece.

- For older children or teens, a loft bed, with a storage or study area below, is also a space saver and can be made if you have some woodworking skills or if you can find a local carpenter or handyman to build one for you. If you have to purchase one, you'll find a wide variety of prices and styles available. Ikea and other stores carry them; usually they come as kits that you bolt together.

have a ball with baskets

You can find cheap baskets at garage sales, flea markets, thrift stores, and craft or fabric stores. When you see a basket for a good price, snap it up; they're amazingly useful. If you are using baskets in a child's room, you can spray-paint them in a color to match the room or to spiff them up.

- Keep a basket for kids' bath toys in the bathroom, tucked in a corner. Make a rule that after baths, all the toys must go into the basket; your bathroom will stay neater, the toys won't get lost, and if you're entertaining, you can hide the basket in a closet.

- Assign each family member a basket (painting each to identify which basket is whose). Place the baskets near the most-used outside door, on a shelf or in a closet, to serve as a handy mitten, hat, and scarf storage spot.

- Toy boxes are really unnecessary and can be dangerous to little fingers. Instead, purchase plastic laundry baskets or big plastic tubs (wait for a Dollar Day sale at your local superstore or drugstore) to hold toys. You can assign a different color tub to each child, which helps keep the toys straight and makes toy pickup faster and easier for the kids, too. If several young children or teens are sharing one bathroom, storing all their toiletries (especially as they get older) can be a logistical nightmare. Give the kids a basket apiece to store their own toiletries in, and have them keep the baskets in their closets or on a dresser.

pillow power

Instead of spending money on child-size chairs that are soon outgrown, try some penny-wise pillow ideas:

- Buy a large foam pillow form at a fabric store and make a simple cover for it. Floor pillows allow a child freedom to cuddle up wherever they wish, and they are safe and easy for children to move.

- Create a pile of old decorative pillows you have on hand or pick up at garage sales. Let your child make his or her own little nest for reading or listening to music.

sitting pretty

Don't spend money on booster seats for those youngsters who have outgrown their high chairs but can't quite reach the tabletop without a little added height. Take your old phone book (just the right height!) and wrap it in an old pillowcase. This trick is also great to remember when you're visiting friends or relatives who are not set up for small children.

- You don't actually need a high chair at all. An infant can be fed in a portable car seat set in its upright position or simply held in your lap. When the child can sit upright

Good Old Ways

When a child was no longer a toddler or baby, they graduated to adult furniture. Though it's tempting to indulge in cute but costly children's furniture. It's a waste of money. If you buy good quality wood furniture in a natural tone, you can soften the look of a child's room with pastel walls, child-geared wallpaper, bedclothes, and curtains in bright fabrics, and collections of stuffed toys or dolls. The furniture will grow with the child and serve him or her into adulthood. The soft furnishings can be changed over time to reflect the child's changing age and interests.

(about the same time you begin introducing solid foods), you can buy an inexpensive three-in-one booster seat ($15 to $20 at discount superstores). This seat, which has a seat belt and removable tray, can be strapped onto a sturdy kitchen or dining-room chair. The tray has a high position and a lower position to accommodate the child's size as he or she grows. When the child no longer needs the tray, it can be removed altogether, and the seat can be used as a booster seat. A bonus is that these seats usually fold up so they can be taken along on car trips with ease.

on their level

To put your child's clothes within reach, add a second, low rod in the closet. Screw an eye-hook into each end of a dowel. Use chains or strong cord to hang the dowel from the top rod, adjusting the height until the lower rod is at a good level for your child. Hang the current season's clothing on the dowel and out-of-season wear on the top rod.

off the wall

Another way to make it easier for children to hang up their clothing is to attach a small rack of hooks at their level in their bedroom to hang coats, hats, pajamas, bathrobes, and other things on. Or screw cup hooks within children's reach just inside a hallway coat closet, on the back of their bedroom door, and on the back of the bathroom door.

a case for books

One simple piece of furniture is absolutely essential to a child's room: a good sturdy bookcase. And it's not just for storing books! A bookcase is so versatile that it can accommodate your child's needs from toddlerhood through the high-school and college years. When you put a bookcase in a toddler's room, be sure to secure it to the wall so adventurous little ones who decide to climb it won't pull it down on top of themselves. A few things to store in bookcases (besides a wonderful supply of books):

art supplies Keep shoe boxes full of crayons, washable markers, glue sticks, stickers, watercolors and other washable paints, modeling clay or play dough, beads, buttons, bits of fabric, ribbon, cording, and so on, neatly stacked for quick and easy access.

stuffed animals Most kids have scores of these and storing them can be a challenge.

often-used toys Put larger or heavier toys, such as blocks and big trucks, on the lower shelves and smaller, lighter toys such as tea sets, dolls, and smaller models, on the upper shelves. This is not only more practical, but safer.

multi-piece sets Dollhouses with dolls, miniature car sets with roadways, train sets with tracks, little town pieces, and more can either be set on shelves ready for play or stored in clear plastic boxes stacked neatly in place.

video tapes, dvds, and games Store child-friendly movies where your child can see and reach them, and keep games they like close at hand, too.

clothing Store piles of T-shirts, shorts, underwear, and such out in the open. Or make it even easier and put together sets of shirts, pants, underwear, and socks so your child just has to reach in and take a whole outfit.

SAFE NET

Computers and the Internet are great teaching tools and fun to play with, but concerned parents need to monitor their children while they're using computers. There are filters, such as CYBERsitter, which look for key words, and software, such as Net Nanny, which limits the amount of time a child can stay online and monitors online activity, blocking specific chat and news groups and search engines. But your best bet is to be sure your child knows these safe surfing rules:

- Never give personal information over the computer.
- Never try to meet someone you've met only online.
- Never respond to offensive or dangerous communications.
- Surf only when a parent or other responsible adult is nearby (preferably in the same room).

www.niehs.nih.gov/kids
The National Institute of Environmental Health Sciences site

www.school.discovery.com
The Discovery Channel's site for teachers and students includes a section providing students with study tools

www.kidsmoney.org
The site provides sections with questions and answers about allowances and kids' money

www.nationalgeographic.com/kids
The National Geographic Society site for kids

http://dir.yahoo.com/education
Yahoo!'s huge education site

www.bigidea.com
VeggieTales info., games, music, etc.

www.pbskids.org
All the Public Broadcasting System favorites, from Sesame Street and Barney to Zoom, Zoboomafoo, Sagwa, Dragon Tales, Arthur, and more

www.scholastic.com
Great kids' publishing site, with areas for parents, kids, and teachers and featuring activities based on favorites such as Harry Potter, Clifford, the Magic School Bus, and more

free-time Fun

KEEPING KIDS HAPPY AND
ENTERTAINED REQUIRES A LITTLE
INGENUITY BUT NOT A LOT OF MONEY.

If we were to believe the commercials on television, we'd think that a child simply can't be happy without the latest toys and expensive video games. Actually, the gift kids love most is your undivided attention, which is free. And though toys and games are fun to have, they need not cost a fortune to be enjoyable. Time spent together as a family can be a treat for all and doesn't have to break the budget. It may require a stretch of the imagination on occasion.

dining in

Once in a while (not just on a significant occasion, such as a birthday), set your table as if company were coming and treat your children like honored guests. Serve their milk in special glasses, light candles, have music playing in the background, and encourage the family to dress up. That doesn't have to mean putting on uncomfortable fancy clothing: Everyone might wear dress-up clothes, pajamas and bathrobes, or Halloween costumes for fun. The whole occasion won't cost you a cent more than a regular meal.

penny-wise picnics

Impromptu picnic meals, out of doors or in, can made a simple meal much more fun and save you money in the bargain. Your kids will enjoy it, too.

● When you are spending the day with your kids at a park or an amusement center, avoid the added expense of buying food there; pack a lunch instead. Include a treat or two so your children will feel that the lunch is special. Save yogurt containers and margarine tubs to use as disposable containers for convenience.

● On a rainy or snowy day (or a real scorcher) when you're stuck inside, surprise your child with an indoor picnic. Spread a tablecloth or old bedspread on the floor, serve picnic foods on picnic plates, and, for added atmosphere, set houseplants around the cloth to create an outdoorsy atmosphere.

at the movies

Unfortunately, taking the whole family out to the local quadraplex for the latest hot movie can really break the bank, even if you look for bargain matinees. (The cost of popcorn alone can top the cost of matinee tickets!) Thankfully, with videos and DVDs, movie night can be enjoyed in the comfort of your own home. Movie rental stores usually have a "cheapie" night or two during the week, and libraries loan videos and DVDs free. Make loads of popcorn, turn out the lights, and curl up with a film that the whole family can enjoy.

cultural expression

You don't have to spend tons of money to introduce your children to art, music, dance, and theater. Just learn to use a few of these tricks:

museums Most museums have a free day, and many have free or extremely inexpensive programs for children. Call the museums in your area and find out what they offer.

theaters Legitimate theaters often charge a significantly reduced price for tickets during previews, which function as rehearsals before an audience. Some have free matinees, aimed at introducing children to live theater, or one performance during a run for which you pay what you can. The same is true for dance companies, symphony orchestras, and even opera companies. Call the performing arts companies in your area to ask for details.

college performances If you live in a town with a college or university, take advantage of student performances. College choirs, symphonies, theaters, dance troupes, and art galleries usually charge very little, and you'll have the thrill of seeing stars in the making. And older children often respond strongly to performers close to their age.

take me out to the ball game

Most kids love going to sporting events. But with the ever-growing price of tickets, taking the family out to a professional sports event can cost almost as much as going to the theater—more if you want to sit anywhere close to the action. Check for promotional days or nights to lower the cost somewhat. Or try the minor leagues or become a fan of your local college teams. The tickets are usually less expensive, the games are scrappier, the fans are more loyal, and the players aren't doing it for the paycheck—yet. Don't just try the men's teams; women's softball, basketball, and soccer are hot right now, as are women's volleyball, lacrosse, and swimming and diving events.

the cost of memberships

Children's museums, science centers, and nature centers generally offer family memberships and are usually a bargain. Though the initial outlay may make you pause, if you live in an area where most of a season (very cold winters or very hot summers) must be spent primarily indoors, a membership in a top notch museum or center will quickly pay for itself. Furthermore, members usually receive advance notice of special events, discounts on those events, and some special benefits including food or gift discounts. And if that's not enough, many museums and centers have reciprocal relationships with centers in other cities across the country, so you will have free access to those when on vacation.

66 Any kid who has two parents who are interested in him and has a houseful of books isn't poor. 99

Sam Levenson, humorist

class distinctions

Classes for enrichment or fun are terrific for kids. You can find excellent classes through most parks and recreation departments for all ages, and the cost is minimal. (The YMCA and YWCA also offer excellent classes, but the membership fees tend to be heftier.) Take a class in a foreign language, modern dance, pottery, step aerobics, basketball, improvisation, Chinese cooking, tumbling, feng shui, or anything else you or your children care to try. Even better, take a class with your child and get to know them better, too.

downloading fun

The family computer is becoming an institution, and with the drop in computer prices, it's become more commonplace to have more than one computer in a home. There are reams of fun sites for children and teens to visit (see pages 162–163 for some ideas), but you want to be the one in control.

- Consider having a family computer set up in a den, a family room, or a corner of the kitchen—some place where a parent is usually available. That way you can be present for help or questions and can subtly monitor the sites your children are investigating.
- If you have more than one child, make sure you set up a schedule for sharing time on the computer.
- It's a good idea to put a time limit on using the computer. Though computers can be interactive and educational, sitting is still sitting, and recent studies show that many children are not getting enough physical activity. But used well, a family computer can provide hours of fun and a learning experience to boot.

making music

It's wonderful when a child expresses an interest in taking music lessons, and it is definitely something to encourage, but you shouldn't invest in a musical instrument until you know this isn't just a passing fancy. Most music stores rent instruments, so call around for the best deal.

FINGER PAINTS

A rainy day (or scorcher) sanity saver!

1-1/4 cups all-purpose flour	1 cup water
3 tablespoons glycerin	assorted food colorings

- Combine the flour and water in a medium-size bowl. Divide the mixture equally among three small bowls.
- Stirring constantly, add 1 tablespoon of glycerin to each batch, along with the desired amount of food coloring. Make fresh as needed.

---

secondhand sounds

Buying a musical instrument secondhand can offer great savings, but be sure to ask a music teacher or someone who actually plays the instrument to check it out before you buy. And be wary of used guitars for sale on the cheap; they are often warped so badly that the strings are as much as an inch from the frets, making them nearly impossible to play.

the sound of your voice

Make tape recordings of your children's favorite stories, or record yourself telling about your childhood or special events or holidays. For extra fun, tape the family singing favorite songs. When you're going out for an evening or are away on a business trip, these tapes can provide a lot of comfort to young children, with very little investment of money. Further, have grandparents make some tapes to keep faraway grandchildren connected.

revisit your childhood

Young children love to hear stories about when their parents or grandparents were little. (Savor this time—it does not last.) Put together an album of your childhood and share those times with your own child or grandchild. Even better, go to a copy shop and make a copy of each photo on a piece of paper with space below. Type or write the story beneath the picture. Purchase an inexpensive album and make a book of your life for your child or grandchild to keep forever.

bowled over

Kids love to bowl, and bowling can be done inside or outside. You can make your own bowling set for practically nothing!

- For bowling pins, save 2-liter plastic soda bottles (or ask friends and family to save them for you) and wash them out. Use any sort of soft ball as the bowling ball. For very small children, leave the bottles empty and use large balls. As the children get older, fill the bottles with sand (to make them tougher to knock over) and use a smaller, heavier ball. If you want to make an impromptu bowling alley in your driveway, garage, or basement, just prop two long two-by-fours (or two-by-eights, if you have them) about 3 feet apart, with a board across one short end to stop the ball.

keeping keen

Many children have more toys than they know what to do with, so at least half the toys sit around collecting dust. Trick your youngsters into greeting each toy as if it were new by boxing up half to two-thirds of their toys and storing them out of sight. When boredom with the current group sets in, whisk out a hidden box and hide the "old" toys.

stacking up savings

stacking cups These are still one of the most popular early toys for tots. But you don't have to buy them. Look through your cupboards for old plastic cups to make your own set. Or check out garage sales for a set of measuring cups.

building blocks Another simple toy you can make is building blocks. Cut small pieces of wood from two-by-fours or four-by-fours (or ask a local lumber store to save them for you). Sand off any rough edges. Either stain to bring out the wood tones or paint in bright colors. (Make sure the stain or paint is safe for children; check the label, and if in doubt, ask for help at the paint-counter.)

long live board games

If you want to extend the life of your favorite family board games (particularly those played often and with enthusiasm by the youngest members of your household), coat the boards on both sides with shellac or polyurethane varnish right after you buy them. The games will last longer, and you can clean the boards easily with a damp cloth. Store the game pieces in plastic self-sealing bags.

chalk talk

● Wrap masking tape around the middle of chalk to keep it from breaking (and to keep hands cleaner).
● Coat chalk or charcoal drawings with hair spray to keep them from smudging.

revive that marker

Give new life to a dried-out marker by dipping the tip in an acetone-based nail polish remover. Replace the cap and let the marker sit for a couple of hours before using.

postcards

Kids love getting mail, and they especially love receiving picture postcards, which cost little to buy and mail. Ask relatives or friends who live out of town (it doesn't matter where the cards come from) to send a postcard for a child's special day (birthday, first tooth out, graduation from preschool, end of baseball season, dance recital). Then designate an area of the child's room as the card wall. Install inexpensive corkboard (to prevent tape or pin marks in the wall) on which the cards can be displayed.

be constructive: don't throw it out!

Save every paper towel roll, toilet paper roll, margarine tub, yogurt cup, plastic bottle cap, soda pop bottle, plastic jar, oatmeal or cornmeal container, coffee can (with plastic lid), and sturdy paper box. Let your kids build castles, forts, mountain ranges, and more with all these free construction materials.

animal cracker race

This is an ideal game for two to four younger children: Use an old checkerboard (or even better make your own). Each child gets one animal cracker. Designate one corner square as the Start position and place hurdles (a chocolate kiss or a marshmallow) on random squares around the edge of the board. Each child rolls a die once, then moves his or her cracker the number of squares indicated by the die. If a player's animal cracker lands on a hurdle, the player must go back two squares—but gets to eat the hurdle! The first animal cracker to make it all around the edge of the board wins. And the winner eats his or her cracker!

story sack

On days when the weather keeps you inside, when you're on a long car trip, or during evenings in hotels, this can be a fun pastime for everyone in the family: Fill a bag with pictures cut from old magazines. Take turns with your children picking out images and making up stories about them. Write out or tape-record the tales you create.

stir crazy

Kids love to help in the kitchen, especially if they get to eat what they make. Assign fun activities they can tackle with their bare hands, such as kneading bread dough or cutting out cookies. Decorating a sheet cake or a batch of sugar

---

PAPIER-MÂCHÉ

An old-fashioned favorite for making piñatas or gifts.

1 cup flour   2/3 cup water
newspaper strips (about 1-1/2 inches wide)

● Combine the flour and water in a medium-size bowl. Stir until it is the consistency of thick glue. If a thicker mixture is desired, add more flour.

● Dip each strip separately in the paste and gently pull it through your fingers to remove any excess paste. Then apply the strip to the surface you want to cover. (Clay, cartons, bottles, or other disposable containers make a good base; if you want to make a piñata, cover a blown-up balloon.) Repeat until the object is completely covered. Let dry.

● When the surface is dry, decorate with poster paint. For a longer-lasting and harder surface, coat with shellac after the paint dries.

cookies is another favorite: Supply the youngsters with an array of sprinkles, chocolate bits, jelly beans, nuts, or fresh berries, and tell them to be creative. Let them eat their masterpieces when they are done.

hold it!

- Make your own crayon or pen holder: Take a foot-long scrap piece of a two-by-four and drill 1/2-inch–diameter holes in a line down the 2-inch side, spaced about 1/2 inch apart. If desired, paint the holder in a bright color.
- Use an old toothbrush cup with holes to hold pens, pencils, markers, and scissors (with the points down) handy for your little artist.

stickers savings

Everyone gets more junk mail than they'd like to, and most of it goes right into the trash. But before you throw away the ads, look through the envelopes. You may find free stickers (showing thumbnail-size magazine or CD covers, for example) that your kids will enjoy pasting on their creations.

greening of the thumbs

Another activity children usually like to help with, if encouraged, is gardening. If you have the space, give your children their own plots on which to grow whatever they fancy: tomatoes, watermelons, sunflowers. Teach them how to prepare the soil, plant the seeds, and care for their plants. If space is limited, buy a window box planter or several small pots and let them learn container gardening.

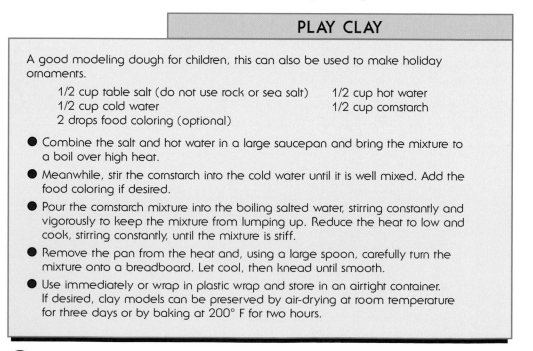

PLAY CLAY

A good modeling dough for children, this can also be used to make holiday ornaments.

1/2 cup table salt (do not use rock or sea salt)   1/2 cup hot water
1/2 cup cold water   1/2 cup cornstarch
2 drops food coloring (optional)

- Combine the salt and hot water in a large saucepan and bring the mixture to a boil over high heat.
- Meanwhile, stir the cornstarch into the cold water until it is well mixed. Add the food coloring if desired.
- Pour the cornstarch mixture into the boiling salted water, stirring constantly and vigorously to keep the mixture from lumping up. Reduce the heat to low and cook, stirring constantly, until the mixture is stiff.
- Remove the pan from the heat and, using a large spoon, carefully turn the mixture onto a breadboard. Let cool, then knead until smooth.
- Use immediately or wrap in plastic wrap and store in an airtight container. If desired, clay models can be preserved by air-drying at room temperature for three days or by baking at 200° F for two hours.

oldies are still goodies

In this day of computer games and high-tech toys, we tend to forget the good old games we played as children. Since there is national concern about the rise in childhood obesity and lack of physical exercise, there is even more reason to revive these two classic games—which are usually played outdoors with minimal equipment:

hopscotch This can be played with others or against yourself. Use a piece of chalk to draw a hopscotch board on a sidewalk, driveway, or patio. The board usually has 9 squares with squares 4 and 5 and squares 7 and 8 paired. To make a marker, link together several paper clips or safety pins into a circle chain.

- **game one** Standing in front of square 1, toss the marker onto it. Hop on one foot into square 1, pick up your marker and hop back to the start. Next toss the marker to square 2, hop onto square 1, then onto square 2, pick up your marker, and return the same way. Repeat until you reach square 9; then hop all the way back to the beginning. If your marker misses the square or is touching any of the lines, if you put down your second foot, or if your foot touches any of the lines, your turn is over. The first player who makes a complete trip up and down the board is the winner.

- **game two** Toss your marker onto square 1. Hop over square 1 into square 2, then up the board, landing on square 9 on one foot, turning on the same foot, and going back down the board. When you arrive back at square 2, bend over, pick up your marker, hop on square 1, then home. Next time, toss the marker into square 2 and repeat. Continue as for Game One, moving up and down the board, hopping over the squares with markers. The first one to make it back, wins. The same rules for ending a turn apply.

dodgeball This is a game for a group. Divide them into two teams of equal numbers. Mark a playing area about 30 feet long and wide enough to let all the players stand side by side. Divide the area in half by chalking across its width. One team takes one half of the court; the other team takes the remaining half. One player has the ball and tries to throw it across the center line to hit an opposing team member. Any player hit by the ball is out and must leave the court. Players try to dodge the ball, but they must not go outside the bounds of court or touch the boundry lines. If you hit someone, your team gets to go again; if you throw and miss, it's their turn. The team that strikes out all their opponents first, wins.

Cent-sational Special Occasions

- penny-wise parties
- the well-planned wedding
- happy homemade holidays
- all good gifts

Your buddy, Rob, dropped you a thank you note for the birthday party you threw him—great eats, best beer ever, and everyone had a blast! He's just worried that it cost you a bundle. Aunt Mary called to rave about that spectacular wedding you helped Cousin Betty to plan—how perfect the dress, the setting, and the food were. How did you manage to stay on budget? Your sister came to hug you for the wonderful Thanksgiving you hosted—the dinner was divine and the decorations were incredible! Did you spend a fortune? You smile; you know the secret to great entertaining, and it has almost nothing to do with money. For Rob's party, each guest contributed their favorite ethnic dish, the beer was home brewed, and the "this is your life" game kept everyone in stitches. Betty's wedding was held in a botanical garden using a member's discount and her dress was made by a local costume designer, which allowed you to splurge a little on the food. And Thanksgiving? Seasonal foods make for a cost-effective yet scrumptious feast, and last year a fabric store yielded day-after decorations at 75 percent off. Lots of money for great entertaining?

Don't be ridiculous!

penny-wise
Parties

AS ANY SUCCESSFUL HOSTESS
WILL TELL YOU, THROWING A MEMORABLE PARTY
ISN'T ABOUT SPENDING GOBS OF MONEY.

A successful party involves creativity, a knowledge of what your guests will enjoy, and an enthusiastic spirit. Although a gourmet feast can be the focus of the event, it doesn't have to be. Similarly, while some folks enjoy an open bar, we've yet to hear anyone tout that as the reason a party succeeded. The best parties are just fun to be at. The conversation is lively, the mood is effervescent, and the sense of welcome and well being goes home with you.

cost-effective entertaining

One way to keep a lid on costs is to think of parties as either theme- or event-based. Your theme can be very simple—such as a TGIF (Thank God It's Friday) or board-game night—or as elaborate as an ethnic feast or karaoke sing-along. Event-based parties are built around a special occasion, from the Superbowl or Kentucky Derby to an anniversary or birthday. Building your menu and decorations around a theme or specific event will help you make a big splash for less money. Why? Because the choices of food and décor will be clearer allowing you to tailor the party for effect, not expense.

where to shop?

Big party stores are all over the place and you can find great stuff there for a good price. But we have found that buying party supplies is less costly if you purchase them over a period of time whenever you see a sale. Having a stock of party stuff on hand will spare you from last-minute shopping—which tends to add up. Also, don't assume that big party stores have the best selection or the best prices. Sometimes little mom-and-pop stores offer more variety and cheaper prices in order to keep your business.

- Check out drug stores for paper plates, cups, balloons and party favors.
- Discount superstores have party aisles, but you'll also find sale items in the aisles where toys, candy, cookies, sodas, and juices are sold.
- Craft and fabric stores often have all sorts of party favor ideas. They also can have terrific sales, especially if you hit them around the holiday season.

candles in the night

Buy candles whenever you see them on sale and keep them handy for entertaining. A good selection of taper-style and column candles can be used to create a warm or elegant party atmosphere with a minimum of fuss. Don't forget votive candles. They are also a beautiful and versatile party accent.

- Greet your guests in style with luminaria lining your front walkway. You can make these traditional Mexican

Christmas candles yourself. Simply pour a thick layer of sand inside white lunch-size paper bags and place a tea lights or votive candles in the sand of each bag. When lighted from within, the lunch-bag candles produce a warm and beautiful glow. Instead of bags, you can recycle 16-ounce cans and use a tin punch to make designs on the sides for the light to shine through.

- Place small scented votive candles in holders in each powder room. This will make the room smell nice and the light will make it easier for your guests to find the bathroom.
- For a more formal atmosphere, use matching candlestick holders or candelabras in pairs on the dining room table or fireplace mantel.
- For an eye-catching, informal look use single candlestick holders of different shapes and sizes set in groups.
- Column candles are effective as a single accent or grouped together, especially if they vary in height.
- Clean out your fireplace and place a collection of different-sized column candles during warmer months to produce a warm inviting look without the heat.

flameless enchantment

Start snapping up strings of indoor/outdoor Christmas lights during post-holiday sales. These tiny lights, whether colored or white, add instant enchantment to any party scene, indoor or out. You can use them again and again, and they can be left unattended—unlike candles. Use them to line your walkway or front door, to outline a gazebo or fence, and string them in trees.

frugal flowers

Of course, serious penny pinchers grow their own cutting flowers so that they never have to spend money on them. But even those of us who depend on store-bought blossoms can find ways to keep costs down.

- Only buy flowers in season—the more exotic the bloom, the higher the cost.
- Buy flowers in bunches; pre-made flower arrangements tend to cost more and limit your options.
- Buy just a few flowers and fill in with greens, preferably from your own garden (herbs such as rosemary or lavender are lovely to use in arrangements).
- Fresh fruit and vegetables, especially different varieties of hard squash and nuts, can be pulled together for a distinctive and unique centerpiece.

making arrangements

Here are a few hints to help you create your own flower arrangements with professional results:

66 My idea of hell is a very large party in a cold room where everybody has to play hockey properly. **99**

Stella Gibbons,
British novelist

● Instead of using floral foam (that spongy green stuff florists use), put a bunch of glass marbles into the bottom of a clear vase to hold flower stems in place.

● To hold arrangements of long-stemmed flowers in place, make a crisscross pattern of cellophane tape just inside and across the opening of a vase. Insert the flower stems into the spaces between the tape.

● Dig out your old plastic hair rollers (or pick them up for pennies at a garage sale). Bind several together side by side with a large rubber band and stand them on end in the bottom of an opaque vase. Slip one or more stems into each roller to hold the stems upright.

hold it!

Your don't have to use a standard vase to hold flowers. If you use your imagination, you can liven up your flower arrangements. Here are some suggestions:

● If you're throwing a baby shower, have friends who already have babies save their old baby-food jars for you. Put one jar at each place setting with a tiny bouquet of violets, sweet william, lily of the valley, and, of course, baby's breath.

● Pick up small and unusual old bottles at junk or antique stores, flea markets, garage sales, or thrift stores—they make eye-catching vases. Set them at each place at a sit-down dinner. Place a blossom or two in each bottle, plus a place card. Or use them to tuck mini-bouquets throughout the house, including the bathroom.

● Sunflowers are easy to grow and make a dramatic statement when used in arrangements—the only problem can be finding a vase to accommodate them. Try using an old milk pail, umbrella stand, or wrap a plastic waste can with burlap and tie the burlap in place with some raffia.

● Line a pretty basket with plastic or find an old plastic container or bucket and trim it to fit inside the basket. Arrange daisies, asters or mums in the basket.

● Hunt through thrift stores, junk shops or flea markets for old cookie, mason, canning, or apothecary jars—all make wonderful containers for flowers.

balloon bouquets

Few things say "party" quite so definitively as balloons. Buy latex balloons in bulk and rent a helium tank from a party store. Filling your own balloons is usually less expensive than buying an already filled bouquet. Buy a big roll of curling ribbon and cut it into long pieces. Tie them to each balloon, then slightly curl the ribbon, making sure the ribbons reach from the balloon at least halfway down to the floor. Then just let them float around the room—instant party!

note Balloons and candles don't make a good combination—for obvious reasons.

- For the Fourth of July: red, white, and blue balloons!
- For a sporting event: balloons in the team colors.
- For a baby shower: pink and blue, naturally.
- For New Year's Eve: black and white balloons decorated with silver ribbons.
- For graduation: the school colors.
- For a birthday: the favorite color (or colors) of the birthday boy or birthday girl.

food for a frugal feast

This is where a price club can save your budget! They offer excellent selections of meat, poultry, fish, vegetables, fruit, wine, beer, hard liquor, breads, crackers, chips, juices, and sodas—everything you could possibly want in bulk and at an excellent price! Plus, you'll find big boxes of frozen appetizers if time is short, and even fresh dips, sauces, sushi, cheese, and enormous desserts (including sheet cakes for special occasions that can be decorated to order). Depending on your budget, you can pick up everything for a gourmet spread or a low-cost blowout and still come out on top financially. Here are a couple of other ways to save money on food:

- If you want to prepare a formal, sit-down meal without breaking the budget, select one course as the star and spend extra time and money on that. Many gourmet dishes actually don't require expensive ingredients—you just have to be able to cook well.
- A big piece of meat, such as a turkey, boneless ham, or roast can feed a crowd easily and fairly economically. Add rice or pasta, vegetables, salad, bread, and dessert (cookies, a sheet cake, fresh fruit with chocolate dipping sauce) for a delicious menu.

eat, drink, and be merry

Planning a party around a particular food or beverage is another easy and low-cost party idea.

wine and dine If you have friends who really appreciate wine, plan a menu, then ask each guest to bring a bottle of wine for each course. Make sure they bring a description of the wine's characteristics. Set a limit on the amount spent on each bottle—wine doesn't need to be expensive to be good.

bring on the brew With the explosion of microbreweries, the variety of beer available is both delicious and exciting. Host a beer-tasting party and invite your friends to bring a six-pack of their favorite stout, pale ale, amber ale, or bitter. Mexican, Indian, and Chinese food are all enhanced by beer. A selection of appetizers from any or all of these cuisines would be fabulous and relatively cheap to make or buy.

FINDING PARTY SUPPLIES ONLINE

www.mypartypal.com
or 1-800-533-7956

There are a number of party supply sites on the Web. Type the words "party" and "discount" in your search engine to locate them. One of the more interesting sites we found was www.mypartypal.com. It has a wide assortment of party goods for adults and children. For example, a Blues Clues party set for eight children (invitations, plates, tableware, cloth, crepe paper streamers, latex balloons, and so on) cost $22.95 at mypartypal.com—that's $3 to $5 cheaper than two other sites that we checked.

The biggest mistake you can make is to put off getting ready for a party until the last minute. Planning ahead lets you keep costs under control—and frees you up to enjoy the party.

3-4 WEEKS AHEAD

- Decide on theme or event.
- Make guest list.
- Set budget.
- Plan menu.
- Mail, e-mail, or phone invitations.

2 WEEKS AHEAD

- Select recipes.
- Check pantry and make shopping list.
- Shop for nonperishables and beverages.
- Make food preparation schedule.
- Start making dishes that can be frozen.

1 WEEK AHEAD

- Plan furniture arrangement.
- Arrange for extra seating if needed.
- Plan decorating scheme and shop for decorations.
- Plan seating arrangement if needed.
- Select music and set up sound system.
- Check tableware and linens.

easy, inexpensive party ideas

All you need is a little imagination to throw a party that's a lot of fun without costing an arm and a leg. Try these ideas:

movie night Let a movie shape the menu: serve fried chicken, collard greens, grits, and iced tea with *Gone With the Wind;* deep-dish Chicago-style pizza with *The Untouchables;* a selection of German or Austrian pastries with *The Sound of Music;* or a vat of Texas-style chili, buttermilk biscuits, and beer with *My Darling Clementine.* Ask your guests to come dressed in costumes for fun.

game night Have a selection of board games that your guests can play in teams. Serve a selection of finger foods, such as mini pizzas, chicken satay, empanadas, stuffed mushrooms, and pot stickers.

so you wanna be a star Rent a karaoke machine and let your friends do their best Elvis Presley, Aretha Franklin, or Frank Sinatra impersonation (the sky's the limit in terms of music). Just warn your neighbors first, or invite them. Serve champagne punch and canapés, and ask everyone to dress in their best "star" duds.

ethnic potluck Ask each guest to bring a dish from a particular country or region such as Greece, Denmark, New England, or the Florida Keys. The host and hostess provide beverages, tableware and linens. Check out CDs of appropriate music and ask a travel agency or the tourist board for posters or brochures to use in decorating.

tgif pajama party Invite your friends to wear PJs or their favorite lounging outfit. Serve fun comfort food, like roast chicken and mashed potatoes, tomato soup, grilled cheese sandwiches, or big messy tacos. And make sure to set a "no talk about work" rule.

the low-cost lowdown on kid's parties

Let's face it—kid's birthday parties have gotten out of hand. How did we become convinced that unless we rent an inflated castle to jump in or have a marionette show and invite everyone we've ever met, little Jimmy or Susie will end up in therapy? Truth is, most children are happy just to have their parents completely focused on them for their special day. Big-ticket spending is unnecessary. When planning your child's party, ask him (or her) what he wants (it may surprise you), keep your child involved in the planning, and remember that imagination counts for much more than dollars spent.

- Keep it short—a two hour party is fine for children under five. For older kids, you can add an extra hour.
- Serve foods that children like: chicken nuggets, hot dogs, squares of cheese, and pizza are always a big hit. Children tend to like "little" food just their size, so make a hit by cutting everything small.

- Plan at least four more games or activities than you think you'll need. If one game doesn't catch the children's attention, switch gears quickly.
- When choosing party favors, think like a child. Things you can play with or sweets usually go over well. Most children are delighted if they get to take home a balloon.
- Unless the children are very small, don't invite parents. The more adults who stay, the less the focus will stay on the birthday child. Do, however, be sure to have enough adult help. If you're having a pool party, hire a licensed lifeguard whose only job is to watch over the children while they are swimming.
- The more of a child's birthday party you can create yourself, the happier you and your child will be. As your child gets older he or she may want you to do less yourself, but you still don't have to go overboard. You never should have to take out a second mortgage to pay for a kid's party.

kid-friendly party ideas

Here's some approaches to try for children's parties:

wild west Have children play pin the tail on the donkey, toss clothespins in a cowboy hat, and try to rope the rocking horse. Introduce children to "partner, may I?" and send them on a "steer hunt" with a cow-shaped piñata. Play classic cowboy music to set the mood. Serve wagon-wheel macaroni and cheese, lil' doggies (cocktail franks), and prairie grass salad (shredded iceberg lettuce). Party favors could be plastic cowboys and farm animals tied up in a red bandana.

desert island Fill a small wading pool with sand and bury "treasures" there for children to find. Let them dive for "pearls" (small white rocks), enjoy a round of coconut "bowling," and send them on a "shark hunt" (shark piñata). Play calypso music, hang bunches of bananas in your trees for the kids to pick, quench thirst with a tropical punch, and serve mini kabobs of pineapple and ham. Party favors could be a small bag of chocolate gold foil coins (treasure) in a cardboard box (treasure chest) the children decorate themselves.

camp birthday If your planning a party for older children, set up tents in your backyard for an outdoor sleep over. Have the children go on a scavenger nature hunt, toss rope rings over cans of beans, and play "black bear scare" (one person is the bear, the rest hide and the bear tries to catch them). Then set up an outdoor fire pit and tell scary stories. Roast hot dogs and have the whole crew work together to make a s'more "cake." Instead of making each s'more sandwich separately, layer graham crackers, chocolate bars, and melted marshmallows into the shape of a cake. For party favors consider getting an inexpensive paperback book about a camping mystery or adventure suitable for their age level.

3-4 DAYS AHEAD
- Make and store extra ice.
- Polish or clean serving pieces, including silver if necessary.
- Start decorating.

DAY BEFORE
- Arrange furniture, set up extra tables and chairs if needed.
- Clean house thoroughly.
- Shop for perishable foods.
- Prepare food as much as possible (chopping, measuring, and such).

PARTY DAY
- Finish decorating (set out fresh flowers).
- Set tables or arrange buffet table.
- Prepare coat and purse storage.
- Give house last once over.
- Finish preparing and arranging food.
- Set up bar.

ONE HOUR TO PARTY
- Open red wine.
- Stock bar with water, ice, sliced lemons and limes.
- Set out appetizers or finger foods.

30 MINUTES TO PARTY
- Get yourself ready.
- Start the music, sit down and relax until your guests arrive.

PARTY TIME

ENJOY!

spinach-feta triangles

These tasty triangles can be made ahead through step 3, then refrigerated for up to 24 hours. To refrigerate, arrange the triangles in a single layer on a wax paper- or plastic wrap-lined baking sheet so they are not touching. Cover with additional wrap and damp paper towels.

① Preheat the oven to 350° F. In a 10-inch skillet over moderate heat, sauté 1 small finely chopped yellow onion in 2 teaspoons of butter or margarine until onion is translucent, about 3 to 5 minutes. Add 1(10-ounce) package of thawed and squeezed-dry frozen spinach and cook for 2 minutes more. Stir in 1 tablespoon snipped fresh dill (or 1/4 teaspoon crumbled dried dill). Transfer mixture to a large bowl, stir in 1/2 cup (2 ounces) of feta cheese, and then 1 lightly beaten egg.

② Lay 1 sheet of thawed frozen phyllo pastry (from a 17-1/2-ounce package) on a work surface. Melt 4 tablespoons of butter, and brush the sheet with some of the butter. Top with a second sheet of pastry, brush with butter, then top with a third pastry sheet and brush with butter again. Using a sharp knife (and ruler if desired), cut the stack lengthwise into six (1-3/4-inch-wide) strips. Cut the sheets in half vertically, so that there are 12 half strips.

③ Place 1/2 teaspoon of the spinach filling at the end of each half strip. Fold the end of each strip diagonally over the filling to form a triangle. Continue folding diagonally along the entire strip, alternating directions as though you were folding a flag. When you make the last fold, you should have a triangular package.

④ Place filled triangles on a parchment-lined baking sheet and bake until they are golden brown, about 25 minutes.
MAKES 24 TRIANGLES.

stuffed mushroom puffs

① Stem 2 pounds of button mushrooms and wipe the caps clean. Chop the stems and set them aside. Roast the mushroom caps in a preheated 450° F oven, uncovered, for about 15 minutes; if desired, toss the mushroom caps with a little olive oil before roasting.

② Meanwhile, in a 10-inch nonstick skillet, heat 1 tablespoon olive oil over moderate heat, add 1/2 cup of finely chopped red onion and 1 minced clove garlic, and sauté the mixture for 2 minutes. Stir in the chopped mushroom stems and cook until most of the liquid has evaporated, for about 5 minutes more. Remove the pan from the heat. Stir in 1/4 cup of finely chopped toasted pecans or hazelnuts, 2 tablespoons each grated Parmesan cheese and chopped parsley, and 1/4 teaspoon each salt and pepper. Let the mixture cool for 2 or 3 minutes, then fold in 1 lightly beaten egg white.

③ Spoon a little mixture into each roasted mushroom cap. Bake, uncovered, at 450° F until they are puffed and lightly browned, about 10 to 12 minutes.
MAKES 6 SERVINGS.

puff pastry twists

Preheat the oven to 400° F. In a small bowl, combine 1/2 cup grated Parmesan cheese and 1/4 teaspoon cayenne pepper. Place 1 sheet (9-1/2" x 9-1/4" x 1/8") of thawed frozen puff pastry on a work surface. Brush lightly with a wash of 1 egg yolk beaten with 1 tablespoon of water. Sprinkle the Parmesan mixture over the pastry and lightly press in place. Using a sharp knife, cut the pastry lengthwise into 15 strips. Slide each strip onto an ungreased baking sheet and refrigerate for 5 minutes. Holding each strip at either end, twist the strips. Return to the refrigerator for 5 minutes more. Bake the strips in the preheated oven until they are nicely browned, about 12 to 15 minutes. MAKES 15 TWISTS.

chili garlic variation Substitute 1 tablespoon of chili powder mixed with 1 tablespoon very finely minced garlic for the Parmesan mixture.

curry twists Substitute 1 to 2 tablespoons of curry powder with 1/2 teaspoon salt for the mixture.

sesame twists Substitute 1 tablespoon sesame seeds and 1 teaspoon Italian herb mix for the Parmesan mixture.

tex-mex nachos

To make these tasty, but not spicy, treats, all you need are a pint of cherry tomatoes, an onion, some olive oil, a bag of tortilla chips, a bunch of scallions, and a package of shredded Mexican cheese-blend. To make them more healthful, get low-fat baked chips and reduced fat cheese.

① Preheat the oven to 450° F. Slice the cherry tomatoes into quarters and cut the quarters in half. Peel and chop one medium onion, and sauté it in 1 tablespoon of olive oil over medium heat until soft, about 5 minutes. Stir in tomatoes and remove from heat.

② Slice up the scallions. Arrange 42 large tortilla chips in a single layer on two baking sheets. Top the chips with the vegetable mixture and scallions. Sprinkle with shredded cheese.

six quick and easy appetizers

canapés
Cut circles of bread. Spread with mayonnaise, mustard, or cream cheese. Add thin slices of cucumber, ham, or smoked salmon, and top with a sprig of dill, pimento, or a few capers.

stuffed cherry tomatoes
Slice red or yellow cherry tomatoes in half and scoop out the pulp. Fill each with guacamole, tuna salad, whipped cream cheese blended with fresh chopped cilantro or parsley, or finely shredded mozzarella with fresh chopped basil.

bruschetta
Slice a loaf of Italian bread. Brush a little olive oil over each slice, top with a slice of Italian tomato, some chopped fresh basil, and dot with a little mozzarella cheese. Bake the slices in a single layer at 350° F for 10 minutes or until the cheese is melted.

melon and prosciutto
Wrap a thin slice of prosciutto or smoked ham around a piece of cantaloupe or honeydew melon. Secure with toothpick.

asparagus wraps
Wrap prosciutto or ham around asparagus stalks and secure with toothpick.

seasoned nuts
Sauté a variety of nuts, such as almonds, pecans, walnuts, or cashews in a few tablespoons of butter or margarine until golden brown. Toss with seasoned salt, chili powder, curry powder, or any seasoning blend.

③ Bake until cheese melts, 4 to 5 minutes. Serve hot. MAKES 42 NIBBLES.

stuffed hard-boiled eggs

Boil 12 eggs until hard; shell and cut them in half. Scoop our the yolks and place them in a sieve over a medium-sized bowl. Press the yolks through the sieve with the back of a spoon. Add 1/2 cup of mayonnaise, 3 tablespoons of chopped capers, 3 tablespoons snipped fresh dill or 1-1/2 teaspoons crumbled dried dill, and 1/2 teaspoon ground white pepper. Stir with a fork to thoroughly combine all the ingredients; add salt to taste. Spoon or pipe with a pastry bag 1 tablespoon of the yolk mixture into each egg half. If desired, garnish each egg half with additional capers and dill sprigs.
MAKES 24 EGG HALVES.

deviled eggs Substitute 4 teaspoons each of yellow mustard and white wine vinegar for the capers and dill in yolk mixture. Add 1 teaspoon each salt and sugar and increase white pepper to 1 teaspoon. Add 1/2 cup finely chopped celery.

curried eggs Substitute 4 teaspoons curry powder and 3 tablespoons chopped chutney for the capers and dill.

chili eggs Substitute 4 teaspoons chili powder and 1 teaspoon ground cumin for the capers and dill.

spicy eggs Substitute 1/4 cup prepared horseradish and 2 tablespoons chopped parsley for the capers and dill.

chicken wings

Because of the popularity of dishes like this, wings are not as cheap as they once were, but you can still find them on sale in large quantities—perfect for a party.

① Remove the wing tips from 4-1/2 pounds of chicken wings; save the tips to make stock. Preheat the oven to 450° F.

Arrange the wings in a single layer, not touching, on 2 lightly greased baking sheets. In a small bowl, stir together 1 teaspoon salt, 1 teaspoon black pepper, and 1/2 teaspoon cayenne pepper. Sprinkle the mixture over the wings. Bake the wings in the preheated oven until they are crisp and brown, about 30 minutes.

② Meanwhile, combine 4 ounces of crumbled blue cheese, 1-1/3 cup reduced-fat sour cream and 1 teaspoon of Worcestershire sauce in a food processor or blender and pulse until smooth.

③ In a large bowl, stir together 1/2 cup hot red or green pepper sauce and 4 tablespoons of olive oil. Add the baked wings and toss to coat the wings completely. Arrange the wings on a platter and serve the blue-cheese sauce in a bowl for dipping. MAKES 8 SERVINGS.

basic sugar syrup

This keep-on-hand wonder is perfect for adding sweetness to chilled tea, citrus drinks, or punches because the sugar is already dissolved.

Combine 2 cups of sugar and 2-1/2 cups of water in a small, heavy-bottomed saucepan. Cook over moderate heat, stirring often, until the mixture comes to a boil and the sugar is completely dissolved. Remove the pan from the heat, cover and let sit for 1 to 2 minutes to allow any remaining crystals to dissolve. Pour the sugar syrup into a 1-quart jar with a tightly fitting lid and store in the refrigerator. MAKES 3 CUPS.

ideal iced tea

Bring 4 cups of water to a boil in a large saucepan or kettle. Rinse a large ceramic teapot with boiling water and place 12 regular-size tea bags (or 4 tablespoons of loose tea leaves) in the pot. Slowly pour in the boiling water. Cover the teapot and let steep for 3 to 5 minutes. Stir the tea once, then pour into a large pitcher, discarding the bags. Add 4 cups of cold water and as much sugar syrup as desired to sweeten the tea. Pour into individual glasses over ice cubes and garnish with mint sprigs or lemon slices. MAKES 8 SERVINGS.

cranberry iced tea Use 24 tea bags and add 4 cups of chilled cranberry juice cocktail instead of water. Garnish with frozen cranberries, strawberries, or slices of lime.

lemon squash

Cut 8 (3-inch) strips of lemon zest into thin slices. Place the zest slices in a large pitcher and add 2 cups of fresh lemon juice. Add sugar syrup (about 1 cup) to the desired sweetness and stir well. Just before serving, add 6 cups of chilled club soda, seltzer, or sparkling water. Pour into individual glasses over ice cubes, straining out the zest slices. Garnish with lemon slices. MAKES 8 SERVINGS.

lime squash Substitute lime zest and juice for the lemon and garnish with lime slices or fresh strawberries.

triple citrus squash Substitute four (3-inch) strips each of grapefruit, lemon, and orange zest and 2/3 cup each of grapefruit, lemon, and orange juice for the lemon alone. Use 2/3 cup of sugar syrup. Garnish with slices of each fruit.

classic sangria

In a large pitcher, combine 8 cups of a fruity red wine (burgundy, for example), 1 to 2 cups of brandy, Cointreau, Cassis, or other fruit-flavored liqueur, and 6 to 8 tablespoons of lemon juice. Stir, then add about 1 cup of sugar syrup to the desired sweetness. Add orange and lemon slices, pitted cherries, or pineapple rings. Chill well before serving. MAKES 12 SERVINGS.

white sangria Substitute dry white wine (chablis, for example) for the red and Grand Marnier or other orange-flavored liqueur for the brandy. Stir in 4 cups of lemon-lime soda. MAKES 16 SERVINGS.

sparkling fruit bowl

In a large, nonreactive saucepan or Dutch oven, combine a (10-ounce) package each of frozen raspberries and strawberries, 6 cups of water, 1-1/2 cups of sugar, 10 whole cloves, 1/2 teaspoon ground cardamom, six (3- x 1/2-inch) strips orange zest, and 1 split vanilla bean. Bring the mixture to a boil over medium-high heat; reduce the heat and simmer, uncovered, stirring occasionally, for about 10 minutes. Strain the mixture through a fine sieve and discard the solids. Cool the mixture to room temperature, then stir in 2 cups of orange juice and chill. Just before serving, stir in 2 cups of chilled club soda, seltzer, or sparkling water. Serve over ice, garnished as desired. MAKES 10 SERVINGS.

raspberry spritzers In a large pitcher, combine 3 cups of chilled dry white wine, 1-1/2 cups of chilled cran-raspberry juice, and 1-1/2 cups of chilled raspberry flavored sparkling water. Serve as is or over ice, garnished with mint leaves, cranberries, or raspberries.
MAKES 8 SERVINGS.

the well-planned
Wedding

AH, WEDDINGS—THE ROMANCE
THE EXCITEMENT, THE COST!

Somewhere along the line, we became convinced that the act of joining two people in matrimony must involve a costly and lavish production of Hollywood-esque proportions. In truth, some of the most touching, lovely, and memorable weddings are simple, sweet, and actually afford-able. The trick is to set a budget and stick to it.

a basic budget

There was a time when the bride's parents were expected to pay for the entire wedding bill. Not anymore. These days, the bride's family, groom's family, and the couple often do a three-way split. Sometimes each family will pay for a partic-ular aspect of the wedding. If the couple is fairly established financially, they may decide to pay for the entire wedding themselves. However you decide to manage your wedding costs, plan for the following:

- About half of the entire budget ends up going toward the reception, including location rental, food, and drink.
- Roughly ten percent will be spent on clothing for the bride and groom, including rentals.
- About ten percent will go toward invitations, special transportation to and from the reception for the bridal party, and various fees, such as those for the clergy.
- The final 30 percent is divided between music and enter-tainment, photography (or videography), flowers, and other decorations.
- Happily, there are ways to save in each of these areas and still have a glorious wedding.

prudent prioritization

- First, decide how much you want to spend on the entire wedding. If the families are splitting the costs, get together and discuss how much each feels comfortable with.
- Next, make a list of the things you'd like to include in the wedding from the biggest to smallest detail.
- Now, the hard part: Prioritize the list, from most impor-tant to least. This will help keep you on budget. Lower priority items that don't fit the budget can be adapted or approached more creatively. For example, if superb food is important to the bride and groom, finding a great cater-er should be given the highest consideration. To offset food costs, you can economize on transportation to and from the reception by decorating cars instead of renting limousines. It's crucial for the bride and groom to agree on a list of priorities. If each family supports the couple's choices, the wedding will be a happier event.

the guest list

The one thing that will determine how costly your wedding will be is the guest list. It is not necessary to invite everyone you or your family has ever known. A bigger crowd doesn't make the day any more memorable. In fact, the more people that come, the harder it will be for the bride and groom to visit them all. First, the couple should decide on how many people they want at their wedding. Then they should ask family members to submit lists of people they would like to invite. There will have to be some bargaining with family members, if the lists go over the preferred number of guests. Deciding whom to invite may not be easy at times. But if you stick to a set number, you'll keep costs down and may even have a more memorable wedding.

religious considerations

Generally, members of a religious group are permitted to hold a wedding in the place of worship for free or at a minimal cost. Along with the place of worship, you'll likely have access to staff musicians and even a wedding coordinator for the ceremony. If you are a nonmember, but wish to be married in a place of worship, the fee will be larger.

- Often a house of worship has an adjoining hall of some kind, which is usually available for a reception at a modest fee. Many halls have full-service kitchens, but often there are restrictions about serving alcohol.

comforts of home

Until the last century, wedding receptions were almost always held at home. The concept is both sensible and lovely. If the bride or groom have access to a special residence belonging to a member of the family, the wedding and reception can take place there free of cost. The money saved on a location rental can be spent on catering and décor instead.

- In cooler weather, have the wedding indoors in front of a fireplace or a window with a beautiful view. The reception can move from room to room.
- In good weather, a backyard gazebo, a pool, a particularly exquisite area of a garden, or even a tent or canopy can make an eye-catching wedding site.

special places for cents

If you want to save money and have something special, throw away your idea of a conventional wedding site and open up your imagination. Get out the tour book of the area in which you are to be married—you may find some terrific ideas for locations there.

city or county parks A well-landscaped park with a community hall can often be rented for a very modest fee. Or you

> **❝A happy marriage is the world's best bargain.❞**
>
> O. A. Battista,
> 16th-century Italian
> architect

could have a "picnic" wedding at a park shelter beautified by flower garlands, white and silver balloons, and so on.

public beaches and parks If you are nature lovers, these venues, and others, like mountain areas, can provide spectacular scenery for a one-of-a-kind wedding. You may have to be creative when it comes to the food. A big old barbecue is great fun and a cold buffet can travel just about anywhere.

historic buildings Historic houses or public buildings are also a good bargain. They have often been renovated so that they can accommodate functions and add a truly unique feel to the celebration.

museums Many art, history, or nature museums are available for functions in their off hours. They tend to have large kitchens and provide truly memorable surroundings. Ask about member discounts for functions.

botanical gardens You can't ask for a more naturally lush location. They frequently have facilities for functions. Plus, the landscaping is always in top form, regardless of the season. Ask about member discounts for functions.

college chapels These and other buildings at colleges and universities offer a particularly cost-effective and meaningful choice if the bride and groom attended the same college. Many colleges have lovely chapels and halls that can be used for receptions. Alumni often receive substantial discounts.

costly convenience

Country clubs and hotels offer an easy way to have a wedding and/or reception—they have large rooms, which are often beautifully decorated, a full kitchen staff, and much more. But you usually pay top dollar for all this convenience. If you really have your heart set on having the reception at a country club or hotel, shop around. Call smaller hotels or country inns and compare their prices to your ideal location. Be sure to get an itemized breakdown of what is included in the price and an estimate of any extra charges.

investing in invitations

This is a great opportunity to trim the budget and express yourself. Instead of traditional engraved invitations, stop by your favorite stationery store to consider different options. You can find exquisite stationery and even do-it-yourself invitation kits. A hand-written invitation on a card that really reflects who you are is much more intimate and evocative than a printed one.

- If you can't hand-write your invitations, have them printed rather than engraved. Good printing looks wonderful and costs about half as much.
- If you've chosen simple, elegant paper, you can still dress up the invitations by adding wax seals, foil, ribbon, and

Anglo-Saxon weddings featured a ceremony in which the father of the bride granted authority over his daughter to her new husband. This act was symbolized by giving the groom one of the bride's shoes. Many moons later, this has transformed into the custom of tying old shoes to the "get-away" car after the reception.

so on. Sprinkle a little confetti or potpourri inside the envelope before you seal it.

- Chose your stamps with care. The post office is usually very helpful in offering a variety of appropriate stamps. Bring a sample of the invitation with you so they can weigh it and determine the correct postage.

getting the dress for less

Spending hundreds to thousands of dollars for a dress you wear once just doesn't make sense to us. Invest that money or save it for a down payment on a house, don't spend it on a dress—even if it is for your wedding.

check the closets If it's still in good condition, the gown that was worn by your mother, mother-in-law, aunt, or grandmother might be a fine choice. You'll honor them by wearing it and get a dress for free. Pay a good seamstress to alter the gown to fit you perfectly and splurge a little on lingerie, shoes, or other accessories. If the dress is extremely dated, have it slightly altered to reflect both the past and the present.

gently used Check antique stores, thrift stores, and consignment shops. You may be surprised at what you find and the price you'll pay.

get dramatic If you really want a one-of-a-kind dress, call the costume shops of your community theater or try the drama department of a nearby college or university. You may be able to hire a costume designer to create a dress for you. Ask to see a portfolio of designs and some garments he or she has created. A school of fashion design may also have graduate students eager to establish themselves by creating a truly unique dress.

buck tradition An elegant ivory suit, a simple white slip dress, a pretty tea-length gown in antique lace, or just a dressy dress that looks great on you can all be wonderful wedding attire. And don't limit yourself to white—it has only been traditional since the time of Queen Victoria. Many cultures use other colors for wedding dresses.

rent it If you really want a traditional designer gown, a less-expensive route is to rent it. Check the Yellow Pages under "Gown Rentals and Sales."

beautiful budget blooms

The rule here is the same for any entertaining: Buy only flowers in season and, if possible, arrange them yourself (or ask a friend or relative who's good at arrangements to do it).

- For simple charm, use flowering potted plants on tables at the reception, lining the aisle, or tucked in various places for color. Tie ribbons or raffia around the pots and encourage guests to take them home. Potted plants cost much less than cut flowers and won't wither and die.

⦿ Go for the greenery! Use pine boughs in winter or luxurious ferns in summer to add texture, color, and elegance to an arrangement for very little outlay. Use ribbons or carefully tuck candles among the greenery.

⦿ Fill glass bowls with fresh fruit and tuck a few flowers among them for maximum effect with minimal cost.

fabulously frugal food

For many, the formal sit-down dinner seems to be a must for a wedding reception. But it isn't really necessary and may actually detract from the event. Weddings often provide people with a chance to catch up with each other. If guests are seated at a table and required to sit there for a few hours while food is brought to them, they may not enjoy themselves nearly as much as if they had the freedom to eat when they want, what they want, and with whom they want.

⦿ A sit-down meal requires a number of servers and you pay for each and every one.

⦿ A buffet can allow you to spend more on the food itself, offer more variety to please many different tastes, is flexible, and requires only those attending the serving tables.

⦿ Don't limit yourself to dinner! A morning wedding lends itself to a sparkling champagne brunch or a light and luscious lunch. An early afternoon ceremony could be followed by an elegant high tea with finger sandwiches and strawberries and cream. A late afternoon service would lend itself to a fabulous cocktail party with delectable finger foods. All of these options can be truly delicious at less than the cost of a formal dinner— and a lot more fun, too.

⦿ Because you will be serving cake, don't feel you must offer other desserts. A platter of fresh fruit is refreshing to the eye, a nice finish to a meal, and a godsend to those who are watching calories. If you want to dress the fruit up, offer chocolate dipping sauce on the side.

the cake caper

You want your wedding cake to look beautiful but you also want it to taste good. It's a good idea to sample a cake first to make sure you like it before serving it at your wedding.

⦿ Rather than go to a private bakery, ask around to find someone who bakes specialty cakes at home. They usually charge less and the cake is often better.

⦿ Check out the bakery department in your local grocery store. Unlikely as it may seem, some of these produce dazzling cakes at an easy-on-you price.

- The least expensive route is to ask a family member who's a great baker to do you the honor of making your cake as his or her wedding gift. To dress the cake up, have your florist make a miniature version of your wedding bouquet as a cake topper.
- For ease of serving, have the actual wedding cake made smaller, and keep a second large sheet wedding cake ready to be served out of sight.

a budget for beverages

Although there are folks who hail an open bar as a sign of a good party, do you really want them at your wedding? Wine, beer, and a good selection of nonalcoholic beverages, plus champagne for the toasts, is a less pricey and ultimately more satisfying approach.

bring your own bottles The markup on any kind of alcoholic beverage is pretty steep so you'll save money just by shopping and buying your own. Call around to see which stores offer the best prices and buy in bulk. And don't forget keg beer, if you're having an informal outdoor reception.

regional references If you live in or close to an area that produces wine, you may want to call some of the vineyards. You may be able to get a great price on a high-caliber wine or champagne by purchasing cases directly from a vineyard. This is also a way to share something special about your home region with your guests. (Some vineyards also offer outstanding wedding facilities!)

microbrewing The same philosophy of regional pride can be adapted to your choice of beer. The proliferation of microbreweries has been astonishing, and you should be able to find one close to home. Again, by purchasing directly, you may get a break on the price of really special brews.

sparkling sips Champagne or another sparkling wine really makes the toasting special, but few people want to drink it throughout a party (unless you buy the highest quality, bubblies tend to promote headaches). Save the sparklers for the toasts—it will set them off as special, and you can then invest in a better quality sparkling wine.

time (and other) factors If you're having a morning wedding, mimosas can be festive; afternoons can call for a tea- or juice-based punch. A winter wedding with a Renaissance feeling could lend itself to mulled wine or spiced cider; the heat of summer in the Southwest could inspire big pitchers of white and traditional Sangria. Let the time, the season, the place, and personal taste dictate your beverage offerings.

options, options Make sure you have lots of nonalcoholic beverages on hand, too. Sparkling water, iced tea, lemonade, fruit juices, or punch—even big pitchers of iced coffee if the bride and groom are known to love their java.

If you've never planned a wedding before, here's a quick course. As always, careful planning pays, saving you not only money but a lot of last-minute hassles.

6-12 MONTHS AHEAD

- Set budget.
- Choose date and time for wedding and reception.
- Book locations.
- Rough out guest list between families.
- Select caterer and begin choosing menu.
- Meet with person who will officiate and discuss ceremony.
- Select and invite wedding attendants.
- Select wedding dress, bridal attendant dresses, and accessories.
- Register for gifts.
- Order invitations or begin writing your own
- Select wedding rings.
- Contract with photographer, videographer, and musicians.

3 MONTHS BEFORE

- Order flowers.
- Plan and book honeymoon.
- Select attire for groom, best man and usher.
- Check requirements for a wedding license with state agency.

thrifty notes

Music is an important part of just about any wedding. Personal taste, venue, and budget will dictate the music you choose. If you're getting married in a mountain park or on a beach, a guitarist, flutist, or other portable instrumentalist is appropriate. If you're hiring a hall for dancing, a band or disc jockey will be needed.

- If you are having the ceremony in a house of worship, they probably have a pianist or organist on staff. You may be required to use this person or pay them a fee if you don't (this is how they make their living). Unless they're terrible (not likely), hiring the staff musician is generally the most cost-effective option.

- If you are planning to have the reception in the same place that you're being married, hiring someone who can play at both may be less expensive.

- Check local schools of music, colleges or universities to hire excellent musicians at a much lower cost. You can also ask about vocalists and student dance bands that might meet your needs.

- DJ's don't all wear disco suits! A disc jockey can be a very economical alternative to live music at your reception. Shop around. You should be able to find someone who understands the mood you are trying to create and can work with you to select the perfect music.

frugal photos

You don't want to break the budget, but you do want to hire a good photographer. His or her pictures, after all, will become your wedding memories. Ask friends and family members for recommendations on good photographers. You may even want to call your local newspaper or photo supply store for leads. Look at portfolios and interview each candidate to find the best match in personality and approach. Talk about your budget honestly and see what he or she has to offer. Often, a package can save you money.

- Ask the prospective photographer if they would be willing to just shoot pictures and deliver you the negatives and proofs instead of a formal package. You'll save tons of money if you can reprint the photos and create a wedding album yourself.

- For great informal shots, put a cheap disposable camera on each guest table.

- If you will be married in a house of worship, make sure that you check with them first about rules for photographers and videographers. They are frequently stricter than you might imagine.

- Ask your photographer to give you digital copies of the pictures on a CD, so that you can e-mail pictures to all.

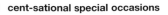

do everyone a favor

Giving a small gift to each wedding guest is a charming custom that can quickly get out of hand. How many of us have little gewgaws sitting in drawers somewhere? We hate to just throw them away, but usually they are useless. Why not take a different approach?

light of love Small scented candles with ribbons in your wedding colors tied around them.

gift of green Packets of seeds, either a flower that was featured in the wedding, or an herb with significance, such as rosemary (remembrance and friendship).

native foods If you're being married in the Southwest, a packet of salsa spice; northeasterners could give tiny bottles of maple syrup.

picture perfect Make copies of your engagement photo or other snapshot that captures the relationship; purchase inexpensive frames and give those as a lasting memento.

pamper your guests Packets of bubble bath, tubes of peppermint foot lotion (relief after all that dancing), and other small indulgences.

share a toast Small bottles of wine or champagne as a toast to family and friends who have gathered to celebrate.

happy endings

The wedding is over, you're off on your honeymoon! Or are you? Don't feel you must rush directly from your wedding to your honeymoon. For one thing, you'll be exhausted after *the* big day. You may want a quiet night at a hotel, or even at home before taking off. By taking the time to relax, even for a day or two, you'll enjoy the trip more. And you'll frequently have to take off days from work around your wedding; if you want a longer trip, waiting may be the answer. We know a couple who waited an entire year after their wedding so they could save up money and vacation days to splurge on a long honeymoon trip to the British Isles.

2 MONTHS BEFORE

- Determine seating arrangements.
- Finalize menu, beverage service, and decor.
- Mail invitations (at least 6 weeks before date).
- Make arrangements for rehearsal dinner.
- Book transportation for wedding party.
- Select gifts for wedding party.

1 MONTH BEFORE

- Arrange lodging for out-of-town guests.
- Final fitting for wedding attire.
- Order wedding cake.

2 WEEKS BEFORE

- Arrange for hair and make-up, if being done professionally.
- Call invitees who haven't responded to determine final guest list.
- Give caterer the final number of guests.
- Schedule wedding rehearsal.
- Confirm honeymoon bookings.
- Have blood tests, get marriage license.

THE WEDDING DAY

- Best man gives officiant the fee.
- Eat a light meal before the wedding.
- RELAX AND ENJOY!

happy homemade
Holidays

IT'S HARD TO KEEP A LID ON
SPENDING AROUND THE HOLIDAYS. IT'S
A TIME OF JOY, OF SHARING, OF SHOPPING.

It simply doesn't feel right to be miserly at holiday time, whether in winter or in spring. But, you don't have to spend a fortune to have fun during the holidays. All it takes is some planning and imagination. Get the whole family involved in preparing parties, decorating, selecting and wrapping gifts, and you'll automatically increase your family time and fun time. And isn't that the whole point?

garage sale decorating

Looking for holiday items (or those that can be adapted) on the cheap? Get thee to some garage sales! We've walked away with exquisite unused table linens, a bevy of candle holders, strings of lights, ornaments, holiday tins (which you can reuse for food gifts or for decorating), artificial trees—and much more. Plus you can look for bowls, cookie jars, and baskets of every size and shape to adapt for any holiday. All for mere pennies! Drop by sales throughout the year and keep your eyes open—you never know when someone is going to clean out their garage, basement, or attic. Chances are, you'll walk away with some sensational seasonal stuff.

fun at the fabric store

Most fabric stores double as craft stores these days. Visiting one of these stores can make holiday decorating fun and easy. Keep an eye out for sales, usually just before and after a holiday. You'll be able to pick up decorations and holiday-themed fabrics for a song, anywhere from 50 percent to 75 percent off the full price. And don't forget to poke through the remnant bins before leaving. You never know what you might find: a piece of lace to use on a small side table, a piece of velvet to wrap around a pillow, or a bright floral fabric to line a spring basket.

'tis the season to spend?

The month of December hits just about everyone in the pocketbook. For many, Christmas, Chanukah, and Kwanzaa have become less about the meaning behind each holiday and more about frenzied shopping so you can shower those you love with loads of gifts. The following activities can help get you back in tune with these sacred celebrations.

quick, easy (and inexpensive) decorations

Most of the decorating ideas below can be adapted to fit Christmas, Chanukah, or Kwanzaa, depending on the colors you choose. Even if you don't celebrate a holiday at this time, these decorations are a wonderful way to celebrate winter. For inventive ideas on gift giving, see pages 198 to 201.

- Pile old or inexpensive glass ball ornaments in a pretty bowl or basket.
- Place a mirror flat in the center of a table. Arrange several candlesticks (they don't have to match) on top of the mirror. Add some greenery, maybe a wire-edged ribbon or strand of curling ribbon wound around the candlesticks, and a glass ball or two.
- Old holiday tins, especially reproductions of antique tins, can be set on kitchen shelves and filled with real or artificial flowers or greens, glass ball ornaments, pine cones, or nuts. They can also be used as holders for large column candles (just make sure they are solidly seated by using melted wax to hold them upright).
- Wile away the winter evenings by cutting snowflakes. Fold a square piece of white paper in half, then in half again. Now fold the square into a triangle. Cut out geometric or other shapes along the outer edges of the triangle. Open up the paper and you have a snowflake. Tape to windows or hang as ornaments.
- Pick up antique toys at garage sales and flea markets and tuck them everywhere; add bows for more color.

natural beauty

Many of the most inviting decorations can be picked up on a walk through the woods or even in your backyard.

- Pick up pine cones, nuts, interesting-looking twigs and leaves around your house, your neighborhood, or on a nature walk. You can spray paint them gold, silver, white, or leave them in their natural state. Arrange them in glass, metallic, or wooden bowls, tuck them along the mantel or on bookshelves and windowsills. You can also attach thin strings to them and then hang them as ornaments on a Christmas tree.
- During fall pruning, set aside any shapely branches or twigs that you cut off. Spray paint them gold, silver, white, or leave them natural and set them in a large container (milk pail, umbrella stand, even a pretty metal waste can). Add a bow and little lights strung through the branches for a truly eye-catching decoration.
- If you are a seashell collector, you can use some of your favorites for holiday decorating. Large open shells, such as clam or abalone, can be used to hold candles. Starfish can be strung as ornaments or set upright on a mantel. Sand dollars make wonderful ornaments, too.
- Don't forget the fruit: A large glass bowl or distressed wooden bowl heaped high with bright red and green apples, golden oranges, or pomegranates makes a charming accent anywhere. If you want, tuck sprigs of holly or pine, and nuts between some of the fruit.

> **❝Never worry about the size of your Christmas tree. In the eyes of children, they are all 30 feet tall.❞**

Larry Wilde, author, motivational speaker and humorist

www.christmasdepot.com

If you'd like to shop online for discount Christmas decorations, try www.christmasdepot.com (or call 1-877-353-5263). They offer a wide selection of everything from artificial trees to music, at fairly good prices. You'll also find decorations for Halloween.

o, christmas tree

A Christmas tree is a veritable must-have for people who celebrate Christmas. However, a traditional pre-cut tree in a stand isn't the only choice available.

cut your own If you really want a fresh tree, your best bet is a tree farm. Usually the prices are good, plus you'll know the tree is fresh and thus will last longer and look better. Selecting and chopping your tree can be a fabulous time for the family. Many tree farms offer hot chocolate or cider to warm you up while you chop and shop. They also sell hand-crafted ornaments, decorations, and gifts.

last minute bargain Start a family tradition of buying and decorating a tree on Christmas Eve, and you'll be surprised at the bargain-basement price you can get for a tree.

trimmings from trees Before setting your tree in a holder, cut off any lower branches that will be in your way and set them aside to use for decorations.

again and again The most economical approach is to invest in an artificial tree. Some of these trees are so realistic you practically have to touch them to realize they are not real. Though the better-looking trees cost more, this is a one-time investment that should pay for itself in a few years. Just think, you'll never have to water or worry about your tree drying out during long holiday trips again. Also, an artificial tree is fireproof, unlike a dried-out real tree.

mini-trees If you live in an apartment or have reached the point where putting up a full tree is more trouble than it's worth, consider a miniature artificial Christmas tree. You can buy them plain, with lights, or completely decorated. They go up in minutes, will serve you well for years, and are relatively inexpensive. They are positively cheap if you buy them at post-holiday sales.

deeply rooted The most expensive, but environmentally friendly option is to buy a tree from a nursery that you can plant in the yard later on. If you have the acreage, you'll be beautifying your property and helping the environment, too. Planting trees helps reduce global warming!

ten terrific uses for old christmas cards

It's really waste to toss all those beautiful cards at the end of the season. Instead, save them and reuse them next year:

get ornamental Cut off the back of the card, punch a hole in the top, and hang it with a ribbon anywhere you need some holiday cheer.

chains of cheer Cut the front of each card into strips and make interlocking loop chains to hang on a tree, edge a mantel, as a window swag, or up a staircase banister.

border lines Use double-sided tape to affix a row of cards around a door frame.

table topper Arrange a selection of your favorite cards on a coffee table. Top with a piece of glass or clear plastic to protect the cards. Or cut out special images from each card and make a coffee table collage.

make a mat Arrange a selection of card fronts or cutouts on 8- by 10-inch construction paper in a holiday color or white. Affix the cards with a glue stick. Cover the front and the back with clear contact paper and trim to the size of the construction paper. Voila! A place mat you can wipe clean!

fun runner Place a bunch of cards down the center of your dining room table, setting them at angles to each other in a pleasing arrangement. Tape together with invisible tape.

new from old Cut off the backs and use the fronts as party invitations or Christmas postcards to new friends.

tag it Cut out images from the card fronts, punch a hole in one edge, and use them for gift tags on packages.

wreathed in joy Cut images or just the fronts of a number of cards. Cut a wreath shape from cardboard and glue the cards to the wreath. Add a bow and hang the wreath on a door, window, or wall that needs some cheer.

hold it! Cut two-inch-wide strips from card fronts and bend them into a circle; glue or staple the ends to secure. Roll holiday napkins and slip them through these unique holders.

thanksgiving

Make this an incredibly fun day—a real celebration of family and friends. And don't let it wear out your nerves or your pocketbook.

the pleasures of potluck If you're not planning a traditional family dinner, host a potluck feast where each guest brings their favorite side dish or dessert. The host provides the turkey and tableware. This can be great fun, especially if your guests bring a favorite family recipe. Because it's potluck, you'll end up with a fabulous meal without the stress of preparing it all alone.

one-man band If you really love cooking all the holiday dishes yourself, you're in luck. Traditional Thanksgiving meals celebrate the foods of the season, so they are usually a bargain. Not only are fall vegetables and fruits, such as sweet potatoes, pumpkins, brussels sprouts, oranges, and apples, at their freshest and cheapest, but many supermarkets will give you a turkey if you buy a certain amount of goods—like $80 or $100's worth—within a certain period of time. (If you don't have enough food purchases, stock up on staples.)

being thankful As part of the holiday meal, have family or friends tell about something that they are thankful about this year. Or, for children, read a picture book—about pilgrims and the first Thanksgiving—or a story about being grateful.

turkey table talk

The classic cornucopia always looks beautiful as the table centerpiece during Thanksgiving dinner. If your table is cramped, you may want to put it on the mantel or a side table instead. Here are some other decorative ideas:

- If you don't have a cornucopia, substitute a rustic basket overflowing with miniature pumpkins, squash, gourds, Indian corn, nuts, pomegranates, apples, or oranges. Tie a big raffia bow around the sides of the basket or the handle, and trail the ends through the autumn bounty.
- Use miniature pumpkins or small gourds for rustic candleholders. Just cut a hole in the top large enough to fit the end of a candlestick.
- Collect and press autumn leaves throughout the fall. Arrange pressed leaves down the center of the dining room table, tuck a few into grapevine wreaths, or tape some to the windows. Also dry some leaves without pressing them flat and gather them in big wooden bowls.
- Pots of mums are usually on sale around this time of year. They last longer than cut flowers and the colors are perfect for Thanksgiving. Buy several small pots, set them in baskets, tin buckets, or wooden bowls, tie ribbons or raffia around them, and place them separately or in groups throughout the house. Later, you can plant them in your garden for year-round beauty.

halloween

Halloween appeals to people of all ages as a time to dress up and pretend, play with friends, and have fun. It's no wonder that it's become one of the most popular holidays. Practically every store you walk into has tons of Halloween decorations for sale. Because you can make them easily yourself, however, why spend the money? You'll find some do-it-yourself Halloween ideas below.

scary stuff

ghosts in the night There are three relatively easy and cheap ways to make ghosts. White plastic garbage bags can  be opened, a ball of wadded up newspaper stuffed into the head area, then a rubber band used to secure the neck. You can draw a face on the head with indelible black marker and hang these plastic ghosts from trees, the eaves of your house, and just about anywhere else. They are waterproof, too—a distinct advantage. You can also pick up white sheets at garage sales throughout the year, make a solid wad of newspaper for the head, and secure the neck with string. Another fabric that makes great ghosts is cheesecloth; use a white or clear balloon for the head and these ghosts will really float.

scarecrow fashion Scarecrow clothes are a cinch to find at garage sales (ratty jeans, plaid shirts, old gloves or mittens, hats, etc.). Because straw can be a bit hard to find, use wadded up newspaper to stuff the clothes. Make the head out of plain muslin (usually less than two dollars a yard at fabric stores), and draw on the face with markers.

ghoulish graveyard Cut headstones out of stiff cardboard or plywood (if you have access to power tools). Attach a garden stake to the back of each headstone, then pound into the ground. Paint the stones white and add goofy epitaphs.

pumpkin patch Pumpkins are easy to grow, so why not grow your own for carving or using in arrangements? The kids will love watching the patch as it develops. If you have to buy pumpkins, you can usually pick them up cheaply—check out farmer's markets for specials.

costumes on the cheap

Years ago people never thought of buying a Halloween costume—part of the fun was making your own. This art can easily be revived with a bit of creativity. Garage sales and thrift stores can be treasure troves for costume pieces.

- To make a wig, glue Easter "grass," raffia, or yarn to a stocking cap, old swimming cap, or old pantyhose with the legs knotted and cut off.
- Clean out old makeup and let the kids use it as face paint.
- To make white makeup for a clown face, combine two tablespoons of cornstarch with one tablespoon of solid vegetable shortening. Add a few drops of green food coloring to get monster decay, a few drops of red food coloring to add a dash of the devil, blue coloring for corpses and ghouls, and yellow for a lion face.
- For extra bulk and padding, wear a large size of pantyhose under the costume and stuff with rags, wadded newspaper, or small pillows.

easter

This is a time to celebrate the return of spring. The holiday is about renewal, rebirth and hope—and usually comes laden with lots of candy eggs and bunnies, too.

- Don't buy a new basket year after year. Choose one sturdy basket with a wide mouth and a broad shallow base and store it with your other Easter items. The night before Easter, have your child set it somewhere (on the back porch, under a special tree or bush, or at the foot of their bed). Then use raffia for grass and fill the basket with toys, books, and goodies.
- Take advantage of sales after Easter to stock up on refillable plastic eggs. You can fill them with small candies, stickers, trinkets, and toys, and reuse them year after year.

GOOD OLD WAYS

Christmas is the season for cookies of all kinds, but most people don't have enough time to make as many as they might like. One option is to host an old-fashioned cookie exchange: Invite six friends and ask each to bake six dozen of the same cookie. At the party, each person takes home one dozen of each type of cookie or six dozen assorted cookies! For an added touch, ask each participant to make six copies of their recipe, so you each get six dozen cookies and five new recipes!

all good Gifts

MOST PEOPLE CHERISH GIVING
A GIFT TO A LOVED ONE. WHAT THEY
DON'T CHERISH IS SPENDING A FORTUNE.

Truth is, the best gifts don't have to cost a bundle. They come from the giver's heart and imagination. Think about the person you're giving to. Hone in on the things that excite them or make them happy. Consider the qualities that make the person special. By doing all these things you'll settle on the perfect present. A thoughtful gift will mean much more to the recipient than the priciest bauble.

shopping smart

Ever thought you could find someone the perfect Christmas gift in the middle of July? What about scoring a divine birthday present three weeks after a person's birthday? Shopping smart means buying things you think a person will like when you spot them and when the price is right. It also means never buying anything in a hurry. If you do, you're likely to spend more than you want to and maybe even settle for a less than ideal gift. A smart shopper is always looking for gifts throughout the year. If you go to a craft fair, don't just think in the short term. If you see a hand-painted vase that would delight Aunt Mary and it's a steal, buy it. Vacation trips, country fairs, flea markets, auctions, gift shops at museums and botanical gardens, are all excellent sources of one-of-a-kind presents anytime of the year. Establish a drawer, closet shelf, or trunk in your home as the gift store. Then when a birthday, special occasion, or holiday approaches, you'll be able to reach in and pull out the ideal present for anyone on your list.

personal gift certificates

One of the nicest and most personal presents you can give is an offer of time or service during the year.

- New parents or parents of small children can always use the gift of babysitting, not just for a much-needed evening out, but for doctor or dentist appointments, to get their hair cut, or just to grocery shop without distractions.
- Seniors may need help with big tasks such as cleaning out an attic or garage, mowing a big lawn, spring cleaning, or fall pruning and weeding.
- Someone who doesn't drive would love a book of trip coupons. Each coupon could be redeemable for a run to the grocery store, the eye doctor, and perhaps a "surprise" trip to somewhere they don't get a chance to go to often.
- Offer dinner on a night of their choosing to someone you know is constantly overwhelmed by work or family needs. Cook up a lasagna, casserole, or stew, add a loaf of bread, salad, brownies and a bottle of wine. Put it all in a pretty wicker basket. They will be eternally grateful.

make a date

A variation on the personal coupon is the offer of a date. Most of us have an awful lot of material things, but we never have enough time with family and friends.

- A husband or wife can present their spouse with the offer of an outing with their best friend. The outing could be to play a sport, go to a museum, dine in a restaurant, or anything that is fun. The spouse promises to take care of all matters on the home front.
- Let's say your partner loves theater, music, dance, or sports. You can surprise him or her with tickets to a live event and a "date" coupon.
- If someone loves to garden, give him or her a gift of gardening time. He or she will appreciate a willing helper to dig, weed, plant, and water. Add a picnic to celebrate your gardening achievements.
- If your spouse loves to be pampered, wrap a bottle of massage oil with a promise to give him or her a back rub. Add a touch of romance with a book of "date night" coupons that includes dinner for two (out or at home), dancing, a movie, or a long walk together.

flower power

Cut flowers are always a lovely gift, but live plants that bloom last longer and continue to give pleasure for years.

- Buy inexpensive terra cotta pots and paint them to suit the occasion or the taste of the person. Transplant a seasonal plant or a personal favorite of the recipient into the pot. Include care instructions on a hand-decorated tag.
- Small tin pails, old cookie tins and jars, old pottery bowls or pitchers, and cheese crocks make eye-catching planters. Use them for a plant and give to a friend who likes these collectibles. They'll be thrilled!
- Create a window herb garden for a friend who's an avid cook. Plant a variety of herbs in a long planter or a group of little pots arranged in a shallow basket or tin tray.

got ya framed

Few people have enough photo frames. Here's how to personalize a simple flat wooden frame for the greatest impact.

the golfer Hot glue wooden tees around a painted frame by laying them flat and alternating the points and heads.

the movie lover Use white glue to hold an attractive arrangement of ticket stubs. Coat with clear polyurethane.

the gardener Spread white glue over the frame and arrange real pressed flowers or leaves. You can also cut out pictures of flowers and glue to the frame. Coat with polyurethane.

the seamstress Buy inexpensive sewing notions and use them to decorate a frame.

66 The manner of giving is worth more than the gift. **99**

Pierre Corneille, 17th-century French dramatist

GIFT GIVING GUIDE

Each wedding anniversary has a symbolic motif, which can be a gift-giving guide.

ANNIVERSARY	MOTIF
1st	Paper
2nd	Cotton
3rd	Leather
4th	Linen
5th	Wood
6th	Iron
7th	Copper
8th	Bronze
9th	Pottery
10th	Tin
11th	Steel
12th	Silk
13th	Lace
14th	Ivory
15th	Crystal
20th	China
25th	Silver
30th	Pearl
35th	Coral or Jade
40th	Ruby
45th	Sapphire
50th	Gold
55th	Emerald
60th	Diamond

scraps of memories

For a milestone birthday, wedding anniversary, graduation, or retirement, make a scrapbook for the guest of honor, with photographs, important papers, and other memorabilia. Then ask friends, family, and/or coworkers to contribute a written memory of an event, encounter, or conversation with the honoree to include in the scrapbook.

memories all year long

Another way to commemorate an anniversary, birthday, or graduation is to select 12 photographs that depict a special moment in the honoree's life and have them made into a personalized calendar. They'll enjoy your gift all year long.

gifts from the kitchen

You don't have to be a gourmet to make a delicious gift to eat as you will learn from these simple and easy ideas.

○ Cookies are welcome just about anytime, especially around holidays. A basic sugar cookie dough is easy to make, and you can buy or make icing to decorate them.

○ Sweet breads such as banana, nut, cinnamon raisin, carrot, and poppy seed make lovely gifts. Wrap them in aluminum foil with a beautiful ribbon to dress them up.

○ Do you have a secret family recipe for chili, pasta sauce, or a dessert topping? Make it and pour it into decorative bottles. Include directions for use and storage.

○ Buy a bag of pretzel sticks and whip up some honey mustard dipping sauce to go with it.

○ If you are a canner, homemade jams and jellies are among the most prized gifts you can give.

○ Do you have lavender growing in your garden? Harvest it for making potpourri, sachets, or drying in bunches. Dried rose petals, marigolds, and geraniums also make lovely potpourri.

○ Does your garden overflow with herbs? Make pesto with excess basil or dry extra rosemary, thyme, and other herbs as gifts. Present your gift in pretty antique bottles (found at garage sales, flea markets and junk stores).

wrap it up

Want a fun project for the kids? Make your own gift-wrap. It's a great way to add a personal touch to giving. You'll need butcher paper or thin brown paper. Then have the kids sponge paint, make potato prints, stencil, finger-paint, or paint designs to create one-of-a-kind wrapping paper.

○ Fabric is excellent wrap, especially for awkward shapes.

○ Aluminum foil or gold foil paper are simple to mold around unusually shaped items, such as a hammer, tennis racket, or football.

- Use a section of the newspaper that reflects the gift, the giver, or the person receiving the gift. Use the sports section for the athlete (active or armchair), book review section for the bookworm, and food section for the cook. The funnies are amusing for just about anyone.
- Decorate white or brown paper bags with paint, markers, stickers, stamps, and ribbons for personal gift bags.

ten blue-ribbon gift baskets

anniversary Do a little research and recreate dishes served at the couple's wedding. Add a bottle of champagne and toasting flutes. Line the basket in the wedding colors.

baby shower Fill with practical items the new parents will need: sleepwear, undershirts, bottles, bibs, diaper cloths, rattles, pacifiers, booties or socks, and so on.

birthday Create a basket based on the person's favorite pastime. If he or she loves tennis, line the basket with a sweat towel, visor, sports drinks, wrist and head bands, tennis balls, fancy tennis shoe laces, and a note promising a game.

bridal shower Line several baskets with pretty tablecloths. Tuck in a recipe box, napkins, candles, and candlesticks. Ask each guest to bring a favorite recipe on a card plus a utensil used in the recipe and add them to the baskets. Distribute so each guest gets a basket with a new recipe and utensil.

graduation Welcome the graduate to the next phase of life by filling a basket with a cookbook of simple recipes, boxes of instant food, a bag of subway tokens, a commuter coffee mug, and other items for a young, newly independent person.

new job Line the basket with a map showing the route to work, add a big coffee mug, gourmet coffee or tea bags, trail mix, a small potted plant, a family picture, and an emergency office grooming kit.

new neighbors Create a welcome basket lined with a map of the area, add a chamber of commerce guide to local businesses and attractions, a contact sheet with neighbors numbers and names, a plant for their yard, or a ready-to-go meal.

starting school For a new kindergarten student, line the basket with a fun T-shirt, add bundles of graphite and colored pencils, a box of crayons, safety scissors, and packs of favorite snacks. Tailor the idea for each level of school.

thank you Line the basket with a picnic cloth and fill it with gourmet foods such as canned oysters, Greek olives, caviar, paté, spreads, crackers, and a bottle of sparkling cider.

wedding Create a honeymoon basket by lining it with fabric used in the wedding or in the wedding colors. Include champagne with two glasses, peppermint foot lotion, massage oil, a box of fancy chocolates, a scented candle (with matches), and tuck loving notes from family and friends.

Going Out and Spending Wisely

- discount fine dining
- bargain culture
- sporty savings
- cheap thrills

There's a whole big world of fun things to do out there, and they don't have to cost a fortune! Whether your bent is toward the symphony or soccer, theater or trail riding, fine dining or art fairs, you can enjoy eating out, culture, sports, and other fun outings at a fraction of the price most folks shell out. Use coupons to enjoy two-for-one entrees at a special restaurant or take advantage of seasonal (or time-of-day) specials. Move into the minor league world and enjoy exciting sporting events for much less, or split a season's subscription and reduce the ticket price for major-league sports. Scout twofers or half-price ticket booths, call the box office about lower cost performances, or get into the community spirit and support local theater, symphony, opera, and dance. Pick up a tour book for your hometown and discover the amazing number of places to visit, things to see, and ways to have fun for practically nothing—all in your back yard. Being a penny pincher means saving where you can, so you can do all the activities you love to do.

Get out and enjoy yourself.

discount fine
Dining

AS A REWARD FOR YOUR FRUGALITY,
YOU DESERVE A NICE MEAL OUT,
BUT DON'T LET IT BUST YOUR BUDGET.

As a dedicated penny pincher, you are already enjoying most of your meals at home, eating a brown-bag lunch whenever possible, and brewing your own gourmet commuter coffee. Every once in a while, however, you deserve an indulgence. Treat yourself to a meal at an excellent restaurant. When you do, the dining experience will become more than just eating. Having a wonderful meal cooked for you will feel like a well-earned and deserved luxury— an experience that you will truly appreciate.

fast food vs. fine food

First, let's explore the direction in which America's taste buds has evolved in the past few decades. Fast-food joints have sprouted like weeds. Often, this option seems awfully convenient, but nutritionally it's almost always a bust, and the cost isn't always so cheap. Wouldn't you rather forgo the greasy fries and fat-laden burgers and treat yourself to mouthwatering cuisine served in a tasteful atmosphere? If you have to have a fast-food fix now and again, make it during a rare occasion like a road trip, and not a few times a week habit. Your arteries will thank you. So will your wallet.

early birds get more than worms

One way to enjoy a great restaurant meal for less is the early bird special. This is basically the same food, served at a time when the restaurant traditionally experiences low volume. It's good business for the restaurant, and for you. You get a great meal and they don't have empty tables. A variation on this is a pre-theater menu. Often, these offers are set menus with a choice between two to three items for a fixed price (excluding beverage). Sometimes you can order a la carte for less. Either way, the discount is offered before shows start (or sometimes after they finish) and the price is reduced, whether you're actually going to the theater or not!

off-season specials

In some parts of the country, tourism falls off during certain times of the year. In many coastal resort areas, for instance, there are fewer tourists in the winter. The same applies to many ski resort areas in the summer. Off-season is an ideal time to take advantage of some great travel and dining opportunities. When tourism season is in full swing, establishments in these resort areas can, and do, charge pretty steep prices. But when tourism dwindles, they are anxious to get bodies in and make a little money. To get you to visit, many will offer terrific room rates and two-for-one entrees, free appetizer with purchase of entree, or other culinary deals. If you live in an area that has a high season for tourism, call and ask about specials during the off-season.

coupons de cuisine

You can find discount coupons for top-notch restaurants many different ways. And you save can a significant amount.

entertainment book This is that thick book of coupons sold by scouting troops, church youth groups, and schools. The coupon book costs from $30 to $50 and contains page after page of coupons. In the dining section, you'll find a number of coupons dedicated to fast-food restaurants, but you will also find a surprising number of excellent restaurants with two-for-one coupons. You buy one entree and get a second one of equal or lesser value for free. Imagine saving $15 to $20 on a fine gourmet meal. Any way you look at it, an Entertainment Book can offer significant savings.

valpak These are mailed all over the country, usually in a blue envelope. Many people toss them—and other similar coupon packages—out as soon as they see them. Don't! Along with coupons for oil changes and dry cleaning, you'll find a number of dining coupons, often to high-quality restaurants. Sometimes the coupons will offer a two-for-one deal; sometimes it will be a fixed-price meal or a special selection of entrees at a discount. Again, the savings can add up quickly.

newspapers Scan your local newspaper (or if you're on a trip, the local paper of the city you are visiting) for restaurant ads. Sometimes they double as coupons for a two-for-one meal or a percentage off the bill. You should check every day, but especially the day the entertainment section comes out (usually Friday). Keep a close eye on the newspaper when the weather has been nasty for a period of time—even the best restaurants may run a special to lure folks back.

chamber of commerce In order to encourage tourists to visit local restaurants, the chamber of commerce may offer a selection of coupons. Call them to find out if any are available. If you're flying to a different destination, don't forget to stop at the airport tourist desk. You'll find flyers for lots of local attractions, sometimes with discounts, and you may find restaurant coupons as well. It's worth a look.

back to school

Another venue for fine dining at an easier-on-you price is a culinary institute. These are schools where students learn to be chefs. Often, you can have extraordinary meals there. Even better, you can sometimes watch the food being prepared—entertainment included with the cost of the meal! But be warned: If you go to one of the top academies, you might pay more. The trade-off is that you will be getting a truly gourmet meal for much less than you would at the restaurant these talented chefs will eventually cook at or start themselves.

> **''Tis not the meat, but 'tis the appetite makes eating a delight.''**

Sir John Suckling,
17th-century English poet

RESTAURANT WEB SITE

www.restaurants.com

This site lists fine eateries in the U.S. and internationally. You enter a city or region and the site offers restaurants with ratings and personal reviews, plus costs for an average dinner. You can download a map to the restaurant, often book a table online, and even give your own input. Plus, they have a link to tell you which restaurants have coupons available.

do the split

Most restaurants serve far more food than just about anyone can consume easily at one sitting. Of course, penny pinchers never leave food behind (doggie bags are hip, you know). One way to expand your taste horizons without blowing the budget is to share either the appetizer or the dessert (or both). As long as you are each purchasing an entree, most restaurants don't have a problem with this (and if they do, don't patronize them!). You'll still savor the flavor, but you'll eat less and spend less.

let's do lunch

If there is a divine restaurant that you've been longing to try but the prices for dinner take away your appetite, consider dining there for lunch instead. The prices on lunch menus can be 25 percent cheaper than the same items on a dinner menu. What's more, many such restaurants have "business specials" at lunchtime that run even less. Also consider trying that restaurant for a less costly weekend brunch.

first in line

This is a technique to fine dining that requires the willingness to gamble a bit. Most restaurants charge less when they first open, then up their prices as their popularity increases. Read the restaurant review sections, talk to friends who eat out a lot, keep your ears always open, and you may be the first on your block to sample next year's rave. The only exception to this is a restaurant opened by a celebrity chef, but even those can have their slow times so . . . be brave, be bold, and be the first!

i dine, you dine

Do you like discount dining but can't remember to bring the coupons? Try **www.idine.com**. This elder statesman of dining clubs has some 7,000 participating restaurantsnationwide, and the discounts are given via credit card. To join, you register up to three of your credit cards online. The membership fee (about $49) is deducted from your savings when you begin using the program. Once the fee is paid, you'll start to see the savings on your credit card bill—and most restaurants offer from 10 to 20 percent off on your entire bill, including tips, taxes, and yes, even alcohol! Naturally, there are restrictions: Many restaurants limit the times the discount applies (not on peak hours and sometimes not on weekends), some require online booking, some only give you the discount on one visit per month, and there is a cap on how much you can spend to get the savings (not usually a problem for a penny pincher). All that being said, this is a good program if you like to eat out relatively frequently.

a family affair

It's nice to take the whole family out once in a while, but the final tally can cast quite a pall on the evening. Before making reservations, call around and check the papers for restaurants that offer a "kid's night" where children (usually under 12) either eat free when an adult meal is purchased or receives a significant discount. This will make the dining experience a pleasure from beginning to bill.

FRUGALLY PRICED ETHNIC CUISINES

Eating out doesn't have yo cost a fortune. At many ethnic eateries you can get a great multi-course meal and still go home with change in your pocket. Many are known for spicy dishes, but they also have milder food for those who don't like hot. Another savings: To keep their overhead low, these places often don't have a liquor license; if you really love a beer with your vindaloo, call ahead to see you can bring your own.

- **Chinese:** From sizzling Szechuan to mellower Mandarin, the choices are many and varied.

- **Thai:** Peanuts, coconut milk, and myriad spices to gently burn or take your head off, plus delectable pad thai, noodles from heaven.

- **Vietnamese:** From the land of fresh herbs and surprising tropical tastes, a veritable Eden of vegetarian delights.

- **Mexican:** Way beyond tacos, savor avocado, chayote, papaya, and even cocoa in choices ranging from Tex-Mex to Mayan- or Aztec-influenced dishes.

- **Caribbean:** As varied and interesting as the islands, from the French-graced cuisine of Martinique to African notes in Jamaican cooking.

- **Cuban:** A heady mixture of Spanish, West African, and native flavors, all well spiced; a Cuban sandwich is a mouthwatering revelation.

- **Ethiopian:** Spice, spice, and more spice, usually in one-pot extravaganzas rich with red pepper (berbere), onions, garlic, and ginger scooped up with flat bread.

- **Indian:** Flavors as varied as the regions of India, from fiery curries and vindaloos to creamy kormas to lightly spiced biryanis, served with fragrant basmati rice and exquisite breads, tandoori delicacies, and more.

- **Middle Eastern:** Taste tantalizing classics as hummus, baba ghanouj, felafels, tabbouleh, and the staple of Middle Eastern cuisine: beguiling, beloved bread.

- **Greek:** Home of tender lamb seasoned with garlic, olive oil, rosemary, lemon, and oregano; outrageously good olives, tart feta cheese, flamed saganaki, and melting moussaka and decadent baklava.

TAKING ADVANTAGE

You've probably already discovered that many restaurants offer senior discounts or special menu sections for seniors — usually with smaller portions at a lower price. Sometimes you have to ask about senior discounts — never be embarrassed to ask! The price of a meal out can really strain a budget, and you should take advantage of any discount you can.

bargain
Culture

DO YOU ENJOY CULTURAL EVENTS,
SUCH AS THE SYMPHONY, THEATER,
DANCE, AND MUSEUM SHOWS?

Do the prices of pursuing culture sometimes give you pause? Then, read on. You'll learn the cheapest way to visit museums and cultural arts performances. You'll also discover the world of free venues. Now you can relish the thrill of live performances or savor the glory of great art without breaking your budget. You may even be able to bring your children along and introduce them to the finer things in life without sacrificing their college funds.

dramatic discounts

Taking a family of four to a Broadway show has gotten to the point where the cost could underwrite the domestic budget of a small nation. Individual ticket prices for major shows have soared to an absurd point. Luckily, there are less-expensive alternatives.

half-price ticket booths In New York City, there is the world-famous TKTS booth, selling tickets to Broadway, Off-Broadway, dance and music events on the day of the show for up to 50 percent off the regular price (plus a $3 per ticket service charge). This is a terrific deal that is well worth the effort, but there is some risk involved. You may end up spending several hours waiting in line. When you get to the counter, you may not get tickets to the exact show you want (so have several in mind that you'd be willing to see). You also may end up with tickets in the nosebleed section. Usually, however, you can score tickets for fabulous seats. Besides New York, many major metropolitan cities now offer half-price ticket booths. Call the city's chamber of commerce to find out if they have one or if there is another way to get discount tickets for a show.

two-fers These are vouchers that you can use to buy two tickets for the price of one. You'll find these ticket-shaped two-fers everywhere if you just look—at the desk in hotels or near the cash register in restaurants and newsstands. Often they are for new shows that need to build an audience or older shows that have been running a while. The hot-ticket shows rarely have vouchers, but you can find them occasionally. The benefit of vouchers is that you don't have to stand in line at a central booth. Instead, you go directly to the box office to purchase the tickets.

previews and matinees Generally speaking, a preview is a dress rehearsal in front of an audience. You may witness some glitches that are still being ironed out, but most often a preview is just like a normal performance—except you pay a little less to see it. You'll also pay less to see a matinee performance because they tend to be less well attended than evening shows. To take advantage of these options, buy the tickets in advance directly from the box office.

student and senior discounts Many theaters all over the country offer lower rates to students with valid ID cards and seniors who have proof of their age.

theater thrift

If you love theatre, you should consider purchasing a subscription. While a subscription requires a big chunk of cash, the savings are significant when compared to buying individual tickets to shows—as much as 50 percent cheaper! As a subscriber you will also be given other benefits: the best seats, the ability to change seats or performance dates easily and without penalty, discounts on tickets for friends, invitations to special events, advance notice of sponsored extras, discounts at nearby restaurants and shops, lost ticket insurance, and more. Since you'll know the dates of the shows well in advance, you can plan for babysitters or dinner out if you want to make a real evening of it.

● Some professional theater companies, in an effort to serve lower-income people, offer one "pay what you can" performance per run. Ask the box office for details.

symphony savings

The same tricks that you use to save on tickets for the theater can usually be applied to music performances as well. Subscribing to the symphony will not only save you on tickets to their performances, but orchestras often have agreements with other musical ensembles that allow you to purchase their tickets at a discount as well.

operatic notes

While opera by and large is not a bargain to attend, you can still see some of the greatest performers and companies for less than full price. Try the same techniques used to procure theater or symphony tickets on the cheap, but if they don't yield enough savings, consider the standing room option. You definitely will need comfortable shoes and a good attitude. But if you're willing to stand, you can see performances at the Metropolitan Opera in New York City for a pittance—and this is true of many opera companies. We caught opera diva Kiri Te Kanawa in Mozart's Cosi fan Tutte for a mere $15 per person. Halfway through the performance, a nice man who had to leave gave us his orchestra tickets for free. We had incredible seats for the second half of the performance!

miserly museum moments

Every museum we've encountered has one day or one evening a week—or sometimes one day a month—that is free to all. For some reason, most museums offer their weekly free day on Tuesdays. Whenever a museum offers these days, take

66 The arts are an even better barometer of what is happening in our world than the stock market or the debates in congress. **99**

Hendrik Willem Van Loon, American author and journalist

advantage of them. You can see the best art in the world, from masterpieces by the classic masters to cutting-edge modern works, all for free.

- If you happen to be a member of a museum where you live and are visiting a museum while on vacation, ask about reciprocity before paying the entrance fee. Many museums around the country will let you in free if you are a member of a sister institution.

community cultural costs

The main difference between professional theater and amateur theater is that professionals are paid. If you love drama, consider your local community theaters—they often produce professional-quality shows and the tickets are considerably less. Plus, the theaters may be closer to where you live, making getting there cheaper and easier.

- Community symphonies, chamber music ensembles, and other music venues are also a great deal. Often, you can hear amazing performances by talented amateurs. Some groups will sponsor a professional guest performer at a few concerts, adding even better value to a ticket.
- Local dance companies are frequently associated with a training program or dance school. The ticket cost is minimal and the performances can be superb.
- Check out your local museum scene, too. In one commu-nity we know, a tiny storefront museum dedicated to wildlife in the area has grown over the past 20 years to become a major educational facility with a state-of-the-art campus. Even so, you can still purchase a ticket at bargain-basement prices thanks to community support.

back-to-school savings

Colleges and universities have some of the best deals going for performing and visual arts.

- College theater can be very exciting. You'll often see talented actors developing their skills. Good theater departments usually employ several artists-in-residence—professional directors, performers, or designers who are training the department's students for a specific performance. With works ranging from classics to experimental shows, college theater can be a stimulating and cost-effective way to see live performances.
- Schools with music departments offers all kinds of performances throughout the year, from symphony to solos, jazz ensembles to a cappella singing groups—all for a bargain price and sometimes free.
- Dance programs at universities and colleges can be just as varied as the music and theater programs, with ballet, jazz, and modern dance all represented. These young

dancers offer a vitality that is truly exciting to witness and you'll be able to afford several performances rather than blow your budget on just one.

- Art departments usually have their own galleries where works by students and often by professors are displayed. If they charge a fee at all, it is usually minimal.

membership matters

Do you belong to **AAA** (American Automobile Association) or a union of some kind? Check your membership benefits— aside from the obvious ones, you may be entitled to discounts at all sorts of entertainment venues. The money you save at theme parks, performance arenas, and sporting events, may be worth the cost of your membership!

booking entertainment

Those Entertainment books have more than restaurant vouchers in them—you'll also find coupons for theater, symphony, opera, and other musical or dance performances. Usually, the coupons offer a two-for-one discount. Occasionally, they will be for specific performances, but mostly they are only limited by availability.

summer freebies

Think summer and images of warm summer nights, fireflies, and brilliant sunsets come to mind. But what about free shows and music? Most cities and many other communities offer free performances throughout the summer, usually in a city park. You can hear the symphony or see theater, dance, and other types of performances for nothing at all. Bring a picnic and your family will enjoy some wonderful evening performances under the stars. Granted the quality may vary from the sublime to, well, amateurish, but for the price, you just can't beat it.

see a show for free

One way to get into theater and music performances absolutely free is to volunteer to work as an usher for a local theater group or symphony. The work is not strenuous nor terribly time consuming, and you will be providing a real service to the theater itself. Your reward: great shows for no cost.

VIRTUAL MUSEUMS
www.mcn.edu

Check out this site if you want to a virtual tour of museums around the country. This Museums Computer Network site provides links to museums across the nation. Through this site, you can find the Web sites, hours of operation, prices, discounts, and free days of hundreds of museums. If you're planing a trip to another city, or just want to be prepared before you visit a museum in your own city, this is a great place to start.

sporty Savings

ENJOY THE THRILL OF LIVE SPORTS WITHOUT PAYING THROUGH THE NOSE.

The skyrocketing prices of pro sports events can chill you from ever wanting to attend again. It's unfortunate, but much of professional sports today is about overpaid players and greedy owners. For many spectators, it's gotten to the point where it isn't nearly as much fun to attend pro games these days. Can you still enjoy sports while saving for your future? Of course! Luckily, there are lots of other options, all of them less expensive and usually more fun—you just have to think outside the box. You can even get involved in a sport—it is cheap and easy to get started. You'll have a blast, and get in shape, too!

professional prices

If you're going to pay professional athletes a gazillion dollars a year, you have to charge sports fans more to see them. Unfortunately, there are not many ways to save on buying tickets to professional sporting events. But we do have a few ideas that you may want to try:

group power Many arenas will offer a discount for a group sale. If you have a group from work, church, synagogue, or other organization, buying in bulk can save you a modest amount per ticket.

sharing the savings You and a friend or a group of friends can purchase a subscription and divide the season's tickets. Subscriptions are slightly less expensive than individual tickets so this approach will reduce your cost. The downside is that you can only go to the games that you and your friends agreed upon before purchasing the tickets.

promo discounts Take advantage of any and all promotional discounts. You'll have to keep a close eye to find and take advantage of these when they're available, but the effort might be worth your while.

get cheap seats Modern stadiums and arenas are designed so well that even the nosebleed seats have good sight lines— you're just farther away. Be sure to bring your binoculars so that you can get a closer look at the action. You can still experience the fun of a live game at the lowest stadium prices that are available.

the finances of food

Even if you score discounted tickets to a professional game, another place where they still try to get you is in the price-gouging food concessions. Avoid them like the plague. Instead, tuck some sandwiches and popcorn into a backpack and drink water. It's healthier and a whole lot cheaper than overpriced hot dogs and sodas.

● More and more stadiums are starting to offer picnic areas where you can watch the game while you eat. This is a real boon to a family—you're still out the cost of the tickets, but you can pack yourself a delicious home-cooked meal, and save on food costs.

minor miracles

As people become more disenchanted with professional teams, they are rediscovering the joys of the minor leagues. Many professional teams have farm teams where they train up and coming talent. Check to see if any of these teams are in your local area. At minor league games everyone gets a great seat because the stadiums are much smaller. These games tend to be more family friendly, and the ticket prices are vastly lower.

spirited school savings

Athletic teams at colleges and universities can inspire tremendous fan loyalty. You can find terrific variety, too — literally a sport for everyone. The only drawback is that it can be hard to get tickets to college or university events because the students and alumns are so very loyal. But these competitions are well worth seeking out if you want to watch some memorable games.

beginner's bargains

Do you have a standout high school team nearby? What about youth football, soccer, or Little League? If you have young children in your family, it especially makes sense to check out some of these games. Because they're usually free, you'll never find a better bargain for spectator sports and the games can be really fun to watch. For adults, community basketball and baseball leagues can be a great deal and a good time, too, whether you play or watch.

outside of the box: think different!

For many years, the most popular American sports were baseball, basketball, and football (with hockey not far behind). Not anymore. Nowadays, the field, so to speak, is wide open and there are a lot more venues for spectator athletics than ever before.

women's team sports In Tucson, Arizona, home of the University of Arizona, the passion for women's softball is beginning to rival that for any of the men's teams. And this is not an isolated phenomenon. Around the country, women's college athletics are rapidly gaining ground, including women's basketball, softball, lacrosse, and soccer. At the professional level, there's the Women's National Basketball Association league (WNBA) during late spring and summer. Most cities that have a NBA team also have a WNBA team. Whether college or pro sports, women's athletics is amazing and there are usually seats available on game day.

soccer This sport, long a favorite in nearly all the rest of the world, has exploded in popularity in the U.S., both in participants and spectators. The games are fast and exciting;

66 Whoever wants to know the heart and mind of America had better learn baseball, the rules and realities of the game—and do it by watching first some high school or small-town teams. 99

Jacques Barzun, cultural critic and historian

the skills breathtaking. See if there's a youth or adult league to check out in your local area.

swimming and diving There are folks who wait for the summer Olympics just to watch the water sports. If you have a college or university nearby (or even a high school) with a ranked swim team, these are extremely exciting events to attend.

gymnastics Another favorite of the Olympics, both men's and women's gymnastic events, are full of heart-stopping moments, graceful routines, and supreme athleticism. Check with high school coaches, college athletic departments, or gymnastic schools to find out about competitions in the area.

martial arts Martial arts schools frequently offer demonstrations and there are competitions between schools. These are exciting to watch and cost little or nothing.

horse shows and dog shows It can be thrilling to watch riders negotiate their horses over huge fences or observe trainers as they make their dogs complete a series of paces. Usually, the cost of attending these events is very low or free. If you have never been to a horse or a dog show, give it a try. Check area stables for event information and local dog trainers for up and coming shows.

working it out

If you really want to have a good time with sports, join a team or get involved in a sport yourself. Although finding a team once you've left school can be more challenging, there are a few places you can check out.

the ymca A local Y will offer teams for every age in just about every sport. Of course, each Y has different facilities, so you may have to search around for one that fits your needs. All in all, they are a good source for team sports.

city or community recreation centers The parks and recreation department in just about every city or community usually sponsors lots of sports teams, from elementary age through seniors. Golf, tennis, swimming, dancing, gymnastics, basketball, baseball, softball, and more are offered for a minimal fee (usually just to cover costs). Call the parks and recreation department nearest you and ask for a brochure of sponsored events.

alumni associations Many alumni associations try to coordinate events to bring fellow alumni together. Some even sponsor sports teams. If your chapter doesn't currently sponsor sports teams, give them a call and suggest it.

religious groups If you attend a house of worship, you probably already know if a team exists. If one doesn't, there may be people who might very well want to form a team or two. Some houses of worship have basketball courts or surrounding fields that can be used for sports.

work Many places of employment have softball and other company teams. If yours doesn't, why not put up a notice asking if folks are interested in starting a team of some sort?

snow-bunny savings

Skiing, especially cross-country, can be a terrific exercise, but it can be very a costly pastime. One way to lower the costs is watch what you spend on equipment.

- At the end of the season (around Easter), search ski shops for last year's model of skis, poles, boots, and clothing. The difference in design from year to year is negligible, and you'll pay considerably less buying skis on sale.
- If possible, visit a ski area at the very end of the season to take advantage of their sales. Most ski resort stores, even posh ones, want to get rid of as much of this year's merchandise as possible and offer outstanding discounts.
- Seek out lesser known or less popular ski areas to lower the cost of a day of skiing. Use the Internet, word-of-mouth, the AAA guides, and a good map to look for places that are off the beaten path and are more likely to want to woo skiers to their resorts.

the low-cost lowdown

If you want a terrific time at very little cost, few things can beat bowling or ice skating. Both sports offer all kinds of specials. Many rinks and alleys have off-peak hours, which are usually cheaper. You can also take lessons or join teams. Best of all, most rinks and alleys are family-friendly environments so the whole gang can join in no matter what their age. Many bowling alleys have bumpers along their gutters designed to keep balls on track even if a wee bowler has thrown it wildly onto the lane. Many ice rinks have shoes with double runners for little ones and a device they can hold onto and push to keep steady on the slippery surface.

Ice rinks offer a cool haven in summertime, and bowling is a good time year round. If you haven't enjoyed either sport in a while, try one of them again. You'll be surprised at how much fun you'll have.

cheap Thrills

IF YOU JUST LOOK,
INEXPENSIVE, ENTERTAINING
EVENTS ARE ALL AROUND.

So what exactly are cheap thrills? They are fun events and places to visit that are either free or don't cost much. We've found that lots of people simply aren't aware of all the interesting, entertaining, or exciting things there are do to in their geographic area. Or they may know about them, but they haven't taken the time or effort to check them out. Once you start looking for cheap thrills, you'll be amazed at how many there are to choose from at any given time during the year.

getting to know you

Even if you've grown up in a town, you probably don't know about all the sites of interest to visit there. If you are a member of the American Automobile Association (AAA), go to the nearest office and pick up a free tour book for your area. You can also try to find one at a secondhand bookstore or your local library. Then sit down and learn about the sites you never knew existed:

- Historic houses—often with beautiful grounds
- National or state landmarks—state buildings, missions, cathedrals, and more
- Living history exhibits—usually connected with a historic house or building, these often include costumed interpreters demonstrating how life was lived during a certain historic period
- Parks—with special gardens, play areas, ponds, lakes, streams, and more
- Caves
- Wildlife refuges—a chance to see birds and animals in their native habitats
- Zoos and other animal parks
- Observatories
- Monuments
- Museums—not just the major well-known places, but little hole-in-the-wall museums as well
- Wineries
- Special ethnic or cultural areas—Chinatown, Little Italy, Germantown, artists' colonies, historic districts, and more
- Scenic drives
- Adventure sightseeing such as trail rides, jeep tours, helicopter tours, or balloon rides
- Shopping areas

For major cities or well-populated areas, you'll also find listings for sporting and performance events, festivals and fairs, special yearly exhibits or shows, and more. All the pertinent information about these events is in the guide, including their prices and any free days or times. Plus, if you are a member of AAA or other type of club, you may be entitled to discounted tickets for many attractions.

botanical garden bargains

Like museums, most botanical gardens sponsor a day each week where people can come and visit free of cost. These gardens are usually extraordinary to stroll through and have much more than trees and flowers to look at. Some have glass greenhouses with exotic plants or a building where they offer special botanical exhibits and courses in gardening. Others have special children's gardens with fun play areas and sculptures to climb through or stations for children to learn about natural science. Some even have sprinkler fountains that youngsters can frolic in on hot days.

you won't snooze at the zoo

Although zoo entrance fees have gotten a bit pricier in recent years, spending a day at the zoo is still an excellent deal. Most zoos today have a lot more to offer than just looking at animals in a cage. In the last 20 to 30 years, zoos have created natural settings so visitors can learn not only about the animals but also about their environments (many of which are endangered). Many have animal handlers who teach and supervise as children experience the thrill of petting or holding a live animal. Some have imaginative play areas for kids, including sprinkler fountain plazas for cooling off. There are also train rides and the occasional merry-go-round. Usually there are lots of picnic tables scattered about. You'll want to pack a lunch; the food sold at zoos is rarely cheap.

66 Every morning, every evening, ain't we got fun. Not much money, oh but honey, ain't we got fun. 99

Raymond B. Egan, songwriter

pick-your-own frugal farms

If you grew up in a rural area, going to a farm and picking your own fruit may not seem that wonderful an idea to you. But for those of us who were raised in cities or suburbs the thought of being able to pick apples, for example, is downright exciting. At pick-your-own farms, there is rarely an entrance fee. You usually get to ride on a wagon to the picking area. Many farms have places for children to play made from hay bales and corn stalks. Often there is a petting zoo where your children or grandchildren can meet goats, sheep, donkeys, and chickens up close and personal. Best of all, most farms offer a large variety of fruit you can pick—from strawberries to pumpkins. When you're done collecting fruit, there's usually a a country store or farmer's stand where you can buy freshly pressed cider, jams and jellies, home-baked goods, and fresh vegetables.

theme park thrift

Yeah, these places can be a lot of fun, but they can really set you back—if you're foolish enough to pay full price and then eat at one of their overpriced concessions. But you don't do that, right? Just about every theme park has off-season

specials, which offer discounts on tickets, a two-for-one voucher, or some other kind of coupon to reduce the cost. In an Entertainment Book, we spotted coupons offering $4 off the price of admission per ticket for up to six admissions to amusement parks like Knott's Berry Farm, Six Flags, Legoland, Sea World, and more. That's a chunk of cash you can save on a family outing— especially if you pack lunch and carry refillable water bottles.

frugal fun parks

Although smaller than your major theme parks, these local places can offer hours of fun—usually for a lot less. And they sponsor discount days during off-peak times to further lower your costs. You can find often coupons—in newspapers and flyers—for go-carts, laser tag, bumper cars, mini-roller coasters, merry-go-rounds, and even one free game of miniature golf with the purchase of one game. One water fun park we visited discounted the entry fee by 30 percent after 3 p.m. to attract more business before the park closed at 7 p.m.

let's go to the fair!

Fairs and festivals offer an excellent opportunity to go out and spend little to nothing, while having a wonderful time. Whether the focus is crafts, music, art, dance, or a specific ethnic heritage, there's a fair or festival to tickle your fancy. Sometimes there will be a small entrance fee, but usually there's not especially if the fair or festival is held in on public land like a park, street, municipal parking lot or campus. The food can be pricey so eat first and carry snacks. If you're shopping for gifts, you may spot some well-priced, unique items. But even if you just walk around and look, fairs and festivals can be big fun for small bucks.

● Keep your eyes open around public holidays, such as Labor Day and Martin Luther King, Jr. Day. Many city and community parks have fairs or festivals at these times. Last year, we went to a Labor Day fair in the park sponsored by local employee unions where everything, including the food, was free. There was music in the band shell, games for kids, antique fire engines, exhibits by many of the unions, blood pressure screenings, and a blood mobile. When it got hot, the firefighters turned on a hose and sprayed the kids down. It was fantastic, fun, and absolutely free.

● County fairs and state fairs are also still a bargain, though they are not as cheap as they once were. The entrance fee is usually moderate but rides can cost you big time. The best bet is to buy tickets for these rides in bulk. If you really want keep the costs down, avoid the rides altogether. Except for the food, just about everything else is free—musical entertainment, animal acts, animal showing pavilions, and special exhibitions. This can be great, inexpensive family entertainment.

● School fairs and church or synagogue fairs are also a lot of fun and very inexpensive to attend. They often include rides or activities for kids, fairly reasonable food, an auction, flea market, or extended yard sale. Keep your eyes open for bargains while you wander.

national and state parks: a real bargain

State and national parks all charge a fee for day use and for camping or other recreational use. When you consider how little you pay for what you get, you'll come to appreciate that these parks offer an amazing deal. From the Cape Cod National Seashore in Massachusetts to the Grand Canyon in Arizona, we have some of the most breathtaking national parks in the world. Luckily, forward-thinking naturalists and statesmen like John Muir and Theodore Roosevelt, have ensured that scenic treasures like these will be preserved for future generations. Whether you pack a picnic and just go for the day, or load up your tents and camp for a week or two, visiting a state or national park will be a guaranteed adventure and good time at a reasonable cost. You will be able to walk, hike, climb mountains, swim in lakes, tube down rivers, drive through the most incredible scenery, spot wildlife, and savor the beauty that belongs to all of us.

speaking of books

Big chain bookstores, like Barnes & Noble and Borders, as well as privately owned hometown stores, have blossomed into dynamic meeting places these days. To draw potential customers into the store, they often host a variety of events throughout the year. Programs include author readings and signings, book discussion groups of all kinds, and kids programs with storytelling and crafts. We recently saw ads for a swing dance exhibition (followed by a lesson), a Shakespeare performance by a local theater company, and music ranging from bluegrass to classical guitar—all for free!

the library: beyond the books

Your public library is much more than just a place to take out books, videos, and CDs for free. Libraries have become community centers that offer computers, book clubs, and fabulous children's programs including story times, craft programs, visits from "celebrities" (like Clifford the Big Red Dog), and much more. Next time you go in for a book, ask your librarian for a schedule of activities.

MUSIC FESTIVALS AND CRAFTS FAIRS

The festivalfinder.com site lists more than 2,500 music festivals in the United States. Every music genre is covered — alternative, classical, rock, blues, jazz, folk, Cajun/zydeco, country, and more. Just point, click, and you have the dates, time, place, and everything else you need to go. If you love to browse (or sell at) crafts fairs, the craftsfaironline.com site offers a simple point-and-click guide to crafts fairs across America. Find one near your hometown or look for fairs in places you plan to visit.

www.festivalfinder.com

www.craftsfaironline.com

more store savings

Bookstores are not alone in their effort to lure folks in with special events. You can find all sorts of unusual entertainment at any number of stores.

sporting goods stores These range from the small, sport-specific store to the mega-complexes. The smaller stores will have smaller events, sometimes in their parking lots and often tied in with a sale. The mega-complexes have rock-climbing walls, simulators, and all sorts of interesting hands-on, try-it-out areas for any number of sports.

music stores As you might imagine, these specialize in musical events that sell CDs, but they can offer wonderful opportunities to hear some terrific local artists (or the occasional guest star) performing for free.

toy stores Many of these kiddie entertainment emporiums, especially the smaller ones, are taking a page from the bookstores and planning events for children of all ages. We've seen Harry Potter events, American Girl teas, storytelling, singalongs, pajama parties, and oodles of arts and crafts mornings, afternoons, or evenings.

food stores Wanting to appeal to more than just the main shopper in the family, you can find health fairs offering flu shots, blood pressure and cholesterol screening, "farmer's markets" with seasonal crafts, foods, music, and more.

mall moves

The village square may have gone the way of the dodo, but the mall has moved in to take its place. No longer merely a conglomeration of stores, the mall has evolved into a meeting place, an eating place, a play place, a movie place, and a place where something always seems to be happening.

fairs We've seen ads for safety fairs at the mall, where you can register your child, have a picture taken for security purposes, check out information, let your children enjoy an interactive learning experience on "stranger danger" and more. We've also visited arts and crafts fairs, both to look and possibly to buy, and farmer's market–type events with foods, crafts, and entertainment.

seasonal specials There are few places in town that compare to a good mall during holidays. At Christmas, you can hear live music from local amateur or professional groups, see children's plays, visit Santa, and shop. At Easter, you may find the Bunny holding court with a big egg hunt for the little ones. Halloween often brings a "safe" treat outing, with various establishments setting up booths for the kids to trick-or-treat for candy and small toys, or you may have access to a not-too-scary and very affordable haunted house.

exercise A most common site at malls during the icy winters is seniors doing mall walks for health and mothers with strollers and toddlers wandering up and down the mall for exercise and entertainment. In the Southwest, you see the same groups in the middle of the 100-plus summer heat.

playtime More and more malls are realizing the value of having a play area for young children. Usually located near the food court, they are sometimes wildly imaginative. There's a mall in a northern suburb of Chicago that has a "tree house" to climb all over, including slides from a number of "knots." All are climate controlled, and most are fenced off so you can safely let your kids run to their hearts content. The idea is that you will eat, the kids will work out their fidgetiness, and then you are more likely to start shopping again. As a penny pincher, skip the lunch, buy an inexpensive treat if you must, let the kids have a glorious time, then go home.

THAT'S ENTERTAINMENT

We've mentioned the Entertainment Book earlier. It's that big coupon book sold by scout troops, church youth groups, and schools that costs from $30 to $50. While half are restaurant coupons, in the other half we found a treasure trove of discounts for family fun:

● Video rental: rent two get one free
● Family fun parks
● Museums: art, children, science, planetarium, and nature
● Water parks
● Comedy clubs
● Symphony
● Theater
● Opera
● Dance performances
● Movie theater discounts: two for the price of one or total of six at discount
● Mountain biking
● Scuba lessons
● Martial arts
● Tumbling
● Golf: both miniature and real
● Ice skating
● Bowling
● Pool and billiards
● Minor league baseball and pro basketball discount tickets
● Family pass to a day at the Y
● Exercise classes: buy one month, get one free.

Thrifty Travel

- up in the air
- discount detours
- savings at sea
- frugal family fun

Let's get one thing straight— we are not into seedy lodgings, substandard food, rickety airplanes, leaky ships, or putting off travel until the kids are through Harvard. Travel is terrific, mind-expanding, entertaining, and enlightening, and frankly it should be a lot of fun. You just have to know how to do it well for the least amount. Probably your biggest aid in touring on the cheap is the World Wide Web. Even if you don't own a computer, head to the library to take advantage of the outstanding specials on airfares, hotels, cruises, restaurants, and more that can be found on any of the sites dedicated to travel. And don't leave your family behind—travel helps your children grow and develop in more ways than you think. Just use know-how to make your family vacation a dream for you all. By finding the best deal on your plane tickets, a hotel for 50 percent off standard rates, or negotiating a family cruise for hundreds of dollars less, you can treat yourself to a five-star dinner, World Cup soccer game, or La Scala—the proper reward for the thrifty traveler.

Get going—the world awaits you.

up in the Air

IF YOU AREN'T ALREADY USING
YOUR PC TO MAKE AIR TRAVEL QUICK
AND CHEAP, GET THEE TO A MODEM!

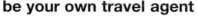

There's no doubt that air travel is the quickest and most convenient way to get from one place to another, especially if you are traveling long distances. But airline tickets can be expensive if you don't know how to find the cheapest fares. With the right tools, you'll discover that there are fantastic bargains still available to take you where you want to go, when you want to go.

be your own travel agent

For years, working with a skilled travel agent was one of the most effective ways to save money. Travel agents still can be effective, but today they have competition: the home computer. These days anyone can search the Web for the best fares, hotels, or tours, and make their own arrangements.

○ To book tickets on a computer, you'll need a printer so that you can have a hard copy of all your reservations. You'll also need time to check out the many Web sites that cater to the tourist industry.

○ To make your research faster and easier, bookmark your favorite sites for bargain travel, hotels, and cars on your computer. This step makes comparison shopping much quicker and simpler every time you want to use the computer to make reservations.

○ What if you don't happen to have a computer to use for your research? Don't despair. You can still find travel information by phone, but it definitely will be slower; getting through to a customer service representative can take time and lots of patience.

no time for research

If you don't want to put the time and energy into research and making your own travel arrangements, then you will want to work with a good travel agent. In order to get the perfect vacation at the right price, make sure the agent understands what is important to you. Also, check up on the agent. Many airline companies offer bonuses to travel agencies that sell the most tickets. Keep in mind that your agent may have an agenda other than getting you the best prices. If you have an agent you know and trust, he or she can be a fantastic source of information and decent fares.

sites for savings

There are dozens of travel sites now on the Internet. Some of the most popular are Travelocity, Expedia, Cheap Tickets, and Orbitz (see Resources box, page 228). You can find wonderful bargains on each of these sites; however, a 2002 *Consumer Reports Travel Letter* article comparing the sites reported that although the cheapest fares were listed on Expedia, getting some of those dirt cheap fares was hard to do. Travelocity had a better track record of fares and flights with good prices you could actually book. Your best bet when looking for the right flight at the right price is to check several sites to see what each can offer at the time.

○ Club costs: AAA and other auto clubs, price clubs, and membership organizations frequently offer full travel services, including airfares. Though we have not had luck getting the absolute cheapest fares with these clubs and organizations, they are worth checking out.

○ Dirt cheap? We found a pretty cool Web site, which is called traveldirt.com. It had links to actual reservation sites, but was also full of information on strategies for finding cheap airfares, saving on parking at airports, credit card mileage programs, and more. They also had pages devoted to travel safety, health away from home, maps, family travel tips, cruises, discounts on hotels, and auto travel. The site is interesting, valuable, and well worth a visit.

going to the source

After you've checked the availability of flights and price of tickets with several of the travel sites, go directly to the airline's Web site or call the airline itself. Let's say you want to fly from Des Moines to Philadelphia. Once you have collected information from the travel sites on the lowest American Airlines fares at the times you want to fly, go to American Airline's Web site directly and check the price they offer for those times. When we've done this, we've gotten a slightly better deal on the flights we really wanted than was shown on the travel site. It doesn't always work that way, but it's worth trying. Most airline Web site addresses are almost always www.airlinename.com (for example, www.americawest.com).

the southwest story

One carrier to always check is Southwest Airlines. Southwest doesn't allow its flights or fares to be advertised on any other Web site than its own (with the exception of Sabre, which can be difficult to access unless you're a travel agent). You will often find the cheapest flights through Southwest—the company that pioneered no-frills flying. Southwest has always kept its fares very low by eliminating food service and viewing air travel as a get-there-fast-and-cheap proposition. So be sure to check the airline's site (www.southwest.com) whenever you travel. By the way, don't be surprised if they fly to less popular airports. For example, Southwest flies into Midway Airport in Chicago, not O'Hare. That, too, is part of their cost-cutting strategy, which we'll review later.

> 66 Imagination is as good as many voyages— and much cheaper. 99

George William Curtis, 19th-century American author

cost-effective charm

If you decide to call the phone reservation numbers instead of booking online, learn these tricks to make the most of your phone time:

○ Do your homework first. Check newspapers or online sources to get a sense of what the best fares are at the time you want to travel, and which airlines are offering specials. You can use this information to spur the agent into topping the deals you've already found.

○ Call very early or very late. If you catch a ticket agent at a time when they're having fewer phone calls, you're more likely to get their full attention and help finding the best fares. What if American is offering a great deal, but you prefer to fly United? Ask the United agent if he or she can match the rival offer.

○ Most important (and this is true of anyone you call wanting a favor), use every ounce of charm in your stock. We've found the greatest strategy is making the agent laugh by being a happy, verbally entertaining, presence in the midst of their shift. By nudging the client-salesperson relationship in a more sympathetically human direction, we've found that we both got a better deal and enjoyed the interaction much more. A win-win situation, wouldn't you agree?

budget airports

One of the reasons Southwest can offer lower fares is because most of their flights originate and land at less-popular airports. This helps the airline keep their costs down and it may work as a bargain fare strategy for other airlines as well. Many airline Web sites have a "check nearby airports" feature that can automatically zip you to a smaller, usually cheaper, destination. For example, instead of flying into San Francisco International, you can fly into San Jose or Oakland Airports—close by and less traveled. You'll usually find good transportation to major city areas from these smaller airports. The savings on airfares can make the change in destination really worth your while.

go small for big bargains

Although everyone knows about major airlines, such as United, American, and Delta, there are many smaller airlines (see Resources box, page 230) well worth checking out.

more for less A greater number of seats on the smaller airlines are sold at a bargain rate, and the difference between the highest and lowest fares isn't as big as on major carriers.

no saturday, no extra charge Some of the smaller airlines have streamlined their booking so that they don't charge the heftier fee for stays that don't include a Saturday night.

small airlines, small airports Following Southwest's lead, smaller carriers tend to fly into a city's secondary airports, thus allowing them to offer lower fares.

small feels good After September 11, wide-spread panic wreaked havoc with the major airlines, causing personnel and service cuts in an effort to lower fares. However, the smaller airlines haven't been as affected and in some cases their business has actually improved. Smaller can feel more secure to nervous travelers.

sensational service Although major carriers continue to rake in complaints about disinterested attendants and agents, smaller airlines rate consistently high on customer satisfaction. Airline travelers feel they get more personal service when traveling with a smaller carrier.

constant savings Great fares on major carriers tend to be short-lived and often hard to get. The fares on smaller carriers change less over the course of the year and are consistently lower.

timing is everything

In many travel guide's tips about saving money, the virtues of making reservations early to save money are extolled over and over again. The travel guides are right. You'll usually get a decent price if you make reservations several weeks in advance, and you're more likely to get the flights you want and the seats you want if you book early. But booking too early has burned us. Most airlines don't offer a supersaver fare until close to the departure date. It's a gamble: Do you wait and wait and hope the airlines drop their fares, or do you take the safe route and buy tickets way in advance? It depends on the trip and your nerves. The smart approach is to keep an eye on normal low fares to destinations you travel to regularly (cities where family members live, for example). Get to know the range of reasonable prices to that destination. Then, if you really need to travel at a certain time, on a specific date, start checking fares about six weeks before your trip. When you see one that you know is reasonable and meets your needs, go ahead and book it. If you wait until the last minute, you may get a further discount, but you'll often have to be flexible about things such as nonstop flights, departure dates, and seats.

In the early days of air travel, no one expected to get a meal when they were flying in the air. Well, everything old seems to be new again. When Southwest Airlines was launched they announced they would offer beverage service and snacks during flights, but no meals. The savings would be passed onto customers through cheaper airfares. In recent years, other airlines have followed Southwest's lead to keep costs down. We recently flew from Tucson to Chicago and happened to notice that our ticket did not mention food. We called American Airlines and were informed by an agent that any flight under four hours (ours was three hours and 50 minutes) no longer had any food service. Because our flight left around 7 a.m., we picked up bagels, cream cheese, and fruit, and feasted happily on board. Fellow passengers who were unprepared ended up paying top dollar for fast food at the airport. If your flight doesn't provide food, pack a little picnic to have while your flying. The food will be better, you can eat when and what you want, and the lower airfares will be worth every penny you save on airline food.

SITES FOR SORE POCKETS

Try one of these Web sites for discount travel, whether you just want to book a flight or a room or buy an entire package.

www.travelocity.com

www.expedia.com

www.orbitz.com

www.cheaptickets.com

www.travelnow.com

www.onetravel.com

www.travelzoo.com

off-peak perks

It is still usually cheaper to fly off-peak, departing on a Tuesday, Wednesday, or Thursday, and staying over one Saturday night. Flying at odd times—very late at night, for example—may also save you some cash. Check carefully and see how much you can save by adjusting your dates and times (if possible), and then determine whether it is worth the inconvenience. Frankly, sometimes we've found the savings to be negligible and the inconvenience considerable. You'll have to decide what level of savings make the extra effort worthwhile for you and your family.

frugal frequent fliers

Just about every airline has a frequent flier program. Even if you don't fly that often, it can still pay to belong to a program—especially since it costs you nothing to join.

○ Join several programs—if you tend to fly on two or three airlines, sign up to get the frequent flier miles offered by all of the carriers you use regularly.

○ To check to see if the program is worth your while, compare the minimum number of miles awarded per leg of each flight. The higher the number of miles awarded per leg, the faster you can score either upgrades or free tickets. The most advantageous frequent flier programs are the ones that require the least amount of miles before awarding you a round-trip ticket.

○ Check out the list of partners for each program. Hotels, car rentals, and other services often offer frequent flier miles that you can use to acquire free airline tickets more quickly. Also, check for partnerships between airlines; many allow miles to be used towards the purchase of tickets on other domestic and international carriers.

○ Many programs have expiration dates on their miles—look for programs that do not make this restriction.

○ Some airlines offer credit cards that accrue miles whenever you use them—usually one mile per dollar spent. You can also find nonairline cards that offer the same program. This can be a great way to get lots of miles fast, but don't sign up for this type of credit card unless you are sure that you can pay off the balance every month. Credit card debt is one of the worst money pits to fall into and definitely not worth the few miles you may accrue by sliding down that slippery slope.

○ Check out programs that offer frequent-flier mileage for long-distance phone minutes: Every time you make a long-distance phone call you pick up miles. But make sure it's a good deal otherwise.

○ Use your miles on tickets that are pricey, not on those that are already discounted. Those big routes, like New York to

San Francisco, inspire ticket wars among airlines so you're more likely to find a discount fare. But trips to some less-frequented cities are almost never discounted because there's less competition. These tickets for less commonly used routes are the best candidates for you to use your frequent-flier miles on.

consolidators and charters: cheap?

If you're planning a trip to a popular vacation destination, it always pays to check these:

consolidators A consolidator buys up blocks of air tickets and then sells them at a large discount. You will see advertisements for consolidators in the travel section of most large Sunday newspapers. This can yield you excellent prices on tickets to major overseas destinations, including Europe, the Caribbean, Australia and New Zealand, and Asia. But you'll find a number of restrictions on the tickets, so you must be willing to be flexible to maximize savings this way.

charter flights These are another way to save money. Usually, these flights are nonstop. They are almost always to highly popular vacation destinations and can be purchased as "air only" or in combination with tour packages that offer discounts on hotels, sightseeing, and other vacation amenities. As with consolidators, there will be fewer options on availability and seating. Because you'll be buying this type of ticket through a tour operator, you might want to use a knowledgeable travel agent to protect yourself from scams and last-minute cancellations.

carefree couriers

If you really want to save money on airfare, consider traveling as a courier. To take advantage of this option, you'll need to travel alone, have a very flexible schedule, and travel really light (carry-on bags only). That's because you'll be traveling with a package (frequently documents) to deliver to a legitimate company. To find ads seeking freelance couriers, check newspapers and magazines, or go online. The Web site run by the International Association of Air Travel Couriers (www.courier.org) contains all the information you need about becoming a courier. Furthermore, you can join the association for $45, fill out the application online, and start checking for flights. By acting as a courier, you can save as much as 85 percent on the price of a regular airline ticket. The more flexible you can be with your schedule, the more you can save. You'll get the best bargain on airfares closest to the package delivery date. This is an increasingly popular way to travel cheap and is becoming more competitive, especially for favorite destinations or times of the year, so research your options carefully before committing yourself.

ASK, ASK, ASK

The airline industry is changing rapidly. It used to be that almost every carrier offered discounts for seniors. Anyone over 62 could get a discount of ten percent or more off the regular airfare. These days, however, the senior discount is not so readily available. Southwest Airlines still offers a senior discount, but few other carriers do. Regardless of age, other carriers are offering supersaver specials instead. If you're a senior citizen and have received discounts on your favorite airline in the past, be sure to ask if it is still available before you book. If it isn't, check other airlines for a discount. It may be time to try a new airline.

fly for free: get bumped

If you have a really flexible schedule and like to gamble a bit, try to get a ticket on an extremely popular flight—one that tends to be overbooked. If there are too many passengers, airline representatives will often ask for volunteers willing to give up their seat in exchange for a $100 to $200 travel coupon or a free ticket good for any destination in the United States. If the later flight keeps you at the airport overnight, the airline will sometimes throw in free accommodations, too. If you're willing to volunteer for this inconvenience, it's a fairly painless way to snag a free ticket.

be assured, you're insured

If you have normal health and life insurance, do not purchase additional flight insurance—it's just a way of getting you to spend money unnecessarily. And the coverage isn't nearly as good as a standard insurance policy. Besides, if your plane does go down (heaven forbid!), you can be assured the carrier's insurance company will be paying your heirs a lot more than any quickie flight insurance policy would.

parking pluses

Unless you have great public transportation or someone willing to get you to and from the airport, you will probably end up leaving your car in a parking lot for a period of time. The closer the lot is to the airport, the higher the parking fees tend to be. Unless you want to pay a ton of money, never leave your car in short-term parking for more than an hour or two. The long-term parking options at most airports are relatively decent, and shuttle buses run frequently between the lots and the departure gates. But the cheapest option is a satellite parking lot on the airport outskirts. They charge up to half what long-term airport lots cost, offer frequent shuttle bus service, and are usually fenced in and guarded.

bargain buses?

Many cities have privately owned shuttle buses that will pick you up at one of several central locations (or even at your home) and take you to the airport. If you are traveling alone, that could be a less expensive option than parking at the airport. If you're traveling with a family or a group of friends, private shuttle bus costs can become more expensive that driving and parking at the airport. If you live in an area with good public transportation to the airport, that will probably be the cheapest option of all—unless, of course, you can get a friend or family member to drive you.

○ If you are going to a city where you don't need to rent a car to get around (such as Chicago, New York, or San Francisco), don't just jump into a cab or an airport bus to get into the city. With your return to the airport, you can easily end up adding another $40 or $60 to the cost of the trip. Most metropolitan areas have excellent cheap public transportation that will take you to the heart of the city. You can get from O'Hare to downtown Chicago, for example, on the Blue Line rapid transit train in 40 minutes for $1.50, and it often beats cars stuck in traffic.

○ If you are not renting a car at your destination, don't forget to check to see if your hotel offers free (except for a tip) airport transportation service for guests.

STRANDED IN CINCINNATI!

Most people who regularly travel by plane have faced this moment: The voice comes over the intercom stating that the flight you've been waiting on for hours has been canceled. Scrambling for options, a planeload of unhappy passengers rush and form a humongous line at the ticket agent's desk. Quick—what do you do?

- **Get to a telephone:** Pull out your cell phone (airport phones can cost more than you think and are often in use) or, if you don't have one, hightail it to the nearest pay phone and use your calling card.

- **Call your travel agent:** This is when going through a travel agent, if you have one, can be a big bonus. He or she can make other arrangements for you and your problem is solved.

- **Call the airlines:** If you don't have a travel agent, start calling other carriers. When traveling, try to keep a list of toll-free telephone numbers for all the major airlines tucked in your wallet so you can call easily and quickly. You can rearrange the flight yourself, while sitting in an airport chair.

- **Seek service:** Instead of standing on line at the gate of the canceled flight, head to a less-crowded customer service desk at another gate and look for an agent who can spend a few minutes helping you.

- **Cash in club privileges:** If you happen to be a member of the airline's airport club, zip in to their lounge for faster, more personalized service.

- **Stand your ground:** When a flight is canceled, an airline will usually try to book you on another one of its own flights. But sometimes, they can't get you on another flight that same day. If you have an important reason to get home quickly, be polite but firm with the ticketing agent and insist that they come up with a reasonable solution, even if it means transferring you to another airline.

discount
Detours

Fortunately, there are lots of ways to keep costs down and travel in style. It requires a bit of research and creative thinking, but if you're willing to make the effort, you can travel the world and come home solvent. Getting the best room rates, lowering car rental costs, sightseeing for a song, or investing in a tour package, will permit you to indulge in the extras you enjoy— specialty shopping, theater, sporting events— without guilt or financial ruin.

touring for savings

Packaged tours can be a godsend to those traveling on a budget. If you're exploring an out-of-the-way destination, they can also be the safest way to travel. On a package tour, the dates and times are preset, and the cost usually includes lodgings, some meals, sightseeing, and transportation to the places in the tour. Airfare is usually extra, though it also may be included. Tours take the hassle out of planning a trip because all the arrangements and details are handled by the tour operators. Tour operators usually take care of any problems during the tour, as well. Because tours are preplanned, you are more limited in your itinerary and may not get to every destination you'd like to, but the savings and freedom from stress can make up for the lack of freedom.

join the club for thrifty travel

Almost every club you can think of offers some sort of travel service, often with some terrific discounts on tour packages. Of course, auto clubs, like AAA have built their reputation on rating hotels and getting member discounts, but they also offer tours by bus and rail. Price clubs, such as Costco and Sam's Club, have pretty extensive travel services and you can locate a good deal through them. To take just one example, surfing the Costco Web site recently, we were struck by the following offers:

- Six nights in Montego Bay, Jamaica, with all meals and beverages, entertainment, water sports, fitness center, and more included. The original price was $1,013; the Costco rebate was $105, for a total cost per person of $908.
- Three nights at L'Auberge de Sedona, a highly ranked resort in the Red Rock country of Arizona with a top-rated restaurant. It included a four-day rental of a compact car. And the total cost was $350 per person.
- Three nights at the Ritz Hotel in Barcelona, Spain, with daily buffet breakfast, for $351 per person.

If you're a member of a price club, it's smart shopping to check your own club for similar types of packages or tours whenever you are planning a vacation trip. Price clubs are not the first place you think of for this, but they can pay off.

travel agent to tour guide

You've already become your own travel agent to save money. Have you ever considered becoming a tour guide to save even more? All you need to do is contact several tour operators and offer to put together a group for a specific tour. Usually, if you get enough people to sign up, your travel costs will be covered completely; if you sign up more than the minimum needed for a tour, you may garner considerable reductions for a companion. To organize a tour, you'll need to gather friends or acquaintances that share a specific interest:

- ⃝ Wine tasting tour of France, Spain, or Germany
- ⃝ Literary tour of the British Isles, visiting all the homes or areas written about by literary giants
- ⃝ Asian art tours of China, Japan, Korea, and/or any other Asian country
- ⃝ "In the footsteps of the Raj" tour of India, exploring Indian royalty and the influence of British occupation
- ⃝ "Following the Mission Trail," visiting as many of the missions in Arizona and California as possible
- ⃝ Music tours, art tours, soccer tours, folk craft tours, walking tours, or biking tours can also be organized to explore regional sites of interest.

sightseeing specials: 50 percent off

When you travel to a city, pay a visit to their tourist bureau to find out about tours the city sponsors. You'll find that many places have inexpensive walking tours with excellent guides that charge far less than big tour operators do. Also check with the local historical society and architectural society to see what kind of tours or educational programs they're sponsoring. Don't forget that city parks, museums, universities, and libraries often have free or discounted tours on specific days or at special times. If you do a little research, you may find several tours for free—our favorite price!

discount dreaming

Regardless of where you're traveling, one of the biggest expenses is often lodging. Although we feel that cleanliness and quiet are the top priorities, you have to determine your own "musts" and how much you're willing to pay for them. A lot will depend on how much time you're planning to spend in a hotel room. If you're staying at a resort, you'll spend more time in a room. If you're touring several cities, you'll probably spend less. In any case, try these tips to get a good hotel room at a traveler-friendly rate.

- ⃝ First search the travel sites on your computer— Travelocity, Expedia, Cheap Tickets, and more—they all have hotel connections to find you deals in the city you're visiting. Check several sites to see which comes up with

❝Be careful going in search of adventure— it's ridiculously easy to find.❞

William Least Heat Moon, American travel writer

the best deal. If you belong to an auto club, check their Web site too. But before you book, call the hotel directly. You may land an even cheaper rate by phone.

○ Don't just call the national toll-free number for hotel reservations, spend a quarter or two and call the hotel itself. Nationwide reservation desks don't always net you the best rate because they aren't aware of special promotions at individual hotels.

○ Check your Entertainment Book—they have a discount hotel number that provides discounts of up to 50 percent on lodging around the world.

○ Open that next blue envelope from ValPak. We found a coupon for 50 percent off every second night at participating Holiday Inns.

○ If you belong to Costco or Sam's Club, check their travel services—Costco was recently offering up to 15 percent off on reservations at Best Western hotels.

○ Ask about corporate rates. Even if you own a small business or work as a freelancer, you may qualify for a discount of as much as 20 percent off the standard room rates.

○ Ask about discounts for seniors, special offers for members of clubs (like AAA), promotional rebates, or anything else that could lower the cost of a room.

○ Try a discount hotel broker by contacting the tourist bureau in the city you want to visit. If one is available, they can lower room prices by as much as 50 percent.

○ Don't forget to haggle, especially if it is off season. Empty rooms cost the hotel money, so see if you can talk them down a bit on the room rate.

sleeping for quarters

For some people, a luxury hotel is the only way to travel, but the wise penny-pincher traveler knows that a place to sleep need only be clean and preferably cheap so that you can spend your money on food, sightseeing, cultural events, sports, shopping, and other enjoyable activities. Here are some ideas on cheap places to rest your weary body after a busy day of sightseeing.

college dormitories Many schools have made it a business to rent dorm rooms to travelers during the summer when there are few students are around. And they charge very modest fees. Of course, you might have a bathroom down the hall, but the savings will more than make up for that. The University of London, for example, will rent a dorm room for about $35 a day, including breakfast. The school is located in the heart of the city within easy walking distance of all major train and subway lines. The rooms are very clean, though they lack glamour—but how much time will you be spending in your room anyway?

hostels Not just for youth, there are hostels for senior citizens, families, couples—you name it! A good source to explore is www.hostels.com, produced by an independent group, not an international hosteling organization. You can find listings for hostels in North and South America, Africa, Asia, the Middle East, Australia, New Zealand, the South Pacific, Europe, and Russia.

religious retreats You can often book a room at a retreat run by a religious organization. Because most people are there for religious reasons, there will be more rules to follow. The facilities are usually very well maintained.

bed and breakfasts Also known as B & B's, these establishments have long been a way to get a room at a bargain rate, especially outside of the U.S. For some reason, American B & B's have evolved into high-end inns—not always at bargain prices. In other countries, however, you can still save money at a B & B. Typically, this is a private home that has set aside one or more bedrooms for paid guests with breakfast included. Sometimes you'll have a private bath; most often, you'll share. The breakfast can be a simple continental affair of bread, rolls, pastry, fruit, juice, and coffee or tea, but in some cases, you might be presented with a hearty home-cooked feast. Ask about the meals when you make your reservation.

other alternatives There are other, off-the-beaten track, places to lay your head. To find out about them, contact the tourist bureau in the city or area you want to visit and ask about alternative lodging ideas.

swapping for savings

Another way to lower the cost of lodging is to consider swapping your home or apartment with someone in another city, state, or country. There are many books written about home-exchange clubs, so check your library or bookstore. Usually, there is a fee to join the club, and then your name will be added to a list of people interested in exchanges.

- When you write up your listing, be sure to include any and all amenities that would make your home particularly appealing: access to public transportation, historic sites nearby, parks, mountains, lakes, rivers, natural areas or wildlife refuges, theaters, sporting venues, amusement parks, museums, shopping, and so on.
- If you have regular access to a health club, swimming pool, tennis courts, beach, special parking or the like, include this information in your listing, too.
- Get it in writing: the home exchange networks have standard contracts available and you should use them. The contract should include a guarantee that swappers will pay replacement value for any damage.

THE ELDERHOSTEL EQUATION

www.elderhostel.org
or 1-877-426-8056

Founded in 1975, Elderhostel is a nonprofit organization that offers education and travel opportunities for people 55 and older. Their motto is: The world is our classroom. A quick perusal of their Web site or their catalog bears that motto out. Elderhostel offers wonderful, unique package tours to destinations all over the world, from the Navajo Country of northeastern Arizona to an "Odyssey" tour of Turkey. In some cases, the lodgings are at a university or college; more often they are at good hotels. Classes and tours are included in the cost, as are many meals. These trips are for seniors who never tire of learning about other cultures, crafts, geography, art, music, natural history, and more. Contact them at the Web site or toll-free phone number above for information or a free catalog.

cars on the cheap

You can find some great deals on rental cars, but you'll have to look for them. This is an area in which a little time spent surfing the Net can yield you great savings (not to mention the convenience of finding bargains this way, compared to calling 800 numbers). Check all the major travel sites, auto club sites, and the home page of each the major rental car companies for specials offered only over the Internet.

coupons, coupons, coupons Next time you get your credit card bill, don't just toss the glossy inserts—you may be throwing away discount coupons for car rentals. Check fliers in the mail, the magazine or newsletter from your auto club or price club, look up your frequent flier Web site, and see if they offer coupons or discounts. Also scan airline inflight magazines on your next trip for clippable coupons.

size cents Always book the cheapest car going, which is usually also the smallest (though not necessarily). Because these cars are limited in numbers, the rental agency will generally offer you an upgrade for the same price. In fact, if they don't have the car you ordered and want you to upgrade, don't let them trick you into paying more for it, especially if you reserved ahead with a credit card. On the other hand, if you get to the car rental desk and they actually have that mini you don't really want to drive for a week, they are always happy to let you upgrade—and may still give you a good deal on it.

rental rip-offs Though each and every car rental office will try it's hardest to sell you insurance while you're driving their car, it's almost always a waste of money. Check with your own car insurance agent, your auto club, or your credit card company. You'll probably find the coverage offered by the rental company is simply duplicating coverage you are already paying for. However, this may not be true overseas.

fill 'er up In the past, the car you rented would always have a full tank and it would save you money to return the car full of gas, preferably from a cheapie gas station. The times have changed, however, and now you'll often be getting a car with only a half tank. Since the rental company simply requires you to return the car with the same amount of gas as at the time of rental (or they'll refill at high rates), it makes no sense to put in more gas than necessary. Ask for details before you rent, then follow the cheapest option.

GOOD OLD WAYS

Going out to restaurants used to be a big deal for the average person; very pricey and reserved only for special occasions. This isn't a bad philosophy to adopt while traveling, especially if you want to save money and spend it elsewhere. Many hotels and resorts provide a mini-fridge, coffee maker, and microwave in their rooms. On a recent stay at a resort, we brought along a bag of fresh bagels, cream cheese, juice, and fresh fruit to eat breakfast en suite. At lunchtime, we'd stop by a local supermarket or farmer's market to buy bread, cheese, and salami for a picnic. Then we'd treat ourselves to a great dinner. We were able to eat inexpensive, delicious, healthy food for two meals and then cut loose a bit for the third meal without guilt.

riding the rails for less

Train trips can be lots of fun. Amtrak (www.amtrak.com) has a number of special deals, including discounts for senior citizens, students, families, special packages, and more. But you can also find coupons for train travel from other sources:

- The Entertainment Book has coupons for special trips, such as two-for-one coupons for the Grand Canyon Railroad, which goes from the town of Williams, Arizona, to the rim of the Grand Canyon—with lots of Wild West entertainment thrown in. Look in your book for coupons on special rail trips in your area. A recent copy of the Entertainment Book included coupons for ten percent off any Amtrak train—a tidy savings at any time.

- Clubs and organizations, such as AAA (www.aaa.com) and Costco and Sam's Club travel services, also offer discounts or packages on rail trips. Through these services, we found ten percent off Amtrak prices for their Superliner service and for their car train (where your car travels with you on the train).

foreign exchange

Exchanging currency can cost a bundle if you don't know how to do it right. Never exchange large amounts of currency where it is most convenient. For example, if you exchange dollars for foreign currency at the airport, you'll pay an absurd service fee. Your best bet will be banks and foreign exchange companies before you leave or in the country you are visiting. Like anything else, you'll want to shop around to get the best rate.

tips on tipping: when not to tip

More travelers squander money with excessive tips than any-thing else. We're not advocating squeezing people when they provide you with good service, but tipping practices vary widely from culture to culture. For instance, many European restaurants include a "seating" or service fee in their final bill. Make sure you check closely to see how much of a tip you're being charged already before you decide to tack on an additional tip. If you want to give something extra, five or ten percent is more than generous. Before you travel, check with a guidebook or travel agent to find out local tipping customs. Setting down the American standard of 15 to 20 percent without a thought is not the penny-pinching way.

**HOME EXCHANGE
THE EASY WAY**

·······················
**www.exchangehome.com
or 1-800-848-7927**
·······················

Out of curiosity, we went online and input "home exchange" into our search engine. We couldn't believe how many entries popped up, and they seemed to cover just about anyone! There were listings for home exchanges for seniors and the disabled. One major site we found was for Exchange Homes. Founded in 1986, this large company offers a yearlong membership for $30. Members can list their homes and can browse possible exchanges online. The company protects the privacy of their members and bars non-members from accessing the exchange lists. They have a useful frequently asked questions area that can give you a thorough overview of how exchanges work.

savings at
Sea

DON'T LET THE PRICES SCARE
YOU AWAY. A CRUISE PACKAGE
CAN BE A PRETTY GOOD BARGAIN.

Sailing off into the sunset sounds so romantic until you start pricing those luxury cruises. As mind-boggling as they might seem at first, you have to keep in mind that the price of a cruise includes just about everything. You get most of the amenities found on board at no extra cost including all meals, live entertainment, movies, organized activities, pools, fitness centers, and more. If life aboard the high seas beckons, full speed ahead!

you better shop around

As with so many things, shopping for a cruise will require effort on your part. Luckily, there are many venues for finding cruise packages so you'll have loads of options. Most of the sources are the same as the ones you would use to find discount airfare, lodging and tour packages: travel Web sites, auto clubs, price clubs, and other clubs offering travel services, consolidators, charters, and so on.

before you sail

Cruises are not for everyone, especially if you don't like being confined to a limited space or if you suffer from seasickness easily. Once you're on a ship, it's very hard to get off before the end of the cruise. Before making a significant investment in this kind of vacation, ask yourself (and your family) the following questions:

○ Are your favorite vacations the kind where you all just kick back and let someone else take care of details?
○ Do you like having a set schedule or itinerary?
○ Do you enjoy vacations surrounded by lots of people?
○ Is it important to know vacation expenses ahead of time?
○ Do you want a whole family experience with special areas or activities just for the kids?

If you answer most of these questions with a yes, a cruise might be your perfect trip.

surfing for sales

Using your computer to check out specials can save you big bucks, even if you end up having to use a travel agent or booking directly through the company. Surfing several sites can give you a good overview of the cost of a cruise and how to save a few hundred bucks.

onetravel This site, for example, was showing a seven-night Eastern Caribbean cruise on the Disney Magic (without airfare) for $940.35; a Western Caribbean cruise was $972.77.

travelocity This site had a seven-night Eastern Caribbean Thanksgiving Cruise for $679 on Carnival, a four-night Western Caribbean holiday on Norwegian for $159, and a seven-night Mexican Riviera on Royal Caribbean for $599.

AAA The AAA site showed a three-night Pacific Northwest cruise from Seattle on Royal Caribbean from $299, and a 12-night Alaska Glacier Cruise from Vancouver to San Diego on Celebrity from $900.

costco The online travel services here offered a seven-day, smoke-free Eastern Caribbean cruise on Carnival from $589, and a Disney Wonder cruise for four nights from $029.

consolidated savings

Consolidators are the middlemen between the cruise lines and the consumer. Each line will usually provide a consolidator with a number of cabins for each cruise. These consolidators will sometimes offer deals that are the lowest around with the advantage of one-stop comparison shopping. You can find ads in the travel section of most major newspapers under either "consolidators" or "discounters." And there are several Web sites now available, too.

○ In a Sunday travel section ad, a consolidator was offering a seven-night Alaska cruise from $549 and a four-day cruise from Miami from $279, though the actual carriers were not listed.

○ Another ad for a "cruise vacation center agency" had a ten-day cruise through the waters of French Polynesia on the Tahitian Princess from $799 (adding on airfare from Phoenix to Tahiti brought it to from $949).

○ GalaxSea Cruises of San Diego offers specials at www.galaxsea.com (1-800-923-7245). On a late October visit to the Hot Deals section of their site, we spotted a seven-day cruise to either the Eastern or Western Caribbean on a five-star ship in a balcony cabin for $899 sailing that fall.

○ Spur of the Moment Cruises has a site specializing in last-minute bookings (www.spurof .com) that can save you 50 percent or more on a cruise. We logged on to their Red Hot Specials section and found an amazing 17-day cruise to South America that included the Amazon and Orinoco rivers on Royal Olympic for only $1,249—leaving within the month.

save on sailing

An agency that specializes in cruises can save you money. They buy up space on certain cruises in bulk at a hefty discount and are able to offer you a better bargain.

○ Check with more than one agency that specializes in cruises. Some agencies will push one cruise line more than another so that they can get a bonus for extra sales. You want the best price for your favorite cruise. But to get what you want, you'll need an agency that is willing to review all your options, not just one.

SAVINGS AT THE SOURCE

After checking your favorite bargain travel sites, it might save you money to check each cruise lines directly (especially if you have access to a computer). Even if the sites don't book travel, you can get a better idea of the ships and the amenities they offer before you buy. The Carnival site includes information about their corporate partners.

Carnival Cruise Lines
www.carnival.com
....
Celebrity Cruise Lines
www.celebritycruises.com
....
Disney Cruise Lines
www.disneycruise.com
....
Norwegian Cruise Line
www.ncl.com
....
Princess Cruises
www.princesscruises.com
....
Royal Caribbean International
www.rccl.com
....
Windstar Cruise Line
www.windstarcruises.com

○ Booking really early or really late can cut costs. Cruise lines give a big discount to those who put money down well ahead. The same goes if you book close to the sailing date when the cruise line my have cabins it needs to fill.

spontaneous savings

Although with most cruises, you're best off booking at least one month prior to sailing to garner a good fair, if you can travel at the drop of a hat, you may find a great deal by waiting until literally the last minute. And there are now Web sites that can help you find those last-minute marvels:

www.site59.com This young site was bought out by Travelocity recently so you will find some packages that appear on both sites. Site59 specializes in last-minute deals —any time from two weeks to three hours before leaving, and they guarantee a savings of up to 60 percent. When you go on the Web site, you'll see a "cruise quick-shop" button to the right of the screen that will take you right to the listing of sailing-soon packages at a deep discount.

www.11thhourvacations.com A few years senior to Site59, this site can offer savings from 35 to 70 percent on cruises and travel packages, as well as airfare and hotel rate discounts. The site also has a frequent-user rewards program, plus two-for-one vacation specials.

www.lastminutetravel.com This site actually has offerings from many different carriers and operators, including JetBlue and Spirit. As its name indicates, the site specializes in last-minute deals, but you can also book in advance here.

fair fares

Most cruise packages include just about everything, except for airfare. Most cruise lines will offer a "discounted" fare with an airline partner—don't automatically buy into this. Use all the tricks from Up in the Air (see p. 224) to find the best price to fly to your departure city. You may save yourself a couple hundred dollars. Of course, you may find that the airfare the cruise line offers is indeed the best. One advantage of booking a flight with a cruise line partner: if the flight is delayed or canceled, the cruise line will honor your booking and get you to the ship another way.

saving cents on cruises

A few before-you-embark tips to keep extra costs from spoiling your cruise experience:

○ Even though all the major things are included on a cruise, tips are not—and they can add up significantly. Drinks (other than coffee and tea) are not included, nor are many shore excursions. Check what is and is not included carefully before you sign on the dotted line.

- Bring your own cans of soda. Most cruises will provide you with unlimited coffee, tea, and sometimes fruit juices. But soda is quite pricey. Better yet, bring bottled water!
- Don't limit yourself to the planned excursions from the ship—contact the tourist bureau of the port you'll be visiting ahead of time and see what they can offer you. Doing your own land tour can be more fun, tailored to your interests, and a lot cheaper. Just be sure to get back on time so the ship doesn't leave without you.
- Inside cabins are just as large as the outside ones and generally cost a lot less. The only thing you'll miss out on is the view from your room, but if you plan to be out and about most of the cruise, this shouldn't be a problem. Spend the money you'll save on the cabin on a shipboard massage or extra excursion.

GREAT RATES FOR FREIGHTS

If you want to check into freighter cruises, try the outfits listed here.

**www.freighterworld.com
or 1-800-531-7774**
....
**www.freightercruises.com
or 1-800-996-2747**

coupons for cruising

Yes, you can find coupons for everything, including cruises. Check the middle of the Entertainment Book—we saw coupons for $100 to $200 off a cruise on the Carnival, Norwegian, and Princess cruise lines.

frugal freighting

If you are the adventurous type, you may want to look into freighter cruises. Now, maybe a freighter lacks the romance of one of those big ships but, then again, if you have a flexible schedule and a taste for something a little unusual, freighter travel can be a great way to go.
- Freighters carry a lot fewer passengers than a cruise ship, generally no more than 12.
- Freighters don't usually allow children under 13 or seniors over a certain age.
- Freighters have fewer amenities, but they often have a small pool, a library with books and videos, a lounge, deck chairs, and even a shop.
- Freighters have an itinerary, but they are subject to change depending on the cargo. The trips are generally longer and they go to more unusual ports of call than a normal cruise ship.
- Freighters are much more casual; there are no big formal dinners, casinos, glitzy shows, or organized activities.
- Traveling on a freighter costs half as much as traveling on a regular cruise line; the fee covers everything on the ship except alcohol. If you're looking for an inexpensive offbeat adventure—a no-frills trip with a small group of like-minded travelers—a freighter cruise might be a terrific option for you.

frugal Family Fun

TRAVELING WITH CHILDREN
CAN BE WONDERFUL AND DOESN'T
HAVE TO COST A LOT, IF YOU DO IT RIGHT.

Children add a dimension to travel—especially in the way they see the world from a child's perspective—that can't be equaled by adults traveling alone. But traveling with children can also be very challenging—especially if they are very young. Unfamiliar places and food, strange routines, and changes in time zones can result in cranky children and frazzled parents. Luckily, there are many options available to minimize stress and make family travel easier.

tips for happy travelers

Before you depart, let go of the idea that you can have the same kind of vacation with children that you did before they were born. Even if you were avid campers, camping with young children is much different than camping with adults. To make traveling easier on everyone, you'll need to adjust and think of your children's needs before your own. Follow these tips and everyone will have more fun.

don't abandon your routines Unless they are infants who sleep a lot, most young children won't cope well with an unpredictable schedule. If they don't eat or sleep on time, they'll likely be ill tempered and unpleasant to be around. Everyone will be much happier if you keep to your home schedule when you are on vacation. But remember that little ones do outgrow the need for routine pretty quickly. The toddler that needs to be in bed by 7 p.m. this year may be more flexible next year.

think like a child What did you like to do when you were little? What does your child like to do? The good news: Most things that entertain kids are cheaper than those that entertain only adults.

don't drag things out Limit excursions or tours to an hour or two and keep an eye on your children—when they start to fade or get antsy, take them somewhere else (preferably outdoors where they can run around for a bit).

avoid fancy restaurants Don't take your kids to restaurants where they have to sit silently for any length of time. Even the best-behaved children get bored. Stick to family-friendly places (lots of ethnic eateries with excellent food are set up for children) and you'll all enjoy the meal more.

always carry snacks Having snacks (and water) wards off hunger and crankiness. Little bodies burn fuel faster than we do. Boxes of dried fruit, cereal bars, pretzels, goldfish, or small crackers in a zip-lock bag fit easily in a pocket or purse.

focus on your children If you try experiencing the adventure from their point of view, you'll have more fun and create better memories than just sitting back and watching.

treat yourselves sometimes Buy a nice bottle of wine to drink in the hotel room (or by the campfire), after the kids are in bed. Also, try taking turns playing with your children to give your partner some time alone. If you care for your children as a team, you'll be surprised by how enjoyable a family vacation can be.

natural thrift

One of the best family vacations is also the cheapest: camping. If you own equipment, the only major outlay will be food and gas. If you don't own any gear, try to rent or borrow some from friends for the first outing or two, that way you'll be sure everyone likes it before investing any money. Campgrounds can range from those that require you to backpack to a remote wilderness site to KOAs (Kampgrounds of America) or other privately owned campgrounds that have sites with showers, stores, entertainment rooms, or swimming pools nearby. You can really pick and choose the type of camping experience that you and your family want. Campground fees will vary considerably too. Some state parks offer a site where you can pitch a tent for as little as $5 a night. Private campgrounds can charge up to $20 or $30 for a site.

- Young children get thirsty fast, especially if they are very active, so be sure the campground provides water. As your kids grow older you can try more rustic sites. Having potable water close to your tent makes a huge difference.
- Some campgrounds will have pit toilets, some vault toilets, and some flush toilets. Which type of facility is best suited for your family will be a practical decision.
- Some campgrounds are tent only, some can accommodate RVs without hookups for water or electricity, some are for tents and RVs with all services, and some are only for RVs.
- Generally, the closer a park is to a major metropolitan area, the more crowded it is on weekends or holidays. On the really big camping weekends—Memorial Day, Labor Day, and July Fourth—even remote, out-of-the-way campgrounds can fill up early.
- Seasoned backpackers or old-time campers may sneer, but using an air mattress can make camping much more pleasant and comfortable. Getting a good night's sleep is important, especially if you have children to care for.
- In many parts of the country, you're likely to experience rain if you camp in the summer. Setting up a tarp over a picnic table will allow everyone to eat in comfort and sit and play games. Remember to bring a tarp, just in case it rains. It's much better than being stuck in a small tent with the whole family for hours.
- Don't try to maintain your living standards at home while on a camping trip. Bring only the essentials for your family's needs and rely on your creativity to fill in the gaps.

❝A family vacation is one where you arrive with five bags, four kids and seven I-thought-you-packed-it's.❞

Ivern Ball, author

Tell stories, sing songs, toast marshmallows, or go on a nature hike. Don't worry about kids or clothes getting dirty. That's all part of the camping experience. Just throw it all in the wash when you get home.

beyond tents

If you don't like sleeping in a tent but still want to have a camping experience, try locating a cabin. Cabins are available in state and national parks as well as private campgrounds such as KOA. Cabins are popular, so be sure to book in advance. Usually they are one-room structures, with wooden bunks, a table and benches, and a wood-burning stove. Some are more rustic than others; all provide you with four walls and a roof to sleep under.

national treasures

The United States is full of extraordinary national parks, all of which are worth a visit. Many of these parks have lodges or some type of hotel, if camping is not for you. The most popular parks tend to fill up during peak times so you should reserve campsites or other lodgings well in advance. (For information, try www.nps.gov or 1-800-365-2267.)

○ If you plan to visit several national parks in a short time, consider getting a Golden Eagle Passport. For a set price, the passport permits you to visit any National Park or monument as often as you like for one year. Passports are available at any national park. Getting one can yield goodly savings, especially if you're planning on doing a lot of traveling and camping.

into the woods

If you want to camp in a less-crowded setting, consider checking out a national forest. There are many of these forests all around the country, mostly in and around national parks. Administered by the Department of Agriculture (USDA), national forests often offer lovely, well-maintained campgrounds. To find out more about national forests, visit the USDA Forest Service Web site at www.fs.fed.us.

state sites

Many people skip over state parks in the rush to secure a campsite in a national park. But these state gems shouldn't be overlooked. Campgrounds, cabins, and even lodges found in state parks provide wonderful opportunities for family vacations. Among other activities, many state parks offer hiking, fishing, boating, and swimming in just about any natural setting from desert to alpine meadow. For example,

Estes Park in Colorado offers great beauty and economy without the crowds that typically descend into neighboring Rocky Mountain National Park. Visit the parks in your state; then branch out to parks found in neighboring states. You'll be pleasantly surprised by what you discover!

one-stop fun for less

If camping isn't your bag and you want a really stress-free vacation for the whole family, shop around for a resort or cruise that is set up for children. Many resorts and cruises now offer a range of children's programs with kid-friendly play areas and even baby-sitting services. Of course, these resorts often have a higher price tag, but if you shop hard and think off-season and off-peak, you'll probably find a program to suit your family at a price you can afford. Although the initial price tag can be daunting, keep in mind that the cost is all-inclusive and can still be a good deal.

off season or off peak

If you want to indulge in a resort vacation or a nice city hotel, look for times during the year when business is down and promotional offers are at their peak. Skiing resorts are located in beautiful mountains with loads of hiking trails. Southwestern spas lose business when the weather turns hot, but their pools, fitness centers, masseurs, and restaurants are open year-round. Hotels in cities that usually do a booming business during the week may be dead on weekends, especially holiday weekends. Call and ask if they have any family specials—you may be surprised.

good deal, dude

A variation on a typical resort, a guest ranch (once known as dude ranches) can be a blast, especially if you and your family like to horseback ride. Some ranches are set up primarily for riding; others offer riding plus a wide range of other activities. A good family ranch can also offer a special program for little ones so they'll be happy while you're off riding on the range. Again, the initial cost will seem high, but everything should be included. There are scores of books you can buy detailing the different types of ranches available. If you want to search the Web, just type "guest ranches" into your search engine.

home away from home

Rather than stay at a hotel, you may find renting a house or condo to be a cheaper, more family-friendly option, especially if you have young children. A house has a kitchen, a washer and dryer, and is a more relaxed setting for little ones than a hotel. You'll have the most luck renting a house in

GOLDEN AGE PASSPORT
www.nps.gov
or 1-800-GO-PARKS

If you are 62 or older, get a Golden Age Passport from the National Park Service. It gives you free entrance for life to any national park, monument, historic site, recreation area, or wildlife refuge run by the NPS. If a park has a car fee, the passport admits you plus all your car passengers. If there is a per person fee, it admits you, your spouse, and children. It even offers the passport holder a 50 percent discount on federal use charges for facilities and services, such as camping, swimming, parking, boat launching, and tours. To apply for a Golden Age Passport, you must show proof of age (driver's license or birth certificate) and must prove you are a U.S. citizen or permanent resident. Passports are available at any NPS facility (national park, historic site, wildlife refuge, and so on) where an entrance fee is charged. There is a one-time $10 charge.

popular tourist destinations. For example, we found a home on the island of Eleuthera in the Bahamas during peak season starting at $60 per night. In Maine, houses or "housekeeping" cottages are available for rent during the summer starting at less than $500 a week. To find house rentals, check with a local real estate office or try typing the name of your destination plus "vacation rentals" in your Web search engine. If there aren't any houses available in the area where you're going, see if any of the motels have kitchen facilities. You're children will love it if you can cook the familiar foods they like. Not only will you save money on restaurants, but you'll have happier children—and that's the key to a wonderful and relaxing family vacation.

get your kicks . . .

One easy way to plan a driving vacation is to travel on one of our country's famous scenic routes. This usually becomes a trip through time and history as well as a family vacation. Route 66 is probably the most famous, but the Natchez Trace Parkway through Mississippi, Alabama, and Tennessee, Highways 1 and 101 along the Pacific Coast, the Beartooth Highway in Montana and Wyoming, the Great Platte River Road in Nebraska, the Lakeside Drive in Upper Michigan, and the Old Kings Highway in Massachusetts are all worth taking a look at. Each and every state has its great old routes so pack a lunch and take to the open road.

culture convergence

One of the most remarkable things about the United States is the wide diversity of cultures within our borders. You don't need to travel abroad to meet an astonishing variety of people—or feel as if you've experienced something wonderfully different from your daily life. Since you can probably find such an enclave within driving distance, you can make this a family trip to remember without breaking the bank.

native american reservations One good example is the Navajo Nation spanning the Four Corners of Arizona, New Mexico, Utah, and Colorado. In this area rich in anthropological interest, you'll find Navajo, Zuni, and Hopi communities, each with its distinctive fascinating culture, extraordinary handcrafts and artworks as well as stunning scenery. Check within your own state—you may be amazed at the areas of interest to visit where your children can be exposed to (and learn respect for) the ancient cultures of our continent's First Peoples. While every state may not have a large reservation you can visit, nearly every state has some historic sites associated with Native Americans.

amish country The most well-known enclave of the Amish is probably in Pennsylvania, but it is by no means the only one. A visit to Amish Country will transport you to another time—when life was much simpler—and introduce you to a culture that thrives in a setting that is centuries apart from most modern communities.

border crossings

If you want to introduce your children to life in a different country, you are in luck. Folks in the Northern states can usually drive up to Canada, and those in the Southwest, can drive down to Mexico. Our closest neighbors offers so many intriguing places to visit, you could spend years in either country and not see everything. Both countries are easy to visit from the States and offer many attractions, including good packages for families. Even if you fly, you can usually find decent rates to the more popular cities or areas.

- In Canada, experience the British culture of Victoria, the old-world French charm of Montreal, the glorious scenery of Banff, or the cosmopolitan delight found in Toronto.
- Mexico offers the sun-drenched excitement of the Mexican Riviera, the awe-inspiring Mayan ruins of the Yucatan peninsula, the splendor of the Copper Canyon, and the thriving metropolis of Mexico City.

FAMILY ADVENTURES

www.familyadventuretravel.com

There are a host of publications and Web sites devoted to family vacations, but one we particularly like is sponsored by Family Adventure Magazine. This bi-yearly magazine not only provides information on family adventure travel, it also lists companies around the country that specialize in adventure travel throughout the world. You can find the magazine at bookstores, newsstands, and some specialty shops or you can order it from:

The Family Adventure Magazine
P.O. Box 469
Woodstock, NY 12498

Thrifty Home Improvements

- cost-saving home care
- do-it-yourself damage control
- reduce, reuse, recycle
- the prudent gardener

We bet you know somebody like this: They constantly moan about their money seeming to disappear, yet they pay hoards of people to service their home from top to bottom. They call a repair-person immediately if something doesn't work, and firmly maintain that they can't possibly take care of their garden. They throw away things right, left, and center, without stopping to consider other uses for them. This is not a penny pincher. We know that maintaining your home is a fairly simple task that can stave off costly repairs—and many repairs are within the scope of the average homeowner. One or two good gardening books that target your region can enable just about anyone to plant and care for a veritable Eden, even one that requires little to no upkeep. And let's face it: Penny pinchers practically invented recycling! Finding new uses for old objects, cutting down on waste, and recycling as much as possible doesn't save just pennies (not to mention our planet)—it can save you hundreds of dollars every year. With the money you've saved, you can replace your old inefficient windows with gorgeous double-paned ones to save even more!

Make your home your castle.

cost-saving
Home care

WHEN IT COMES TO HOME MAINTENANCE,
THERE IS NO QUESTION THAT A STITCH—
OR NAIL—IN TIME SAVES NINE.

The best way to avoid repair bills or exorbitant replace-ment costs is to get in the habit of taking care of the things you own. Investing in good-quality products— especially those that will take a lot of abuse, such as siding or doors, or those that will lower your energy bills, such as insulated windows—is more than penny-wise; not taking the time to maintain these high-end items is truly pound-foolish.

up on the roof—with care

A leak in your roof can mean much more than trouble up top; it can lead to damaged walls, floors, and belongings. A well-sealed roof requires regular care to do its job proper-ly, but it will pay off in the long run. If your roof is steeply pitched, it's best to hire a professional roofer to do repairs.

- If you have an unfinished attic, start your inspection there. Use a strong flashlight and look for signs of water along the rafters and framing or in the insulation.
- Next, choose a sunny day to do an outdoor examination of your roof. Check carefully for any bare spots on asphalt surfaces, broken shingles or tiles, lumpy or wavy areas indicating buckling, or asphalt shingles starting to curl up or curl down (clawing). Use binoculars to get a close look without having to climb up on your roof.
- Check the flashing around chimneys, vents, and anywhere there's a joint in the roof, because leaks frequently begin around flashing. Small holes can be temporarily repaired with roofing cement, but if the flashing is wearing out, it should be eventually replaced.

straightening the curls

You can fix curling asphalt shingles yourself. Choose a day that is dry and warm so the shingles will be flexible. Gently lift up the curled section of the shingle and apply roofing cement beneath it, following the manufacturer's directions. Press the shingle back in place and weight it (a brick works well) to hold the shingle flat while the cement dries, about 30 minutes.

replacing a worn asphalt shingle

Do repairs to asphalt shingles on a dry, sunny day when the temperature is between 65° F and 80° F so that the shingles will be flexible but not hot.

- Lift the shingle above the damaged one and insert a pry bar to remove the nails holding the damaged shingle in place. Carefully pull out the damaged shingle.
- Brush away any debris and slide in a new shingle. If necessary, gently pry up the surrounding shingles slightly to insert the new one fully.

- Use roofing nails to attach the new shingle, being careful not to damage the shingle above the new one. Using a putty knife, apply roofing cement under both the new shingle and the one above; then press each in place.
- If you don't have a replacement shingle, you can often repair a damaged shingle by cutting a piece of sheet-metal flashing to fit under the shingle. Coat the bottom of the metal patch with roofing cement and slip it into place; then coat the top of the patch with roof cement and press the shingle to it.

replacing a wood shingle or shake
- Using a hammer and a chisel, carefully split the damaged wood shingle along the grain. Gently pull the pieces out. If needed, insert small wedges under the upper shingles to hold them in place while you work.
- Instead of removing the old nails, use a hacksaw to cut them flush to the surface.
- Using a caulking gun, run a bead of roofing cement over the back of the new shingle and over the top of the shingles underneath. Slide the shingle into place; if necessary, place a piece of scrap wood at the base of the shingle and use a hammer to gently tap it fully into place.

flat roof fix
Reflective coatings of aluminum (silver) or fiberglass (white) help protect a flat roof from damaging UV rays and reflect the heat away from the house. Inspect your flat roof at least once a year, looking for blisters, cracks, tears, and storm damage. Repair any damage immediately.

great gutters, houseman!
One of the best and easiest ways to protect your house from water damage is by installing good quality gutters and then maintaining them. Gutters keep water from rotting your siding and help prevent seepage into your basement and possible erosion of your house's foundation. Four times a year, look for and remove any blockages in the gutters and the downspouts. Examine seams for leaks and look carefully for spots of rust.
- Wearing heavy-duty gloves, scoop out any leaves or other debris from the gutters. Begin at the downspout end and work your way up the gutter. As you work, mark any sections that may need maintenance or repair so that you can see them as you walk around the house.
- When the debris is all gone, flush the gutters using a hose and starting at the highest point.
- Many people use mesh screens to keep leaves out of gutters, but this hampers cleaning them. Putting a leaf strainer in the top of each downspout is more practical.

❝Home is a place you grow up wanting to leave, and grow old wanting to get back to.❞

John Ed Pearce,
author and journalist

SEASONAL CARE & REPAIR CALENDAR

In most parts of the country, spring and fall are the times to take care of regular maintenance or outdoor seasonal repairs.

SPRING

chimneys Clean and inspect flues when the seasonal use ends.

gutters and downspouts Clear debris and flush with water. Straighten and correct the pitch of misaligned gutters. Reset downspouts and tighten fasteners.

ironwork Remove rust and paint as necessary.

masonry Repair cracks and seam. Clean crumbling mortar from joints; remortar.

pests Check foundations for termite tunnels. Check vent louvers, chimneys, and other protected nooks and crannies for bird and insect nests.

roofing Repair winter-damaged shingles (or tiles) and flashing. Recoat reflective roofs.

siding and trim Renail loose pieces. Caulk. Touch up damaged paint. Wash all exterior surfaces.

windows Remove storm sashes; repair and clean before storing. Clean and unstick sashes. Repair damaged putty. Install screens in windows used for ventilation, and put up shading devices on south-facing windows.

siding lines

If your siding is starting to look a bit dingy, don't immediately decide to repaint or replace it. It may just need a good bath. And even if a new coat of paint is on the bill, cleaning the surface is the first step to a good paint job, so your washing efforts will pay off one way or another.

● Once a year, give your siding a bath to preserve it and its finish. For painted wood siding and aluminum siding, use a solution of 1 cup extra-strength detergent (sold at paint or hardware stores or home centers) and 1 quart chlorine bleach in 3 gallons of water. Apply with a brush or sponge, and wear rubber gloves, safety goggles, and protective garments. After washing, rinse the siding thoroughly.

● To spruce up vinyl siding, just hose it down and sponge-wash it with a mild liquid detergent. Rinse with spray from your hose.

● Always begin washing your siding from the bottom and work your way up—the siding soaks up less detergent that way and is less likely to streak.

● For easy washing, use a long-handled car-wash brush attachment on your hose.

masonry musts

A once-a-year bath can help keep any stone- or brickwork on your house looking great.

● Use a power washer (you can rent one) on a low-power setting to spray masonry walls clean.

● To kill mold and mildew, add 1 cup of bleach to each gallon of water. Rinse the masonry with plenty of clean water afterward to flush away the bleach solution.

the point of repointing

Repointing (renewing the mortar between bricks) should be done as needed. First, chip out any loose or damaged mortar, using a small sledge hammer and a cold chisel (wear safety goggles). To make filling the joint easier, fill a grout bag (similar to a pastry bag) with mortar. Wearing work gloves, insert the tip of the nozzle in the joint line and, as you pull the nozzle along the joint, squeeze the bag to force mortar out. This lets you get the mortar well into the joint. Go over the mortar afterward with a pressing tool, known as a jointing tool.

up the chimney

Because chimneys take a beating from wind and weather, it is prudent to inspect them at least once a year.

● Check the mortar and replace any that is crumbling or loose. If the disintegration is extensive or if there are cracked bricks or stones, it's best to hire a professional mason to do the repair.

- Inspect the flashing between the chimney and the roof for damage or signs of wear, and replace as needed.
- Hire a licensed chimney sweep to clean and inspect the flue at least once a year.

everlasting decks

A deck can add innumerable hours of pleasure in your garden, functioning as an outdoor room. But until recently, a deck required a goodly amount of upkeep, including staining and resealing regularly. New products for building decks make such maintenance obsolete. Composite lumber, which is made from waste wood products, requires no staining or sealing, is weather- and insect-resistant, can take years of strong sunlight without problem, will not rot or deteriorate, and is splinter free. There are several products available now (Trex is one brand name) for beautiful, maintenance-free decks, and though they cost more than real wood does, the long-term benefits far outweigh the initial costs. Plus you'll be helping the environment by using composite lumber rather than regular lumber!

ironwork makeovers

Each spring, check your wrought-iron railings and cast-iron patio furniture for signs of rust and repair them promptly.

- For quick rust removal, use a wire brush attachment on an electric drill. Or if the rust is really thick and hard to remove, use a product such as Rust-Oleum's Rust Reformer or Duro's rust converter, which converts rust into a hard, paintable surface.
- Use an enamel-based spray paint with a rust retardant for quick, even coverage.

windows on the world

Your windows let in light, air, and views, and they keep out air that's too hot or too cold along with insects and other unwelcome critters—at least they do if you take care of them. Windows, like the rest of your house, require regular maintenance to work properly.

- If a double-hung window—the most common type of window—moves but doesn't slide easily, clean out the sash channels with steel wool. Then vacuum the area until no dust remains and lubricate the channels by rubbing them with bar soap or paraffin, or use a silicone spray.
- Old paint can often be the culprit if windows are sticking to the point that you can't open them at all. After checking to make sure that the window isn't nailed or screwed shut, use a utility knife to cut around the sash, breaking the paint seal evenly. Gently tap the sash with a rubber mallet (not a hammer!) to loosen it.

SUMMER

driveways Repair holes and cracks in asphalt. Protect the blacktop by applying asphalt sealant.

gutters and downspouts Clear debris at midseason.

pests Check foundation for carpenter ants and eaves for wasps' nests.

yard Check wood fences and posts for decay and wood-boring insects.

FALL

gutters and downspouts Clear debris and flush with water.

outdoor water supply In frost-prone areas, shut off supply, drain the lines, and leave valves open.

siding and foundation Patch and seal open cracks. Seal openings where animals may take refuge. Close vents of unheated crawl spaces.

windows and doors Put storm sashes in place. Clean and repair screens; spray with protective coating. Inspect and fortify weatherstripping and caulking. Clear debris from basement window wells.

WINTER

chimneys Clean and inspect flues in midseason if you use a wood stove or fireplace frequently.

gutters and downspouts Keep clear of ice.

before the storm

Add-on storm windows, either wood or aluminum, help retain heat in the winter and protect against heavy weather in colder regions. But they require periodic maintenance. When you remove storm windows in the spring (and again before you put them on in the fall), inspect and clean them.

- Wearing heavy gloves (preferably with rubber finger grips) and goggles, carefully remove the storm windows.
- If the frames of your aluminum storm windows have oxidation deposits, use a lightly abrasive household cleaner, a mild detergent, or fine steel wool to rub the deposits away. After cleaning, apply automobile paste wax to the frames. Reapply the wax annually.
- On a wooden storm window, pry out any loose and crumbling glazing compound and apply fresh compound.
- Check and tighten any hanger hardware and unclog weep holes at the bottom of the sash.
- Wash your storm window glass inside and out. Rubbing alcohol is an excellent glass cleaner.
- If you will be repainting wood-framed storm windows, be sure to check the fit first; extra layers of paint can make the windows too big to reinstall.
- If the corner joints of wooden storm windows have become loose, use small mending plates on the inside corners to reinforce the joints and strengthen the corners. Drill pilot holes first to avoid splitting the wood.

keep out dirt: clean your screens

- Dirty window screens block out sunlight and make spots on windows whenever it rains. Regular maintenance should include vacuuming them or brushing them while they are in place. Once or twice a year, wash them.
- Lay the screens flat on a smooth, cloth-covered surface, such as an old sheet on a picnic table. Scrub the screen gently with a brush dipped in soapy water and rinse with a hose. Let air-dry.

fixing a hole

- If you find a tiny hole in a window screen, there's no need to patch it; just dab a little rubber cement or clear nail polish on the opening to keep out bugs.
- To mend a larger hole, cut a piece of screening 1/2 inch larger than the hole and unravel its edges to leave points all around. Bend the points at right angles to the patch. Slip the points through the screen and bend them back flat to hold the patch to the screen. Affix the patch by coating its edges with clear glue or nail polish.
- To repair a small hole or tear in a plastic or fiberglass screen, use a No. 18 tapestry needle and very fine nylon

fishing line. Zigzag-stitch over the hole or tear; do not pull the line taut or you may pucker the screen. Paint over the stitching with clear glue or nail polish.

drive on!

Keeping your asphalt driveway in good repair will benefit your car and your property values. Do repairs when the weather is 60° F or above; the asphalt will be softer and easier to use and will set more quickly and form a better bond.

- Every few years, coat the entire driveway with an emulsified asphalt or coal-tar sealer. Sealer comes in ready-to-pour 5-gallon pails (enough to cover 400 square feet) at home centers or hardware stores. Read the directions before you begin; different manufacturer's recommend different approaches. The sealer will fill any tiny cracks.
- Fill cracks up to 1/2 inch wide as soon as you spot them—before frozen precipitation can cause more damage. Clean out the crack with a wire brush. Then fill it with driveway crack filler sold in caulk-gun cartridges. If the crack is deeper than 1/4 inch, partially fill it with sand, then finish filling with caulk and smooth with a trowel.
- Patch cracks wider than 1/2 inch with a sand and sealer mix. First clean out the crack with a wire brush. In a disposable pan, combine the sand and sealer until it is the consistency of putty. Use a trowel to pack the mixture into the crack and to smooth the top.
- Patch big holes with cold-mix asphalt compound. Have extensive damage repaired by a pro with hot-mix.

pest patrol

The most effective way to deal with pest infestations in your home is to block them from occurring. Insects look for food, water, and shelter. Deny them these, and you'll stop the problem before it happens.

- Store food in tightly sealed containers.
- Clean up spills and crumbs as soon as possible, and limit the areas of the house in which food may be taken. (Ban food from bedrooms.)
- After cleaning the sink, wipe the sink area until it is almost dry; sinks should be kept dry between use.
- Wipe down counters after each food preparation; wipe out cabinets regularly.
- Wash out garbage cans regularly; empty the kitchen garbage once a day.
- Caulk cracks and crevices in walls, floors, and foundations. Don't overlook any gaps around pipes.
- Repair tears and holes in window screens.
- Top your chimney with a spark-arresting screening.

DO-IT-YOURSELF ANT TRAPS

Combine 1 cup sugar, 4 teaspoons boric acid, and 3 cups water, and use to saturate cotton balls. Wearing rubber gloves, pack the cotton balls into jars with screw-top lids, filling each about half full. Poke two or three holes in each lid with an icepick. Place the jars near the ant colony but out of the reach of children.

Other natural ant repellents: talcum powder, cream of tartar, borax, powdered sulfur, oil of cloves—and growing mint around your home's foundation.

do-it-yourself
Damage Control

HOME REPAIRS CAN EAT UP A CHUNK
OF YOUR INCOME IF YOU CALL SOMEONE
EVERY TIME THERE'S A PROBLEM.

The truth is, just about anyone can do most of his or her own repairs—even if the person isn't a dedicated do-it-yourselfer or devotee of such shows as "This Old House" or "Hometime." If you're on top of your home maintenance, you will save even more by fixing that sticky door, repairing your burnt carpet, or tackling some of the other simple fix-its in this section.

doors that stick

If a door is sticking, first check the weather. Dampness can cause wood to swell. On a dry, cool day, check the door again; your problem may have gone with the humidity. If not, try the following:

- First, check the screws in the hinges and the strike plate. They may need to be tightened or reinforced.
- Second, make sure the hinges are properly mounted. If not, open the door and slip a wedge under the bottom edge to hold the door steady at the right height. If the door is sticking along the top edge, remove the screws from the bottom hinge on the side attached to the door frame (not the door). Slip a piece of cardboard (a shim) under the hinge to raise it slightly and then reinsert the screws. If the door is sticking along the bottom, insert a shim behind the top hinge on the frame side.
- If the door still sticks after shimming the hinges, sand or plane the door edge along the area that's sticking.
- If the door still sticks, remove the door from the frame and plane the entire edge, always working with the grain. Plane from the outer edge toward the center. After planing, check the edge you trimmed down with a straight-edge, and sand any irregularities you find.
- Once the door opens and shuts smoothly, sand its edges, then prime and repaint the door to prevent it from absorbing moisture and swelling again.

squeaky doors

One at a time, remove the pin from each hinge and apply household oil or silicone spray to the hinge barrel; then replace the pin. Open and shut the door a few times to work the lubricant into the hinges.

slip-sliding doors

- A sliding door that rattles when you open or shut it may have faulty bottom door guides, or they may be missing altogether. Replace them if necessary.
- A sliding door that sticks may have dirt in the track. Try vacuuming the track first. If this doesn't work, slip an old

sock over the head of a flat-head screwdriver and use that to probe into and clean the track.

- Do not use household oil to lubricate the tracks of sliding doors; only use spray silicone.

fixing the door warp

A door that has become slightly bowed in the center can be fixed in one of two ways:

- If the bow is slight, try adding a third hinge at the point at which the door is bowed. In time, the pressure may straighten the warp.
- If the warp is more pronounced, remove the door from its hinges. Place the door, bowed side up, on four support bricks or cement blocks. Place additional bricks over the warp and let the door lie there until the warp has straightened out.

keep wood floors shining

Preventing problems before they occur is both time saving and money smart.

- Sop up spills—don't let liquids sit on a wood floor, especially alcohol which can eat through floor wax quickly.
- Use slides—rubber or plastic casters or stick-on felt protectors all work to keep your furniture from scratching the floor. Use them even under larger furniture feet.
- Screen the sun—sunlight can discolor and bleach floors. Close the drapes when the sun starts shining on the floor or install sheers to let in light but keep out sun.
- Prevent planter problems—use glazed ceramic (not porous terra cotta) or plastic coasters under every plant to catch excess water. And check underneath often to be sure rings aren't forming.

66 Old houses mended, cost little less than new before they're ended. **99**

Colley Cibber

rug repairs

These are amazing simple fixes to make, but work carefully.
small stain or burn in pile carpeting Use small scissors to trim away the damaged tufts. If this will leave a noticeable hole, cut matching tufts of the carpet from a hidden area of the carpet, such as a closet floor or under a bed or sofa. Use a toothpick to dab rubber cement both in the hole and on the ends of the tuft. Insert the tuft in the hole and press lightly into place. Work the tufts upright with a clean toothpick. When the cement is dry, use the toothpick to blend the fibers into the surrounding carpet.
deeper burn, hole, or worn spot Use a carpet knife to cut out a square or rectangle around the damaged part. Using the damaged piece as a pattern, cut a matching piece from a carpet scrap or from a hidden area. Check the patch for fit, and trim as needed. Spread a thick layer of carpet glue over

the back of the patch and carefully place the patch in the hole. Press the patch into place and brush the carpet pile with your fingertips to hide the seams. Let dry for several hours or overnight before vacuuming.

restoring resilience

Resilient floors (no-wax vinyl or standard vinyl) are amazingly forgiving if you take care of them.

stubborn stains or ground-in dirt Use a solution of 1 part household ammonia to 10 parts water and a plastic scouring pad to scrub the area lightly. Make sure the room is well ventilated and wear vinyl gloves. If this doesn't remove the stain, try an extra-fine (#0000) piece of steel wool. Once the stain is gone, use wax or polish to restore the shine.

black heel marks Rub with either silver polish on a soft cloth or white appliance wax (available at appliance stores). Remove any excess polish or wax with a clean soft cloth.

flattening curled tiles Occasionally, a vinyl tile will develop curled edges or corners. Set a steam iron on low and cover the curled area with a doubled cotton dish towel or rag. Gently press the warm iron on the towel and move it back and forth just until the glue underneath is softened. Carefully pull up the edge of the tile and apply fresh adhesive. Press the tile back into place, wiping off any excess glue, then place weights (bricks or books are good) over the reglued area until it is set.

replacing a tile Use the iron and cotton cloth as above to soften the glue under the entire damaged tile. Using a putty

KEEPING YOUR COOL WHEN POWER GOES OUT

Power outages are more than just inconvenient. If they last for too long, food in your refrigerator and freezer can start to spoil. If you face this situation, try the following:

- Keep the doors closed. The fewer times the door is opened, the fewer chances the cool has to escape. Most modern refrigerator-freezers are well insulated. If you keep the door closed, a unit will hold the cold air for a long time. A fully stocked freezer with the door kept closed should keep the food frozen for 48 hours. If the freezer is only partially full, the food may keep for only 24 hours.

- After two days, think dry. Dry ice, that is. If the power outage has lasted 48 hours, and there is no sign of power returning, check with your local provider of clear ice to see if they stock dry ice. Wear heavy-duty gloves when handling dry ice, keep it in cardboard containers, and never let it touch skin or food. Twenty-five pounds of dry ice will keep an average 10-cubic-foot freezer cold for about three days.

- After the power returns, evaluate. Check all foods once the unit is working again. Don't re-freeze any frozen item that has completely defrosted, but you can cook it and either refrigerate or freeze the cooked dish. Use your nose: If some thing smells funny, odd, or off, throw it out!

- If you end up with lot of spoiled, unusable food, check your homeowner's policy. You may be covered for the losts up to a certain limit, like $200.

knife, pry up the tile, being careful not to lift up any surrounding tiles. Check the fit of the replacement tile and trim as needed with a utility knife. Spread adhesive over the exposed floor, warm the replacement tile with the iron and cloth, and carefully set the new tile in place. Wipe away excess glue and place weights over the entire tile until it is set and the adhesive is dried.

chilling out

One of the most-used appliances in your house, the refrigerator-freezer must be kept in good working order to do its job of keeping the food you and your family eat safely cold.

check the gaskets Of all the parts on a refrigerator, the gaskets are usually the first to wear out and need replacing. To check yours, put a 150-watt floodlight on an extension cord in the refrigerator or freezer compartment. Check one edge at a time. Point the bulb toward the suspect edge with the cord coming out the opposite edge. With the light on, the door shut, and the kitchen lights off, check for light coming through the edge. If any light leaks out, the gasket is worn and should be replaced.

repairing a cracked gasket If the crack is small, you can usually fill it with a little silicone caulk (check the directions carefully to be sure the caulk is approved for use around food). Roll the gasket back and fill the crack with a tiny bit of the caulk; be careful not to apply too much.

replacing gaskets Check with your local appliance store to see if they have the right gasket for your particular model in stock; if they don't, they can special-order it. Most gaskets are held in place by a retainer strip and screws, some by just a retainer strip and some just by screws. Roll the gasket back and remove the screws, then remove the old gasket. Thoroughly clean the area under and around the gasket. If the new gasket has kinks in it, soak it in some hot tap water to remove them. Beginning at the top of the door, slip the new gasket over the retainer, working from one corner to the opposite. Continue around the opening until the new gasket is in position. Carefully reinsert the screws and tighten them gently, starting with those in the center of each side, then the corners, and then in between; don't overtighten the screws.

on the level

A refrigerator, like most other appliances, works best when it's level. If it's not, it's likely to be noisy or have a sagging door. Place a carpenter's level on top of the refrigerator and check it from side to side and from back to front. Inspect the legs or casters to be sure all are firmly on the floor. If one is not on the floor or if the refrigerator is not level, adjust the legs until the unit is level in all directions. Here's how:

- Take off the grille at the bottom of the unit (it is usually held on by clips and pops off when you pull up on the bottom edge). If the legs are threaded, simply change the height by turning the legs with a wrench. If you have casters, turn the leveling screw (clockwise to raise, counterclockwise to lower) until the unit is level. While working on the legs, rest the refrigerator on a 2 by 4 scrap for easy access. After adjusting the legs, check again that the refrigerator is level.

cookin' with gas

A gas cooktop and oven are ignited either by separate pilot lights or electronic spark igniters. Pilot lights especially may need a little adjustment from time to time. Burners can also need adjustment. All you need is a screwdriver.

- A pilot light system has one or two continuously burning small flames that spark the burners; the oven has a separate pilot light. If your stovetop burners won't ignite because a pilot light keeps going out, the pilot light flame needs to be adjusted. To adjust it, follow the gas-supply tube from the pilot light until you find an adjusting screw near the front of the range. Gradually turn the screw—counterclockwise to increase the flame—until the flame is a sharp blue cone 1/4 to 3/8 inches high.

- To adjust the oven pilot light, take off the cover over the bottom of the oven. Look on the safety valve or under the thermostat knob for the adjusting screw. Adjust the flame as for the cooktop pilot light.

- If burners with electronic spark igniters won't light, the most likely cause is a lack of power. Before calling for service, check for an unplugged power cord, a tripped circuit breaker, or a blown fuse.

- If your cooktop burner's flame is uneven—either low, yellow, and sooty or too high and noisy—you may need to adjust the mixture of gas and air: Open the range top and look for the air shutter (usually a sleeve with an opening on the burner tubes). Loosen the screw that holds the sleeve. Then turn the burner on high and open the shutter until the flame is loud and flickering. Slowly close the shutter until the flames are a small circle of uniform, 1-inch-high, steady, blue flames with tiny orange tips. When the flames are right, tighten the retaining screw. Be careful working around open flames.

in your element

Electric cooktops and ovens have their pluses and minuses, just as gas versions do. Ongoing upkeep, particularly keeping

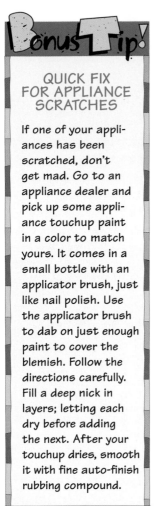

Bonus Tip!

QUICK FIX FOR APPLIANCE SCRATCHES

If one of your appliances has been scratched, don't get mad. Go to an appliance dealer and pick up some appliance touchup paint in a color to match yours. It comes in a small bottle with an applicator brush, just like nail polish. Use the applicator brush to dab on just enough paint to cover the blemish. Follow the directions carefully. Fill a deep nick in layers; letting each dry before adding the next. After your touchup dries, smooth it with fine auto-finish rubbing compound.

the elements and drip pans clean so they can work efficiently, will benefit the cook and the cooking equipment.

- Out hot spot! If one of the cooktops elements has a spot that gets redder than the rest of the ring, the ceramic insulation sheathing on the coil has broken down. You should replace the element with a new one from a home center or hardware store. You can usually remove an element (make sure it's cool and turned off!) by simply lifting it up and pulling it out of its socket. Some older elements are wired directly with screw terminals.

- If the bake or broil element in your oven burns out, save money and replace them yourself. Unplug the unit. Remove the screws that hold the element to the oven wall; then disengage any brackets holding the element and gently pull the element out until the terminals are visible. The wires will be attached to terminal screws or slip-on clips; disconnect each wire noting which terminal it goes to. Remove the old element and put the new one in place. Attach the wires to the appropriate terminals; then screw the element back in place.

foiled again

It may be tempting, if you don't have a self- or continuously cleaning oven, to cover the oven floor with aluminum foil to catch drips. Bad idea! Since foil reflects heat, it can throw off your cooking times, or even worse, it can cause the baking element to burn out. Don't cover an oven rack with foil either. It will trap heat in the lower part of the oven, keeping it from reaching the sensor at the top. This can damage the element, the oven lining, and even glass in the oven door.

just exhausted

Your kitchen exhaust fan works hard to keep the grease and dust and steam out of your kitchen—and it probably looks like it does. Cleaning this hardworking fan may seem daunting, but it's not that hard, and it will add years of use to the fan.

- Turn off the power source (the circuit not the switch). If the grille is removable, detach it and soak it in a mild dishwashing detergent solution. If not, use a soapy sponge to wipe it clean.

- Unplug and remove the fan-and-motor unit and lay it on old newspaper. Wipe off the heavy grease with a soft, dry cloth. Do not immerse metal and electrical parts in water.

- Wipe out the fan opening with a soft, dry cloth (do not use water); then replace the clean fan-and-motor unit and plug it in. Dry and replace the grille if you've removed it. Turn on the power.

- If you can't remove the fan-and-motor unit, remove the grease filters. Soak them in a detergent solution. Clean

REPAIR HELP ON THE WEB

If you encounter a home repair problem that you're not sure how to handle, try these Web sites, which are filled with step-by-step instructions, hints and tips, and expert advice as well as catalogs of goods they hope to sell you.

www.doityourself.com

www.handymanusa.com

www.homedepot.com

www.home-repair.com

www.hometips.com

www.lowes.com

the fan with the crevice tool of your vacuum. Wipe the hood with the solution before replacing the filter.

dishwasher in distress

Look for these signs and prevent dishwasher problems before they start:

- Yellow or brown stains on your machine's interior and on dishes? The problem may be iron in the water. To stop staining, install an iron filter in your water supply.
- Chalky deposits in your dishwasher? Start the machine without dishes or detergent on a rinse-and-hold cycle. During the fill, add 1 cup of white vinegar and let the machine finish the cycle. Then add detergent and run the empty machine through a cycle.
- Dish rack jammed? The rollers may be sticking. Turn them by hand to loosen them. If they are worn and no longer round, replace them. Some can be removed by taking out screws; most simply pull off. If a rack sticks because it is bent, replace it.
- Chipped rack prongs? Pick up some inexpensive rubber tip covers at a home center or dealer.
- Not sure the spray arm is working? Note the position of the arm at the start of a cycle, stop the machine during the wash, and check to see if the arm has moved.

  - Clogged spray arm? Remove the racks, unscrew the hub cap holding the arm, and lift it off. Use a stiff wire to open the holes fully. Rinse the arm well under running water.
  - Clogged filter screen? Remove the spray arm and any clips securing the screen. Hold the screen under running water and scrub with a stiff brush.

washing machines out of whack

Many problems are simple fixes for you but pretty pricey to pay a pro to repair. Be sure to unplug your washer before attempting any repair. If you must move the washer, disconnect the water hoses first.

- Uneven-steven: Vibrations from running your machine can throw it off the level; you'll notice an increase in noise. Use a carpenter's level and adjust the leg heights until the machine is on an even keel again.
- Balancing act: When you overload or unevenly load a machine, the weight of the wet clothes can cause the machine to go off balance, so that it becomes noisy and wobbly. Stop the machine and redistribute the load.
- Belt up: If your machine's drive belt is loose, you may notice problems during the wash or spin cycles. Open the machine's rear access panel and press on the belt; if it bends more than 3/4 inch, tighten it. If it shows signs of

real wear, replace it or have it replaced. (On a top-loader, loosen the motor's mounting nut and move the motor along the slotted opening, increasing tension on the belt. Then retighten the nut.)

- Drips and dribbles: Check all the hoses while the water is running to spot leaks. If a hose is worn or has a leak, replace it.
- Tears and snags: If your clothes are taking a beating in the wash, slip an old nylon stocking over your hand and run your hand lightly over the washer tub and agitator. If you find any sharp edges or rough spots, use fine sandpaper to smooth them.
- Agitated wash: A cracked or broken vane on an agitator or a loose or worn agitator can be hazardous to your clothing. Replace the agitator or have it replaced.

do-it-yourself dryer fixes

speed thumps Rotate the drum by hand. Slow thumping that varies with the speed of the rotation often means the drive belt is worn out and needs replacing.

multithumps Rotate the drum by hand. Many thumps each time you rotate the drum usually mean a worn support roller. Replace it following the directions in your owner's manual or have it replaced.

leaky door Move a piece of tissue paper over the door's edge while the dryer is running; if the paper is drawn in, the seal needs to be replaced. (A damp door is also a sign of a bad seal.) You can get a seal for your model from an appliance parts store. Usually you can just pull or pry off the old seal, remove any old adhesive with mineral spirits, and attach the new seal with the special heat-resistant adhesive, which is usually sold with the seal.

an essential bit of dryer maintenance

To keep your dryer running efficiently, make it a point once a year to clean out the vent duct:

- Turn off the power to the dryer (usually two circuits) and remove the duct. Shake out any built-up lint. If necessary, run a wadded cloth on a stick through the duct.
- When replacing the duct, make sure to reseal the joints with fresh duct tape. Try to set your vent duct so that it is straight; dips and kinks collect water and lint, blocking air flow.
- Outdoors, clean the damper and its hinge by inserting a length of straightened coat hanger into the vent hood.

drains: open and shut

Don't spend money on expensive drain openers. They can cause severe burns to your skin and may make the drain problem worse. Take these steps to open a clogged drain. Call a (licensed) plumber only if all else fails.

plunge Remove the sink stopper or strainer. Clean out any material stuck in the top of the drain or on the stopper. If there is an overflow hole, block it closed and fill the sink about half full. Place a plunger over the open drain. Rapidly pump up and down with the plunger ten times, then jerk it up and away on the last pump. If the water rushes out, you've unclogged the drain; if not, repeat several times.

clean the trap If you can't plunge away the blockage, place a bucket under the sink, directly under the trap. Using a wrench, remove the plug on the bottom of the trap; let the water run out. If there's no plug, remove the trap itself by unscrewing the two coupling nuts, top one first. Once you locate the blockage, clear it out by hand or use a straightened wire hanger. Replace the plug or the trap.

use a plumber's snake Snakes can be purchased at hardware stores and home centers. Remove the stopper or strainer and insert the end of the snake in the drain. Twisting the handle of the snake clockwise, push it in and pull it back as you work the snake down the drain. When you reach the blockage, push and pull until it breaks up and the snake moves easily in and out.

unclogging a toilet

When you flush a toilet, if the bowl stays filled and won't drain, the toilet is clogged. If the bowl is more than half full, bail out water until you reach the halfway mark.

- Rub some petroleum jelly around the lip of a plunger before using it to help stabilize the plunger's position on the drain hole.

  - Secure the cone of the plunger over the drain hole and rapidly pump the plunger up and down about ten times. If the toilet is still clogged, wait about an hour and repeat.
    - If plunging fails, try a toilet auger (similar to a snake). Insert the bent end of the auger in the drain hole. Turn the handle clockwise to move the auger through the drain to the clog. Turn the handle a bit more to force the auger through the obstruction; then slowly pull out the auger, still cranking the handle clockwise.
- If neither the plunger nor the auger works, call a plumber.

quick fixes for leaky pipes

Dripping water can pose an electrical hazard and can cause other damage, so even minor leaks should be repaired promptly by a licensed plumber. But leaks don't always happen at times when plumbers are available, so for some temporary quick fixes, try the following:

- Shut off the water supply to the pipe.
- Using steel wool, sand off any rust from the pipe, wipe the pipe clean, and dry.
- To seal a small crack or puncture in a waste pipe, wrap layers of electrical tape around the pipe from one side of the leak to the other.
- For a small leak, wrap a rubber pad around the leak and cover it with a hose clamp.
- For a larger leak, wrap a rubber pad around the leak, then cover the pad with a pipe clamp, and bolt or screw the clamp in place. Make sure the clamp is centered directly over the leak.

getting into hot water

Keep an eye and ear on your water heater to spot any problems early. It'll save you money in the long run.

- Noisy plumbing? If you hear a lot of noise when the hot water is running, the temperature may be too high, causing steam in the pipes. Reset the water temperature.
- Dirty hot water or a long wait until the water gets hot? Either of these could mean sediment in your water heater's tank. Turn off the gas or power and the cold-water inlet valve on the tank. Open a hot-water faucet in your tub. Attach a garden hose to the water heater's drain valve and empty the tank water into a floor drain; this may take several hours. Reopen the cold-water valve and let water run through the empty tank until the draining water is clear. To prevent sediment buildup, drain the tank two to four times a year.
- No hot water from your electric heater? Check the circuit breakers or fuses. If they aren't causing the problem, turn off power to the heater, remove the access panel, and press the reset button on the upper thermostat. Replace the access panel; then restore power and test.

clean showers

If a shower is sluggish, mineral deposits from the water may be clogging the head. Unscrew the head and disassemble it. Put all the pieces in a bowl of white vinegar and let them soak for a few hours. Use a brush to remove any stubborn sediment and rinse all the pieces well. Reassemble the shower head and screw it back into place.

HOME INVENTORY

For your own protection in the event of burglary, fire, flood, or other natural disaster, you want to have a detailed record of your possessions. One way to do this is to photograph them, write the estimated value on the back of the photo, and keep the records in a fire-safe box or safe-deposit box at your bank. Another method is to have someone videotape you as you walk through your house, stopping at significant possessions and explaining them in detail, including estimated value.

reduce, reuse,
Recycle

TO ANYONE BENT ON SAVING A DIME,
CONSERVING ON ENERGY AND RESOURCES
AND REUSING THINGS IS SECOND NATURE.

Making the best use of natural resources, reducing our energy and water consumption, and learning clever uses for old things is more than good for the environment; it makes smart money sense, too. For a long time, we were a throwaway society. Now, with energy costs going through the roof (literally), water becoming increasingly an issue in many parts of the country, and the amount spent on everyday items rising steadily, it is the rare penny pincher who isn't finding ways to conserve and cut costs.

insulation issues

A surefire way to lower your heating and cooling bills is to improve the insulation in your home. As you review your insulation needs, be sure to take into account walls or floors that separate living spaces from garages, basements, attics, or crawl space as well as outside walls.

● Check at a home center for the specific insulation recommendations for your area. Or try the Department of Energy's Web site (**www.energy.gov**), which gives recommendations by zip code. These recommendations are based on installation costs and energy savings. Don't put in more insulation than is recommended, because it won't save you extra money.

● Insulation is measured in R-values, which indicate the resistance to heat loss your insulation should have in ceilings, walls, and floors. The highest R-values are recommended in the North, because of their cold winters, and in the South, because of their hot summers.

● Fluffy fiberglass blankets in either batts or rolls are very popular, but there are also rigid foam sheets, as well as sprayed-in foam and blown-in loose-fill insulation. Any type you choose will require a vapor barrier to keep damp air from condensing inside the wall, causing damage. Some insulation has the vapor barrier built in; some vapor barriers must be installed separately. Always place the barrier so it is facing toward the heated interior wall. If you live in a hot, humid area, however, the barrier may need to face the exterior wall, or it may not be needed at all; check with a local builder.

● Urethane foam insulation is rapidly gaining in popularity, both in new construction and in retrofitting older homes. This insulation is pumped into existing walls through a small hole (less patching) or sprayed in new walls. Foam provides excellent insulation and forms its own vapor retarder, but a licensed contractor must install it.

weather stripping and caulking cut costs

Another excellent and relatively simple step toward reducing your energy bills is to add weather stripping to all doors and windows and to caulk all cracks and leaks. The average heating bill can be reduced by as much as 30 percent just by preventing outside air from seeping through miniscule cracks.

- The most common sources of air leaks are plumbing penetrations, chimneys, fireplace dampers, attic access hatches, recessed lights and ceiling fans, missing plaster, electrical outlets and switches, windows, doors, and baseboard moldings.
- One of the biggest culprits in heating or cooling loss (up to 15 percent!) is air loss around ductwork. Either contact a qualified licensed contractor or check all the accessible air ducts in your home and caulk any cracks or leaks.
- Before applying weather stripping, lay a bead of caulking; this acts as an adhesive and stops any drafts caused by surface irregularities.
- Another easy-to-use and effective option for plugging leaks is expanding foam sealant, sold in cans at hardware stores and home centers. Follow the manufacturer's directions carefully.
- Self-sticking weather stripping has a tendency to peel off eventually. Add a few tacks or staples to reinforce the weather stripping the next time you put some up.
- To weatherproof a door, tack metal-backed door weather strips along the stops on the jamb. Then screw a bottom strip with a sweep onto the door. Trim both strips with a hacksaw and be sure each fits snugly.

66 Use it up, wear it out; make it do, or do without. **99**

Traditional saying

thrifty thermostats

Lowering your thermostat during the winter or raising it during the summer (if you have central air-conditioning), even just a few degrees, can appreciably reduce your energy bills. During the cold months, a thermostat that is set at 66° to 68° F is perfect; in summer, aim for 78° to 80° F. If everyone is out of the house during the day, it's prudent to invest in an automatic thermostat timer that brings the heat up about one hour before you get up, lowers it 5 to 10 degrees for the hours the house is empty, and then turns it back up just before you get home. (The settings would, of course, be different for the summer months.)

filter savings

Get into the habit of checking your furnace filter once a month during the heating season. And do the same with your air conditioner during the summer. Choose a specific day of the month or do it the day your bill arrives (highly motivating). Cleaning or replacing the filter monthly can help keep your heating and cooling systems working efficiently, since clogged filters waste energy and make your systems work harder and run longer—money out the window.

energy-efficient windows

The cost of replacing your old single-glazed windows with new double-glazed ones that have argon gas between the panes can be fairly daunting. Although new windows represent a big investment, the long-term benefit in lowered heating and cooling bills, especially with the cost of energy continuing to skyrocket, makes it worth considering.

● If your old windows are basically sound, consider adding permanent combination storm windows. Because they have sliding screens, you won't have to change your storm windows with the seasons. And they double the energy efficiency of windows. Look for solid construction, resilient pile weather stripping, and three tracks instead of two. Make sure they are easy to open and close—and to get at when you want to wash them.

● Have your older windows professionally treated with low-E (low-emissivity) film. A low-E coating blocks and reflects heat and usually lasts about five years.

● The least expensive option to seal windows against winter cold is to install clear sheets of plastic. You will not be able to access the windows once these are in place, and you will be putting tiny holes in the plastic at the points where you attach the sheets, but they will still help lower your heating costs to an extent.

● Make your curtains an ally in energy efficiency: Light-colored curtains will keep a room warmer than dark-colored ones because the light-colored ones let sunlight come into the room. Line the curtains with an acetate or acrylic fabric so that your warm air doesn't pass through the curtains and out the window.

here comes the sun

You can use passive solar energy to heat your house in winter, and these same tricks work in reverse to keep your house cooler in summer:

cold weather During the winter months, allow as much sun as possible into the house. Remove and store window screens. On sunny days, open blinds, shutters, and shades and tie back curtains. Trim evergreen trees and shrubs that shade the windows. As soon as the sun starts to go down, close the blinds to hold the heat inside.

hot weather In the summer take the opposite approach: Plant trees to shade the house and especially your air conditioner. (A shaded air-conditioning unit uses 10 percent less energy than one in direct sunlight.) In addition, install awnings over south-facing windows and close your curtains early in the day. (Leave them closed all day if you will be gone.) If it cools down after sunset, open up the house to take advantage of the breezes.

lighten up

Invest in compact fluorescent bulbs for frequently used fixtures. These produce the same amount of light and fit in the same sockets as an incandescent bulb but use only about one-quarter of the energy. They also last ten times as long as their incandescent cousins—double savings indeed.

cooking energy

- Adjust the burners on a gas cooktop so that the flames just touch or are slightly lower than the bottoms of pans. Flames curling around a pan waste energy.
- On an electric cooktop, place a pan on a coil that is closest to it in size. Place the pan so that its bottom lies absolutely flat on the burner.
- When cooking on an electric cooktop, set the burner on high first and then lower it to finish the cooking. For most dishes, turn off the burner altogether at the end; the element will continue to hold the heat for several minutes.
- The oven vent on an electric range is generally under one of the burners. When the oven is in use, you can feel the hot air coming through the vent. Set dishes you want to warm on that burner.
- Before you turn on the oven to bake something, adjust the oven racks; you won't get burned and you'll save heat.
- If a dish is to cook for an hour or more, you do not need to preheat the oven. (The exception is turkey, if you want a crisp skin.) Instead, start the oven when you put the dish in it. If the time is just under an hour, extend the cooking time slightly. Preheating is required only for dishes with a short baking time.
- Use a timer! Every time you open the oven door to peek at a dish, the oven loses as much as 25 degrees in heat, which your oven then has to make up again.
- When you're baking sequentially (cookies, for example), always have the next item ready to go before the timer goes off so that you can put another in as you pull one out, keeping the oven door open for as little as possible.
- If you have an oven with a self-cleaning cycle, start the cycle right after you take a meal out of the oven, while it's still warm.

small savings

Using small appliances can actually save energy (thus lowering your bills). A toaster oven can bake a potato or cook a small-size portion of food; a microwave can cook anything liquid in less time using less energy than a stove can. Look for models of small appliances that have a lower wattage rating to further your savings.

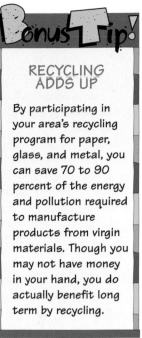

Bonus Tip!

RECYCLING ADDS UP

By participating in your area's recycling program for paper, glass, and metal, you can save 70 to 90 percent of the energy and pollution required to manufacture products from virgin materials. Though you may not have money in your hand, you do actually benefit long term by recycling.

hot tips for water heaters

Except for your home's heating and cooling units, your water heater is your largest energy user. So it pays to control its cost.

● Unless you need a higher temperature for a dishwasher, set the thermostat on your unit at 120° F. This simple step can cut your hot water costs by as much as 50 percent! Turn the unit to the lowest setting if you will be gone a week or more.

● If your water heater runs out of hot water often, you may be doing tasks that consume a lot of hot water too close together. One bath, for example can completely use up a common 40-gallon tank, and it can take nearly an hour to reheat. To find out how quickly your water heater recovers, look for a plate on it that says how many gallons it can heat in an hour.

● If you have an electric water heater, find out if your power company offers off-peak rates. Then try to schedule bathing, laundering, and dishwashing for those periods, whenever possible.

● Unless you have a fairly new, superinsulated unit, buy an inexpensive water heater cover from your home center or hardware store. These covers come as kits and wrap around your water heater, keeping it insulated and the heat where it belongs. A cover can cut 15 percent off your hot water costs. If your unit is gas, be careful not to cover the top or to block the airflow to the gas burner at the bottom.

BAG IT!

The most economical and earth-friendly kind of bag is one you can use over and over again.

● Canvas shopping bags are ideal for grocery shopping. They hold anything and will not break. If they get dirty, you can just throw them in the washing machine.
● String shopping bags are great for keeping in your purse or briefcase to have when you're picking some things up on the way home, and they expand to accommodate a surprising amount.
● Paper bags are useful for collecting newspapers for recycling. Or you can unfold them and use the paper for wrapping packages, covering books, or anything else that requires heavy-duty paper.
● When you do end up with some plastic bags—they're unavoidable—reuse them as garbage pail liners. Or see if you can return them to the store for repayment. Some stores will pay 5 cents per bag.

showered with savings

Installing inexpensive low-flow shower heads and faucets in your home is a simple fix you can do yourself and will reduce the amount of water you use by half, without decreasing the performance. Follow the manufacturer's instructions; you'll need only a wrench or pliers to do the job.

● Just taking a shower instead of a bath can save water: A three-minute shower uses one-fourth the water of a bath. With a low-flow shower head, you save even more.
● Check out shower heads with an off-on switch that lets you interrupt the flow while you soap up, shave, or shampoo and then resume the flow to rinse.
● Turn off the water while you soap your face or hands, shave, or brush your teeth. Get into the habit of turning off the tap when you're not continuously using it.

- Keep an old milk jug under each sink. When you have to run water to get it hot, use the jug to catch the water instead of letting it go down the drain. Then use the water in the jug for your houseplants or humidifier.
- When you replace a toilet, get a new low-flow model (which is now required in all new construction). These toilets use only 1.67 gallons of water per flush, compared with the 3.5 gallons the old type used.
- If you're not ready to replace your toilets, fill old plastic soda pop bottles with water and put one in each toilet tank to reduce the amount of water per flush.

appliance dos and don'ts

DON'T buy the most expensive appliances automatically. Check *Consumer Reports* for models with high energy efficiency and low water usage that are in the medium-price range. Higher prices of appliances sometimes mean you're paying for bells and whistles you don't need; really low prices may land you with a model that eats energy or water, costing you more in the long run.

DO look for dishwashers that have water-miser and no-heat drying features when you are shopping for a new one.

DON'T run your dishwasher or clothes washer until it is full.

DO run dishwashers at night, when many power companies offer lower rates. In the summer, running a dishwasher at night when it's cooler also conserves on cooling costs.

DON'T rinse off normally soiled dishes before you put them in the dishwasher. Just scrap off the food. Also, don't use your dishwasher's rinse-and-hold cycle except when dishes must be held overnight and odors may result.

DO use the lightest washing cycle for dishes that aren't very dirty. It uses less hot water and energy.

DON'T use more detergent than you need in either your dishwasher or your clothes washer. Experiment to see how little you can use and still get things clean.

DO use nature for drying—a clothes-line for laundry and the no-heat setting for dishes. (Open the dishwasher door while the dishes are drying to add humidity to a dry house.)

the prudent
Gardener

A GLORIOUS GARDEN NEED NOT COST A SMALL FORTUNE.

As with so many things, working with nature will make your garden look better with less work and less monetary investment. Planting native varieties, using low-flow watering systems, making your own compost for soil amendment, and using natural options rather than expensive chemical fertilizers and pest controls will save you money while helping you create a veritable Eden in your own yard.

plans for pennies

Planning a landscape design is an exact art. The cheapest way is to do the design and installation yourself. If you are an avid gardener and very familiar with the plants in your area, this is probably the way to go. There are myriad books detailing landscape design that you can consult. But if you are new to gardening or to a particular region, you may want to invest in having a professional landscape design done and then do the work yourself. This option will mean more outlay of cash up front, but the resulting design and selection of appropriate plants will be more assured.

- Professional landscape designers can charge more than $1,000—though you can find those who charge less.
- Some nurseries have a landscape designer on staff. If you contract with them, they will charge very little or nothing for the design with the agreement that all the plants will be purchased from that nursery.
- Check with the nearest university or college to see whether it offers a major in landscape design. Students, either undergrad or graduate, can often be hired for less than well-known professionals charge. A student will also have a higher stake in coming up with a beautiful and work-able design that will help launch his or her reputation.
- The real saving is in doing the work yourself: preparing the soil; building the paths, decks, arbors, and so on; installing a drip-irrigation system; and putting in the plants. If you have a detailed professional design to follow, you're more likely to end up with a garden that functions well and plants that thrive.

nursery costs

Plant nurseries will be, by and large, the most expensive option, though they generally have good sales. Their strong point is the quality of the plants, the variety to choose from, and the expertise of their sales force. For focal plants in your landscape, those you'd have to invest a bit in anyhow, you may want to opt for a professional nursery. By getting a healthy plant and installing it correctly, you'll be less likely to have to replace it (double the cost).

home centered

Big home centers with attached garden centers, such as **Lowe's** and **Home Depot**, are convenient when you're planning a landscape. You can pick up almost everything there, from path and arbor materials to plants to deck furniture. You can also take classes there, often at no cost except perhaps a materials charge. You can learn how to install drip irrigation (the easiest, most water- and energy-efficient way to water your garden), which plants will thrive in your region, how to install a brick or tile patio, and much more. In terms of money savings, the prices at home centers will vary but are generally pretty good. And the folks who work there generally (there will always be exceptions) take great pride in being able to help customers and are trained in their area of expertise. And if you are planning a really big project, you can take advantage of the "new credit card" discount; just buy as much as you can to make it worth your while.

super savings

Superstores such as **Wal-Mart** and **Kmart** almost always have a garden center attached where the prices, on bedding plants in particular, can be fabulous in season. You'll also find a large variety of furniture, arbors, edgings, trellises, and so on. If you shop at the end of the season, you will find terrific clearance sales. But be careful not to wait too long. The stock at most of these stores is determined by a corporate headquarters, and when executives decide the sales peak has been reached, they want to clear out the seasonal stuff fast. While the season lasts, however, these stores offer great prices and a fairly wide selection.

garage gardening?

An area in which garage sales excel is garden supplies. This can be a seasonal opportunity, when folks start cleaning out their storage sheds or garages. Watch ads closely and call ahead to find out whether the sale will include any garden tools, machines, or furniture. Remember, that rusty cast-iron patio set can be revived easily with a little muscle and paint.

bulk savings

When purchasing supplies for your landscaping, remember to buy in bulk for savings in time and money. Topsoil, mulch, gravel, and so forth can be ordered from a landscaping company and delivered by the truckload to your driveway. Though the initial cost may give you pause, try adding up the cost of buying the same stuff in those bags at a nursery, and the savings will quickly become apparent. To save more, ask around your neighborhood to see whether anyone else is getting ready to do a large landscaping job, and buy together.

66Spring is nature's way of saying, let's party!**99**

Robin Williams

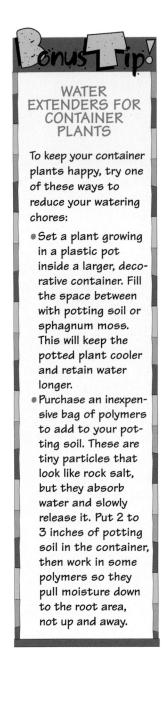
seasonal supplies

Like clothing, gardening supplies usually go on sale at the end of the season. Check the newspaper during late summer, when lawn mowers, edgers, gardening tools, and furniture for your garden are likely to be offered for considerably less than in late spring or early summer. Also watch the ads in late winter or very early spring, because sometimes centers want to get rid of last year's stock before putting in new merchandise. You might find clearance sales on all sorts of gardening supplies.

in the zone

Before you plan a garden, get to know your temperature zone. You can find zone maps in many gardening books, with some slight variations. Each zone is based on an average minimum temperature (how cold it gets). The freeze factor pretty much determines whether a plant can survive in a given region. When you buy plants, you may find the recommended zone indicated on the pot or stake. You may also find information about whether the plant likes sun or shade, as well as watering recommendations and other important tips for successful cultivation. If you read and follow this information, the plant will have a better chance of surviving where you put it.

- Within a general zone, there are microclimates. Even in as small an area as a backyard, one place will get more sun and be drier, another will be deeply shaded and moist, and so on. You can often use microclimates to grow plants that don't normally thrive in your zone.

embrace xeriscaping— or a reasonable facsimile thereof

The fastest-growing trend in gardening is also the cheapest, the most consistently successful, and the easiest: xeriscaping. This word comes from the Greek word *xerós*, meaning **dry**. Xeriscaping is landscaping that requires a minimal amount of supplementary water. Although xeriscaping is generally practiced in drier climates, the concept can be adapted to just about any region.

- One of the hallmarks of this landscaping approach is its reliance on native or acclimated plants that thrive on a particular region's normal rainfall. You can get a list of these plants from local horticultural societies. If you use a plant in your garden that is either native or adapts easily to the normal conditions of your area, the chances that it will thrive are greatly increased, the plant will usually cost less than an exotic variety, and the care needed will be minimal. It doesn't get much better than that, right?
- Xeriscaping also involves replacing water-thirsty lawns with patios and hardy groundcovers, using mulches to

prevent evaporation and erosion, and amending the soil with compost or peat moss to help it retain moisture. All are low-maintenance tricks that will save not only water, but money and time in the long run.

go green

Like xeriscaping, organic gardening is both better for the environment and much cheaper than gardening with chemicals. But it does require some self-education. Learning to compost will save you money, because you won't need to buy soil enhancers and you will have a year-round source of fertilizer. For a healthier garden with fewer pest problems and vegetables you can serve right out of the ground without fear, try companion planting. Plant basil among your ornamentals, for example, to discourage aphids. Or plant yarrow near your fruit trees to lure bees. Natural pest-control measures contribute to the health of your garden. Planting angelica and morning glory will attract ladybugs and lacewings that eat other insects. Organic gardening makes sense and saves cents.

the veggie machine

A vegetable garden is one of the best garden investments you can make. It will cut your food bills and provide your family with delicious meals for the entire growing season—and beyond, if you can or freeze your homegrown produce. Choose a plot that gets at least six hours of full sun a day and make sure the soil drains well. If necessary, amend the soil by adding organic matter, such as compost, peat moss, or composted manure. Organic matter helps relieve soil problems, whether they be caused by an excess of clay or sand. If space is limited, many vegetables grow beautifully in containers or raised beds. And if you learn about companion planting, you can mix flowers with your vegetables to improve the health of each and the beauty of your garden.

GARDENING ON THE WEB
www.garden.org

There are any number of gardening sites on the Web, but the site listed above is particularly helpful to both the neophyte and the experienced gardener. The site is run by the National Gardening Association, and it is chock full of ideas, help, and product information. The features that you will find include:

- National zone map with information about your particular region
- New products like a planter that holds water for a week
- Plants for sale
- A section on organic gardening
- Question and answer of the day
- A how-to section
- Pest control
- Online gardening courses

THE THREE KEYS TO ORGANIC GARDENING

1. **Great soil makes great gardens.** Most soil is either too full of clay (drains poorly) or sand (doesn't hold water and loses nutrients). Work in lots of compost several times a year for any type of soil. If you have clay soil, work in some sand. If you have sandy soil, work in sphagnum peat moss.

2. **Give frequent care.** Be sure your plants get enough water (but not too much), weed regularly, and walk through daily to catch problems before they cause trouble.

3. **Embrace imperfection.** Only nature is perfect. Don't fall apart because a pest invades your garden or a plant dies. Figure out your next step and see your garden as a constantly changing pleasure.

water wisdom

Investing in a watering system will end up saving you time and water. By putting your system on a timer, you can automatically water at the best time for the plants, whether you're awake or not. You can even water when you're away.

- Drip-irrigation systems deliver water directly to the plant roots, resulting in less evaporation and lower water use. Drip systems are available at garden centers, and not all of them are expensive, especially if you factor in the cost of water in a region where it's scarce.
- Soaker hoses, some of which are manufactured from recycled car tires, have small holes down their length. You can put them wherever you want to water plants at their bases (perfect under a hedge or in a flower border). A soaker hose slowly waters an area up to several feet on either side.
- New and improved sprinkler heads are smaller than traditional heads and can be placed more closely together. This improves the delivery of water to plants, which saves water.
- Give plants that need deep watering, such as tomatoes, their own watering system. Rinse out a 1-gallon plastic beverage jug and poke one or two small holes along its sides with a nail. When you put a tomato plant in the ground, bury the jug up to its neck a few inches away. When the plant needs watering, simply fill the jug. The water will steadily seep out the holes over a day or so.

compost: garden gold mine

Making your own compost is easy, environmentally sound, and absolutely free! There are two methods: cold composting, which is simply making a pile of materials and letting them break down naturally (over one or two years), and hot composting, which requires more work but will be ready to use in a few weeks. In hot composting, you layer carbon-rich materials (dry) and nitrogen-rich materials (damp or wet), turning and watering the pile every few days to keep it moist. The heat is caused by microbial reaction and will kill bacteria and even weed seeds.

- Easiest site: Make a single pile in one bin. Fancier but more useful: three bins—one for new yard waste, another for partly decomposed compost, and a third for ready-to-use good stuff. Choose a level, well-drained, shady or partly shady area, preferably near a water source, for the bins.
- What can go in compost: Most yard waste (grass clippings, leaves, and such), eggshells, vegetable and fruit peels, coffee grounds, potato and onion skins.
- What cannot go in: Weeds, meat scraps or bones, bacon fat, dog or cat feces (or litter).

know your grasses

Choosing the right grass for your area and needs is imperative for the eventual success of your lawn. The northern and mountain regions of the United States (Zones 3 through 6) require cool-season varieties; the southern half to bottom third of the country (Zones 7 though 10) should use warm-season grasses. A local nursery or Cooperative Extension Service can be an invaluable resource for selecting a type of grass that will thrive in your particular environment.

cool-season grasses Kentucky bluegrass, perennial rye, and fescues (best used in mixtures with other types of grass).

warm-season grasses Bermuda, Zoysia, St. Augustine, and turf-type tall fescues.

four steps to great grass

1. choose the right grass As noted above, the climate zone you are in will determine what kind of grass (or mixture) you should plant. Though you may just love the look of Kentucky bluegrass, if you live in a warm-season climate, your bluegrass will not grow well.

2. mow it often, mow it high If you let lawn grass grow too long it will become thin, and if you cut it too short, it can kill the grass. If you have cool-season grass, set your mower blade 2-1/2 to 3 inches high; if you have warm-season grass, set the blade 1-1/2 to 2 inches high. Then keep an eye on your lawn and mow it to keep it as close to that height as possible.

3. water well Set your sprinkler system to water to a depth of at least 1 inch to encourage the development of a deep root system—which means a more drought resistant root system. Once your lawn goes dormant (usually turning brown in late summer, early fall), leave it alone until the weather cools. If you water during the dormant stage, the lawn may come out of dormancy too early and become stressed.

4. feed it right and on schedule A rule of thumb for most turf grasses is to use a complete fertilizer formulated for lawns containing nitrogen, phosphorus, and potassium. Make sure the entire lawn receives the same amount of fertilizer (about 1 pound of nitrogen per 1,000 square feet of lawn per application), but don't overfertilize it. Cool-season grasses thrive on a spring and fall fertilization schedule; warm-season turfs prefer a spring and summer feeding. Check with a local nursery or Cooperative Extension Service for recommendations on the best schedule, methods, and mixtures for fertilizing the grass in your yard.

COOPERATIVE EXTENSION SERVICE

www.reeusda.gov

The Cooperative Extension Service's primary mission is agricultural, but it also has a lot of useful information for the home gardener. Sponsored by the Department of Agriculture and affiliated with a major agricultural school in each state, it has an office in nearly every county. The Web site above will lead you to your main state site, which in turn will lead you to your nearest office.

Cheap Car Talk

- the best car buy

- car care

- auto alternative

"Cars" and "cheap" in the same title—what's going on? Are we talking about old junkers here? Or too-good-to-be-true slimy sales deals? No, here is where you can find just about every trick for saving on the cost of a new or used car. You'll find out about surfing the Web for information, money-saving months (and even days of the month) to buy, different purchasing venues, how to use your option choices to negotiate, and the fine art of haggling down to the dirt. Once you've driven your new toy home, you'll need to know how to take care of it. Ignorance in this area is not bliss, it is excessively expensive! Like your home, year-round attention (and good driving techniques) will make your car run better, last longer, and need fewer major repairs over the years. Just in case you are in the mood for alternatives, we offer a slew of them from commuting strategies such as car-pooling, the unexpected pluses of public transportation, and even the pros of pedal power.

Zoom, Zoom!

the best
Car Buy

IF YOU DO YOUR HOMEWORK
AND BARGAIN, YOU CAN GET
YOUR DREAM CAR FOR A LOT LESS.

Other than buying a house, a car may be the most expensive purchase you'll make in your lifetime. The experience can be frustrating, especially given the fact that your spanking-new car will drop about twenty-five percent of its value the minute you drive it off the dealer's lot. It's not uncommon to experience "buyer's regret" after a car purchase: Did I buy the right car? Should I have gone for the extended warranty? Did I pay too much? But don't despair. If you have done your research and use some basic bargaining techniques, you can drive away in the car you want without loosing your shirt.

research, research, research!

The first and most important step to selecting and buying a car, whether new or used, is to gather as much information as possible about the models you are interested in.

● Don't limit yourself to one car manufacturer when you begin your research. That will automatically reduce your bargaining power. Instead, make a list of features that are most important to you (safety record, gas mileage, reliability, engine size, all-wheel drive). Then try to prioritize the list in order of importance.

● When you have a better idea of what kind of car you want, read magazines (such as *Consumer Reports* and *Car and Driver*), surf the Web (see Resources box, page 283 for good sites to check), and try to identify two or three manufacturers with models that fit your needs.

the real price

Once you've identified the car models you're interested in, the most valuable piece of information you can find out is the **wholesale price**—what the dealer paid for the car from the manufacturer. This price includes the base price as well as the "goodies" the manufacturer offered the dealer, including discounts, rebates, incentives, and special financing. There are a number of easy-to-access sources to find out a car's wholesale price, including *Edmunds' New Cars & Trucks Prices & Reviews*, a paperback book available in most local libraries. The same information is also available on-line at **www.edmunds.com**. Once you know what the dealer paid, you can tack on a modest profit—say $500—for the dealer and get yourself a terrific deal. You always want to start with the lowest price and bargain up. Never bargain down from the sticker price.

'tis the season

At the end of the year, most car dealers are eager to get rid of last year's models to make room for the new line. November and December are often **great months to buy** because dealers are more willing to negotiate aggressively in order to ensure you will drive an older model car off the lot.

But never buy the upcoming year's models in November because you'll pay for the newness. Also, wait for bad weather. If the dealership has been a ghost town for a week because of the storm of the century, they will be more anxious to sell a car—at a better price for you.

it pays to shop around

When purchasing a car, most folks automatically think of the traditional dealer working out a showroom. However, there are more places to shop for a car these days, and they're all worth checking out. It pays to know what these various options are offering because the more information you have at your fingertips, the better deal you're likely to strike on the car you want.

the dealer This option requires legwork and time as you go from one showroom to another, hearing sales pitch after sales pitch. If you're willing to do your homework first and haggle fiercely, you can usually get an excellent price on the exact car that you want.

internet services On the Web, car shoppers can use a free dealer-referral service (see Resources box, page 283). You input a description of the car with the options you want and a participating dealer will send back a no-obligation quote, which you can then try to bargain down. This method can get you the car you want with minimal human contact—a real plus for some shoppers.

club services These are member-only car-buying services offered through price clubs and other organizations. They put you in touch with an affiliated dealer, who then offers prospective buyers a pre-arranged quote with a flat markup above the invoice. While convenient and a blessing for those who can't bring themselves to haggle, you'll probably end up paying more for the privilege of using a buying service.

over the phone Rather than visiting a dealership, let your fingers do the walking and offer a price over the telephone based on the wholesale price of the car you want. Call other dealers to see whether they will do better than the first accepted offer. Once you've gotten the best deal you can, visit the dealership to make sure that it has the exact car you've agreed to buy. Be aware, though, that most dealerships won't really get down to their rock-bottom price until you are sitting in their showroom.

floor models

Buying a floor model or loaner vehicle can be an effective way to save money on a car. The price of an automobile that has been used as a floor model can usually be negotiated down considerably. Just make sure that you get a new-car warranty with it for better coverage.

❝The car has become the carapace, the protective and aggressive shell, of urban and suburban man.❞

Marshall McLuhan, media theorist

popularity contest

Car models that are popular and in high demand may be bought at a better price through a car buying service or an auto broker. Either one is likely to get you a better price than you'll be able to negotiate yourself. For example, AAA Wheel EZ (1-877-943-3539 or **www.aaa.com**) will negotiate the deal, handle the trade-in on your old car, arrange financing, and even offer insurance options.

it's optional

Be very picky about which options you select when you buy a car. Don't let a salesperson seduce you into an option package that has gizmos that you don't need or actually want. Keep a list of "must haves" with you and refer to it often. Those shiny mag wheels and deluxe speakers can significantly increase the price of the car.

testing, testing

Make sure that you test drive at least three different cars before you make a final decision. And make sure the test cars have the same engine, transmission, and preferably the same options that you're looking for.

car talk terms

Learning the lingo can really help keep you on top of the bargaining process:

base price This is the cost of a particular model of automobile without any additional options at all (the standard package plus factory warranty).

invoice price This is how much the manufacturer initially charged the dealer for the car. The invoice price is generally higher than the dealer's final cost because car dealers often get rebates, allowances, discounts, and incentive awards from manufacturers. Also, the invoice price will often include freight charges — check this point carefully if you're using the invoice price as your base price. You don't want to be charged for the freight if it has already been paid for!

dealer sticker price This sticker is affixed to the window of the car by the car dealer. It shows both the Monroney sticker price (described below), and the suggested retail prices of any dealer-installed options, plus the charges for preparation and undercoating.

monroney sticker price (msrp) Federal law requires this sticker to be on every new car's window, and only the purchaser can legally take it off. It lists the base price, the manufacturer's installed options with suggested retail prices, the transportation charge, and the fuel economy of the vehicle (mileage per gallon based on city and highway driving).

the dos and don'ts of haggling

Unless you want to pay more than you should, you will need to learn how to haggle for a car. It is expected and it is necessary. If you simply can't bring yourself to bargain hard, try to get a tougher-minded family member or close friend to help you out (good cop, bad cop can work well with bargaining). These tips will help you too:

DON'T wait to shop until your current car is on its last legs. Being in need puts you in a very bad bargaining position. Desperation tends to show and can lead you to make hasty decisions you may regret later on.

DO be prepared. Have your research firmly in your head or at your fingertips with models, options, and prices.

DON'T worry about bargaining too hard and offending the dealer. They take care of themselves. You can be friendly. In fact, making a buddy of the dealer can work to your advantage. But don't mistake a friendly feeling for good bargaining. Salespeople, even the nicest kind, are there to sell their product and make money. Take care of yourself.

DO be discreet. If you've really fallen in love and have your heart set on a particular car, continue to bargain as if you are undecided between two or three. This will give your more bargaining power.

DON'T do the salesperson's work. During the course of bargaining, a salesperson may ask you to name a reasonable profit. Don't take the bait. That isn't your job, that's their job, and it's their problem! You need to focus on getting the best car for the lowest price.

DO be willing to walk away. Trust your gut instinct if the deal isn't good enough or if some of the details don't feel right. If you don't feel good about the deal or the dealer, chances are you are picking up something subliminally and should walk out the door.

DON'T glide over the details. Most contracts include a charge for paperwork or an advertising fee. If you have agreed on a good price, ask the dealer to waive these fees. If they won't do that, suggest free servicing or complimentary extras (floor mats, for example) to offset the fees.

DO express negative feelings. If you decide to walk, the dealer will probably ask why. Tell them. You may see a radical change in their attitude, resulting in a better deal.

DON'T pay any mind when the salesperson asks, "What amount would you like your monthly payment to be?" It's one of the oldest dealer tricks and one of the most effective. Paying $219 a month is no kind of deal if the payments stretch on for an extra 24 months. Make the negotiation on the price of the car.

DO keep your trade-in out of the negotiation until the end. Many clever salespeople will give you a huge bargain on the

NETTING THE BEST DEAL
....
**www.consumerreports.org
or 1-800-205-2445**
....

Consumer Reports offers comprehensive pricing information and charges $12 for the first report; $10 for each additional one. Here are some other helpful sites:

For model and price info:
....
www.bbbonline.org
(Better Business Bureau)
....
www.carfax.com
....
www.carbargains.org
....
www.carprice.com
....
www.edmunds.com
....
**www.kelleybluebook.com
or www.kbb.com**
....
www.intellichoice.com
....
www.nadaguides.com

For dealer referrals:
....
www.autobytel.com
....
www.autovantage.com
....
www.autoweb.com
....
www.carmax.com
....
www.cars.com
....
www.carpoint.com
....
www.carsdirect.com
....
www.costcoauto.com
....
www.samsclub.com
....
www.stoneage.com

new car; then fleece you on the trade-in. Get a firm price on the new car first, and then get the best price you can for your old one (you will always do better selling it privately if you are willing to make the effort).

no deposit, no return
There are dealers who, once the deal is just about made, will press you to put a deposit on a car. Unless you know for certain that this is The Car, don't put any money down. Ignore threats of the car getting away. You could end up making a commitment you'll regret.

let's make a deal
If possible, try to close a deal on a Saturday at the end of the month. At some dealerships, the sales personnel can make a bonus for hitting a sales number (usually determined weekly or monthly or both). If your sale can help put that person in place to win, they will be more motivated to bargain and seal the deal then and there.

signing on the dotted line
You've done your homework, you've haggled with the best, you're ready to sign the contract. Wait. Consider these:
- Be sure there is a clause in the contract that allows you to void the agreement if something goes wrong, such as a delay in delivery.
- Once you've read over the contract and agree with it, be sure the manager or general manager signs the contract with you. A salesperson will not have the authority to make certain contractual changes so you want the highest official signature possible.

close inspection
When you go to pick up your new car at the dealership, go over it with a fine-toothed comb and test-drive it before finalizing the contract.

the art of financing
The best way to buy a car is to use cash and pay for it outright. Cars depreciate upon purchase so borrowing money to buy a car is bad debt. However, few of us are in a position to pay all cash. If you do need to finance a car, don't automatically go with the manufacturer's or dealer's financing. Although convenient, they don't usually offer the best deal. You can save a lot of money by shopping around. Here's some tips:
- Compare the annual percentage rate (APR) and the length of the loan when shopping for financing—don't just fixate on the monthly payment. The final amount

SAFETY FIRST
www.nhtsa.gov or
**1-888-DASH-2-DOT
(1-888-327-4236)**

The National Highway Traffic Safety Administration maintains a Web site and a toll-free phone number to offer the public information about the safety features of vehicles, any recalls, crash tests, and other auto safety topics.

1-800-424-9393

If you are thinking of buying a used car, call the number above first. This is the U.S. Department of Transportation's Auto Safety Hotline. By calling, you can find out if there have been any recalls on the vehicle model that you're considering.

you'll end up paying will be determined by the negotiated price of the car, the APR, and the length of the loan.

- Put down the largest down payment possible and opt for the shortest term loan possible.
- If you are a member of a credit union, contact them to see if they offer loans for major purchases and ask about the terms of the various loans.
- Check with your bank about the various loans they offer and what it would take to give you the best deal.
- If possible, consider taking out a home equity loan. You can deduct the interest paid on a home equity loan on your taxes—and who doesn't like lowering their taxes?

lose the lease

Think twice about leasing a car. It's often a bad financial decision. Over time, you will end up paying more leasing than you would buying. You pay the big payment at the end rather than a larger down payment at the beginning. Lease payments are tax-deductible only if the car is used exclusively for work (and don't let a salesperson tell you differently; check with a tax expert). With so many negatives, it's usually just not worth it.

secondhand sensations

A good used car can be the best automotive bargain of all. You can often buy it outright, sparing yourself years of debt. Just make sure to check reliability ratings in *Consumer Reports* or on-line at **www.edmunds.com** (also see Resources box, page 283) to find out which used cars to avoid. Here are some suggestions on buying a "preowned" car:

venues Independent used car lot, new-car dealership that also sells used cars, auctions, used car superstore, or private seller.

cost vs. worth Always know the market value of the car before negotiating (*Kelley's Blue Book* is an excellent source, either in print or on-line; see Resources box, page 283). Make your first bid slightly lower than the market price and go up from there, but set a limit for yourself and don't go above it. As with new cars, it is almost impossible to bargain down.

get a history A nonnegotiable requirement for buying a used car should be a detailed service history. This should list any potential problems including past accidents, damages, and odometer discrepancies. You can obtain a history on your own using the 17-digit VIN (vehicle identification number) from the state or a private company specializing in vehicle history reports. Search on the Web for "vehicle history."

get a check up Have your mechanic check out the car before you buy it.

car Care

BECAUSE A CAR IS SUCH
A BIG INVESTMENT, IT PAYS
TO KEEP IT IN THE BEST POSSIBLE SHAPE.

**Taking care of a car means purchasing good insurance and servicing your car regularly to keep it running well. It also should include frequent inspections to insure the tires are correctly inflated, the oil and water levels are where they should be, the lights are in good working order, and so on.
If you commit to ongoing care of your car, you will save thousands of dollars in the long run. Maintaining a car is relatively inexpensive, but major repairs are not.**

the ins and outs of auto insurance

Trying to find the best auto insurance can be an overwhelming process. There are a lot of choices out there. Depending on where you live, the insurance rules in your state, and your driving record, the options will be many and varied. A few rules of thumb from the United States Office of Consumer Affairs, however, can help you make the right choice and get the most for your insurance dollars:

shop around Insurance premiums on identical policies can vary by hundreds of dollars. For unbiased information about auto insurance companies, ask family and friends for recommendations or call your state insurance department or an insurance-rating firm like A.M. Best (see Insurance Information box, page 289). Consumer guides can tell you which companies offer the lowest rates, but cost should not be the only determining factor. You want to make sure that you are getting good service for your insurance dollars. If you should ever need to use your policy, you want an agent or company who's on your side and makes it easy for you.

up your deductible To lower the monthly cost of car insurance, offer to increase your deductible—the amount you would pay in the case of collision, fire, or theft before the insurance company has to pay anything. This can lower your insurance costs considerably.

less coverage on older cars At some point, having a lot of insurance on a car that is no longer worth that much invokes the laws of diminishing returns. Drop, or significantly lower, both collision and comprehensive (fire and theft) on any car that is worth less than $1,000.

check for double coverage Chances are you already have good health insurance, so you don't need this type of coverage in your auto insurance. Check with your state insurance department (see Insurance Information box, page 289). Getting rid of duplicate coverage could lower your auto policy's personal injury protection (PIP) cost by up to 40 percent.

opt for the ordinary A car that is listed as "high theft" or that is expensive to repair generally will cost a lot more to insure than one that isn't. Be sure to check the insurance rates before you buy a high-end car.

low miles, low cost Ask your insurance company if they give discounts for low mileage—if you don't drive that much, why pay more?

good drivers get good rates Most insurance companies offer discounts for drivers who are over 50 years of age and for those with good driving records (no accidents in three years). Some will reduce rates if you've taken a driver's education course and will even offer discounts for student drivers who have gotten good grades. All of these discounts can add up to big savings.

safety first discounts The other area that might net you a discount on auto insurance is the safety of your car. Do you have automatic seat belts, air bags, an antitheft device, or antilock brakes? Does your car rank high on safety features with *Consumer Reports*? Ask your insurance agent if these features could mean lower rates for you.

three months or 3,000 miles

Memorize the above—it's the formula for oil changes. The most important fluid in your car is that dark, syrupy liquid that lubricates your engine. Perhaps the most critical thing you can do to keep your engine working well is to change the oil regularly. Be sure to use the correct weight and grade of oil recommended for your particular vehicle. If you use a heavier oil, it won't lubricate the bearings; if you use too light an oil, it can cause hammering in the engine when you start it cold—and that can eventually damage the engine. The exception to the three months or 3,000 mile rule is if you are using synthetic oil. Then the formula changes to every six months or 7,500 miles. When your car's oil is changed, make sure to check the car's other fluids (brake fluid, power steering, transmission, and such) replace the oil filter, and check all the belts and hoses.

a maintenance primer

Preventative maintenance will keep you from making many costly trips to the automobile mechanic for repairs. Here's a basic maintenance laundry list to follow:

air filter Check every other month and replace if dirty. Definitely replace this every 10,000 to 15,000 miles (generally part of a tune up).

antifreeze/coolant Check the level monthly or when changing the oil and keep topped off (most reservoirs are transparent so this is easy to do). The best mixture is a 50-50 combination of antifreeze and water. Once a year, have the system flushed and new coolant put in.

battery Check the battery every three months along with the oil change—if your car's battery is accessible. Some batteries are sealed and can't be checked.

> 66 And the gilded car of day, His glowing axle doth allay In the steep Atlantic stream. 99

John Milton

belts and hoses Check occasionally or at oil change intervals. If you can depress the belts more than a 1/2 inch, tighten them. Check and tighten hose clamps. Any belts or hoses that are worn, frayed, glazed, bulging, rotting, or brittle should be replaced immediately.

brake fluid Check the brake fluid when you have the oil changed. Brake fluid should be flushed and replaced every two years or 24,000 miles.

fuel filter Replace the fuel filter every 10,000 to 15,000 miles (if applicable).

lights Check your lights at dusk regularly, including brake lights, turn signals, and emergency flashers. Wipe off lenses whenever you wash your windshield and replace nonworking bulbs immediately.

oil Check every other time you fill-up with gas. If the oil is low, add more of the correct weight and grade. Change oil and filter regularly as discussed earlier in this section.

power-steering fluid Check when changing oil, replacing as needed, and inspect the pump and hoses for leaks. Always check this before any long trip.

shocks Check at oil change intervals. If your car's ride becomes bouncy or if your car begins to dip into turns, you may need to replace the shocks. Test shocks by bouncing the car: It should stop bouncing quickly when you step away. Replace worn or leaking shocks immediately and always in pairs.

tires Check regularly for uneven tread wear, cuts, bulges, or sharp objects lodged in tires. Keep tire pressure up to the recommended level and check the pressure frequently, especially after significant weather changes. Rotate the tires every 7,500 miles (after 5,000 miles the first time).

transmission fluid Check every three months with oil change. Replace once a year along with the transmission filter (if applicable).

windshield wiper blades and fluid Inspect the blades whenever you clean the windshield and replace them at least once a year, or whenever they leave smears when working. Check the fluid based on use, and keep it topped off.

in tune

Unlike earlier generations of automobiles, most cars today don't need regular tune-ups. A general engine checkup done once a year by your mechanic should suffice and pick up any potential problems. If you own a car made before 1980, however, you'll probably still need to have it tuned up once or twice a year—ask your mechanic. For newer cars, it's always a good idea to have a mechanic or dealer perform the manufacturer's suggested major servicing at 15,000 miles, 30,000 miles, and so on.

batteries not included

The battery in your new car was installed at the factory and is probably not a top-rated battery. They don't usually last that long, so don't be surprised when yours suddenly quits working. Don't let your battery lose too much power before you replace it. This can cause the charging system to work way too hard and the starter motor to overheat. Save money (and wear on your engine) by planning ahead and start checking your battery at least six months before the warranty runs out.

● Buy the longest-lasting battery your car can take. It'll help prevent problems with the starting, charging, and electrical systems in the long run.

● Check the cold-cranking amp (CCA) rating! If you're replacing a battery, get one with the same or greater cold-cranking amp rating (the temperature at which the battery can be charged for 30 seconds at 0° F). Make sure the rating is measured in Fahrenheit (F), not Celsius (C). This is important because 0° C is actually 32° F. Making a mistake could mean the battery wouldn't be guaranteed to work at a lower temperature.

fuel facts

Some people have the idea that premium gas is better than regular unleaded. Not necessarily. If your car's engine isn't designed for high-test fuel, buying premium gas is a big old waste of your cash. With the exception of a few high-end

INSURANCE INFORMATION

You can get information about all sorts of insurance issues from the National Insurance Consumer Help Line at 1-800-942-4242. You can write to the Insurance Information Institute at 110 William Street, New York, NY 10038 (212-669-9200). Another reliable source of information is A.M. Best (www.ambest.com, or 1-908-439-2200), a firm that rates insurance companies. Or call your state insurance department:

AK: 907-465-2515	ID: 208-334-2250	MT: 406-444-2040	RI: 401-277-2223
AL: 205-269-3550	IL: 217-782-4515	NC: 919-733-2032	SC: 803-737-6160
AR: 501-686-2900	IN: 317-232-2385	ND: 701-224-2440	SD: 605-773-3563
AZ: 602-912-8400	KS: 913-296-7801	NE: 402-444-2040	TN: 615-741-2176
CA: 213-897-8921	KY: 502-564-3630	NH: 603-271-2261	TX: 512-463-6464
CO: 303-894-7499	LA: 504-342-5900	NJ: 609-292-5363	UT: 801-538-3800
CT: 203-297-3800	MA: 617-521-7777	NM: 505-826-4601	VA: 804-371-9741
DC: 202-727-8002	MD: 410-333-6200	NV: 702-687-4270	VT: 802-828-3301
DE: 302-739-4251	ME: 207-582-8707	NY: 212-602-0203	WA: 206-753-7301
FL: 850-413-3100	MI: 517-373-9273	OH: 614-466-2658	WI: 608-266-0102
GA: 404-656-2056	MN: 651-297-7161	OK: 405-521-2828	WV: 304-558-3394
HI: 808-586-2790	MO: 314-751-2640	OR: 503-378-4271	WY: 307-777-7401
IA: 515-281-5705	MS: 601-359-3569	PA: 717-787-5173	

cars, most cars today are designed to run on regular unleaded fuel. Cars requiring high-test fuel will say so under the gas gauge found on the dashboard. Unless the car manufacturer requires it, premium fuel is not better, it doesn't produce more power, improve engine performance, save fuel, or contain any additives that help your car. It just costs more.

maximizing the mileage

You want to aim at getting the mileage per gallon estimated by the government for your vehicle. If you're close, you're doing fine. If you're not, one of the following could be the culprit. With the price of gas today, it's worth taking steps to improve your car's fuel efficiency.

- If your brakes are even slightly rubbing, you can burn extra fuel without even noticing the excess heat or wear on your brakes.
- Every time you switch on an electrical device (headlights, for example, or defogger), you use a little more gas. But the greatest gas-sucking device of all is your car's air conditioner. The more you use it, the worse your mileage.
- The type of tires and their air pressure can affect your car's fuel efficiency. Big tires have more contact with the road resulting in more friction and more gas burned. During cooler months, your tire pressure may go down more rapidly than you notice. A tire that is inflated correctly at 70° F will be under-inflated by as much a five pounds per square inch (PSI) at 20° F. This also produces more friction with the road.
- A faulty transmission linkage means the information that the car needs to work efficiently is not getting to the computer and, especially at highway speeds, this can significantly reduce fuel economy.
- Harsh wind, weather, and terrain can lower your car's fuel efficiency, as can a heavy load, stop-and-start traffic, and rough road conditions.
- Distance matters when it comes to fuel economy. Short trips of five miles or less reduce mileage and are harder on your engine, especially in cold weather. That doesn't mean you should drive farther, but it does mean you should take the time to warm up your car before you get started.

wiper wisdom

Even if your car is so high-tech that you really can't work on it at all, you can replace your windshield wipers—and it's surprisingly important to do. The rubber edges wear out pretty rapidly so check them at least every six months or so, depending on your climate conditions.

general smearing This means your windshield or wiper blades (or both) are dirty, the blades are worn out, or your

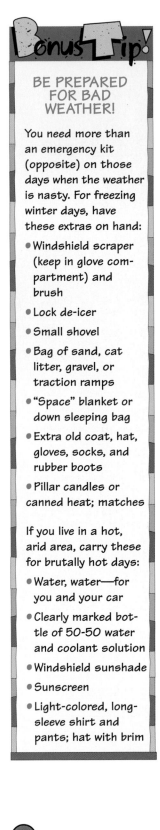

BE PREPARED FOR BAD WEATHER!

You need more than an emergency kit (opposite) on those days when the weather is nasty. For freezing winter days, have these extras on hand:

- Windshield scraper (keep in glove compartment) and brush
- Lock de-icer
- Small shovel
- Bag of sand, cat litter, gravel, or traction ramps
- "Space" blanket or down sleeping bag
- Extra old coat, hat, gloves, socks, and rubber boots
- Pillar candles or canned heat; matches

If you live in a hot, arid area, carry these for brutally hot days:

- Water, water—for you and your car
- Clearly marked bottle of 50-50 water and coolant solution
- Windshield sunshade
- Sunscreen
- Light-colored, long-sleeve shirt and pants; hat with brim

washer solution is not great. First, clean the wipers, checking the edges. If they're just a bit abraded, use fine-grade sandpaper to smooth them out. If they're shot, replace them. Replace the washer solution.

one-direction smearing This usually happens when the rubber blades are the wrong size or they have hardened due to extreme temperatures or just old age. Replace the rubber blades, making sure to buy the correct size for your car.

talking back When your wipers make a chattering noise, it generally means that your blade has frozen from the cold or the wiper arm is bent. If the cause is cold, thaw out the blade or replace it. If the arm is bent, either straighten it (see below) or buy a new arm and blade.

bent If your wiper blade has bent out of shape, turn on the wipers and stop them at midstroke. Using two pairs of pliers, grip the arm on either side of the bend, then carefully twist it until the arm is parallel to the windshield. If the tip of the arm is bent, remove the assembly to straighten it.

excess beading When water just beads all over your windshield, this means there's an excess of oil, grease, wax, or grime. Try cleaning the windshield with rubbing alcohol and clean cloths; repeat until the windshield no longer beads.

fog eraser

Pick up a cheap felt chalkboard eraser and keep it in your car. You'll find that it makes a terrific wiper when your car windows have fogged up.

wash 'n' dry

Taking your car to a professional car wash might be quicker and easier, but it will cost you. Washing your own car can be fun (make it a family affair!), and can be combined with an inspection to insure your car is running properly.

cool down Always wash in the shade and let the engine cool before you start. A hot surface dries the water too quickly and will leave unsightly spots on your car.

in balance Like your skin, your car needs a balanced pH cleanser. Dishwashing detergent will work just fine, but don't use too much soap. You can also add a tablespoon of baking soda to neutralize any acids.

water wise Rinse the car once with a hose to loosen dirt. Have one bucket of soapy water and one bucket of clean water as you wash the car.. Then use the hose again to do the final rinse. If you leave the hose on all the time you'll waste a lot of water and your money.

top to bottom Start washing the roof and work down. Wash one section at a time, using a back and forth pattern. Rinse frequently with clean water and a clean sponge.

to finish Dry the car with a soft, clean, lint-free cloth.

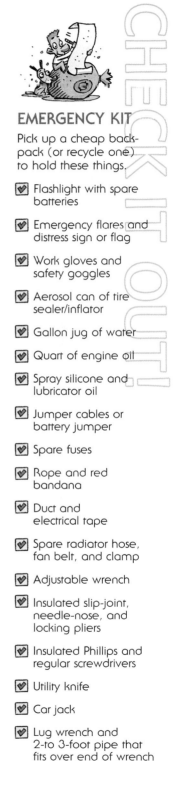

EMERGENCY KIT

Pick up a cheap backpack (or recycle one) to hold these things.

- ✔ Flashlight with spare batteries
- ✔ Emergency flares and distress sign or flag
- ✔ Work gloves and safety goggles
- ✔ Aerosol can of tire sealer/inflator
- ✔ Gallon jug of water
- ✔ Quart of engine oil
- ✔ Spray silicone and lubricator oil
- ✔ Jumper cables or battery jumper
- ✔ Spare fuses
- ✔ Rope and red bandana
- ✔ Duct and electrical tape
- ✔ Spare radiator hose, fan belt, and clamp
- ✔ Adjustable wrench
- ✔ Insulated slip-joint, needle-nose, and locking pliers
- ✔ Insulated Phillips and regular screwdrivers
- ✔ Utility knife
- ✔ Car jack
- ✔ Lug wrench and 2-to 3-foot pipe that fits over end of wrench

get it off!

When certain sticky substances or objects adhere to your car, just washing your vehicle isn't enough. Specific measures are required to get rid of them:

splattered bugs Even good old soap and water sometimes doesn't take off those squashed insects, so try combining 1/2 cup of baking soda with 2 cups of warm water in a clean spray bottle. Saturate each little carcass with the solution and let it sit for about 2 minutes. Then hose off the car using a sponge to remove the bugs. (Baking soda neutralizes the acid in the insect carcass and makes it easy to remove without hurting the car's finish.)

pine sap Love the smell of pines, hate the sap sticking to your car. First, use a plastic spatula to break off as much of the sap as possible being careful not to damage the finish. Wearing rubber gloves, soak a cloth in very hot water and dishwashing detergent, then apply the cloth to the sap. Rub hard until the sap starts to break off. Repeat until all the sap is gone, then rinse thoroughly with clean cold water.

WHAT'S THE LEAK?

With the exception of water, puddles of any kind under your car spell trouble. Often you can identify the source of the problem by the liquid's color, smell, or viscosity. To get a good look at the fluid, cut the bottom off a clear or white plastic jug and place it under the drip. Or you can place a piece of white paper where the leak is— just don't let it sit too long or the paper may dissolve.

Antifreeze: Newer coolant is usually green or yellow, sometimes orange. If older, it may be rusty or brownish. It has a distinct sweet odor.

Automatic-transmission fluid: Generally light red or rust red with an oily consistency. To confirm, check oil from the leak against oil on the transmission dipstick.

Battery acid: The smell will warn you first —sulfur or rotten eggs. This is an extremely corrosive substance. Don't touch it; wash it off immediately if you come into contact with it.

Brake fluid: Danger sign! If you notice a thin, watery, clear liquid, it could be brake fluid. Take your car to a mechanic immediately!

Diesel fuel: If you think you're smelling cooking oil, you may have a leak from the injector pump, fuel filter, or fuel line.

Gasoline: If you've ever pumped gas, you'll know what it smells like. Highly flammable and poisonous.

Gear oil: Though very light brown when fresh, this oil usually looks dark brown or even black. It has a heavy consistency and is used in manual transmissions, axles, and differentials.

Grease: Just like it sounds—thick and gooey. If your car has recently had a grease job, a little leakage is normal.

Power-steering fluid: If you have an old car, chances are transmission fluid is used in the steering system. Newer cars use a special steering fluid that is similar to fresh motor oil in color, but has a lighter consistency and a very different odor. If the fluid has turned to a silvery-gray color, it could indicate an internal failure; get it checked immediately.

Windshield wiper fluid: Usually light blue or greenish blue and smells like ammonia. It is also poisonous. If you notice leaking, you could have a cracked reservoir or a hole in a hose going from the reservoir to the nozzles.

bumper stickers Grab your trusty hair dryer and blow on a bumper sticker until the glue softens, then carefully peel off the sticker. Rub the remaining adhesive with your thumb; it should ball up and come off. If it's particularly stubborn, use rubber cement thinner or alcohol on a paper towel to get rid of the glue, then rinse the area thoroughly.

shine on!

Rubbing alcohol can keep your car windows bright, grease-free, and sparkling. Be sure the car is in the shade while you clean because rubbing alcohol dries extremely quickly. You can also use a solution of vinegar and water to clean the inside of a windshield that is dirty.

not just for miss kitty

Keep a bag of cat litter in your garage—even if you don't have a cat. This highly absorbent material is perfect for sopping up oil or other car fluids. If you have an oil stain on the garage floor, coat it with paint thinner and then a layer of cat litter; leave the door open while you do this. Let the mixture sit for a few hours while the litter absorbs the oil, then just sweep it up and discard it.

parts for pennies

Okay, you can't really get new car parts for pennies, but you can cut down on repair costs if you have a little information on your side. The most important distinction to remember when purchasing new parts is that between original equipment manufactured **(OEM)** and **after-market parts**. The OEMs tend to cost from 15 to 20 percent more than the after-market variety. So what's the difference? It's similar to the difference between name-brand drugs and generic ones.

- After-market parts are generally produced under the same standards as OEMs; however, the after-market parts come with mounting hardware that allows them to be installed in a number of similar vehicles, not just one or two. This helps lower the cost of the after-market part.
- The warranty on OEMs is usually twice as long as that of after-market parts and if the part goes bad, the OEM is replaced by the car dealer for nothing, including installation. Basically, if a longer warranty and the newest gizmo are important to you, go with OEMs; if you want to save money, use after-market varieties.
- Car dealers usually get the "latest and greatest" parts from the manufacturer; it may take longer for an after-market version to become available.

auto
Alternative

If you live in an area that has good public transportation, chances are you are already taking advantage of mass transit. If the area you are in is less well served, you can still cut down on the individual use of your car, plan your travel routes for maximum efficiency, and walk whenever possible. You'll save money, get some exercise, and help the environment, too.

to drive or not to drive?

Most urban dwellers enjoy excellent public transportation and thus opt not to own a car, sparing themselves the daily battle for parking spaces, whopping garage bills, and ghastly insurance premiums. If you live in a major city, it probably makes more sense and is a whole lot cheaper not to own a car. When you need to drive, a rental will be more convenient and inexpensive all the way around. For those who live in areas with little public transportation, the need to have a car becomes more critical. Next time you're looking for a place to live try to think about how close you are to shops, parks, schools, and other places you need to go. If you're within walking distance, you might be able to reduce the amount you use your car considerably.

plan ahead for savings

The worst kind of gas-guzzling travel comes from those quick trips to the grocery store for milk followed by a stop at the post office, then the drugstore, and so on. Most of us just jump in the car and zip off on the spur of the moment, but those little trips add up to big costs. One way to cut down on them is to sit down every morning (or the evening before) and make a list of where everyone has to go and what everyone has to do for the day. Then plan out the most efficient routes to keep everyone on schedule with the least amount of traveling. You'll save money, time, and frustration, too.

mass transit math

Because commuting by car can be costly, it may pay to turn to local mass transit for your transportation needs. You may even be able to lower the costs further by following some of these suggestions:

● Ask your employer if they participate in a plan for discount passes for trains, subways, or buses. If not, lobby to start such a program.
● If you know a group of people who all use the same means of public transportation, see if you can buy passes at a group discount from the transit authority.
● Try to take advantage of off-peak train and bus prices.

Ask your employer if you can adjust your work schedule so you can commute during off-peak hours. Many commuter trains discount tickets during off-peak hours by 15 percent or more from peak rates. Another benefit to traveling during off-peak hours is less-crowded trains and buses so you'll always get a seat.

park and ride
Look for these signs around metro area train or subway stations—generally these parking lots offer you a convenient place to leave your car so you can commute the rest of the way by bus or train. With this option, you can catch up on the news or paperwork while someone else drives.

jump in the pool
Participating in a carpool saves you money and reduces fuel emissions that pollute the environment—a good deal all around. With carpools, the more is definitely the merrier. If sharing the commute with one other person cuts your travel expenses in half, just think about dividing it by four. If you carpool, you'll also be able to travel on high-occupancy-vehicle (HOV) lanes. HOV lanes are available on many major highways and allow carpool drivers to zip past heavy traffic, leaving solo commuters stuck, losing money, and lonely.
- Check with your employer to see if they offer a program to help employees develop carpools. If they don't offer one, start one yourself. Also, ask whether the company ever provides a car for groups that carpool, or if they can arrange transportation if there is an emergency. Ask if the company offers any other incentives, such as a better parking space or flexible hours.
- Call your county government or regional transportation agency to see if either one offers a program for matching up people interested in forming a carpool.
- Watch for highway signs with a number to call for more information about carpools.

a big pool
Carpools are not just for commuting to work. Anytime you can find a group of people who all want to go to the same place at the same time, you can start a carpool. Other carpool destinations might include:
- Schools
- Sports
- Extracurricular activities (drama club, debating, cheerleading, volunteer work)
- Church, temple, and/or religious school
- Choirs, community theater, or dance groups
- Clubs (scouting, book, sewing, crafting, and so on)

❝Take most people. They're crazy about cars . . . and if they get a brand new car already they think about trading it in for one that's even newer. ❞

J.D. Salinger

rules of the pool

Be sure everyone involved in your carpool agrees on a few basic principles:

driver, driver Some carpools rotate drivers and some have one driver with the rest contributing for gas, tolls, parking, and so on. Make sure everyone agrees on the rotation or the amount paid each week or month.

contact sheet Each member of a carpool should have a sheet with everyone else's home and work phone numbers (including pagers and cell phones) in case of an emergency or unexpected change in schedule.

money matters More friendships are killed over money than just about anything else. Discuss the handling of money carefully before starting a carpool. Some lawyers advise against charging a set amount, which might be interpreted as running a fee-for-service business in a liability action.

pickup times and places Agree to the same time and same place every day, otherwise it becomes a logistical nightmare. Set rules for what to do when someone is running late—how long will the carpool wait?

contingency plans Just about everyone has a day where they must work longer than expected to finish a project or meet a deadline. Be sure to have contingency plans for unexpected occurrences.

carpool rules Will smoking or eating be allowed? Talk about these issues ahead of time—including what to do about burns, spills, and stains.

noise or sweet silence Some people love to chat during the ride, while others want to ease quietly into the day. Some enjoy listening to tunes, while others want all-news radio all the time. Be sure to set very specific ground rules about this to avoid problems later on.

Some of these issues may be difficult for people to discuss openly. But if you want your carpool to run smoothly, it's essential to get these matters out in the open and agreed upon (preferably in writing) before you start. That way you'll avoid arguments down the road—literally!

carpool cash

There are more benefits to being in a carpool than might immediately spring to mind. Aside from reducing the wear and tear on your car and commuting nerves, there may be other incentives:

● Check with your insurance company. There are policies that offer reductions for people who carpool.

● Check with your parking lot. They may offer better spaces, discounts, or even free spaces for carpool drivers.

● Tax breaks? Ask your accountant or tax adviser what you can deduct for carpooling expenses.

finding a ride on the web

Many areas have developed Web sites to help people join or start a carpool. On your computer search engine, enter your city and the word carpool. These sites usually have a form where you fill in the particulars of where you live and where you need to commute. Then they match you with others who are looking to carpool from your area to a similar location.

pedal power

The cry that early motorists heard used to be "get a horse!" But that's not terribly practical in this day and age in most parts of the country. However, most folks can ride a bicycle and it's amazing how much you can cut down on travel expenses when you start pedaling.

- If you live reasonably close to where you work, try commuting on your bike instead.
- If your work is too far for you to commute by bike, try pedaling to the train station.
- If you must use a vehicle to get to work, try using your bike to run errands in your neighborhood. Put a basket on front of your bike and a saddle-basket on the rear so you'll have lots of room to tote your groceries or other purchases. Don't get fancy. Ride a simple bike so it will be a lot less attractive to thieves.
- Cancel your gym membership—with all this biking, you'll be in fabulous shape!

SPECIAL SAVINGS

Most mass transit agencies have special discounts for seniors and other people with special needs, notably students, children, or disabled individuals. It can really pay to check into these lower fares, which can be as much as half the regular fare. Call your local transit authority or look at brochures or printed schedules to see if any discounts apply to you.

Money-Savvy Medicine

○ medical insurance

○ doctors and hospitals
and HMOs, oh my!

○ eyes, ears, and teeth

○ drugs for less

Yikes! Medical costs just seem to go up and up and consumer options seem to be fewer and fewer. What's a penny pincher to do? Use good research, cost-cutting tricks, and some common sense to get the best health care possible at a reasonable rate. Don't let the medical establishment cow you—there are ways to lower insurance rates, keep a lid on hospital bills, cut surgery costs, and find dedicated physicians for the right price. And you can extend this savvy to eye health, hearing equipment, and topnotch dental care—you just have to know how. Once you've got the whole insurance-HMO-doctor thing down, it's time to tackle one of the most pernicious penny-pinching problems: lowering the cost of drugs, both prescription and over-the-counter. Whether you choose to halve tablets, buy big, go for the generic, seize samples, or make a run for the border, you'll find solutions to your pricey pill problems. You can't put a dollar sign on your health, but you can control costs.

Make every medical penny count.

medical
Insurance

HEALTH INSURANCE IS A MAJOR BUDGET ITEM FOR EVERY FAMILY. HERE ARE SOME WAYS TO MAKE THE MOST OF YOUR COVERAGE.

The best (and cheapest) way to deal with the vexing health insurance issue is to do everything you can to get and stay healthy, even if that requires changes in diet, exercise, and preventive medicine. However, reality dictates the need for health insurance, because you can't predict accidents, disease, or many medical conditions. Determining the absolute best deal in health insurance would require a company-by-company and policy-by-policy search. But we have a few rules of thumb to help you keep a cap on costs while maintaining adequate medical coverage.

how do you choose?

Choosing the right health coverage for you and your family can be really hard. Most people get their coverage through their employers, which puts a limit on the number of choices. Another limiting factor is the number of plans offered in the area where you live. Even so, there are many factors to consider, not the least of which is cost.

- The first step is to learn as much as you can about the plans offered by your employer or, if you are buying insurance on your own, the plans available in your area.
- **HMOs** (health maintenance organizations) and **PPOs** (preferred provider organizations) make the most sense for families with children at home, since kids tend to visit the doctor more frequently and unexpectedly.
- HMO and PPO plans also make sense for individuals who expect to spend a lot on health care (preventive or for existing or anticipated conditions).
- Individuals or families who don't expect to have a lot of health care expenses may find it less costly in the long run to select a health plan that has higher deductibles and higher copayments.

comparing health plans

The best way to compare health plans is to spread out all the information you've accumulated. Then get out a pencil and pad so that you can make a comparison chart and ask yourself the following questions:

- What would my premium be with each plan?
- How much would my copayment be with each plan?
- How much would my deductible be, and could I make it larger in order to lower my premium?
- What kind of coverage is offered?
- What health care needs do I think that I and my dependents might have? (List possible needs.)

finding the best hmo or ppo

If you buying health plan on your own, instead of getting it through your employer, choosing an HMO or PPO is an area where using a licensed insurance agent might save you money. Because of the great number of options and rapid changes in the systems it can be tricky to decide what's best on your own. Here are few key points to keep in mind:

- Health is more important than saving money. You can't put a price on your health, so go for the best, not the cheapest, plan you can afford.
- Check out the plan thoroughly. You want to be sure the insurance company and its network have a good track record. The Better Business Bureau, your state's department of insurance, and other policyholders can help you evaluate a company's performance.
- Preventive medicine should be included in the plan. If the National Committee for Quality Assurance (**www.ncqa.org**) gives a plan a high rating, it means the plan provides extensive screening (cancer, diabetes, and the like) to catch conditions early, when they are more likely to be easily and successfully treated. A low rating means the plan's records include an inappropriately high number of heart bypasses and angioplasties, indicating that the plan's emphasis is on fixing damage after it's done rather than on preventing damage. Clearly, preventing problems is better than fixing them, both for your health and your pocketbook.
- Does the organization have staying power? Look for a group that's been around for 15 to 20 years.
- Do you have a wide choice of doctors? Are they located reasonably near you? Are most of them taking new patients? You want to have a choice of doctors, but you don't want to have to travel far in an emergency. And you want a plan in which about 90 percent of the doctors are accepting new patients.
- What do you do if you need to see a specialist? Make sure the plan offers an adequate choice of specialists.
- Are doctors unhappy with the organization? If there is high turnover (10 percent or more), it usually means the doctors don't like dealing with this organization.
- What if you have a pre-existing condition? Are there restrictions on your coverage?
- What can you do if you don't agree with a doctor's diagnosis or treatment plan and want a second opinion? What recourse do you have?

medical savings accounts (msas)

Not unlike an IRA, an **MSA** is an account set up to help you save (tax free) for eligible medical spending. The MSA legislation was passed in 1996 for people who are **self-employed** or who work for a small company (50 or fewer employees) that doesn't offer health coverage. How it works:

- You buy your own private health insurance policy with a

> 66 Look to your health; and if you have it, praise God, and value it next to a good conscience; for health is the second blessing that we mortals are capable of; a blessing that money cannot buy. 99

Izaak Walton, English writer

large deductible (in 2001 they ranged from $1,600 to $2,400 for individuals and from $3,200 to $4,800 for families). The maximum out-of-pocket payments are limited—no more than $3,200 a year for an individual; no more than $5,850 for a family (subject to inflation, so check current figures beforehand).

● You open an MSA at a bank, insurance company, or other approved holder. In 2001, individuals could deposit up to 65 percent of their deductible; families, up to 75 percent. The money in the account earns tax-free interest. When you turn 65, you'll have to pay taxes only on any excess money deposited and the interest. Because seniors have a lower tax rate, the bite won't be as big.

● When you have eligible medical treatment, you pay by making a withdrawal or with a check from your MSA. Any money remaining at the end of the fiscal year can be left in the account, tax free, until you reach age 65 or you take the money out early for noneligible reasons.

● If you take out the money before age 65 for noneligible reasons, you will be penalized and taxed.

an umbrella for my umbrella?

If your employer offers only hospital coverage, it's a good idea to look into buying an HMO or PPO plan for yourself and your family. Look for a plan with the best doctors and most convenient features, but don't worry about the hospitalization coverage, because you're already covered for that.

retiree recommendations

● Don't depend entirely on Medicare. It has way too many gaps in coverage, and the gaps are always changing and are not always easy to figure out.

● Don't just drop your major medical insurance when you retire. As you're approaching retirement, check with the program you're in; if you continue the coverage, the insurer will often keep it at the lowest possible rate. If you let your major medical drop and then try to get new coverage, it will be much more expensive and, after age 65, hard to get. Your major medical should cover any gaps in your Medicare.

● Scrutinize any policies that claim to supplement Medicare; some actually cover the same stuff. You want a policy that fills the gaps.

● Use group power. Organize a group of 50 seniors and approach a doctor. Offer a written agreement whereby the entire group will use only that doctor as its primary physician if the doctor will accept whatever Medicare agrees to pay. The physician may agree if the guaranteed patient volume seems to make the deal worthwhile.

medicare hmo?

This works just like a regular HMO. You sign up and agree to use a network of approved doctors. Then you don't need to buy Medigap coverage, and you only pay the usual small copayment. Medicare reimburses the other expenses. But be warned: In many states, insurance companies are closing Medicare HMOs because they are not profitable enough.

long-term care insurance pros and cons

We never want to think we'll end up in a nursing home, but there are no guarantees in life. Long-term care insurance can help protect you and your family by covering the costs of care where Medicare leaves off. But think twice before signing up for long-term care insurance.

● Although widely promoted as essential for everyone, this form of insurance is mainly of real value for people who have considerable assets that they want to preserve for their families and who want to avoid depleting their wealth on nursing home bills.

● Before buying this kind of insurance, analyze whether you can pay the premiums for the rest of your life; many policyholders on fixed incomes are forced to cancel their long-term care policies as they grow older and their premiums increase. They can no longer pay the premiums— just when they are more likely to need long-term care.

● If you do want a long-term policy—and you no longer have dependents—you might want to consider converting your life insurance to long-term care insurance.

scam alert!

Not every insurance company is what it appears to be. Be especially wary of insurance companies that advertise on the Internet and TV.

● If it seems too good to be true, it probably is. Those slick-looking Web sites that offer bargain-basement insurance rates may be selling stuff you really don't want.

● Check that the company selling in cyber-space is licensed in your state. If it's not and it fails, you lose.

worst-case scenario The company is a total sham and takes your money and runs, shutting down its Web site.

defense Always check with your state department of insurance to confirm that a company is licensed to do business in your state before signing anything or sending any money.

too much coverage

If you are married and both you and your spouse are eligible for full medical coverage (including family members), decide which is the better insurance. Then the partner who has the inferior coverage should ask his or her employer about a credit for the portion of the premium that the employer would normally pay.

fighting back

Though insurance companies sell peace of mind, when it comes to actually shelling out payments, they can become mulish in the extreme. And the higher the amount of your claim, the more likely the insurer is to put up a struggle. Common problems include the following:

scenario: You've had surgery that was approved. You file a claim. Mr. Insurer sees the big bill and orders an audit of your medical records to see whether you made any mistakes on your application so that he can deny the claim or cancel your policy.
best defense: Avoid the problem in the first place by filling out your applications yourself, being careful to provide all of the information requested.

scenario: You put in a claim, and Mr. Insurer wants to keep costs down, so he denies it without a full investigation.
best defense: Get written statements from your doctors to help support your claim. If Mr. Insurer still balks, appeal again with more documentation or to higher level. (See Making the Most of an Appeal, facing page.)

scenario: Your doctor says a procedure or treatment is necessary. Mr. Insurer gets his own doctor to say it isn't and therefore he doesn't have to pay for it.
best defense: Get a second opinion! And before you go for treatment, make sure your doctor is willing to fight for you in this kind of situation.

scenario: You're a writer who develops severe carpal tunnel syndrome, which prevents you from using a keyboard. You file a disability claim because you can no longer do your job. Mr. Insurer denies the claim, saying you can do other jobs.
best defense: Be sure your policy covers you for your specific line of work, not just any job. Tell your doctor what it is you do at work and why you can't do it anymore.

scenario: Your doctor says you need a certain operation. You call the insurance company, and the nice lady you talk to says OK. You have the operation and file a claim. Mr. Insurer denies the claim, contending that it's not the standard treatment and that the nice lady was only a clerk, not someone qualified to give approval for treatment.

best defense: Get the approval for treatment in writing from a claims adjuster. Be sure the adjuster includes his or her name, title, the specific procedure, and amount covered.

making the most of an appeal

We've all heard the horror stories: "I'd just given birth and they were trying to push me out the door.""I really needed the operation, but my HMO just kept saying no.""My insurance won't pay for the brand-name medication, even though the generic doesn't work as well for me." As mentioned, health insurers want to make money and every time they pay for something, it costs them. But just because the first person you ask says no doesn't mean the proverbial buck has stopped there. You can appeal—and appeal and appeal and appeal—until you most often get what you want or need. In September 2002, *The Wall Street Journal* reported that at two of the major California HMOs, patients that appealed initial negative decisions for emergency care were successful about 95 percent of the time. Good news for consumers: The squeaky wheel usually *does* get the grease. But there are two key things to remember. One, be calm; don't get angry and emotional. Two, write letters, don't call.

- The first time an insurer denies your claim, write a polite letter. Indicate that you understand that you have been denied, but then carefully explain why you think they should reconsider. Attach copies of your medical files to support your arguments.
- If you are denied again, write another letter. This time include more evidence in your favor: a letter from your doctor, a second opinion from another physician, any articles from medical journals (do a Web search) supporting the treatment, and so on.
- If you are denied a third and "final" time, write another letter. This time ask to be referred to a higher office since you feel you have tried all the normal channels. Make it clear that you are not giving up.
- If that third letter receives a denial, you have three options: arbitration, an independent review board, or taking the insurer to court. Arbitration may be your only course of action if your contract plan has a clause requiring it instead of legal redress. Forty-two states allow you to send your case to an independent review board. No lawyer is needed, a judgment is usually timely (about 2 months), and you can find instructions on how to file on your state's Web site (usually in the form www.state.ny.us; substitute your state's postal abbreviation for "ny").
- Going to court should be a last resort and considered only when a substantial amount of money is involved, otherwise you could really end up the loser.

CHECKING YOUR BENEFITS
www.benefitscheckup.org

There may be Medicare or Medicaid benefits that you are qualified for and aren't taking advantage of, or you may not be getting free health insurance counseling that you are entitled to. The National Council on the Aging wants to help. They have set up this Web site to help older Americans determine at no charge their eligibility for federal and state benefits. Beyond health benefits, you can find information about programs to help with food stamps, utility bills, transportation services, property tax abatements, and even home weatherization (insulation, weather-stripping, heating systems, and other similar services).

doctors and hospitals and
HMOs, Oh My!

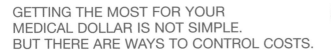

GETTING THE MOST FOR YOUR
MEDICAL DOLLAR IS NOT SIMPLE.
BUT THERE ARE WAYS TO CONTROL COSTS.

Doctors are often portrayed either as miracle workers or as grossly incompetent money grubbers who threaten your life at every visit. Hospitals are seen as impersonal factories for the sick, and health plans are said to care only about the bottom line. Although you'll certainly find examples of these extremes, most doctors, hospitals, and health plans aren't out to do you in. Your best bet is to gather enough information to make intelligent and economical health care choices.

back-to-school bargains

If you live in an area with a medical school or teaching hospital, you're in luck. Medical residents—men and women who have earned medical degrees and are receiving postgraduate training—must gain clinical experience and spend part of their time working in outpatient clinics. Such clinics often provide top-quality care, and the residents work under the supervision of attending physicians who are fully trained and licensed (usually with a number of years of practice behind them). Occasionally, a medical student will observe or perform an examination, under the tutelage of a resident or an attending physician. Because medical schools are generally up to date on the latest research, technology, and techniques, you can benefit from excellent care at discount prices at clinics run by medical schools and teaching hospitals. And you will be helping these young doctors develop exemplary bedside manners—good for them and good for you.

a word of caution If you are in a hurry, avoid teaching (medical school–affiliated) hospitals in the month of July. Why? July is the beginning of the medical year, so all the new residents and medical students are just starting. Though you will get excellent treatment, it will probably take longer because of the learning curve.

call me! let your fingers do the walking

Remember the old Yellow Pages ad? That slogan can save you big bucks in terms of medical consultation. Instead of running to your doctor's office when you have a nonemergency problem, try calling first. Many medical offices keep nurses on staff just to talk to patients over the phone. Their job is to determine whether and when you should see the doctor. Sometimes they can give you immediate information, and sometimes they consult the doctor and call you back. Either way, they often make an office visit unnecessary, saving you money, time, and effort.

● Most cities have information lines that you can call with questions about health care. Look in the Yellow Pages under the listings for Health Resources, Health Education, or Health Information.

testing, testing

A sad fact of life is that doctors who work for large private practices order about twice as many chest X rays and electrocardiograms as do their counterparts at HMOs or PPOs. It's a money thing: Tests make money for the practice, and each doctor's fee structure is based on how much income he or she brings in—which can encourage a doctor to order needless tests. HMOs and PPOs generally use a fixed prepayment structure, so there's less pressure to order expensive tests, and sometimes just the opposite. Be sure to ask about any tests ordered for you and expect a courteous, easily understandable answer.

surgery cents

It has been estimated that about a fourth of the surgical procedures performed in the U.S. each year are not really necessary. One reason may be that medical schools are producing more surgeons than ever, and surgeons are more prone to see surgery as the solution to a condition than not. Protect yourself by being an informed consumer. Ask your doctor:

- Why do I need this operation now?
- Are there alternatives that do not involve surgery?
- What are the risks of the surgery versus not having it?
- Can I have a same-day surgery?
- If not, how long will I be in the hospital?
- What can I expect during recovery in the way of pain and the ability to move around?
- Will I require rehabilitative care?
- Will there be any residual effects of the surgery?
- When can I resume my normal routine?

same-day savings

Having surgery and leaving the hospital on the same day avoids the discomfort and expense of a hospital stay (not to mention the risk of secondary infection), and you can recuperate in the comfort of your own home. Procedures suitable for same-day surgery include hernia repair, tonsillectomy, adenoidectomy, cataract removal, some plastic surgeries, removal of a tissue lesion or cyst, tubal ligation, dilation and curettage (D and C), some laparoscopic procedures, and drainage for glaucoma.

the price of a second opinion

Getting a second opinion can save you money and pain. This is not a rejection of a good doctor you like and trust; it is just plain common sense. Here are some guidelines:

- Avoid the old-boy network trap. Though most doctors will refer you to someone they feel is well qualified to answer your questions, there are those who will refer you to

66 Who shall decide when doctors disagree...? **99**

Alexander Pope

colleagues they're confident will simply back them up.

- Call a medical school or teaching hospital and ask for the department of surgery. Ask the administrative assistant if the department has referral lists for second opinions.
- If a teaching hospital isn't available in your area, call a local hospital that's not affiliated with the doctor.
- The American College of Surgeons (633 N. Saint Clair Street, Chicago, IL 60611, **www.facs.org**, or 312-202-5000) can provide you with the names of board-certified surgeons in your area.
- Ask the second doctor the same questions that you asked the first one. (See list on previous page.)
- If the two opinions conflict, it is probably a good idea to seek a third and maybe even a fourth opinion.
- If you want to eliminate any question of whether the surgery is necessary, get an opinion from a medical doctor who isn't a surgeon; he or she would have nothing to lose by being honest.

nonprofit hospitals for peanuts?

A for-profit hospital (usually privately owned and operated) is almost always more expensive than a nonprofit (city, county, or state university) hospital. One study found that, in the year surveyed, the average bill from a for-profit hospital was 22 percent higher than the bill from a nonprofit institution. Surprisingly, the basic room cost was nearly the same at both kinds of hospitals, but the cost of ancillary services, such as drugs and medical supplies, was significantly higher at the for-profit institutions.

check-in costs

Never check into a hospital on a weekend for tests or elective surgery (unless medically necessary). Chances are you will lie in bed for the weekend at a cost of up to **$1,000 a day!** Doctors try to discharge patients by Friday, so hospitals want to fill up the empty beds (which cost them money) on weekends. For your monetary and physical health, insist on checking in as close to the test or surgery time as possible. The same rule applies to holidays.

Bonus Tip!

A WEB OF INFORMATION AND MISINFORMATION

To make informed choices about your health care, you have to educate yourself. Whether you're seeking general health information or specifics of a particular condition, the Internet can be a valuable resource for the most up-to-date research available. But consumer beware! Unfortunately, anyone with the right equipment can create a Web site, and they can look amazingly professional. Before you plunge into a site and believe what is written there, first ask yourself the following questions:

- Whose site is it, anyhow? Check the credentials of any site carefully. Some sites that sound reputable really have an agenda and skew information to fit it.
- How old is the site, and how often is it updated? Make sure you're getting the most up-to-date information.
- Can you link up to other health or medical Web sites from this site?

Red flags: If it sounds too good to be true—look for such words as miracle, revolutionary, secret, and breakthrough—it probably is. And if a site is pushing a particular product or remedy, it's a sure sign of a marketing ploy.

rub out billing errors

Here's a shocking statistic: It has been estimated that well over ninety percent of hospital bills contain errors, and only a small part of those errors are in a patient's favor. A few years ago, the New York Life Insurance Company estimated that the average hospital bill contained about $600 worth of erroneous charges. And it's not only the insurance company that ends up paying for these errors. You do, too! The problem is that patients (or their families) tend to pay medical expenses without checking the bills. If you went to a restaurant or a car repair shop and were handed a hefty bill, you'd probably go over it with a fine-toothed comb. Do the same with your medical bill.

four billing-error red flags

The most frequent errors in hospital billing tend to be found in the following areas:

respiratory therapy After you stopped using an oxygen tank, the equipment charge continued to go on your bill.

pharmacy charges You actually didn't need a particular drug, so it was returned to the pharmacy, but no one bothered to remove the charge from your bill.

lab tests A lab test was ordered, then canceled, but the cost still went on your bill.

central supply A staff person or nurse ran out of something for your roommate and borrowed it from your supply. They meant to note it in your chart but forgot, and it went on your bill. It happens more often than you think.

avoid overbilling

write it down Bring a notebook and keep track of everything that you use, that's given to you, or that's done to you during your stay. If you can't do this, ask a family member.

question everything Ask about anything that is given or done to you—tests, medications, therapies. If the doctor doesn't answer to your satisfaction, ask a nurse.

itemize When you are checking out, ask for an itemized bill that lists every service and charge so you can check it carefully against your own record.

double-check data Examine the room-and-board charges, make sure the number of days and type of room are correct, and check the rates.

don't overlook extras Scrutinize charges for phone calls and TV rental. Again, check the number of days.

examine the doctors' bills Many doctors don't prepare their own bills, and changes in visitations or in-office services are not always conveyed to the billing agent.

get an estimate in writing Whenever possible, ask ahead of time for a written estimate of what everything will cost.

ONLINE INFORMATION

Here are some good Web sites run by reputable institutions that you can visit for sound medical information and referrals. To make sure that any information applies to you or your condition, check with your doctor.

American Medical Association
www.ama-assn.org

American Academy of Pediatrics
www.aap.org

Centers for Disease Control and Prevention
www.cdc.gov

Mayo Clinic
www.mayoclinic.com

National Fraud Information Center
www.fraud.org

Obstetrics and Gynecology
www.obgyn.net

U.S. Department of Health and Human Services sites

www.nih.gov
(National Institutes of Health)

www.healthfinder.gov

www.4woman.gov

eyes, ears, and Teeth

EYE, EAR, AND TOOTH CARE
ARE OFTEN UNINSURED,
MAKING COST CONTROL ESSENTIAL.

The cost of eye care, hearing care, and dental care can eat up money almost without your being aware of it. From eyeglasses to contact lenses (the care for which can really add up) to hearing aids to the myriad dental costs that aren't covered by any insurance, the bills are enough to drive a penny pincher to distraction. But there are things you can do to keep a lid on these costs.

eye care: paying the price of training

Depending on your eye care needs, you will select one of the following, and your choice will affect the final cost:

ophthalmologists Generally the most expensive choice, these are medical doctors who specialize in the diagnosis of diseases of the eyes and the treatment of eye disorders. Ophthalmologists do everything from examining eyes and writing corrective prescriptions to performing eye surgery and treating eye injuries and diseases.

optometrists These have a doctor of optometry degree (O.D. rather than M.D.) plus specialized training. They examine eyes, write prescriptions for corrective wear, and diagnose diseases of the eye. In some states, they can also treat certain eye diseases and prescribe medicines, although they can't perform surgery; in other states, they must refer patients to an ophthalmologist.

opticians Only about half the states require opticians to be licensed. Opticians usually fill prescriptions for corrective eyewear written by ophthalmologists or optometrists.

dollar days at school

As in other health care areas, if your eye care is not covered by insurance and you want to save a little, call a teaching hospital or medical school and ask if they have an ophthalmological outpatient clinic. At the clinic, you will be seen by a resident who is doing post-M.D. training in ophthalmology and who is supervised by a fully trained ophthalmologist. The care at a hospital or medical school clinic is excellent, and the cost significantly less than elsewhere. Any time you go to a teaching hospital or a clinic run by a teaching hospital, you may also have a medical student examine you or be present at your examination. The students are never allowed to do anything without supervision.

you'd better shop around

The best plan is to have an ophthalmologist or optometrist examine your eyes and give you a prescription for glasses or contact lenses. Generally, it is cheaper to fill the prescriptions elsewhere. Though glasses must be fitted to you, once you have a prescription for contact lenses, you'll save a bundle by purchasing them through one of the many suppliers now available over the phone, by mail, or on the Internet. (See page 313.) Good contact lens prices are also available at Costco and similar stores, for sometimes as a little as a third of the price that the same lens brand would cost if bought from an optician.

gains on glasses

If you are an eyeglass wearer, it's usually best to opt for old-fashioned glass in your eyewear. Glass is very durable and hard to scratch, unlike many plastic lenses (even those that purport to be scratch resistant).

- If you play heavy-duty sports, you may want a pair with plastic lenses, which don't break as easily. It's often a good idea to get a pair that adjusts to the light or a pair of prescription sunglasses to wear when playing sports and buy the cheapest variety available.
- Metal frames tend to be stronger than plastic frames, and the styles change less rapidly than those of plastic frames. If you are particularly style conscious, get the cheapest pair of stylish frames possible with glass lenses. When you need a new style to keep up with the times, have your existing lenses put in new frames (if your prescription hasn't changed).

keep 'em clean

Clean your glasses gently, using soapy water or a drop of vinegar, vodka, or rubbing alcohol. To prevent scratches, do not rub plastic lenses until you've rinsed off all the dirt.

glasses coming unhinged?

If you're out and about, and you lose one of the little screws that holds the earpiece (more properly called a temple) to the glasses frame, use a small safety pin or paper clip to hold things together temporarily. Most optical stores (like those in every mall) will replace a missing screw at little or no cost.

in a fog

If your glasses always mist up when you come in from the cold, fogproof them. Before going out, put a drop of liquid soap on each lens and gently rub until the lens is thinly coated; do not rinse off the soap. Gently polish the lenses with a clean, lint-free cloth until they are clear.

saving your eyes

Like your skin, your eyes can be damaged by exposure to the sun, and you won't know about it for years. So do your eyes (and future vision) a favor and put on a pair of sunglasses

> 66The best doctors in the world are Doctor Diet, Doctor Quiet, and Doctor Merryman.99

Jonathan Swift

whenever you are outside in the bright, direct sun, regardless of the time of year. And here's something that a penny pincher can appreciate: It doesn't matter whether you spend a lot on sunglasses or buy those cheapies at the drugstore. Because sunglasses tend to take a lot of abuse and generally need to be replaced more often than regular glasses, it makes more sense to buy cheap. The key test of good sunglasses is their ability to filter UVA and UVB rays. And higher cost doesn't equal better protection. Look for labels that guarantee complete UV protection; you should be able to get a great pair for under $15.

reading matters

If you are over forty and are beginning to have trouble seeing things close up, like the print (fine or otherwise) in books or newspapers, you may just need a pair of reading glasses. Reading glasses are basically magnifiers, and you  can pick up a pair for under $15 (usually closer to $10) at most drugstores and at many other retail stores. Most displays have sample reading matter that helps you select the best magnification power for you. But if you have other eye problems and are already wearing glasses to correct for them, you may need to get prescription bifocal glasses or contacts; check with your eye doctor.

taking care of your hearing

More than 20 million people in the United States have some form of hearing impairment. Outer- or middle-ear impairment can be caused by a variety of factors, from buildup of earwax to birth defects, and most can be treated with drugs or surgery. Inner-ear impairment is due to nerve damage from infection, heredity factors, trauma, or aging and can rarely be fixed by medicine or surgery, but can be helped by a hearing aid. If you are having trouble hearing properly, follow these basic guidelines:

● Have a full examination by a medical doctor. He or she may either treat the condition or prescribe a hearing aid.
● To find a good hearing-aid dispenser, ask your doctor, friends or colleagues who wear hearing aids, or your local chapter of the AARP. Before proceeding, check the dispenser's reliability and service record with the Better Business Bureau.
● Never ask advice of someone who is selling hearing aids. They want your money and may skew the truth to suit their sales pitch.
● Get all the details of any service agreements in writing. Check the warranty.

- Make sure the service agreement includes a trial period and gives you the option to return the hearing aid if you are not satisfied with it.

hear now, for less

If your doctor prescribes a hearing aid and money is really tight, call **1-800-648-HEAR**. This is the number for a group called Hear Now, which offers a bank of new, used, and revamped hearing aids for lower rates.

thrifty tooth therapy

Every dentist will tell you that preventive care is the most important part of ensuring healthy teeth, and the most economical approach to a great smile. The cost of toothbrushes, toothpaste, and dental floss is minuscule compared to the cost of fixing or replacing rotting teeth.

- Brush at least twice a day for at least two minutes each time. Use a soft-bristled brush and fluoride toothpaste. Brush up and down, front and back and reach under the gums and behind the back molars. Most important is brushing along the gum line; the biting surfaces of your teeth are basically self-cleaning. It's also a good idea to brush your tongue; the debris that builds up there is the source of most bad breath. Replace your toothbrush every three months or sooner if it becomes frayed.
- Floss your teeth thoroughly at least once a day. Experts recommend that you do it before brushing. Flossing is even more crucial than brushing in the fight against plaque buildup—and the tooth decay and gum disease that results from it. If you have bridgework that makes it difficult to floss, use a small interdental brush to clean between those teeth.

discount dentistry

Again, a professional school or teaching hospital can save you big bucks. Look for an institution with a school of dentistry and call to find out when they have clinics. You can get wonderful dental care for a fraction of the normal cost. And again, the work of these apprentice dentists is closely supervised by fully trained dentists.

caring for dentures

A solution of 1 tablespoon household bleach and 1 teaspoon water softener in 1 cup of water makes an excellent cleaner for removable full dentures with no metal parts. Remember to brush the dentures after soaking to remove plaque. When you're away from home, try using a small piece of nylon net for a quick scrub without removing the dentures.

RESOURCES

CONTACTS FOR LESS

To save on contact lenses, order them through the mail. Here are three suppliers to check out:

Contact Lens Supply
www.lens1st.com
or 1-888-536-7178

Lens Express
www.lensexpress.com
or 1-800-536-7397

1-800-Contacts
www.1800contacts.com
or 1-800-266-8228

drugs for Less

THERE ARE WAYS TO KEEP DOWN
THE COST OF BOTH PRESCRIPTION
AND OVER-THE-COUNTER MEDICATIONS

The outlandish prices of prescription medications are making headlines almost every day, but no significant changes seem to come of it— except that the pharmaceutical industry is making more warm and fuzzy commercials to counter its negative image. So what can the average penny pincher do? Actually, quite a bit. Educate yourself about the various prescription drugs, learn the questions to ask, and do a little foot- (or finger-) work, and you can significantly reduce your drug costs.

make your doctor your penny-pinching partner

When your doctor prescribes a brand-name drug, ask why. Tell him or her that you are trying to keep your drug expenditures down, and ask if there is a generic form of the drug available that could treat your problem just as well. The drug may still be under exclusive patent, so there may not be a generic form available yet, and your doctor may not have another drug available that would produce the desired result. But it is important to ask, because generic drugs are often half the price of name brands.

sample these savings

You can often get free drugs simply by asking for them. Salespeople from drug companies regularly visit doctors and leave samples of new or favorite drugs they want the doctor to prescribe. Most doctors are happy to give you a starter dose from these samples. If you're starting a new medication, the samples give both you and your doctor an opportunity to see whether you will experience any side effects before you invest in a full prescription.

when half is half as much

If you take a prescription medicine that comes in solid pill form, ask your doctor about prescribing them in a higher-dosage size so that you can cut the pills in half. Pill cutters can be bought at most drug stores and are fairly inexpensive. And doubling the dosage and the halving the pill can result in a significant discount.

do a brown bag check

If you take a number of prescription medicines or regularly take an over-the-counter drug, put all of them in a brown bag and take them along on your next appointment with your primary care doctor. This is particularly important if you are seeing several doctors. Your primary care physician needs to know about all the medications that you're taking to make sure there are no dangerous or debilitating interactions. This also gives your doctor the chance to review the drugs to see whether there are any that you no longer need to be taking and whether there are newer, less expensive versions of the drugs that are now available.

mail order from aarp

If you are over 50 and are a member of AARP, check with the group about filling your maintenance prescription by mail. A maintenance prescription is one for any medicine that you take regularly for a chronic condition, such as high blood pressure or high cholesterol. Though this process takes a little longer, you may see a significant reduction in costs, because the drugs are ordered wholesale and the savings are passed on to you. Call 1-800-424-3410 or visit their Web site at **www.aarp.com** for more information. Some other sources are listed in the Resources box on the next page.

bargain border crossings

If you are lucky enough to live near the border, consider going to Mexico or Canada to purchase your prescription drugs. It may sound crazy but the same drugs often sell for considerably less in our neighboring countries. Some groups even charter buses to go to border towns expressly to let passengers buy prescription drugs, and going with a group is an easy way to avoid hassles, at least initially. If you can't find an ad for a group, try contacting a senior center for information about one. The cost of the trip may be worth it in the savings on the prescriptions. But here are some precautions:

- Before you try buying across the border, get a legal prescription from a medical doctor in the States, which you must show both when you purchase the drugs and when coming back over the border. Canadian pharmacies can fill only prescriptions written by doctors certified in Canada. Going with a group is one way to obtain Canadian prescriptions. Some American doctors have become certified in Canada just so that they can write prescriptions for their patients or for groups.
- Be sure to check beforehand with Customs about possible restrictions on drugs you intend to buy. Remember you have to declare prescription drugs at Customs, and Customs also doesn't allow stockpiling.
- Mexican pharmacy employees do not always have pharmaceutical training, so check that the dosage and formula are what your U.S. doctors prescribed. Also in Mexico, the quality control and authenticity of the drugs sold may be questionable at some outlets, which is another reason to go with a group.
- Never buy antibiotics or other prescription medications without a prescription (which can be done in Mexico); taking them without a doctor's guidance is unwise.

66 The desire to take medicine is perhaps the greatest feature which distinguishes man from animals. **99**

Sir William Osler, early 20th-century Canadian physician

RX: INTERNET

You can find information and even buy some drugs via the Internet. These sites may be helpful:

www.1800prescriptiondrugs.com
Information site
....
www.rxlist.com
Information site
....
www.drugstore.com
Sales site

otc generic gains!

Don't fall into the trap of buying brand names on your nonprescription over-the-counter (OTC) drugs, either! Store brands of OTC drugs are almost always less expensive than the name brands, and the key ingredient is the same. Read the labels of your preferred OTC remedies and learn to recognize the key ingredient. Then read the labels of the store brands, and you'll find out they are the same. But cheaper! See the box on the facing page for some money-saving listings of brand names and their generic equivalents.

big bottle bargains at big box stores

Price clubs such as Costco and Sam's Club offer OTC drugs in really big bottles. Do a cost comparison with a smaller bottle at your drugstore. You may find that buying that really big bottle of acetaminophen (which you use fairly frequently and always want to have on hand) is the much better buy, both in terms of cost per pill and convenience. But always do the cost comparison to make sure that you're getting the best buy.

a penny pinch of caution

Although generic drugs are usually the cheapest alternative available, it is not always true. Pharmacies pay less for generics, but some mark them up more than they mark up brand-name drugs. And if you have a good coupon, you may get the better deal buying the brand name. Each time you shop you should do some research and do the math instead of assuming that you'll always save by picking the generic.

combo costs

It is tempting to buy an all-in-one concoction to treat your cold or sinus headache, but it's often a waste of money and, worse, you could end up overdosing on one ingredient. Acetaminophen (Tylenol, etc.) overdoses are particularly worrisome because they can result in liver failure. Overdosing can occur from taking a multisymptom medication, such as Nyquil, which contains acetaminophen, and then an extra dose of acetaminophen on top of that.

You have two choices: Purchase only single-ingredient medications and take them to treat each symptom. For example, if you have a sinus headache, you can take a normal dose of acetaminophen, aspirin or ibuprofen, plus a decongestant such as pseudoephedrine. Or, purchase a multi-symptom medication and just take the recommended dose of that; do not supplement it with other medications. The first choice may well save you money since generic versions of basic medications usually cost less than name-brand multisymptom medications. However, many drug store chains produce low-price generic versions of multi-symptom medications, so you have to do the math and choose the approach that works best for you.

throw it out!

Though we love to save just about everything, even the most devoted penny pincher knows to throw out the following:

- Any medicine past its expiration date.
- Prescription medicines from a former illness.
- Aspirin that has developed a vinegary odor.
- Over-the-counter drugs that you are not longer taking.
- Anything without a label or not in its original container.
- Toss them in a bag and take it to your next doctor's visit. Ask them to dispose of the medications as hazardous medical waste (flushing them puts them into the water supply and throwing them into the garbage puts them in landfills).

DECIPHERING OTC DRUG LABELS

Whether you are looking for a quick nonprescription remedy for a cold, an upset stomach, or a rash, you can save a lot by buying generic store-brand over-the-counter drugs instead of the brand names. Here is a list of some of the more common brand-name OTC drugs and the generic name of their main ingredient. With these and many others, all you have to do is compare the ingredients listed on the store brand with the ones on the brand name. Also make sure that the amount of the active ingredient is the same. They usually are. The generic brands are nearly always complete knock-offs of the brand names. Indeed, many drug stores put them side by side, and generic packages often are designed to resemble brand names.

Brand name	Generic name	Brand name	Generic name
Advil	ibuprofen	Gas-X	simethicone
Afrin	oxymetazoline	Imodium	loperamide
Alka-Seltzer	aspirin, citric acid, and sodium bicarbonate	Kaopectate	attapulgite
		Metamucil	psyllium
Aleve	naproxen	Midol	acetaminophen, caffeine, and pyrilamine maleate
Bayer	aspirin		
Benadryl	diphenhydramine	Motrin	ibuprofen
Bufferin	aspirin	Sudafed	pseudoephedrine
Chlor-Trimeton	chlorpheniramine	Sudafed Sinus Headache	acetaminophen and pseudoephedrine
Cortaid	hydrocorisone	Tagamet HB	cimetidine
Cortizone	hydrocorisone	Tavist-D	clemastine and phenylpropanolamine
Contact	pseudoephedrine		
Dimetapp	brompheniramine and phenylpropanolamine	Tinactin	tolnaftate
		Tums	calcium carbonate
Excedrin	aspirin, acetaminophen, and caffeine	Tylenol	acetaminophen
Excedrin P.M.	acetaminophen and diphenhydramine	Tylenol Sinus	acetaminophen and pseudoephedrine

Frugal Finances

○ the working life

○ home accounting 101

○ retire like royalty!

Living well—what does that mean to you? Do you want to indulge in a really nice car now, Starbucks every day, and plan for the future . . . uh, tomorrow? Do you envision early retirement so you and your honey can sail off to exotic ports of call, free of financial worry? Do you sit up at night and play with figures to leave your children a sizable inheritance to remove money cares from their future? Whatever living well means to you, you have to take control of your finances to achieve your goals. For most of us this requires a balancing act between savoring the now and anticipating needs and desires down the line. Fortunately, once you've mastered the basics, made yourself aware of how your money works, come up with a livable budget, and started a serious savings program, these systems are relatively self-perpetuating—they just need a good once-over every year or so. So take a deep breath and plunge in.

It's your money and it's your life.

the working Life

EVEN ON THE JOB YOU HAVE TO WATCH YOUR
PENNIES AND MAKE THE MOST OF OPPORTUNITIES.

Whether you work in an office, a factory, or a retail store, being a part of the working world comes with a price tag. In order to work, you have to lay out money for clothing, commuting, and food. Or if you work at home, you have other expenses, such as a home computer or phone service. If you employ the right techniques, however, working doesn't have to cost a fortune. By controlling what you spend—and making the most of your benefits—you can make every penny of your paycheck work for you.

a working check-list

Most people work for someone else. If you are an employee, you have already found lots of ways to save money on work-related expenses in earlier chapters about clothing, insurance, cars, commuting, food, and even that morning cup of commuter cappuccino. Here's a quick review of what we've covered earlier as it applies to work:

clothing If you have a uniform, you are actually lucky. You spend almost nothing on working clothes. For the rest of us: Buy the best quality clothing you can afford and take good care of it so that it will last. Avoid impulse shopping and be sure any clothing or accessories you purchase can work with your current wardrobe.

commuting If at all possible, use public transportation, carpool, walk, bike, or find alternatives that will save you on commuting costs. Driving alone to work is a cash drain.

food Eating out is an enormous waste of money. To get an idea of just how much buying lunch at work costs, keep a written account of what you spend on each bagel, sandwich, or salad for just one week. You'll be surprised at how quickly it all adds up. Instead, save your money for a nice dinner or lunch out with a co-worker or friend, and start carrying lunch (and breakfast, if necessary) to work. Most workplaces have a refrigerator, coffee maker, and microwave available to employees, so your brown-bag options are pretty broad. Not only will you save money by bringing food from home; you'll probably eat healthier compared to the fast food you can buy at work. If you feel as if you're missing out, make a date with a work colleague to eat your sack lunches together at the park or in the office. If you prefer to go solo, bring a great book you're dying to finish while you eat.

coffee Oh, what we will pay for a cup of Joe. We don't know whether to laugh or scream when we look at the prices for these so-called gourmet cups of coffee. It is easy and a lot less expensive to make and tote your own in a thermal mug. It's even cheaper to buy the instant special coffees and make them at the office. It makes absolutely no sense to spend $3 a day ($15 a week, over $700 a year!) on a cup of coffee. No coffee is that special!

another alternative If you really feel deprived at the thought of not eating out or buying that gourmet cup, at least cut down. Make lunch out a Friday event. Or have one special cup on Monday morning to start off the week. If you don't indulge every day, your savings will still be significant.

the benefits bargain

Have you been offered a job, but aren't sure it's the best offer you can get? Before you make a decision, make sure to consider the benefits package the company has offered you very carefully. Sure, your salary is important. But with the cost of medical insurance soaring, so is a comprehensive insurance package. If the company isn't offering good medical coverage, you'll use up a big chunk of your paycheck frighteningly fast. Other company benefits, such as educational discounts, should also be factored into your decision.

maximize your paycheck

Many people sign a contract with their employer and leave the details of their paycheck to the accounting or human resources department. Don't make that big mistake! It's up to you to be in charge of the money you earn. Only then will you be sure that every penny is working for you.

scrutinize your withholdings Ideally, when tax time rolls around, you want to make sure you've paid the right amount in taxes with every paycheck. You don't want to owe money and you don't want to get any money back. Although it may feel great to get a big tax refund, this actually means you've been lending your money to the government, not putting it to work for you. That $2,000 tax refund could have been in a CD or money market account earning you interest.

inspect your insurance Make sure the coverage offered through the company is cost effective by checking with an insurance agent you know and trust. You'll want to check if you're paying too low a deductible or have more insurance coverage than you need. This is especially important for married couples who both work and have insurance.

take charge of retirement planning (see pages 336–341 for details): More and more companies are shifting the responsibility of retirement planning from the company to the individual. This will only benefit you in the long run, especially given the number of corporate scandals involving employee pension plans that have made headlines recently. If your company sponsors a 401(k) plan where it matches your contributions, it still may be a good investment. But never put all your retirement eggs in one nest. Diversify! Be sure to spread your assets around to safeguard your future. And keep a careful eye on how your plan is doing (see page 337 for tips on protecting your pension).

> 66 By working faithfully eight hours a day, you may get to be a boss and work twelve hours a day. 99

Robert Frost

ASSOCIATED BENEFITS
www.hoaa.com
or 1-800-809-4622

There are many pros to having a home-based business, but there are also many cons — especially when you can't leverage a large company discount for things like medical insurance and bulk mailings. The Home Office Association of America (HOAA) is trying to change all that. Through the combined clout of the association, you can purchase insurance (medical, disability, life, dental) at a group rate, obtain a discounted schedule from the United Parcel Service, access collection agencies, get a credit card, receive hotel and other travel discounts, purchase insurance for your equipment, and more.

automatic savings

If your employer offers it (and most do), sign up for automatic deposits of your paychecks. Many banks will lower or even drop checking fees entirely if you use direct deposit. This method of payment is faster, safer, and the money is available to you immediately.

working at home

Saving money while working at home is an entirely different subject. If you're planning to set up a home office, either to supplement your outside work or as the base of operations for your own business, you can save yourself time, aggravation, and money by the choices you make.

office space

If you want to claim your office as a deduction, you can't just designate a corner of the family room as the office. The IRS is getting more and more particular about this deduction. A better and more professional option is to set aside a room as your office or create a semiprivate area in the home that is used exclusively for business. If you see clients, having a real office will look more professional. If you have ongoing projects that you need to organize and spread out, you'll be less likely to lose important documents with a real office. Ideally, your office should have a door, enough electrical outlets, and at least one phone jack.

furniture facts

The furniture you choose for your home office will be determined by several factors, including your budget, the type of work you do, and whether or not you entertain clients. First and foremost, you'll need a desk. The components of a desk can range from a hollow-core door sitting on two filing cabinets to an armoire-style computer desk built to accommodate a printer, office files, a memo board, and more. Some of the desks we've seen:

- Costco has a wide variety of computer desks, though their availability varies depending on the season. The store seems to have the biggest selection during the late summer/early fall; you can also check their stock online (www.costco.com). We found everything from a utilitarian rolling laptop stand for $59.99 to a handsome Mission style credenza with hutch (plus three letter-size filing drawers and two utility drawers) for $879.99. Sam's Club offers similar variety and prices.
- Target, Wal-Mart and Kmart all sell office-type furniture, with Target offering the most stylish pieces. If you're looking for a simple computer desk, any one of these stores can provide you with what you need for a good price.

- Office Depot had an ad for a $39.99 (after a $30 instant rebate) basic student desk with pullout keyboard shelf and computer main unit storage.
- Office Max offers a slew of computer desks, ranging from simple units with basic storage that cost $59.99 to a $299.99 L-shaped desk with hutch offering both a computer area and desk area, plus lots of file drawers.

You will also want a comfortable, ergonomically sound chair, especially if you spend lots of hours at your desk (a bad chair can ruin your back). The stores just mentioned carry desk chairs in wide price range. Just remember you don't need the super deluxe, teak-and-leather executive model. In fact, a simple secretary's chair may be just the thing you need.

going-out-of-business breaks

Keep your eyes open as you drive around town, check newspapers or junk mail for office supply stores that are going out of business and selling everything. You can pick up desks, chairs, filing drawers, staplers, hole punches—at a big discount. Don't forget to check out restaurants and stores that are going out of business; they usually have office equipment as well, which you can pick up for pennies.

supply trick

If you have a home office, you'll need to stock it with basic supplies. The big office supply stores are often your best bet because you can buy everything you need to conduct your business in bulk. One trick to keep in mind: Look for damaged boxes. Office supply stores will often give you a discount on a damaged box if you ask for one (they need to get rid of them and many folks simply won't buy a damaged box even if it contains something that can't be hurt by the exterior flaw). So look for those slightly dented or broken-cornered boxes. Who knows? You may save more than you bargained for.

- Price clubs stock a large assortment of office supplies; it's a major part of their business. Troll the aisles and pick up yellow legal pads, pencils, pens, dry-erase markers, bulletin boards, file cabinets, tape, and much more, in really big amounts. Just be sure you have the space at home to store these items.

surge saver

Do yourself a favor and invest in a good quality surge protector. You can pick them up at superstores, hardware stores, home improvement centers, and office supply stores. They usually aren't very expensive, but they can save your investment in computer equipment. If you use your phone line for your Internet connection, get a protector that protects against surges through your phone line as well.

TEN DEDUCTIONS FOR HOME-BASED BUSINESSES

All these are deductible, but be sure to keep records of your purchases and payments and to follow the IRS guidelines for business expenses (see Publication 334 at www.irs.gov).

1. Office space (must be used only for business)
2. Car (mileage, parking fees, tolls)
3. Utilities (share of phone and electricity used)
4. Computers and related items (printer, scanner, Internet service)
5. Software (word processing, spreadsheets, databases, and such)
6. Professional books and subscriptions (e.g., trade magazines, directories, and periodicals)
7. Office equipment (fax machine, calculator, recorder, answering machine, etc.)
8. Educational expenses (courses related to your business)
9. Travel (airfare, hotels, meals, and so on)
10. Office supplies (letterheads, business cards, paperclips, etc.)

electronic equations

More and more you're seeing machines that can do multiple functions and take the place of machines that can do only one. Machines that combine the functions of a printer, scanner, and copier or of a printer and fax are especially common. Is this such a good investment? Maybe not, especially because technology changes so rapidly. Often, a multifunction machine doesn't do all its functions as well or as quickly as a single-function machine. For example, a machine that prints, scans, and copies may not print as fast a regular printer or scan with as fine a detail as a regular scanner. A larger, more complex machine might also be more expensive to fix or replace if it becomes obsolete. Plus, if one function breaks down in these complex machines, the other ones often stop working too. In the long run, it is usually cheaper and easier to fix or replace a machine with a single purpose.

computer costs

Fortunately, computers are a lot cheaper today than they were five years ago. You can pick up a basic model for about $500, which can link you to the Internet, provide you with e-mail, and allow you to play games, run word-processing programs, spreadsheet programs, and more. The more expensive computers will offer more features and run faster. It's easy to pay too much for a computer, especially when all the high-tech bells and whistles look so fun and exciting. In order to avoid overpaying for a computer, you'll need to think honestly about the way you will actually use it, what features are necessary, which are fun, and which you will never use and can live without.

read, read, read There are bookstores full of books devoted to every type of computer, software, and accessory imaginable. Computer magazines can also be a terrific source of information when you're researching which computer or components to purchase. And of course the Internet is filled with information about computers and accessories as well as shopping sites that will do instant comparisons of different models of computers.

talk it up Ask family members, friends, and work colleagues about their favorite computers and software. But be aware that PC users and Mac users are frequently passionate about their choice. Don't be surprised if you get conflicting and biased information from your sources.

order direct Gateway and Dell will ship custom-configured systems to you. This is a way to get your computer personalized but not pay for extras you won't use. Check out Dell's computer products at **www.dell.com** or call 1-800-www-DELL. Gateway has stores nationwide; their Web site is **www.gateway.com** or call 1-800-846-4208.

FULL-FEATURED OFFICE PROGRAM FOR FREE!

Microsoft Works, the basic suite of office software that comes with many PCs, is often all you need for a home office. But if you need more features and can't stand the idea of paying $400 or more for Microsoft Office, consider getting OpenOffice. Like MS Office, it comes with a full-featured word processor, spreadsheet, slide-show program, and more. Produced by a group of "open-source" programmers and sponsored by Microsoft rival Sun Microsystems, it's a highly compatible clone of Office, and it's free at www.openoffice.org. If you want a printed manual and helpline access, get Sun's version StarOffice; it's $76 at Staples and other office and software stores.

salesperson standards If you're shopping in a store, make sure the salesperson listens fully to your list of needs before offering his or her ideas on what system might be best for you. If you sense a salesperson is trying to steer you to a "bigger, better, more expensive" system, find someone else to work with who is interested in actually helping you. A smart salesperson knows that a happy and satisfied customer usually comes right back when ready to upgrade or buy more components.

twice as nice (or nasty)

Buying used computers is tricky. It is almost impossible to know how much actual wear and tear a computer has been exposed to and whether it will work well for you. That being said, we picked up a relatively recent-model hard drive at a university sale for $50. At such a cheap price, it can be cost effective to take the risk on a used computer. If you are not a computer whiz, try to enlist a friend or relative who's well versed about various systems to help you shop.

● American Computer Exchange is a well-respected service that offers an index of used computers and their prices. They will even try to match buyers and sellers for a small fee. To find out more call 1-800-786-0717.

frugal phone facts

There are so many phone service options available now that it can really be confusing to choose the best option for you and your home business. Depending on the size of your business, it may be a good idea to keep your home and business services separate for ease of deductions at tax time. Here are some general hints:

review rates About every six months, sit down with all your telephone bills and list how many local, toll, long distance, and international calls you make. Once you've assessed how you use your phone, call several services and ask them to come up with a calling plan that meets your needs. Compare the plans and the rates to find the least expensive option.

wireless wonders We know a couple from Montana who lived in New York while one of them was doing postgraduate training. They made a lot of long-distance calls to family back home and their cheapest option turned out to be their wireless service. They paid for local service through the local phone company, but all long-distance calls were made on a cell phone. With all the competition between wireless companies these days, this may be your best option, too.

ax the options Phone companies are very fond of selling you service options you don't need or use. Scrutinize your bill to be sure you're not paying for an option you don't want. Each one you drop could save you over $40 a year or more.

dump the operator Dial all long distance calls directly, even if you have to use an operator to get the number. This can save you up to $10 per call.

the scoop about on-line services

The above comments for phone services could almost be repeated word for word when you're shopping around for online service providers: the choices are many and varied. At one time, America On Line (AOL) was the only way to go, but times have changed. Today, there are a host of companies large and small vying for your dollars and you should use this to your advantage. Make a list of the features you are looking for in an on-line service, then call at least five companies and see who offers the best deal. One caution with smaller providers: You often get better, more personalized customer service from a smaller company, but it is not unusual for these firms to be bought out by a larger company. It that happens, it may impact the service that they're willing to provide you.

discounting disability

Disability insurance provides income in the event you are unable to work at your job due to injury or illness. Unfortunately, it is one of the most overlooked types of insurance. Most disability policies will cover between 60 to 80 percent of your former income; if your employer only offers a policy covering 60 percent, you should consider a secondary policy to cover the remaining 20 percent. No one ever thinks they will suffer a disabling injury, but it occurs more often than you might think. Protecting oneself from the unexpected is essential to financial security.

careful cars

Your automobile insurance is not just about repairing or replacing your car in case of theft or accident. It also protects you or someone else in the event of an accident, provides you with lost income if you can't work due to an accident, and even covers you in case of potential lawsuits after an accident. After reviewing your other insurance policies, check your automobile policy to see if it covers gaps in health, life or disability policies. If not, adjust your policies to ensure you are well protected.

make extra money with your hobbies

green thumb If you're a talented gardener, offer your expertise for a fee to community businesses or to your horticulturally challenged neighbors.

chef for a day If you're a whiz in the kitchen, utilize your gourmet skills and start your own small catering firm. Cook for parties and special occasions, make cakes for birthdays and weddings, or make takeout for time-stressed individuals.

sew simple Sewing is fast becoming a lost art. Use your sewing talent to do alterations, make custom children's clothes, fancy curtains, or create special quilts for newborns.

be handy Do you spend your free time puttering around the house doing fix-its? Take your handyman skills and charge others for your know-how and services.

knock on wood If you're a fan of TV's "Yankee Workshop" who's good at building things with power tools, hire yourself out to make custom bookcases, cabinets, desks, tables, or anything else someone wants to commission.

number cruncher Are you really good with numbers? Come tax time, sell your services and help folks prepare their returns; or provide customized budgets.

sunday driver Hire yourself out as a part-time delivery driver or offer to display advertising on your vehicle.

animal lover Help people on vacation or at work care for their cat or dog by feeding, walking and playing it.

tutor time Start tutoring or helping children with their homework. Call area schools to see if you meet their requirements and ask if they can recommend you to parents.

party on If you love to entertain or know how to throw great kids' parties, you can start a business as a party planner.

caution Before starting business, consult with a lawyer or tax adviser about taxes, bookkeeping, licenses, and liability.

trying on new hats

Just because you retired doesn't mean you no longer want to work. It's the perfect time to try on a hat you always wanted to wear but never had the chance.

- Corporate downsizing has created a new, more flexible type of workforce. Check out banks, insurance companies, hardware and home stores, grocery stores, superstores, price clubs, nurseries, and other business to see if you can work on a freelance or part-time basis.
- If you had a great relationship with a company before you retired, ask them about doing consulting work, piecemeal projects, substituting, or other freelance opportunities.
- Expand your skills by taking courses (community colleges often provide fabulous, inexpensive classes in everything from computer technology to cooking). This is also a terrific way to meet other retirees with similar interests.
- Surf the Net to see what's out there. The AARP Web site (**www.aarp.org**) offers information on volunteer opportunities and post-retirement employment. Another good Web site for seniors is **www.wiredseniors.com**.

HELP FOR SMALL BUSINESS IS ON THE NET

The U.S. Small Business Administration bills itself as "America's Small Business Resource," and that is precisely what it aims to provide: information about starting, financing, and running your small business successfully. Affiliated with the SBA is the Service Corps of Retired Executives (SCORE), an organization that offers experienced business people as mentors to new entrepreneurs. It even offers direct e-mail counseling that provides advice on business plans, financial matters, marketing, human resources, and more. You can find links to several other organizations that maintain Web sites just to help small businesses at these two sites.

www.sba.gov
or 1-800-827-5722

www.score.org
or 1-800-634-0245

home accounting 101

FEW OF US KNOW HOW TO MANAGE MONEY. BUT FINANCIAL PLANNING IS A NECESSITY—AND EASIER THAN YOU THINK.

Most of us just muddle along and learn how to manage our money as we go, befuddled by the plethora of options, decisions, and expertise that today's economic world encompasses Take heart. There really are a few fundamental financial truths that don't change over time. If you master them and keep informed of current trends, you can live well for less and save for a financially solvent future.

calculate your net worth

Let's start at the beginning: Before you do anything else, it's essential to figure out just how much you are worth. The easiest way to do it is to get a pad and pencil and make two lists—one of your assets and one of your liabilities.

your assets Start by adding up the current value of everything that you own or have coming to you:
- Cash: Total of your checking and savings accounts, money-market funds, and CDs (certificates of deposit)
- House: The market value of your home.
- Other things of value: This includes jewelry, automobiles, home furnishings, art, vacation home, and such.
- Insurance: Figure out the cash value of all your policies.
- Investments: The current value of stocks and bonds, any rental properties, real estate partnerships, oil and gas partnerships, gold and silver, company stock options, personal collections (stamps, coins, antiques, and such), notes receivable, and the book value of a business.
- Retirement savings: IRAs, Keoghs, pension and profit-sharing plans, 401(k)s, any deferred compensation, and company savings plans (only count the money you could take if you left the company tomorrow).

your liabilities Now add up all your debts—the amounts that you owe to others:
- Mortgage: Be sure to include home equity loans.
- Loans: Bank, car, and any other loans or notes.
- Credit card balances or any other outstanding debts.

your net worth Once you have your two lists and have totaled them up, subtract your total liabilities from your total assets. The result is your net worth. Write that figure down. Memorize it. That's the number that will tell you when you can retire and how far along your are toward reaching your financial goals. Chances are you net worth is more than you think; however, if you find out that you are worth less than you think, let it serve at a wake-up call to revise your budget fast.

get with the budget

Every household should have a written budget. Some people have the feeling that if they balance their checkbook regularly that should suffice. But focusing only your checkbook is not a realistic, safe, or forward-thinking way to approach your financial well being. It is also crucial to be honest about your budget, even when you overspend. Again all you need is a pad and pencil.

total income Add up all the money that you can expect to receive during the year:
- Regular paychecks and bonuses
- Part-time or freelance income
- Interest
- Dividends
- Other income: Rent on properties, benefits, and so on

fixed expenses Next add up all the payments that you make a regular basis during the year:
- Mortgage payment or rent
- Electricity, gas, and water
- Telephone: Home and cell phone
- Internet service
- Garbage
- Alarm service
- Cable or satellite dish
- Insurance: Life, medical, dental, disability, homeowners, and automobile
- Debt payments: Home equity and car loans
- Commuting expenses: Tolls, train or bus tickets, and such

variable expenses Now add up all the payouts you make that vary more widely from month to month:
- Food and beverages
- Paper goods: Toilet paper, paper towels, and so on
- Car maintenance: Gas, oil, upkeep
- Home maintenance and improvement
- Furnishings and appliances
- Clothing
- Personal grooming: Hair cuts, beauty products, etc.
- Recreation: Dining out, sports or cultural events, movies, museums, and so on
- Vacation
- Gifts and contributions
- Health care not covered by insurance

the moment of truth Subtract all your annual expenditures from your total annual income. If the total expenditures are less than the total income, you are living within your income;

❝ I made money by selling too soon. ❞

Bernard Baruch,
Wall Street millionaire

if the expenditures are more than the income, you need to go through your variable flexible expenditures—and some of your fixed expenditures as well—and reduce your spending.

savings and spending

When you are working out your budget, keep in mind that the recommended savings rate is **10 percent** of your take-home pay. If this isn't happening, you may be ill-prepared for retirement. Start by writing down everything you spend for about three months. This should give you a pretty good idea of how much you spend on food, gas, personal items, recreation, and all other variable expenditures. It's also a good idea to take out the past year of utility bills to get an idea of the seasonal rise and fall of expenditures there. Once you start seeing where your money is really going, you can look for ways to cut back and save more.

think small to build big

A lot of people only think in big terms for savings—feeling that if they're not putting away $500 a month, then the effort is just not worth it. That kind of thinking is really destructive. If you're not used to putting away any money for savings, start small. Can you find $25 a month to go into a savings account? Most people can find that much just by cutting out a movie, a dinner out, or even a really lengthy long-distance phone call. If you can free up $25 per month to go to savings, you'll be $300 a year richer; if you can free up $25 a week for savings, you'll be $1,300 a year richer. Because the money you put aside will be earning interest, you'll be surprised at how fast even small amounts of savings will grow. Put it in perspective: If you save just $1 a day, by the end of the year you'll have $365. In an account with a four percent interest rate, that would actually become $372 (you've made $7 by doing nothing). In ten years, you'll have saved $3,650 or, at the same interest rate, $4,487. As you can see, over time it all adds up.

sneaky savings

Another trick to help you save more (or pay down debt much faster) is to take an amount from a debt payment that has been paid off and continue paying it—either into a savings account or into another debt. For example, let's say you have two car payments, one for $300 and one for $230. Once you pay off the lesser debt, just begin adding the $230 to the second debt and make new payments of $530. You'll be amazed how quickly you pay off the second debt (and save on the loan's interest as part of the bargain). Once that second debt is paid off, try tucking that payment into a money market savings account and watch your savings take off.

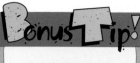

UNEXPECTED INCOME?

When you have a windfall—bonus, gift, extra cash for extra work—use the rule of thirds to determine how you'll use it.

one third for the past Use one third to pay down a debt.

one third for the present Use a second third to make a home or personal improvement you want.

one third for the future Put the final third immediately into some sort of savings or investment.

If you follow this rule, you'll see your debt shrink, your savings grow, and you won't feel deprived.

Because you are already budgeting for the $530 to be unavailable to you each month, this strategy may be the most painless way to build up your savings.

safety margin plan for a rainy day

Conventional wisdom dictates that you set aside three to six months of living expenses in case of an emergency. To safeguard this critical safety net fund, you'll want to put the money into a money market account or short-term certificate of deposit (CD). That way you won't be tempted to dip into it. Only bank your money with institutions that are insured by the Federal Deposit Insurance Corporation (FDIC), which will protect your money up to $100,000. If you have more than this amount, spread your money among different banks so all your savings will be covered.

d is for diversify

As we discussed in the Working Life section, you never want to have all your assets in one place. The safest approach to saving and making your money grow is to diversify—invest your money using several different strategies so that if one fails, you are not back to square one. The fiasco at Enron proved the danger of putting all your retirement eggs in the company basket. Most companies administer their pension plans honestly and carefully, but even so, you need to approach money management with a well-thought-out plan to cover contingencies.

savings accounts This is where you should have your liquid emergency and contingency money. Savings accounts are insured by the FDIC (up to $100,000) and are easy to access when you need your money. Savings accounts pay interest, but the rates tend to be on the low side.

money market deposit accounts These accounts pay slightly higher rates of interest than a savings account and will allow you to withdraw money relatively easily with a few restrictions. You may be required to deposit no less than $1,000, and there may be a limit on the number of withdrawals per year.

money market mutual funds This is similar to a money market in that it is relatively easy to access your money (they often have a few checks linked to the account) but it is administered by a large family of mutual funds. Often this type of account is tax free and offers even higher rates of interest than a money market deposit account.

certificates of deposit (cds) These usually earn higher rates of interest, though the rates vary with the time frame or terms of the account (the longer the term, the higher the interest). CDs are considered very low risk and are insured by the FDIC. But there are penalties for early withdrawal.

TEN MOST COMMON MISTAKES IN PERSONAL FINANCE PLANNING

1. Only one family member is involved in financial affairs.

2. Life goals are not put down on paper.

3. There is no budget for the family.

4. There is insufficient cash available to handle emergencies or new opportunities.

5. The family has no excess liability (or umbrella) insurance.

6. Contents of home are not insured up to their replacement value.

7. Employee benefits are poorly understood and mismanaged.

8. Investments are not diversified.

9. Tax reduction is used as a goal and no projections are made.

10. Income earners do not have adequate life or disability insurance.

stocks When you buy stocks, you acquire a share of a company's profits. This is a riskier investment because, as we all know, the stock market can be volatile. However, in a diversified portfolio, you should have some investment in stocks because they can give you the highest returns, too. Think of stocks as a long-term investment where you can ride out the roller coaster of the market until you decide it is profitable to sell your shares.

bonds When you buy a bond, you are lending money to a company or to the federal, state or local government. The loan is for a fixed period of time ("term") and you are promised repayment on a set date with a set rate of interest. Bonds are lower in risk than stocks because bondholders are paid first if a company goes under. However, if interest rates have gone up since you bought your bond, you will earn less than the rate of inflation.

mutual funds This represents a pool of money from many investors that is managed by a professional. The money in a mutual fund can be invested in stocks, bonds, money markets, and other securities. The fund manager determines when it is best to invest and sell. By combining your money with that of other investors, you reduce individual risk.

annuities These are financial contracts made with an insurance company. A "deferred" annuity focuses on accumulating money for retirement; an "immediate" annuity offers regular income during retirement. Annuities can be very complex and are best approached with a professional's help.

your home This is often the single greatest investment a family makes over a lifetime. Your home's value can fluctuate over time based on its condition, square footage, yard, features, style, surrounding neighborhood, school district, and even stores and businesses moving in and out of the area.

savings at the bank

Fees, fees, fees! They are the way that your bank makes money, and they add up fast. Unless you scrutinize your bank's statements (which you do, as a good penny pincher), you might not even be aware of some of them.

● Scout around for a bank that will give you a checking account with a low or no minimum balance requirement—then make sure you keep that amount in the account. Some banks will allow the minimum balance to be that of the combined checking/savings accounts. This means you can park more money in savings and have it earn interest before you need it to pay bills.

● Ask for a detailed list of all the bank fees, including ATM fees. If there is no fee for using your own bank's ATM, avoid using ATM machines from other banks so that you won't be charged every time you withdraw your money.

Take out larger amounts of cash, if need be, to avoid using other banks' ATM machines.

- Ask if your bank will drop or lower your checking fees if you use it for the direct deposit of your paycheck (or your Social Security or pension check)—many banks will, but only if you ask them.

getting on line

If you are already paying for Internet service, you should definitely look into going online to manage your money at the bank. You'll have instant access to your accounts (so you can avoid ever bouncing a check again), you'll save on postage and potential late fees, you'll use and buy fewer checks, and you'll be able to easily transfer money between accounts to keep most of your funds in the highest interest-bearing accounts possible. All major banks now offer this service, sometimes for no extra charge.

go for broker

Once you make the decision to begin investing in stocks and/or bonds, you will need to use a broker or join an on-line service. A broker (discount or full-service) is licensed to monitor investments and give paid advice on stock purchases. Broker's fees can be a percentage of your portfolio or a set amount for each transaction. They can also make commissions on some of their products. Because you're giving a broker a lot of power over your money, you'll want to make sure that your broker is a member of the Securities Investor Protection Corporation (SIPC). This nonprofit organization can protect investments up to $500,000 if the broker goes out of business.

- Call the National Association of Securities Dealers' (NASD) at 1-800-289-9999. They have records of disciplinary actions against brokerage firms or representatives.
- If you decide to use an on-line service, be sure you are willing to do the homework. With this option, you will be buying your own stocks, bonds, and mutual funds for much lower fees than with a broker. But you will also be taking on added risk because you are making all your own investment decisions. Research any service you're thinking about using thoroughly: the fees, the research provided, the quality of customer service, the commission schedules, and whether the quotes are delayed or real-time.

good money advice

Financial planning can be daunting for the lay person. It can be tempting just to turn your financial planning over to a "professional" but be careful: Unless you do significant research, you may end up paying more for advice than you

CREDIT CHECK

It is wise to check your credit rating, if for no other reason than to remind yourself how precious a good rating is, especially when it comes time for major purchases such as a home or car. Since more than one credit bureau may have a file on you, try the three majors first:

EQUIFAX
P.O. Box 740241
Atlanta, GA 30374
1-800-685-1111
www.equifax.com

EXPERIAN
(formerly TRW)
P.O. Box 949
Allen, TX 75013
1-888-397-3742
www.experian.com

TRANS UNION
P.O. Box 390
Springfield, PA 19064
1-800-916-8800
www.tuc.com

make in investments. If you feel you need financial advice from a pro, here are some guidelines:

personal financial advisor A certified financial planner (CFP) and a chartered financial consultant (ChFC) are essentially the same. In order to be certified, a planner or consultant has to take courses in financial planning and pass a simple exam. They also need at least three years of experience and should continue to take courses to keep abreast of financial trends and economic changes. But beware: Many planners and consultants get commissions for the investment products that they sell. To find a "fee only" financial advisor, someone who charges a flat rate for each service and doesn't get commissions for products sold, try **www.napfa.org** or 1-800-366-2732 or write to:

The National Association of Personal Financial Advisors
355 West Dundee Road, Suite 200
Buffalo Grove, IL 60089

certified public accountant A CPA can be a real help if your portfolio and tax preparation is very complicated. They go through significant training and a rigorous examination to obtain their credentials. They also have to take a number of courses every year to maintain their license. Their fees can vary dramatically, depending on the area or the size of the company they work for. Many (though not all) will also provide financial advice on a fee only basis. To locate a CPA, try **www.aicpa.org** or 1-212-596-6200 or write to:

The American Institute of Certified Public Accountants
1211 Avenue of the Americas
New York, NY 10036-8775

(Note: There are also offices in New Jersey, Washington, D.C., and Texas.)

double checking duty

One of the biggest mistakes a couple can make is for only one person to be the manager or keeper of the money. Though the practice may have been common when most wives stayed at home, it is not a wise arrangement. Both partners need to be actively engaged in meeting financial needs and plans.

- In most couples, one person ends up managing daily finances or paying bills. If that's the case, the other partner should take on the balancing act: When the bank statement comes in, he or she takes the checkbook and balances it against the statement. By doing this, the non-bill-paying partner gets to see exactly where the money goes each month. If both partners are involved, they are much more likely to catch errors. Working together this way is also a perfect opportunity to discuss purchases and figure out discrepancies.

keeping ahead of credit card debt

Credit card debt is the worst kind, because the interest rates that credit card companies charge are ridiculously high. Always pay off your credit cards as soon as the bill arrives. And if you have built up a credit card debt, consider getting a much lower interest bank loan to pay it off. Once you get all those nasty credit cards debts paid off, there's a simple way to keep ahead of the game: After you purchase something with your credit card, write the amount in your check register as a deduction. Then when your bill comes in, you'll have the money set aside to pay it in full.

TEN SOLID TIPS FOR INVESTORS

- **Shop around:** Compare fees and investment options at a variety of banks, credit unions, planners, brokers, and investment houses.

- **Question authorities:** Be sure you understand every investment, especially the risks and benefits involved Ask questions until you feel satisfied. Ask yourself: Can you explain the investment and how it works to someone else?

- **Get it in writing:** Have everything pertaining to your investment in writing, particularly fees, services, and the investment product itself.

- **Get educated:** Too many people assume they won't be able to understand complex investment or financial matters. Nonsense! Your library is a fine place to start. Start with books written for the lay person, like the Dummies or Idiot's guides. Then branch out to investment and financial publications such as the Wall Street Journal, Money, Smart Money, and Investor's Business Daily. If you need extra help, take a class on investing at your community college or local university.

- **See a specialist:** A financial advisor, accountant, or tax advisor can help you set goals and grow your money with less risk. Their knowledge can especially help you with tricky investment products and negotiations. But be sure any financial advisor charges a set fee for services, rather getting a commission for selling you a product.

- **Just hang up:** Never buy a financial product from a salesperson over the telephone. For that matter, never let a salesperson pressure you into making an immediate decision. Ask for any information in writing and tell them you'll call back if you're interested. Then hang up.

- **It's too good to be true:** If it sounds too amazing, start running and don't look back. Salespeople who offer the moon (or an incredible rate of return) are scamming you, pure and simple.

- **Gimme a "D":** We've said it before, we'll say it again: diversify, diversify, diversify. It's safe, sound financial planning.

- **Don't get it, don't bet on it:** If after reading all the literature and talking to the salesperson you still don't understand how a product works, don't invest in it. It's your money. You have to understand where it goes.

- **Regular maintenance:** Give your financial planning regular reviews, especially when you've had a major life change (marriage, birth, divorce, family death, job change, house move, and so on). Because you have to start gathering financial information in January to prepare your taxes, this might also be a good time to review your financial plan and see where changes or improvements could benefit you and your family.

retire like
Royalty!

YOU NEED TO USE ALL YOUR
MONEY-SAVING TRICKS TO MAKE
YOUR RETIREMENT YEARS ENJOYABLE.

Nearly half a century ago, retirement wasn't an option unless you were rich. Most people worked until they couldn't any longer or until they died. The Federal Insurance Contribution Act (FICA), better known as Social Security, changed all that. It was designed to provide the average working American with a little financial help during retirement. But Social Security is only supposed to account for one-quarter of your retirement income, so you need to take control of your financial future.

retirement reality check

The first—and probably hardest—step toward a financially secure retirement is to come up with a realistic figure of what you'll need after you stop working. Some experts estimate the average person will need 70 percent of their pre-retirement income, and lower-wage earners will need up to 90 percent or more, just to live with some degree of comfort and security. However, the statistics are frightening: Less than half of Americans today are putting away money just for retirement. Many workers who have access to a 401(k) plan through their employer aren't taking advantage of it—even though the average person spends 18 years in retirement! These sobering statistics should make you stop and think.

security check

Most people see the FICA deduction in their paycheck and don't give it a second thought. Fact is, the Social Security Administration is a huge organization run by an enormous number of people, and like all organizations, mistakes in accounting do occur. The only one who can catch and correct these errors is you. And don't wait until you're on the verge of retirement. You can do it at anytime. Here's how to check:

- Call your local Social Security office or call 1-800-772-1213, and ask for a Personal Earnings and Benefits Estimate Statement (PEBES). You can also download a request form at www.ssa.gov. The report is free and will be sent to you about five weeks after your request.
- If you find a discrepancy, dig out your old tax returns and W-2 forms and take them to your local Social Security office. After you support your claims, the agency should make an adjustment to your records.

employee advantage

Recent corporate scandals involving employee pension funds have made caution the word for anyone considering employer-sponsored plans. But you should definitely take advantage of them—especially if the company adds to or matches the money you invest in the plans. To protect yourself, make sure you remember to diversify your retirement funds.

pension plans Usually only pretty big companies or government agencies offer a defined-benefit pension plan— where you receive a set monthly amount during retirement based on how many years you worked for the company. Ask your employer for an individual benefit statement to see what your current benefit is worth. If you're thinking of changing jobs, be sure to find out what becomes of the money already invested in the pension fund. Call previous employers and ask if you are eligible for benefits from them (that is, if you worked long enough to qualify).

401(k) In recent years, many employers have shifted corporate contributions for retirement away from traditional pension plans in favor of a tax-sheltered savings plans called 401(k)s. Under this plan, you can automatically contribute a portion of your paycheck's gross income up to a maximum of $12,000 per year (increasing up to $15,000 in 2006). This can be a terrific savings opportunity because, in many cases, your employer will also contribute or even match your investment up to a limit. Money in a 401(k) plan can be invested in stocks, bonds, mutual funds, and CDs. You defer paying income tax on the money until you begin to withdraw, and the interest earned is also tax deferred. There are penalties for early withdrawal, though some plans allow withdrawals for "hardship" reasons such as medical emergencies. Last, but not least, because you're contributing from your gross income, your taxes are lower in the years you are investing in a 401(k). A definite win-win scenario.

403(b) Also known as tax-sheltered annuities, these plans are similar to 401(k)s, but are set up to serve nonprofit organizations such as schools, hospitals, or social service agencies. Again, you can set aside pretax money that is tax-deferred until you begin making withdrawals. The maximum amount you can contribute in a given year is determined by how long you've worked, how much you make, and how much you've already contributed.

protect your pension

The past few years have been a wake-up alert that trusting your company for your retirement may be a gamble you can ill afford to take. This means you have to be an active watchdog. Luckily, there are places to go for help.

get in the know Federal law requires each company or union to publish a Summary Annual Report, a yearly overview of how the company has managed employee funds. It details the amount in the fund, profits or losses for the past year, and administrative costs. If you see big investment losses or high administrative costs, you may be spotting trouble ahead. You can demand a more detailed summary (Form 5500), which will specify where all the money is or has gone.

66 Retirement, we understand, is great if you are busy, rich and healthy. But then, under those conditions, work is great too. 99

Bill Vaughan, author

If you find anything that sends up red flags, contact the Department of Labor's Pension and Welfare Benefits Administration (PWBA). If there is anything illegal going on, this is the agency to attack it. The national office is in Washington, D.C, (202-219-8776), or you can look in your phone book for a local bureau.

free publication *Protecting Your Pension—A Quick Reference Guide*, published by the PWBA, is available by calling 1-800-998-7542. This explains Form 5500 in detail and offers other ways to safeguard your retirement funds.

web site The Department of Labor Web site, **www.dol.gov**, offers information about your rights, retirement, and more.

do-it-yourself accounts

One of the best ways to set aside money for retirement is to set up an individual retirement account (IRA).

regular ira Currently, you can put up to $2,000 a year into a regular IRA (this amount will go up to counter inflation in coming years). You pay no taxes on the interest earned until you retire. If you are 50 or older, you contribute even more. Depending on your income and whether you are contributing to other retirement plans, you may also be able to deduct your IRA contribution from your income tax and not pay taxes on the amount until you withdraw it.

roth ira Money put in a Roth IRA is not tax deductible and must come from income you've earned. But the interest earned by the Roth is not taxable when you withdraw it. There are no age limitations and you don't have to start withdrawing at any particular age. After an initial five year period, there are also fewer restrictions on withdrawing. For example, you can withdraw money from a Roth IRA to make a down payment on a first house. Whether you can set up a Roth depends on your income. It's best to consult with a financial advisor to determine if you are better off with a Roth or a conventional IRA.

self reliance

If you are self-employed or work for a company with no retirement benefits, consider these plans for your future:

sep-iras Simplified Employee Pension Individual Retirement Account, better known as SEP-IRAs, are just that: simple. There is little paperwork, fuss, or bother to set one up and they let you set aside 15 percent of your earnings. One great feature is that you can change the amount you contribute each year. In a good year, you can contribute the maximum; in a less-profitable year, you can contribute whatever is comfortable. For a self-employed person whose income varies greatly from year to year, this flexibility is a real plus.

keogh plans Another separate retirement account, Keoghs usually require a bit more paperwork to set up, but you can contribute more to them in any given year. You can usually put up to 25 percent of your net income, up to a maximum of $30,000 tax-deferred, into a Keogh plan.

analyzing annuities

For most folks, annuities are an option to consider when you have reached your maximum limit on contributions to 401(k)s and IRAs. There is no cap on contributions to annuities. You buy an annuity from an insurance company, either with a lump sum or with payments. The insurance company guarantees to grow your investments at a specific rate, on a tax-free basis. On an agreed date, you begin to receive regular payments from the annuity that will continue for the rest of your life. The size of the payments are based on how much you invested over the years, how long you left the money in the account, the agreed rate of return on your investment, and whether your spouse or other heir continues to receive some payment after you die. Basically, annuities are part investment and part insurance.

- Contributions to a nonqualified deferred annuity are not tax deductible; however, a qualified annuity supporting an IRA, 401(k), 403(b), or other qualified plan, may allow contributions before tax or be tax deductible. Taxes on the interest earned in either case are deferred until you begin receiving payments.
- Immediate annuities allow you to invest a large sum of money, then immediately begin receiving payments on a monthly or other regular basis.
- Deferred or immediate annuities can be paid out based on a fixed or variable interest rate. A fixed annuity will pay you at a fixed rate of interest. Fixed annuities protect your investment from dips in the market, but won't allow you to take advantage of upswings. Variable annuities are designed to take advantage of upswings in the market and, hopefully, make you more money over time if the interest rates are high. But if the market dips significantly, your investment isn't protected.

insuring financial freedom

Many folks don't think about insurance when planning their financial future, but it can be one of the most important retirement investments you can make. From insuring your health and life to insuring your home, these policies should protect you from the unexpected and provide for your family in the event of a long-term illness and death. Make sure you do some research so you can consider all your options and make the right choice for you and your family.

that's life

It's never easy to consider this sobering fact, but you need life insurance in case you die earlier than expected. Life insurance can provide for your loved ones and help their financial future. It is important to have life insurance if you are married and critical if you have dependents.

term life The most straightforward type of life insurance, it guarantees a fixed payment to your beneficiary if you die during the policy's term. Premium cost goes up as you age.

whole life Instead of coverage for a fixed term, this is a life-long policy that guarantees a benefit when you die, as long as you have paid the premiums. Some whole life policies claim to pay increasing dividends based on the accrued cash value of the policy, but often these increases are not guaranteed.

universal life A variation on whole life with a bit more flexibility, universal life insurance allows the policy holder to set the premium amounts and payment frequency (with certain restrictions), and to adjust the policy as life needs change. The policyholder accrues interest from the premiums and cash value of the policy.

variable life Somewhat similar in flexibility to universal life insurance, variable policies provide even more decision-making power to the holder by allowing them to select where their investments will go; however, this form of insurance is subject to greater fluctuation in cash values depending on how the selected investments perform.

safe house

When it comes to planning your retirement, you may not think of your homeowner's insurance policy as being an important facet to consider. But having a good homeowner's policy is more important than you may realize. It will protect one of the biggest retirement investments of your life—your home. If your home is damaged or its contents are ruined, a good policy will cover repair or replacement. The policy may also protect you if someone has an accident on your property. Be sure your policy covers the most common natural disasters for your geographic region, including protection from earth-quakes, floods, brush fires, and tornadoes. If at all possible, try to buy a policy that covers 100 percent of your home's contents and replacement costs.

a will is the way

Because many people don't want to think about death, they expose their partners or dependents to unnecessary financial risk. A will that is legal and binding is essential to protecting your loved ones and equally crucial to protecting your inter-ests. Without a will, the state will decide who raises your children and how to distribute your estate (for a fee).

Features of a thorough will should:

- Include specific instructions on what happens if you and your spouse die together, including designating legal guardians for your children and distribution of property.
- Include a no-contest clause which requires anyone who feels you didn't leave enough for them to forfeit his or her share if they decide to contest your will.
- Try to leave each beneficiary a bequest that takes into account his or her particular situation and age. For an adult, this may mean outright cash and for a minor, it may mean a trust fund.
- Try to avoid leaving joint ownership of anything, especially when one partner is clearly more powerful.
- Specify percentages of your estate to be left rather than exact dollar figures, which may change with inflation. This is especially important if you are young and want your will to stay current over a number of years.
- Include a living will that spells out the care you desire in case you become critically ill and instructs your family how to proceed with such issues as life support measures.

GIVE SOMETHING BACK

Years ago, when a person retired it meant the time had come to give something back to the community, primarily through volunteer work. For retirees, volunteer work can be a tremendous opportunity to use their skills to help others and add real meaning to their days. No matter what your age, volunteer work can be wonderfully enriching. Some groups that need volunteer help:

- **American Red Cross (1-800-HELP-NOW):** Help with disaster relief, blood drives, collections, and more. One lively 80-year-old we know used his talents as a former engineer to repair the dummies used by the Red Cross to teach CPR.

- **Habitat for Humanity (1-800-422-5913):** Help build housing for those who can't afford to buy a decent home. There are ongoing projects all over the U.S., and there is a special band of retirees, the Habitat Gypsies, who travel around the country in their RVs offering their help at various sites.

- **Teach for America (1-800-832-1230):** Dedicated to bringing teachers to under-served regions, both rural and urban, this organization offers paid positions.

- **Peace Corps (1-800-424-8580):** You don't have to be a college age student to go off to an exotic region and help carry out this organization's mission. From teaching to farming, there are many opportunities for a wide span of age ranges in underserved areas or countries.

- **National Forest Service (1-800-281-9176):** You can help maintain hiking trails throughout the United States or work on archaeological digs. Another alternative is to call or check Web sites for the National Park Service and your state's parks to find additional volunteer opportunities preserving our national treasures.

- **National Trust for Historic Preservation (1-800-944-6847):** Volunteers can help with everything from fund raising to hands-on restoration of America's historic homes and public buildings.

If this list doesn't inspire you, create your own. There is no shortage of organizations that need volunteer help. Think about the kind of work that you would enjoy doing; then identify local or national groups that would be a good fit for you.

index
penny pincher's almanac